Dr. Kipnis documents and describes the decision-makers' fatal choice to ignore global and regional changes, which led Israel to an unnecessary war and the loss of many lives. This book is an essential lesson about the heavy price of political arrogance and strategic stagnation.

—**AKIVA ELDAR**
Veteran Israeli Journalist
Correspondent, *Al-Monitor*

Yigal Kipnis knows the Yom Kippur War both as a pilot who flew helicopters in combat and, more importantly, as a scholar who dares once again to go into harm's way. He challenges the conventional wisdom of the past forty years, which pinned most of the blame for Israel's failure to anticipate the coordinated Egyptian-Syrian invasion on intelligence and military officers. Kipnis makes a convincing case for holding the political echelon—Prime Minister Golda Meir, Defense Minister Moshe Dayan, and a close circle of confidants—accountable for pushing Anwar Sadat into a desperate but limited military move aimed at unleashing a diplomatic process.

Rather than realizing that by making the Nixon administration wait until after elections in Israel to launch a peace offensive, Golda and Co. should have expected war and been seriously prepared for it, they were vastly over-confident and complacent. They even kept to themselves, rather than share with their uniformed subordinates planning contingencies, secret undertakings between Washington and Jerusalem which tied Israel's hands regarding pre-emption.

Kipnis flies nap-of-the-earth over this complex terrain. It's one hell of a ride for whoever is interested in how nations stumble into unnecessary wars, conduct secret diplomacy at the highest levels and watch their civil-military relations rip apart at the seams for an entire generation.

—**AMIR OREN**
Defense Correspondent, *Ha'aretz*

A gripping read, taut with the tension inside Israel's inner circle of decision-makers in the countdown to war in October 1973. Kipnis provides fascinating new details that have come to light as archives have opened up. Especially intriguing is the enigmatic role of Ashraf Marwan in the unfolding drama.

—**JANICE GROSS STEIN**
Director, Munk School of Global Affairs
University of Toronto

Yigal Kipnis's *1973: The Road to War* is a revelatory account of the myopic diplomacy that caused an unnecessary war. Based on extensive research in the US and Israeli archives, Kipnis shows how military overconfidence and erroneous political judgments led US and Israeli leaders to dismiss Egypt's peace overtures and force Egypt's Anwar Sadat to launch a war he had tried to avoid. These same errors also led Israel's leaders to disregard the signs of imminent war in October 1973 and allowed Egypt to achieve near-complete strategic surprise. This gripping narrative will fascinate anyone interested in the history of US Middle East policy or in the long and bitter struggle between Arabs and Israelis.

—STEPHEN WALT
Robert and Renee Belfer Professor
of International Affairs
Harvard Kennedy School

This pathbreaking work replaces the conventional military paradigm that has dominated analyses of the 1973 Yom Kippur War with a political one which is already significantly altering the narrative of the war and its aftermath. Political blinkers—supplemented by arrogance, suspicion and secretiveness—may have been the key cause of the most traumatic event in Israeli history. The possibility that this war could have been averted if Israel's leaders had, forty years ago, agreed to pursue a diplomatic option is especially pertinent today, when mistaken preconceptions threaten to stymie the road to a just and lasting accord between Israel, the Palestinians, and the Arab world. Kipnis's book is a must-read for anyone concerned with understanding past patterns of Israeli-Arab relations and with preventing their repetition today.

—NAOMI CHAZAN
Former Deputy Speaker, Israeli Knesset

*1973: The Road to War* is a blockbuster for anyone concerned about the tragic slaughter which flowed from surprise attacks by Egypt and Syria on Israel on Yom Kippur, the holiest day of the Jewish year. Refuting long widespread public understanding of the war's origins as a colossal intelligence failure in both Tel Aviv and Washington, Yigal Kipnis produced this meticulously documented account of the pre-war diplomatic minuet between Cairo and Jerusalem, orchestrated and conducted by Henry Kissinger while Nixon retreated slowly toward his Watergate whirlpool.

Kipnis reveals how even the closest conceivable American-Israeli diplomatic collaboration could not dent Golda Meir's conviction that Israel would easily repulse any Egyptian attack, and that was preferable to any political concessions to Sadat's importuning or Kissinger's forebodings.

This book is important on many levels for historians and for policymakers. It is a demonstration of the limits of American influence on Israel's leaders, even when they enjoy maximum intimacy with the White House; a depressing look into the way Golda Meir held vital political/diplomatic information to a tiny circle, leaning entirely on Moshe Dayan and Yisrael Galili and excluding Yigal Allon, other key cabinet members, and her military and intelligence chiefs from her decision-making circle; confirmation that this bloodiest of Israel's wars of self-defense was, in the words of Bill Quandt's excellent introduction, *an avoidable war;* and as another example of how many years must elapse before historians can gain access to the secret documents needed to piece together the diplomatic prologue to war.

Kipnis's work is truly groundbreaking and an extraordinary achievement that, now finally available in English, merits a wide readership.

—HON. SAMUEL W. LEWIS
Former US Ambassador to Israel
Former President, US Institute of Peace

As one who fought in, studied, and published about the October 1973 war, I felt that nothing could surprise me any more about it. Yigal Kipnis has done that, however. While he confirmed some of my earlier assessments, he put others into question. His mining of the newly available documents made the road to October much more understandable. The 1973 war changed the Middle East, and Kipnis's book helps us understand that change.

—ABDEL MONEM SAID ALY
Chairman and Director
Regional Center for Strategic Studies, Cairo

# 1973:

## The Road to War

Other works by
Dr. Yigal Kipnis

*Ha-Har She-Haya Kemifletset: Ha-Golan Bayn Surya Ve-Yisrael*
*[The Mountain that Was as a Monster:*
*The Golan Heights Between Syria and Israel].*
Jerusalem: Magnes, 2009. Hebrew.

*1973: Ha-Derekh La-Milhamah [1973: The Road to War].*
Or Yehuda: Kinneret, Zmora-Bitan, Dvir, 2012. Hebrew.

*The Golan Heights: Political History,*
*Settlement and Geography since 1949.*
Oxford and New York: Routledge, 2013.

# 1973:
# THE ROAD TO WAR

## YIGAL KIPNIS

Translated from the Hebrew by
### BARBARA DORON

Foreword by
### WILLIAM B. QUANDT

JUST WORLD
BOOKS

CHARLOTTESVILLE, VIRGINIA

Typesetting by Jane T. Sickon for Just World Publishing, LLC.
Cartography and cover design by Lewis Rector for Just World Publishing, LLC.

### Publisher's Cataloging-in-Publication
*(Provided by Quality Books, Inc.)*

Kipnis, Yigal.
    [1973 ha-derekh la-milhamah. English]
    1973 : the road to war / Yigal Kipnis ; translator,
Barbara Doron ; foreword by William B. Quandt.
    pages cm
    Includes bibliographical references.
    LCCN 2013945978
    ISBN (pb.): 978-1-935982-30-2
    ISBN (hc.): 978-1-935982-31-9

    1. Arab-Israeli conflict—1967-1973. 2. Israel-Arab
War, 1973—Diplomatic history.   I. Doron, Barbara,
translator.  II. Translation of: Kipnis, Yigal. 1973
ha-derekh la-milhamah.  III. Title.

DS128.12.A1513 2013          956.04'8
                      QBI13-600124

# Contents

# Foreword

William B. Quandt
Professor Emeritus, University of Virginia

Early on the morning of October 6, 1973, the phone rang in my apartment in southwest Washington, D.C. The 6:00 a.m. caller was a duty officer in the White House Situation Room. I had become acting head of the Middle East office at the National Security Council (NSC) the previous day and had left word that I should be called if there were any major developments in the tense Arab-Israeli arena.

The previous day had been filled with alarming news of preparations for war, yet the Israelis, with a reputedly excellent intelligence service, seemed calm; my quick survey of American intelligence assessments had confirmed that view. These signs of war, I had been told, were just exercises. "We're watching things closely, don't worry," was the bureaucratic answer I received when I asked why the Egyptians were evacuating patients from hospitals on the front lines and why alert levels had gone to unprecedented heights on the Egyptian side of the Suez Canal.

As I picked up the phone, I was pretty sure that the news would not be good. Sure enough, the caller said he had a flash cable from the US embassy in Tel Aviv, which he proceeded to read to me. Prime Minister Golda Meir had just met with US Ambassador Kenneth Keating and had started the conversation by saying, "We may be in trouble." Several "totally reliable" sources had informed Israel that "Syria and Egypt were planning a coordinated attack against Israel today in the late afternoon."[1] The most important of those sources was Ashraf Marwan—about whose role Dr. Yigal Kipnis tells us a lot more in the material that follows. In fact, the war began shortly before 14:00 Israel time, 08:00 in Washington.

I participated personally in many of the meetings that Henry Kissinger and top US policymakers held in the lead-up to October 6, and in most

---

[1] For a photocopy of the cable, see http://www.gwu.edu/~nsarchiv/NSAEBB/NSAEBB98/octwar-09.pdf.

of them during the war itself. Later, I did a lot of research and writing of my own on these events. I was not expecting to learn much new about US policy during this period in a book by an Israeli scholar. After all, most of the American sources have been available for some time now; Kissinger has written at length about the crisis; and just last year the Nixon Presidential Library held a conference on the occasion of the declassification of several hundred additional documents from its archives.[2] What more could one hope to learn?

The answer is that the most sensitive aspects of Israeli policymaking and US-Israel relations did not come into the public domain until quite recently. Yigal Kipnis's *1973: The Road to War*, published in Hebrew in 2012 and now in English, is the first account that mines both the rich American archives and, crucially, the recently released documents from the Israeli war cabinet. What we see is an intimate account of how key Israeli decision-makers—especially Prime Minister Meir and her defense minister Moshe Dayan—saw the events leading up to the war. We can read their remarkable communications with Henry Kissinger.

Although I worked on Kissinger's NSC staff during this period, I understood that he handled the Israeli account as almost a private matter. The Israeli ambassadors in Washington—first Yitzhak Rabin and then Simcha Dinitz—had a direct line to his office, a privilege shared by only one other ambassador, Anatoli Dobrynin of the USSR. When Kissinger spoke on the phone with these individuals, he would sometimes record the conversations; those tapes have been transcribed and are available to researchers. But when Kissinger met face-to-face with Rabin or Dinitz, there was often no American record of what transpired. The Israeli ambassador, however, would report in detail to the prime minister, who would usually respond, often with revealing and detailed instructions. These are the resources that Kipnis has examined and on which he bases much of his analysis.

So what is new in this account? First, we get a better idea of the origins of what I have previously labeled "standstill diplomacy," the period from about 1971 to the outbreak of the Yom Kippur War, when Kissinger was initially determined to thwart State Department initiatives, then slowly came to realize that something must be done to respond to Egyptian president Anwar Sadat's overtures.

We now know, thanks to Kipnis, that in December 1971, on the eve of President Richard Nixon's reelection campaign, Nixon and Kissinger met with Meir and Rabin in Washington and reached an understanding that the White House would not press Israel for diplomatic concessions during 1972

---

[2] The conference program is available at https://www.cia.gov/library/publications/historical-collection-publications/arab-israeli-war/nixon-arab-isaeli-war.pdf.

(for US electoral reasons) or 1973 (for Israeli electoral reasons). In return, Israel agreed not to launch preemptive military operations. Kissinger told Meir there would be no joint US-Soviet proposal for an Arab-Israeli settlement and that a regular supply of arms would be forthcoming; in return, Meir said that Israel might eventually be willing to withdraw to the Mitla and Giddi passes in Sinai as part of a future interim settlement. In short, the Arab-Israeli conflict would be frozen for a two-year period, during which Nixon and Meir would tend to their own political needs and the US would work on its delicate détente relationship with the Soviet Union, while also winding down the war in Vietnam and beginning its engagement with China. If there was to be an American initiative on the Middle East, it would come from the White House—and not until the end of 1973.

As Nixon, Kissinger, and Meir seemed to see the Middle East scene, as long as the Americans kept Israel strong, the Arabs could do little to challenge the status quo. In time, Kissinger thought, this might lead them to abandon their dependence on the Soviet Union and turn to the United States. Only then might he be ready to get involved diplomatically in trying to broker some form of Arab-Israeli peace. Nixon's views were a bit different. He was more inclined to see the need for joint US-USSR pressure on troublesome small powers whose parochial quarrels might disrupt superpower relations. He was not averse to thinking of a sort of superpower condominium. But by 1973 Nixon was deeply involved in the Watergate affair and it was Kissinger, not the president, who shaped US Middle East policy. We now know that Kissinger did so in very close coordination with the Israelis.

On the American side, only Kissinger, his deputy Brent Scowcroft, and his assistant Peter Rodman were fully involved in managing the relationship with Israel, and thus Middle East policy writ large. Nixon and his chief of staff, Alexander Haig, were kept aware of the broad lines of strategy, but the details were handled by a very small inner circle. On the Israeli side, those in the know were the prime minister, Dayan, Yisrael Galili (Minister without Portfolio), Mordechai Gazit (Meir's chief of staff), and first Yitzhak Rabin and then Simcha Dinitz, the two Israeli ambassadors to Washington during the period covered in this book. As Kipnis makes clear, those in the intelligence business were not part of the Israeli inner circle: although they had access to important parts of the overall picture, they were not privy to its most sensitive political dimensions.

In the spring of 1972, the White House tentatively began to explore a new "back channel" relationship with Sadat. In the summer, Sadat unexpectedly expelled some fifteen thousand Soviet advisers. Kissinger and Nixon took notice and began to exchange more messages with Sadat through his national security adviser, Hafez Ismail. The Israelis were kept apprised of the content of these exchanges. Once Nixon secured his reelection in November 1972, it was just a matter of time before he and Kissinger would meet with Ismail. This happened first in February 1973, and then Kissinger held a second face-to-face meeting with Ismail in May.

The upshot of these meetings was that the White House began to see the possibility of working with Egypt on some kind of diplomatic step. Kissinger had in mind a secret track of diplomacy that might get under way after Israeli elections, then slated for late October 1973. He would try to persuade the Israelis to recognize Egypt's sovereignty over Sinai and to make a significant territorial withdrawal in return for Egypt's agreeing to extensive security arrangements (demilitarization, some continued Israeli outposts at sensitive locations for an indefinite period), all wrapped up in an agreement to end the state of war, but not necessarily a full-fledged peace. Kipnis refers to this as a plan. My sense at the time was that it was little more than some broad guidelines that Kissinger was thinking about, but it might well have become a plan after the Israeli elections. In any case, Golda Meir would have none of it. She did not trust Sadat; she did not want to recognize Egypt's sovereignty over all of Sinai; and she did not think that war was likely if she rejected a diplomatic track. But even if it was, she was confident that Israel would easily prevail and that it was Egypt that should worry about war, not Israel.

Sadat's response to the first hints of a new approach from the White House was one of interest, but also skepticism. (Unfortunately, the Egyptian and Syrian parts of the story cannot be fully told because the relevant documentation is not available. The memoirs and partial accounts we do have leave many unanswered questions.) Kissinger did seem to feel some urgency and tried to persuade the Israelis to give him something to work with, but they refused. So he essentially acquiesced and played for time, hoping that after Israeli elections he might find more flexibility on the Israeli side.

The Egyptians and Syrians signaled their frustration in spring 1973 by staging quite realistic military exercises. There was a real concern in Washington that war might take place, but it all turned out to be a bluff. The next warning came during the US-Soviet summit in San Clemente, California, in summer 1973. Soviet leader Leonid Brezhnev told Nixon there that war in the Middle East would occur before the end of the year and that the two great powers should act jointly to prevent it. Kissinger was not eager to work with the Soviets, but he did begin to watch for signs of war. He tasked the US intelligence agencies to watch carefully. A huge amount of information flooded in, but no clear picture emerged. Meanwhile, the Israelis, confident that they had a reliable source in Sadat's inner circle, showed little sign that they were worried about war.

This brings us back to the mysterious figure of Ashraf Marwan. Who was he? Marwan was an Egyptian intelligence operative who also happened to be the son-in-law of Egypt's historic president, Gamal Abdel Nasser, who died in office in September 1970. Marwan contacted the Israelis in 1969 and offered his services. After testing the information he provided to them, some in Israeli intelligence came to believe that he was for real. Others were less sure. But by 1973, the most important Israeli decision-makers seemed to trust him. Several times during 1973 he provided warnings that Egypt and Syria were contemplating war. He also made it clear that Egypt preferred a political settlement, but would insist on getting all its territory back. On October 4, 1973, Marwan told his Israeli contact that he needed a high-level meeting immediately. The head of the Israeli intelligence service (the Mossad), Zvi Zamir, flew to London and met with Marwan, who told him that war would begin at the end of the day on October 6. This was the crucial tidbit of information that convinced Prime Minister Meir that war was indeed on the horizon. Kipnis reviews in detail, in a fascinating appendix to this book, the argument over whether Marwan was a genuine Israeli-controlled asset, as top Israeli officials believed at the time, or was really a double agent, working for Sadat to mislead the Israelis about the precise timing of the onset of the war. The evidence is inconclusive, but it is clear that at the crucial moment in October 1973 the top Israeli leadership had come to depend heavily on their favorite spy in Sadat's inner circle.

Kipnis concludes his comprehensive analysis of the evidence he has amassed by stating that the war could have been avoided. If Israel had been more willing to engage diplomatically, if the US had pressed its ideas more insistently, he believes that Sadat would not have gone to war. There is a school of thought that disagrees with this view and argues that Sadat needed the war in order to become the peacemaker he subsequently became. We will probably never know exactly how Sadat calculated the odds, but we can see that for much of 1972 and up until mid-1973, he seemed quite eager to pursue a diplomatic strategy instead of a military one; it was only when the US-Soviet summit of summer 1973 ended with no sign that anything would be done to address the Arab-Israeli conflict that he made up his mind to go to war.

By September 1973, the signs of war preparations were certainly there for all to see. I saw them, as did many others. But most of us were wedded to the notion that Israel was so strong militarily that it would be suicidal for Egypt and Syria to attack. Deterrence would work. Sadat would not start a war that he could not win. But he did. This book concludes that the war, with all its human, economic, and political costs, could have been avoided if the political leaders in Israel and the United States had read the signals from Cairo more carefully. But these leaders were bound to preconceptions that kept them from seeing clearly. The material Dr. Kipnis presents also affords us a new appreciation of the nearly incestuous relationship at the highest level between Israeli and American leaders—and of how this very closeness led them to reinforce each other's misconceptions.

The October 1973 war may seem far in the past to many people today. But it had a huge impact—on détente, on oil prices, on Israeli and Arab politics. It also led Kissinger to reassess his views on Egypt: shortly after the war he embarked on an intense period of shuttle diplomacy, finally delivering on his promise to turn his attention to the problems of the Middle East, and a few years later, President Jimmy Carter built on the groundwork Kissinger had laid to conclude a final peace agreement between Egypt and Israel, transforming the strategic geography of the whole Middle East. But that is another story. For the moment, it is worth reflecting, on this fortieth anniversary of the October 1973 war, what the Middle East and perhaps the world would have looked like had the war been avoided by an imaginative round of diplomacy in early 1973. It may be worth reflecting, too, on whether there are other situations in the Middle East or elsewhere in which the fixed preconceptions or misconceptions to which policymakers have become overly attached might similarly be blocking the path to a possible diplomatic opening.

No one who wants to understand how war came to Israel and its neighbors in 1973 can afford to ignore this pathbreaking book. Yigal Kipnis has done all serious scholars, concerned citizens, and policymakers a real favor in spelling out so convincingly the steps that led to this avoidable war.

# A Note on Sources

The development of the research and historiography of the events of 1973 leading up to the Yom Kippur War is at a turning point. The forty years that have passed represent the period of time necessary for the disclosure of a significant amount of archival material in Israel and the United States and for researchers to assemble and classify the newly available documents, integrate and verify the information they contain, and ultimately, summarize it in writing to inform the public of the findings.

The dramatic events of that period led to a great amount of writing. In Israel and in Egypt, even writing that dealt with the period preceding the war focused on military and intelligence aspects and was mainly characterized by an apologetic approach or, dualistically, an accusatory one.[1] This body of written material enriched research because each of the writers selectively, and in many cases tendentiously, revealed a great amount of information in his or her possession which would not have been otherwise officially released for publication. Integrating and verifying this information constituted a suitable substitute for archival documentation, which was still secret.

Another important source of information for investigating the intelligence and military dimensions of events that led to the war is the documents issued by the Agranat Commission, established in Israel immediately after the war. The commission was empowered to investigate the conduct of the intelligence and military systems, but not to examine political conduct. Its conclusions were published in 1974, but the full report was released for publication only in 2006. The testimony of the hearings only began to be published in 2012.

The great amount of accumulated information about the intelligence-military domain has led to the dominance of this narrative over the years

---

[1] For example, in Israel, Braun 1992, who defended Moshe Dayan; Bartov 1978 and 2002, who defended Israeli chief of staff David Elazar; Bar-Yosef 2001 and 2011, who focused on intelligence and personal accusations against Eli Zeira; Zeira 2004, who expressed his position and blamed Dayan. In Egypt see, for example, Shazly 1987, el-Gamasy 1995, and Heikal 1975.

in personal and collective memory, in writing, and in the accompanying public discourse.

Another type of information consists of the personal accounts of the major figures of the period and of writings based on interviews with them.[2] These sources should be approached with caution, as memory, in all of its elusiveness, biases, and deceptions, cannot be used as the primary basis for information but can only support or complement it.

Unlike intelligence-military conduct during the period leading up to the war, only a privileged few knew of the political events that took place, and even fewer have chosen to share their knowledge with the public.[3] Those who combined this personal information with academic writing were limited in their ability to base their writings on suitable documentation.[4]

Declassified documents from the US national archives led to a new stage in researching the events of 1973. They have revealed many details about the secret political track established between Henry Kissinger and Anwar Sadat through Hafez Ismail, and between Kissinger and Golda Meir through the ambassadors Yitzhak Rabin and Simcha Dinitz. Kissinger's position as a central pivot in these secret contacts lends added importance to the documentation in the US national archives and the Nixon presidential archives; to a great extent, this fills the gap created by the absence of documentation from states like Egypt and the Soviet Union.

The scope of the documentation necessary to investigate the political conduct of 1973 is enormous. The publication of *Arab-Israeli Crisis and War, 1973* in 2011 has been of great assistance.[5] However, the researcher or reader who does not make the effort to study the large number of archival documents and to do independent research must examine this volume with great care, as many important documents that may change their understanding of the events of the period have been left out. This recognition grows when American archival material is integrated with Israeli archival documentation. The declassification of Israeli documents of the period for researchers began only in 2011. These documents include notes from the most sensitive war cabinet meetings as well as the communications between Prime Minister Golda Meir and then–US National Security Adviser Henry Kissinger, conveyed by the Israeli ambassadors in Washington. These documents were not available to researchers who had by then completed gathering their material and whose works have recently been published. They were also unavailable to the editors of *Arab-Israeli Crisis and War, 1973.*

---

[2] For example, Meir 1975; Sadat 1978; Seale 1993 (biography of Assad); Stein 2003.

[3] For example, Rabin 1979; Ismail 1987.

[4] For example, Kissinger 1979; Kissinger 1982; Quandt 2001.

[5] *Foreign Relations of the United States*, 1969–76, Volume XXV, July 2011.

At the beginning of 2013, the US Central Intelligence Agency (CIA) published its review *President Nixon and the Role of Intelligence in the 1973 Arab-Israeli War*.[6] This survey reveals the almost complete identification between the American and Israeli intelligence assessments. This may lead to the conclusion that the two intelligence organizations were relying on the same sources or that they were supplying each other with assessments, to the detriment of each side's ability to make independent judgments.

The story of 1973 is inseparably intertwined with that of Ashraf Marwan, close advisor to President Sadat, who operated as an agent for the Israeli Mossad during this period. Important material relating to Marwan can be found in the Ahron Bregman papers located in the Liddel Hart Centre for Military Archives at King's College, London.

Research and writing based on historical research methods about the complex of events of 1973 that led to war has only just begun. The important sources are those mentioned: early writing that focused on military-intelligence aspects; literature based on memories of the main figures of the period; research literature that added to these; up-to-date publication of Agranat Commission documents; national archival material of the United States; and documentation from the Israeli State Archives.

The book *1973: The Road to War* is based on research that has made use of all of these sources, integrated them, and added personal interviews with key actors of the period.

Many sources have been abbreviated in the footnotes for the sake of space. The following is a list of the most common sources and their abbreviations:

Lamed Vav: documents sent from the United States to Israel

Vav Lamed: documents sent from Israel to the United States

ISA: Israeli State Archives, Jerusalem

FRUS: *Foreign Relations of the United States* documentary record

LHCMA: Liddell Hart Center for Military Archives, Kings College, London

US NA: United States National Archives, College Park, Maryland

NA RN: Richard Nixon Presidential Materials at Nixon Presidential Library in Yorba Linda, California

LOC: Library of Congress

NSC: National Security Council

HAK: Henry Kissinger

---

[6] Nixon Presidential Library and Museum, January 30, 2013.

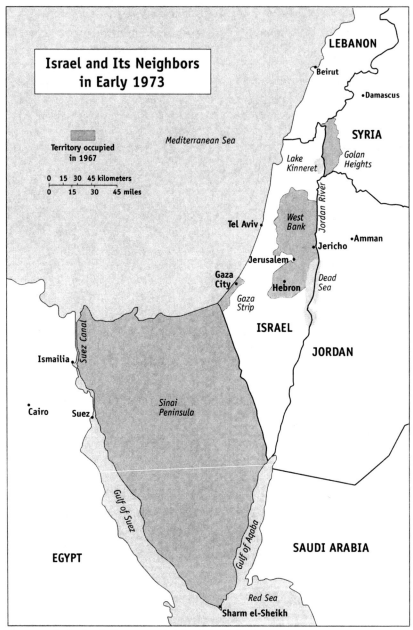

Israel and Its Neighbors
in Early 1973

LEBANON
• Beirut
• Damascus

Territory occupied
in 1967

Mediterranean Sea

0  15  30  45 kilometers
0  15  30  45 miles

SYRIA

Lake
Kinneret

Golan
Heights

Jordan River

Tel Aviv •

West
Bank

• Amman

• Jericho

Jerusalem •

Dead
Sea

Gaza
City •

• Hebron

Gaza
Strip

ISRAEL

JORDAN

Suez Canal

Ismailia •

• Cairo    Suez

Sinai
Peninsula

Gulf of Suez

Gulf of Aqaba

SAUDI ARABIA

EGYPT

Red Sea
Sharm el-Sheikh

Cartography by Lewis Rector, © 2013 Just World Books

# Introduction

"I do not want to blame anyone," said Secretary of State Henry Kissinger to Israeli prime minister Golda Meir in one of their discussions after the Yom Kippur War (also known as the October War in the West and the Ramadan War in Egypt and the Arabic-speaking world), "but over the course of 1973, the war could have been prevented."[1] Kissinger viewed the war which had broken out in October as the "culmination of the failure of political analysis."[2]

Decision-makers in Israel had been mistaken in thinking that their military superiority and deterrence, along with the political support of the United States, would both prevent a political process which they did not want and uphold the favorable (to Israel) status quo. The Israeli prime minister and minister of defense did not comprehend that, in order to ensure Israeli security, military superiority was not enough; a peace agreement was also necessary. At the "culmination of the failure of political analysis" in October 1973, in the days leading up to the war, they erred in their misconception that political considerations would prevent Egyptian president Anwar Sadat from starting a war and that he would wait for a political process to begin a month later, after the Israeli elections. It was convenient for them to base this illusion on the Israel Defense Forces (IDF) leadership's assertion that, if an attack did take place, the standing army could bring it to a halt and that the IDF, without any great effort, could transfer the fighting to the other side of the Suez Canal or deep into Syrian territory.

The American secretary of state perhaps did not want to blame anyone, but he reminded the prime minister of the effort that he had made in coordination with Israel throughout that fateful year to avoid discussion with Sadat about an agreement—or, as Kissinger put it, "to buy time and to

---

[1] Golan 1976, 142.
[2] Kissinger 1982, 459.

postpone the serious stage for another month, another year" and "to calm Sadat down in order to give him a reason to remain passive."[3]

After Meir rejected his plan to formulate the principles of a peace agreement between Israel and Egypt before September 1973, Kissinger had submitted to Israeli pressure and used his great diplomatic skill to maintain the political deadlock. The United States, with his maneuvering, deliberately chose not to advance Sadat's peace initiative. Their moves succeeded—and the war broke out.

Finally, after more than 2,650 Israelis and tens of thousands of Egyptians and Syrians had died,[4] the United States again undertook to advance the Egyptian president's peace initiative from which Prime Minister Meir's government had fled. Following the war, it required all of Kissinger's skill, status, good will, and energies to revive the initiative, which was finally implemented in similar form to what Sadat, via his envoy, had proposed to Kissinger before the war. But the prime minister on the Israeli side who ultimately signed the agreement was no longer Golda Meir, but a Likud prime minister, Menachem Begin.

"Is it worth my while to become a central figure in dealing with the Middle East?" Kissinger consulted with the Israeli Ambassador to the United States, Yitzhak Rabin, eight months prior to the war, just before Kissinger opened a channel for secret talks with Sadat.[5] Rabin, knowing the position of Prime Minister Meir, did not hesitate to answer: Israel had no interest in advancing a political process in 1973. So "he, Kissinger, must not undertake the responsibility for achieving a political solution. Nonetheless, it would be more than essential, perhaps fateful for Israel," if Kissinger led US policy in the Middle East.[6] In that way, he could assist Israel in delaying Sadat's political initiative and, at the same time, act to strengthen Israel militarily and economically in order to deter Egypt from taking military steps against it.

This intimate conversation between Rabin and Kissinger took place on February 22, 1973, and is not included in the American transcript of their meeting.[7] Kissinger had requested that this part of the discussion be considered a talk between friends. Rabin reported on the discussion in writing to the prime minister, as he did with all of the conversations he had by

---

[3] Golan 1976, 142.

[4] The number of Israeli dead includes victims of the war up to the separation-of-forces agreements with Egypt (January 1974) and Syria (May 1974).

[5] Rabin to Meir, February 22, 1973, Lamed Vav/415, Israeli State Archives (ISA).

[6] Ibid. At that time Kissinger was the national security advisor to the president and was not yet secretary of state. Only a month before the war did Kissinger fill both positions.

[7] NA RN, NSC Files, Box 135; FRUS XXV, *Arab-Israeli Crisis and War, 1973*, Doc. 60.

Photo: CIA

*A destroyed Israeli M-60 tank during the Arab-Israeli War, October 1973*

telephone or face to face with senior members of the American administration. His successor, Simcha Dinitz, rigorously continued this practice.

The few preliminary research studies investigating the political events of 1973 have tended to cast responsibility for not preventing the war on Kissinger—for missing the opportunity to advance Sadat's peace initiative.[8] This inaccurate conclusion could be drawn from a consideration of a number of the documents. However, a deeper look clarifies that it was not Kissinger who led this strategy of non-cooperation; rather, he was acting to assist the Israeli government, sometimes under protest, in its policy of not promoting political progress. He was not the one who orchestrated Meir's refusals, but he definitely served Israeli policy interests when they were presented to him as unchangeable realities.

On February 28, 1973, two days after he had received Sadat's ground-breaking initiative through the secret channel he had opened, Kissinger spoke with Golda Meir at a clandestine meeting.[9] The prime minister had not come to talk peace. She demanded that Kissinger keep his promise that, until the end of 1973, the United States would not put pressure on Israel to reach a peace agreement that would force Israel into returning Sinai to

---

[8] See, for example, Vanetik and Shalom 2009, 205–45.

[9] Minutes of the meeting between Meir, Kissinger, and Rabin at Rabin's home in Washington, D.C., February 28, 1973, Aleph-7064/8, ISA.

Egyptian sovereignty. Kissinger replied: "In the talks with [Sadat's envoy Hafez] Ismail, I can apply my regular delaying tactics." On that note, Meir concluded her visit to Washington.

Kissinger had many good reasons not to give in to Israeli demands to relate to Egypt with contempt. It was in his interest to promote the political initiative. After all, a secret political process led by the United States would serve his ultimate aim of continuing to weaken Soviet influence in the world in general and in the Middle East in particular. Promoting such an initiative would also prevent an armed conflict in the Middle East that would damage the thaw in relations between the United States and the Soviet Union for which Kissinger had strived. On a personal level, as well, conducting such an initiative would have enabled him to supplant the State Department (before his appointment to stand at its head) in managing US policy in the Middle East. So, in contrast to the arguments blaming him, it is difficult to believe that Kissinger would have rejected and delayed Sadat's initiative if the Israeli government had responded to it at all positively. Indeed, immediately after his discussions with Sadat's envoy and with Meir, he updated President Nixon about his intention to achieve what he called "heads of agreement" for peace between Israel and Egypt and to formally announce an agreement before the Israeli elections. If Israel agreed, he said, "we are in business." "We've got to tell 'em we're not squeezing them," directed President Nixon, "and then squeeze 'em."[10]

But Meir, via Rabin—and later Dinitz, under her direction—pointedly clarified to Kissinger Israel's interest in maintaining the political deadlock. Kissinger had coordinated the steps to keep his promise to them. The Israeli representatives in Washington kept watch over his moves, lest he attempt to deviate from this policy, and did not hesitate to comment to him if it seemed to them that he had.

Kissinger, for his part, presented the general outline for a political process based on Sadat's initiative to President Nixon and, later, to Israel as well. He tried several times during the following months to change the Israelis' attitude toward his tentative plan and to convince Israel to accept it. But he met with refusal. Thus Ambassador Dinitz could report to Meir later: "Shaul [Kissinger's alias in the secret correspondence] is sure that [the Egyptians] will request [an additional] meeting and he will agree, but in the meanwhile another few weeks will go by and the [US-USSR] summit will be approaching, and so we may possibly get through summer without undue pressure."[11]

---

[10] US NA, Nixon Presidential Materials, White Tapes, Conversation No. 866-16; see also FRUS XXV, *Arab-Israeli Crisis and War, 1973*, Doc. 36, 114–16.

[11] Lamed Vav/555, Aleph-7052/1, March 30, 1973, ISA.

Later, on April 11, after a meeting with Kissinger, Dinitz reported to Meir: "All [Kissinger] asks for is for us to give him ammunition to continue to play for time as he has done up to now."[12] The tight Israeli supervision over the American national security advisor was consistent and continuous. On July 4, 1973, after a discussion with Kissinger, Dinitz reported to the prime minister: "All that [Kissinger] intends to do in his reply [to Egypt] is to propose another meeting. That cannot take place before September. This will again make things easier for him in his contacts with the Russians as he will be able to play one against the other and he can gain time."[13]

At the beginning of September, immediately after Kissinger was named secretary of state, he began to prepare Israel for his intentions to promote the political initiative and end the deadlock. In reaction, on September 25 (two weeks before the war broke out), Meir instructed Dinitz to tell Kissinger: "We are not of the opinion that the present situation is the ideal. But a period of election is not a convenient time for serious discussion. After the election and the composition of the new government, we will consult together [on] what can be done."[14] Kissinger's reply, transmitted by Dinitz on September 30, a week before the Yom Kippur War broke out, was as follows: "Here Naftali [Kissinger's alias] mentioned that when he had formulated the common strategy with us two years ago, he had adhered to it completely and neither of us had lost as a result, but that horse was dead. It is important right now to formulate a new common strategy."[15]

Sadat did not know the details of the coordination between Kissinger and Meir, but he knew the results well—a continuing delay in discussion of his initiative. In June 1973, after the summit between Soviet leader Leonid Brezhnev and US president Richard Nixon in San Clemente, California, had not led to political developments, he began to moderate his threats of war and to intensify his preparations for it, as the only alternative left for him to set the political process in motion. On October 6, six days after Meir received the message that "the horse was dead," Presidents Sadat and Assad gave orders to Egyptian and Syrian forces to start the war.

[12] Dinitz to Meir, report on April 11, 1973, discussion, Lamed Vav/608, Aleph-7052/1 April 12, 1973, ISA.

[13] Dinitz to Meir on his face-to-face discussion with Kissinger in San Clemente on July 3, after an update on the summit between Nixon and Brezhnev, Lamed Vav/765, Aleph-7046/9, July 4, 1973, ISA.

[14] Gazit to Dinitz. Instructions for an answer to Kissinger on the political subject, September 25, 1973, Vav Lamed/738, Aleph-4996/2, ISA.

[15] Dinitz to Meir regarding his meeting with Kissinger, who invited him urgently to the White House on Sunday, September 30, 1973, Lamed Vav/934, Aleph-4996/2, ISA.

*Anwar Sadat, October 1973*

Photo: CIA

On November 7, immediately following the end of the war, Kissinger arrived in Egypt and met with Sadat for the first time. (Until then all contact with him had taken place via his envoy, Hafez Ismail.) The two met privately for four hours, an exceptional amount of time for political meetings. Later Kissinger characterized the meeting as historic and stated that Sadat understood the situation better than he did and was superior to him at delineating his objectives.

Months later, when he had closely experienced Sadat's method of political decision-making, Kissinger described his impressions of Sadat to Ismail Fahmi and Ashraf Marwan: "He is really very farsighted, he is one of the great political leaders I have met."[16] Kissinger defined the Israeli political elite at the time, in contrast, as having a low ability to analyze complex situations and to conduct a long-term policy and compared their decision-making to that of the Syrians, in that "they are preoccupied with the domestic situation."[17]

The policy of repudiation Meir and her "kitchen cabinet" conducted in 1973 and their recoil from promoting discussion of any initiative were based on the public atmosphere in Israel and the Israeli elections which were to take place in late October. Minister of Defense Moshe Dayan's well-known

---

[16] Minutes of the meeting between Kissinger, Ismail Fahmi, and Ashraf Marwan on February 17, 1974, in Washington, DC. NA RN NSC Country Files, Middle East, Egypt, Vol. X, Box 133.

[17] Ibid.

statement that he "prefer[red] to stay in Sharm el-Sheikh without peace than to give them Sharm el-Sheikh with peace and return to the former lines"[18] was based on (or formed the basis of) the position of the Israeli public. The findings of a public opinion poll taken at the beginning of the year found that 96 percent of the population was unwilling to give up this strategic and exotic location in southern Sinai, even for full peace.[19]

A number of years later, most of the Israeli population joined the remaining 4 percent to express widespread support for the peace treaty between Israel and Egypt, which of course included withdrawal from Sharm el-Sheikh along with the rest of Sinai. Dayan himself, who had been minister of defense and a dominant figure in Meir's government, was then serving as foreign minister in Begin's first government and became a coordinating figure in formulating and promoting the treaty. He had been an active partner in Israel's rejectionist policies, but had changed his mind after the war and was heading the peace process on the Israeli side—which in time directly led to a conspiracy theory, according to which Dayan had wanted the war to take a heavy toll in Israel in order to prepare the public for the necessary withdrawal. The emergence of this theory demonstrated how difficult it was for public opinion to accept the political earthquake and the military collapse—and the change of direction which came in its wake.[20]

There was no conspiracy. Dayan did not want Israeli victims; Golda Meir certainly did not either. But Israel was forced to pay a price for the "common strategy" to which Meir had succeeded in recruiting Kissinger and its objective of refusing the Egyptians' peace feelers, at least until after the Israeli elections. The Americans, in return for foot-dragging, required Israel not to open a preemptive attack or escalate the tension by mobilizing large sectors of the reserves, if Egypt were to create such tension. In retrospect, many wondered at and lamented Meir's and Dayan's inaction in not launching a preemptive strike and in not calling up the reserves in the days prior to the war. This inertia was an expression of Israel's clandestine

---

[18] Moshe Dayan, in a speech to a Moshav Movement Conference, June 27, 1969, quoted in *Davar*, June 27, 1969. Dayan repeated his statement in the Knesset on July 15, 1969, in answer to a question by Meir Wilner (Israeli Communist Party). See minutes of Sixth Knesset session 427, July 15, 1969.

[19] Institute for Applied Social Research and Hebrew University Communications Institute, as reported in *Ha'aretz*, April 12, 1973.

[20] This is a very common conspiracy theory in Israel. One of its proponents is historian Uri Milstein. See "Conspiracy, Why Not?," *Ha'aretz*, April 17, 2011, http://www.haaretz. co.il/opinions/1.1171401. In addition, there are those who tie it to the murder of the Israeli air attaché, Joe Allon, in Washington in July 1973: see *Who Killed Joe Allon?*, Channel One, Israel Television, April 6, 2011.

obligation as per the understandings of December 1971 between Israel and the United States.[21]

The secret progression of events in the political track between Sadat, his envoy, and Kissinger and between Kissinger and Meir and her close associates, which has until now not been fully investigated, sheds completely new light on the Yom Kippur War and its causes, on Israeli steps before the war, and on the surprise and shock on the Israeli side following the war's outbreak. The facts which will be revealed here demonstrate that it was the collapse of Dayan's and Meir's "political conception," as it came to be called, not an intelligence failure, that dictated Israeli moves in the days preceding the war and led to failure by preventing Israel from making appropriate preparations for an attack against it.

The deficient "intelligence conception" that led the heads of the Army Intelligence Branch to estimate a "low probability" of war carries its own shame, but had almost no effect on decision-making. The question is not what the intelligence system knew or estimated on the eve of the war but what the political echelon had decided on the basis of events in the secret track—and what was hidden even from the army chief of staff and the head of army intelligence.

The war that finally did break out cost Israel more than 2,650 deaths, hundreds of prisoners of war and missing in action, many thousands of wounded, and great personal suffering for hundreds of thousands of families and friends. Its financial cost was tremendous, but more importantly, on a national level Israel lost its deterrent power. The leadership on all levels lost the trust and the credit to lead.

This book ends with the siren wails that punctuated the Israeli cabinet meeting on the afternoon of Yom Kippur, 1973. This work does not deal with the war but, rather, with its roots. For the first time, the reader is presented with the stories of the complex events of 1973 that led to the Yom Kippur War. An appendix discusses the controversial case of Ashraf Marwan, a Mossad agent who was active in the Egyptian elite.

The book was conceived when, in the framework of my MA and PhD research dealing with the historical geography and political history of the Golan Heights, I became privy to documents of the period, especially material in the US archives. Those documents referring to 1973 were both

---

[21] For further information, see the discussion of the understandings of December 1971 in Chapter 2 and the details of the debate that took place in Israel during the hours preceding the war in Chapter 8.

fascinating and insomnia-producing. I made several trips to Washington. During the day I photographed as many documents as I could, and at night I saved them on my computer. I barely managed to have a look at them, but what I hastily read was enough to agitate me. Some of what I read was already known, but most had yet to be made public. The documents available in the Israeli archives at present have completed the picture. On the face of it, it appears that the Israeli elected leaders of the period, although well-meaning, failed to understand realities and acted with arrogance, with overconfidence, and with political blindness. They wanted the maximum for us but caused us to lose much more.

The documentation indicates that in contrast to the common assumption, it was not an intelligence failure which caused a renewal of war. Intelligence is not responsible for the fact that the State of Israel, whose army was well equipped and well trained, stationed on the banks of the Suez Canal and on a strategic line in the Golan Heights with the political and military support of the United States, was hurled into the grim predicament of the Yom Kippur War with no ability to control events. A committee of inquiry with Israeli Chief Supreme Court Chief Justice Shimon Agranat at its head examined the military's responsibility for the severe results of the war, but not having access to the political material, the committee was limited in its ability even to investigate intelligence and military events, at least those aspects which required an integrated view of both the military and the political. This was all the more true as the committee was unable to examine or to draw conclusions about the conduct of the political system and could not adequately judge regarding the division of responsibility between military and political bodies.

Preliminary historical accounts in Israel, which were by nature partial and biased, assigned responsibility for the failure to foresee the outbreak of war to the intelligence services and the military. Personal blame for the highly charged events of the Yom Kippur War was a heavy burden for any person to bear; this burden overwhelmed and defeated David (Dado) Elazar, who had served as the Israel Defense Forces' chief of staff during the war. The others upon whom the Agranat Commission cast responsibility have continued to deal with this burden, each in his own way. It was convenient for many, especially the political leaders, to limit the personal conclusions to military personalities. However, Golda Meir and Moshe Dayan, who resigned from the government after being elected directly after the war, knew more of their own failures than the public knew then—and more than the public knows today.

Historical research and writing are only possible decades after the events under study. Until then our memories and understandings about what occurred are based only on partial information that, in many cases, is missing, or that focuses on a narrow view of the events and adopts only one narrative of them. In addition, this information is frequently biased and mistaken. That is the main reason why almost forty years after 1973, the Israeli public still does not know much about the real circumstances that led to the war.

The dramatic events of that year naturally led to unceasing examination, but the research, writing, and discussion have focused on their military and intelligence aspects, on the failure of the intelligence evaluations, on the battles with the Egyptians and Syrians, and on the "war of the generals." If these writings touched on political aspects, this was only marginal to the intelligence and the military realms and did not teach the reader about the political events of the period.

However, the central dimension of 1973 was the conduct of the political level: both the political developments that took place and those that were prevented from taking place before the war. As the months went by without anything happening, Sadat deliberated between two alternatives, one diplomatic and the other military. Both were meant to set a political process in motion. In June, following Israel's and Kissinger's coordinated policy to perpetuate the political deadlock by merely avoiding a response to his initiative, Sadat apparently felt he was left solely with the second alternative—war.

The political echelon in Israel who had pushed Sadat into this corner had not prepared to deal with its risks and did not caution the operational and intelligence echelons. They had even tied the hands of the IDF in return for American cooperation in futile diplomacy whose only objective was to thwart a political process.

The great amount of documentation which has recently been publicly released in the United States and Israel and the integration between the two have led to a turning point in historical investigation of the period. We are on the threshold of historical research and writing that will examine the political aspects of 1973. The time has come to investigate the conduct of the political system in 1973 during the period preceding the Yom Kippur War. Updated research resources are now for the most part available, and the importance of the need to research this period extends beyond merely getting to know the past.

Despite the fact that the book discusses the events of 1973, the attention of many readers will be directed toward the present. History, as is well known, does not repeat itself, but it is important to be familiar with it, as such knowledge assists us in better evaluating current events. The actions of the prime minister and the minister of defense that led to the Yom Kippur War evoke thoughts about the role of a national leader, about the relations between decision-makers and evaluation bodies, about the price of silencing a mobilized or a paralyzed media, about the price of the "national euphoria" that characterized Israeli society in the "euphoric period" between the Six-Day War and the Yom Kippur War, and, particularly, about the price of a conviction that time is working in Israel's favor.

# 1

# In Israel—Fear of an American Initiative

*"In my assessment, we have gained a considerable amount of time
for the United States not to act in the Middle East."*
—**Ambassador Rabin to Prime Minister Meir**[1]

At the beginning of 1973, with a clear lack of enthusiasm, Israel awakened
to a new political reality. Since the Six-Day War had ended, the Middle East
had been humming with attempts to set a peace process in motion and to
reach an agreement, but apparently only an informed few could distinguish
between the missions, various attempts at mediation, documents and
plans, and range of initiatives. For many, concepts like the "Jarring mission," "Rogers plan," "Rogers initiative," "Sisco initiative," and others were
all one and the same. All were consolidated in the memory as one chapter
in the period of unsuccessful attempts. They were all pointless moves inasmuch as, in the reality of the period, decision-makers in the White House
were interested in not reaching a peace agreement in the Middle East. This
reality began to change at the beginning of 1973, but many observers still
err and include the first nine months of that year within the preceding
years of sterility. In order to understand what changed, the spotlight must
first be turned on the leader who initiated the change—President Anwar
Sadat of Egypt.

---

[1] All documents from the Israeli State Archives have been translated from the original
Hebrew. Lamed Vav/237, December 22, 1972, Aleph-7061/5, ISA.

## The Challenge of Sadat

When Anwar Sadat was appointed president of Egypt following the death of President Gamal Abdel Nasser in September 1970, no one considered him Nasser's heir, only a temporary caretaker. His advantage was his weakness. There were no expectations that he could, either sooner or later, reach the status of his predecessor as one of the major leaders of the Third World countries, as the principal leader of the Arab world, and as a figure who was admired by the masses. No one expected that Sadat would be successful in dealing with the severe internal problems of Egypt or, even less, in coping with the legacy of the Six-Day War—the national necessity of returning Sinai to Egyptian sovereignty, a mission at which Nasser had failed, both diplomatically and through the use of force. Only a month before he died, Nasser had accepted the failure of his military attempts with regard to the Suez Canal when he signed the ceasefire agreement. The agreement put an end to the War of Attrition, which he had initiated in order to lead the superpowers to impose an agreement on Israel to withdraw from Sinai. Sadat, Nasser's successor, was not perceived as a military leader in war, nor as a personality who could force Israel into an agreement it did not desire. As a person widely believed to be without much political power, Sadat seemed likely to be at best a transitional figure until Egyptian politics would eventually bring to the fore a stronger figure.

Sadat was a surprise. As 1973 approached, two years after he had been chosen without much credit, it appeared that he was surviving successfully, removing his political rivals, and strengthening his status in Egypt as an authoritative president. However, at the same time, in Israel, the United States, the Soviet Union, and the world community, Sadat was not perceived as being endowed with the unique combination of three qualities: first, the ability to observe, to consider, and to plan for the long term, well beyond the ability to view either the internal Egyptian environment or the external political conditions; second, the ability to maneuver and navigate his moves in the immediate and short terms as well as on the long road to achieving his objectives; and, third, courage. His arrival in Israel in November 1977 is one example of these three qualities. His ability to carry out his threats and to initiate war in 1973, a war which appeared to many to have no chance of achieving results, is another example.

The goal Sadat set for himself upon assuming the presidency may seem simplistic—to advance Egypt. All of his moves should be judged in light of this aim. After 1971, his first year in office, which he defined as "a year of decision," ended with no results, Sadat began to adopt a new

Photo: CIA

*Anwar Sadat and Henry Kissinger in Egypt, November 1973*

line of action. Its objective was to solve Egypt's problems and develop the support and patronage of the United States, in addition to assistance from the Arab oil states, which were under US influence. Already in April 1972, even before he cut off the Soviet umbilical cord, Sadat initiated communication with Henry Kissinger with the help of the CIA; clarifications between them continued throughout June and into the beginning of July.[2]

In order to advance in his new direction, Sadat had to take three difficult preliminary steps. First, he had to disengage Egypt from Soviet influence and from its dependence on the Soviet Union; second, he had to reach an agreement with Israel. These were necessary conditions for building ties to the United States and for making the US an ally. The third step, returning Sinai to Egyptian sovereignty, was essential in order to moderate internal opposition in Egypt so that he could survive in office and receive support for his actions.

---

[2] Kissinger 1979, 1293; see also CIA documentation summarizing the process of creating a presidential track, NA RN, NSC files, HAK files, Box 131, and FRUS XXV, 4–5; also, meeting between Kissinger and Rabin, October 6, 1972, Lamed Vav/93, Aleph-7061/5, ISA. Rabin's report to Meir on this subject is not mentioned in the American minutes; they spoke privately.

The return of Sinai to Egyptian sovereignty could not be achieved militarily. Sadat, like the heads of the Egyptian armed forces, knew this well. Only negotiation could return the territory conquered by Israel in June 1967. In order to advance this goal, Sadat initiated two alternative courses: the first, which was preferred, was the political track. The second, only necessary in the absence of conditions leading to diplomacy, was a military move which would set a political process in motion.

## The Expulsion of Soviet Advisors

As the first essential step to execute his strategy, Sadat made a swift and aggressive move. On July 6, 1972, Sadat hosted his vice president, Dr. Mahmoud Fawzy, at his farm and surprised him by informing him, with no preliminary discussion, that he had decided to expel the Soviet military personnel and advisors who were active in Egypt. On July 17, his decision was publicized and was immediately implemented.

This dramatic and significant step is an example of the interdependence of the political and the military tracks. As long as Egypt was dependent on the Soviet Union, Sadat could not earn the trust of the United States and expect it to advance negotiations impartially for an agreement in the Middle East. In addition, to strengthen ties to Saudi Arabia, he would have to distance Egypt from the Soviet Union. And considering the longer term, Israel, as well, would be unwilling to risk an agreement as long as the Soviets had influence in Egypt and army personnel and experts on Egyptian soil.

However, Sadat had no doubt, nor did the commanders of his armed forces, that if military action was required, it could not be carried out without increased Soviet assistance. In the opinion of the army commanders, insulting the Soviet Union and undermining the links between the two states would take its toll on military activity. They were surprised by Sadat's move, had difficulty understanding its meaning, and disagreed with it. "You certainly understand how dangerous this decision is," Chief of Staff Saad el-Din el-Shazly responded to the Egyptian defense minister when he was told about Sadat's decision. "No one can doubt that this will significantly affect our operational capabilities," he added. In order to moderate their opposition, Sadat had prepared them in advance to accept his decisions submissively. "We must separate politicians and military people." he stated on June 6, 1972, to the small group of members of the Supreme Council of the Armed Forces in Egypt. "You, as the military, must concentrate your efforts on preparing the army for the war which is to come." In order to focus them on their role, he emphasized that he was aware that it was not possible to initiate war as long as Egypt could not defend the home front or use weaponry capable of harming the Israeli home front (to deter it from attacking in Egypt as it had done in 1970, during the War of Attrition). Thus, he said, "The problem facing us is what we should do if the political situation forces us to go to war before we have achieved this deterrence."[3] As mentioned, one month later, it became clear to the army commanders that they would have to respond to this question after the Soviets, on whose weaponry and assistance Egypt relied, had been expelled in disgrace from Egypt.

It was not only the heads of the army who viewed Sadat's move as greatly damaging Egypt's preparation for war. Both the United States and Israel had difficulty in understanding Egypt's action and estimated that it had lessened the chances of a resumption of war. As in other cases, Sadat had made this move without consulting with his advisors or close associates.

Sadat severed relations with his patron, the Soviet Union, without backing himself up by any commitment from the Americans. This was unheard of in the political system, and there are those who believe it was also irresponsible. But turning his back on the Soviet Union was calculated not just to open doors to the White House (and this indeed occurred slowly to begin with) but also to open the purse of Saudi Arabia, and more importantly, to access the weapon of oil which was made available to him.

On July 19, 1972, immediately after he announced the expulsion of the Soviets from Egypt, Sadat turned to the United States and requested an open discussion. Secretary of State William P. Rogers and his associates in the State Department immediately responded positively, but National Security Advisor Henry Kissinger reacted with coolness and proposed that the president delay the Egyptian initiative until after the US presidential election in November.[4] There were additional important reasons for Kissinger to ask Egypt to wait: the formulation of a peace agreement in Vietnam, which demanded most of Kissinger's time, his desire to take responsibility for dealing with the Middle East, and his hope to be appointed Secretary of State during Nixon's second term.[5] Sadat accepted the postponement of discussion with understanding

---

[3] Shazly 1987, 116.

[4] A series of telegrams from and to Cairo from July 20, 1972, to September 1, 1972, NA RN, NSC, Boxes 134 and 658; Saunders to Kissinger, July 29, 1972, ibid.; draft copy of a reply from Kissinger to Ismail, December 20, 1972, ibid.; Kissinger 1979, 1295–99.

[5] "Why don't they wait until I am the new Secretary of State? Why do they have to deal with the issue now?" Kissinger complained to Rabin about the Egyptians at a meeting at the White House on October 6, 1972, exactly one year before the war broke out. NA RN, NSC, Box 610.

and even preferred that Nixon be elected for a second term. He was especially anxious that his partner in discussions be Kissinger. He too had already learned that, at the time, two policy systems were operating in the United States (the State Department, headed by Rogers, and the policy directed from inside the White House by Kissinger) and that they were not in coordination. He understood that his interests would best be served by the system operating from the White House, and if necessary, behind the back of the State Department, despite its sympathy for Egypt's position.

Up until the elections, Kissinger and Sadat exchanged letters via the Egyptian intelligence chief at the time, Ismail Ali, in order to coordinate expectations from the track which was to be created. "All Egypt wanted . . . was some assurance that we would meet with 'open hearts.'"[6] Kissinger heard Egypt's demands and replied in this spirit of modest expectations— to meet in an atmosphere of goodwill, to clarify all possibilities, and to begin a continuing exchange of serious and open opinions. However, when the Egyptians proposed two possible dates in October 1972, Kissinger, still involved in the last stages of the Vietnam negotiations, managed to put them off until early the next year.[7]

Sadat waited until after the US elections and then again initiated direct contact with the White House. On December 19, 1972, his national security advisor, Hafez Ismail, requested a meeting with Kissinger in a third country in Europe. Kissinger responded positively, confirming that the meeting would be secret and could take place at the beginning of January.[8]

Despite the promise of secrecy, the Egyptian initiative did not remain unknown to Israel. Rabin, who was well acquainted with Kissinger's schedule, reported to Golda Meir on the following day: "Shaul [Kissinger] is extremely busy and it appears that he has no time for any other subject at this critical stage in the external and internal struggle over Robert's [President Nixon's code name] policies in Vietnam." On the previous days, he had already reported to her: "Perhaps it is unpleasant or immoral to say this, but as long as the president is busy with Vietnam matters, the United States will not be able to find the time to deal with the Middle East. . . . In my estimation, we have gained a considerable amount of time for the United States not to act in the Middle East."

---

[6] Kissinger 1979, 1299.

[7] Ibid., 1300.

[8] NA RN, NSC, Box 131.

Despite Israeli optimism, Kissinger brought Rabin up to date at their meeting on December 22, after he had accepted Ismail's request, "in order to prevent Egyptian requests to others."[9] It is possible that he was referring to "others" in the American government rather than persons or entities outside of the United States. As Rabin had estimated, Kissinger did not have time to meet with Ismail at the beginning of January, but on January 23, precisely the historic date on which a ceasefire agreement was signed in Vietnam, he initiated an attempt to set a date for a meeting between them. For the next two weeks, the two exchanged a series of messages in which Ismail at first pressed for a meeting that month in London and Kissinger postponed the date of the meeting to a month later, at the end of February, and requested to have it at Camp David rather than in Europe. Kissinger explained to Rabin that he had insisted that the meeting take place in the United States and not in a third country in order to reduce any responsibility he might have for the long process of setting a date for the meeting.

In the end, they decided on two days of meetings in the United States. The meetings were coordinated and organized by the CIA for February 25 and 26. It was agreed that they would be completely secret; Secretary of State Rogers and his associates would not know about them. But Rabin, and as a result, Golda Meir and her cabinet did know about the meetings. Kissinger even determined the dates after conferring with Rabin, who preferred that they take place before Meir's visit to Washington. Moreover, Israel acted to prepare Kissinger for the meeting with the Egyptians and had great influence over the content—and, especially, the results.

Simultaneous to these secret moves, Sadat opened a public "diplomatic attack" during which, on January 12, 1973, he met with President Josip Broz Tito of Yugoslavia on the idyllic island of Brijuni in the northern Adriatic (the coast of Croatia today). Accompanying him at the meeting were his advisor Hafez Ismail and Ashraf Marwan, his representative for special missions and the son-in-law of President Nasser. Marwan was then already working as a Mossad agent. Full details of the content of the meeting reached Israel from Marwan,[10] "Zvika's friend" (Zvi Zamir, the head of the Mossad), and became the subject of meticulous study. A month later, the Israelis decided to use this information to prepare Kissinger for the tactical steps Ismail would take in the discussions. Zamir firmly opposed this decision, fearing exposing his source, but he had to comply with the order of the prime minister,

---

[9] Rabin, December 11, 1972, Lamed Vav/237, Aleph-7061/5, ISA.

[10] See appendix for a discussion of Ashraf Marwan's role as a Mossad agent.

who had been convinced that this would thwart Ismail's mission and Sadat's initiative.[11]

One month later, Ismail visited Moscow and immediately after that, London. In the meanwhile, European heads of state were being invited to Egypt, where they heard declarations and details of Egypt's peaceful intentions—and also about its right to use force if these were not accepted.

## The Egyptian Army Changes Strategy

In October 1972, while Sadat was waiting for his emissary's meeting with Kissinger, preparations for war in Egypt were significantly changing direction. President Sadat was called upon to respond to three practical problems:

1. Equipment. How was the military to be equipped and advanced after severing ties with the Soviets?

2. What should the war plans be?

3. Personnel. Who would make up the leadership to advance the military preparations for war? Who would lead the army into war, if necessary?

In everything connected to armaments, the Soviet Union was and would remain the key. At the beginning of October 1972, relations between the two countries were at their lowest point. Even before the expulsion of the Soviet advisors, the Kremlin had no interest in renewing the war in the Middle East, for two reasons. First, the Soviets estimated that Egypt and Syria would lose the war this time as well, which would mean another

---

[11] Dinitz to Rabin, February 18, 1973, Lamed Vav/348; Dinitz to Rabin, February 19, 1973, Lamed/349, Aleph- 7061/6, ISA; Dinitz to Rabin, February 25, 1973, ibid. Zamir took care to oppose transmitting information that arrived from Marwan; more than once, his attempts to protect Marwan usually resulted in discussion in a limited forum of decision-makers. For example, at the end of November 1972, Marwan transmitted to Israel an alert on Egypt's and Syria's intention to initiate a coordinated military action. Rabin, who was in Israel at the time, was permitted to read the information Marwan provided and was instructed to pass it on to Kissinger and Nixon. However, when Rabin returned to Washington, an urgent telegram reached him about a change in instructions "after consultation with the prime minister, the minister of defense, the chief of staff, and the heads of the Mossad and Aman (the army intelligence unit)." The new instructions to Rabin were to pass on only general information: "Tell Shaul that, at the time of your visit in Israel, you managed to meet with various groups. The security organizations are of the opinion that Egypt is preparing a renewal of fighting and they intend to involve the Syrians in this action. . . . The prime minister has concluded that, at this stage, you should not transmit what you read during your visit to your friend." See the document that replaces Lamed Vav/197, Meir to Rabin, January 12, 1972, Aleph-7043/16, ISA.

failure of Soviet arms against American weaponry. Second, the thaw in Soviet relations with the United States and American economic support under the cloak of the trade agreement provided the Soviet Union an escape from its economic crisis and the accompanying damage to its prestige. The Soviets feared that a confrontation in the Middle East would cause damage in this respect.

This also proved how effective Sadat's dramatic and incomprehensible step was. Distancing the Soviets from a position of influence in Egypt weakened the USSR's status in the Middle East. Egypt's preparations for war, which had previously alarmed the Soviet Union, now attracted it as a way of returning to the Middle East and regaining Egypt's dependence while distancing the United States. Sadat effectively took advantage of this temptation and on October 15, 1972, the inhabitants of Port Said again witnessed Soviet ships anchored in the port north of the Suez Canal—and this time, they were carrying tanks for the Egyptian army. Two weeks later, Sadat returned from Moscow, bringing with him a commitment to supply two squadrons of the advanced MiG 23 and Sukhoi 20 planes, as well as a battery of Scud missiles.

The issue of a war plan still remained, in addition to finding the right people to lead the Egyptian army. On October 24, Sadat convened the Supreme Council of the Armed Forces at his home at Giza. The discussion was frank and open.[12] Sadat updated his senior officers that, despite détente (the moderation of the Cold War between the United States and the Soviet Union) and in spite of the humiliation caused by the Soviet advisors' expulsion, the Soviet Union would continue to support Egypt both politically and militarily. Following this meeting, Sadat replaced the high-level military echelon and appointed Ismail Ali as defense minister and commander-in-chief of the army.

Both Chief of Staff Shazly and Ali preferred a limited plan for crossing the canal and capturing a strip of land of only eight kilometers wide on the eastern bank (the "High Turrets" plan), and they were willing to prepare to implement this in a military move that would be coordinated with Sadat's political plans. From the standpoint of Egyptian preparations for war, this was a turning point—recognition that a more ambitious military plan, such as capturing the Sinai mountain passes at a distance of 45 to 60

---

[12] Shazly 1987, 24, 126–34. On December 12, the chiefs of staff of the Arab nations assembled in Cairo and agreed on the details of military and financial assistance to Egypt by the states that were not on the confrontation line, especially making Western-made flight squadrons available to Egypt (Saudi and Kuwaiti Lightnings and Libyan Mirages). Later, the Soviets completed the acquisitions which would be necessary to implement the limited war plan, MiG 23s, batteries of Scud ground-to-ground missiles, anti-tank missile launchers, a battery of SAM 6 anti-aircraft missiles, advanced artillery, and armored personnel carriers.

kilometers from the canal (or to use the plan's code name, "Granite 2"), would not be practical. This was a change in the Egyptian strategy—active planning to implement a limited military alternative.[13]

However, this limited plan did not solve the problem of Syria. The Egyptians feared that if the Syrians learned of their limited plans and understood that the aim was to implement political moves rather than militarily regaining all of the captured territories, they would be deterred from participating in a joint war. In order to ensure their participation, Sadat would have to deceive them and order preparations for an extended war. Shazly and Ismail Ali accepted this, clearly knowing that the plan that would be implemented would be the limited one. When the date of the war was determined at the end of September 1973, they demanded and actually received a written commitment to that end from Sadat.[14]

## What Did Marwan Know?

Did Ashraf Marwan, who was recruited by Israel as a spy, hear of the existence of two plans? From his reports, it is difficult to answer decisively. The previous extended Egyptian war plan was well known to Israel, down to its very details, because of information received from Marwan. Marwan also transmitted to Israel the protocol of the meeting that took place in Giza on October 24, but the document was general and did not include details of the decision or the war plan.

Later, in November, Marwan transmitted an oral report to his handler that gave a more detailed version of the decision. In that report he stated that in December 1972, Egypt would begin specific combat activity east of the canal, which would be characterized primarily by air attacks with artillery support and commando raids using helicopters. The objective of these moves, as he reported, was to cause Israel as many losses as possible. He added that, in mid-December, a plan of general attack would be concluded to cross the canal in order to capture territory in Sinai. This plan would be implemented only after December 31, 1972, in coordination with the Syrians and after heating up the sector. Marwan also reported on Sadat's instructions to determine that the missions on the other side of the canal would only accord with the realistic abilities of the Egyptian forces. He explained that, by saying this, Sadat meant that operations deep in Sinai would be carried out if and when conditions enabled such action. Marwan's report on the October 24 meeting did not include information about a change in "conception" during 1973 and up until the war. This

[13] Ibid.
[14] Shazly 1987, 27.

missing information was significant in the army intelligence unit's evaluations that there was a "low probability" of war.[15]

The updated and detailed Egyptian war plan was known only to a very limited few. It would appear that Marwan was not among them. In retrospect, Zvi Zamir estimated that Marwan was not close enough to Sadat to be privy to all of his considerations and privileged information.[16] (The matter of Marwan and his role in the events of that year will be examined separately later in this book's appendix.)

As noted, Sadat prepared the military alternative for two reasons. Externally, the war plan was an accelerating factor that would motivate a political process if the United States did not support the Egyptian peace initiative. Internally, it provided practical content to his statements about returning Sinai to Egyptian sovereignty and helped to moderate criticism toward him at home. Egypt's military preparations for war can be investigated with the understanding that they were enacted parallel to a preferred political alternative. But the Egyptian military system was not party to the secret of that alternative,[17] nor was Israeli intelligence. The tendency in Israel to analyze Egypt's moves focusing only on the military realm led to a double error: first, the assumption that the expulsion of the Soviets from Egypt also reduced the danger of war; second, that Sadat's political moves were a ploy meant to camouflage his war planning, to moderate United States support for Israel, and to halt or slow down its supply of American armaments.

The beginning of Egypt's practical moves towards preparation for war in October 1972 increased Sadat's military capabilities and, in parallel, his need to make use of the threat of war. It would appear that it was not by chance that (false) warnings of war increased as Kissinger procrastinated in coordinating his meeting with Ismail. However, Israeli army intelligence was not party to what was happening between Ismail and Kissinger, which was known to only a very small number of political figures in Israel; therefore, the intelligence system could not make the connection between Marwan's warnings and Sadat's way of creating an atmosphere of war when important political steps were being taken. Perhaps if the

---

[15] Author's interview with a knowledgeable source.

[16] Author's discussions with Zamir on February 7, 2011.

[17] The military commanders were told that the limited war was a first step in a step-by-step process to free Sinai, and their understanding was that this would be carried out by military moves. Interview with Mohamed Abdel Ghani el-Gamasy on February 24, 1997, given to the BBC for the series *Israel and the Arabs, Fifty Years of War*, Liddell Hart Center for Military Archives (LHCMA), King's College, London. Ahron Bregman and Jihan El-Tahri used these interviews in writing their book *The Fifty Years War*. I would like to thank Dr. Bregman who enabled me to study this material, now located in the archive, filed under the title "Bregman's materials."

*Defense Minister Moshe Dayan, January 30, 1973*

Israeli political system had included the army intelligence apparatus in this information, it could have understood Sadat's pattern of action. Such a distinction might have assisted it in the period leading up to October 1973, when Sadat moderated his threats, and might have led it not to view this as a calming sign but rather as the opposite: another suspicious sign that war was approaching.

## Meanwhile, in Israel

"We have no wish to enter a war of attrition and if they [the Egyptians] renew the war, we will hit them hard," said Moshe Dayan on December 1, 1972, at a meeting of the prime minister's "Kitchen Cabinet," in a discussion of the possibility that Sadat would fan the flames of war as a method to bring about negotiations.[18] The chief of staff, the prime minister, and the defense minister intended to react aggressively to any Egyptian threats, no matter what their purpose.

In February 1972, the IDF prepared one of the largest and most complex war games it had ever conducted, the objective of which was training for a potential canal crossing. They called it the "*Oz* [Courage] Exercise." In Sinai, near Abu Agila at the Ruefa Dam in the El-Arish valley, a miniature "Suez Canal" was dug with great investment of resources and complicated engineering efforts and a division of the IDF organized to train in crossing it. Participating in the exercise were paratroopers, helicopters, air support and airlifted supply forces necessary for such a complex mission as breaching the canal, crossing it, and capturing a bridgehead on the other side. Large formations of the IDF took part in preparations for the exercise. The prime minister looked on from a special observation stage set up on the banks of the crossing site. She listened to the chief of staff's review and to the explanations given by the exercise commanders, Generals Ariel Sharon, Avraham Adan ("Bren"), and Shmuel Gonen ("Gorodish"), and learned about what Israel would do if Sadat renewed fire. After the exercise, in a closed forum, Dayan referred to an Israeli response and said that he did not see the capture of Cairo and Alexandria as a realistic goal in the next war, but that crossing the canal was both realistic and practical.[19] When, a year later, Dayan referred to Israel's intentions if war broke out, he said, "I don't rule out planning to reach the Nile."[20]

Throughout 1972, the IDF continued to train for the eventuality that Egypt would initiate a sudden war. About a year before the war, it conducted a military exercise entitled "Iron Ram." Its opening conditions were based on a situation in which reserve forces reached the canal only two days after the beginning of an attack and Egyptians had captured Israeli strongholds and were holding a bridgehead on the eastern side of the canal. By the third and fourth days of the exercise, General Sharon had crossed the canal at the head of his forces and the combat was taking place on the west side of the canal. Sharon's desire to re-enact this operation during the actual October 1973 war as well did not suit the conditions as they then existed. His insistence on doing so nonetheless led to conflict among the senior army command during the war and harmed its functioning.

In July 1973, three months before the war and after he had completed his term as head of Southern Command and been released from the IDF on his way to a political career, Ariel Sharon spoke out publicly about potential

---

[18] Braun 1992, 18.

[19] Ezov 2011, 66–67; also Bartov 2002, 191–92.

[20] Braun 1994, 28.

combat procedures for Israel. Readers of the daily newspaper, *Ma'ariv*, viewed his statement to Dov Goldstein: "I don't believe that there is any military or civilian target between Baghdad and Khartoum, with all of the area of Libya, that the IDF cannot capture."[21] In answer to an interviewer who asked what he could tell Sadat about the price he would pay if he initiated war, Sharon replied,

> A terrible price, terrible! A price that Egypt would not be able to withstand. In the Six-Day War, Egypt had somewhere to retreat—to the canal, and that was so in the Sinai campaign. In the next war, the Egyptian line of retreat will be Cairo. They have no other line. And that will involve terrible destruction of Egypt. Complete destruction. It's unnecessary, in my opinion. We do not need it. But we will never return to a war of attrition. Despite the fact that we won. The Egyptians will absorb a terrible blow.[22]

Despite the preparations for war, in February 1973, just before the discussions between Kissinger and Ismail, Israel estimated that war would not be renewed in the near future. This appraisal was based on Egypt's lack of military readiness for an attack and on the fact that it would be illogical of Sadat to open fire at this time. As Dayan put it, "Considering the borders which we hold today, in the short term, there is no security danger. In other words, if we are attacked—they will be defeated." Dayan was analyzing the situation in a symposium that included seven past IDF chiefs of staff who agreed with his opinion. Regarding peace, he added, "We can achieve peace, and now, but in return, we must retreat entirely to the Green Line. Including relinquishing control of the Gaza Strip."[23]

Israel's confidence that it would receive sufficient warning if Egypt planned to initiate a war was further strengthened on the night of February 16–17, 1973, far from the headlines and from Washington—in the Jabel Ataka, west of the city of Suez. After almost a year of preparations and training under the code name "Consulate," after sundown on Friday night, four Yasur CH-53 helicopters crossed the Gulf of Suez and landed a special IDF unit of motorized forces. Other Yasur helicopters left toward morning and evacuated the soldiers after they had completed their mission. Two weeks later, when the teams from the special unit and the crews of the helicopters assembled to mark the success of the operation, they

---

[21] *Ma'ariv*, July 20, 1973.

[22] Ibid.

[23] *Ma'ariv*, February 15, 1973. Symposium of chiefs of staff with the participation of Yigael Yadin, Mordechai Makleff, Moshe Dayan, Haim Laskov, Tzvi Tsur, Yitzhak Rabin, and Haim Bar-Lev.

were told by senior decision-makers that they had brought Israel a few years of quiet.[24]

The sense of security among the elite Israeli defense and political echelons was derived from Israeli military superiority, the support of the United States, and the fact Egypt's military secrets were being revealed by a qualified agent like Ashraf Marwan. Now another level was added—"special means," in the form of listening devices on Egyptian military telephone lines. These were meant to supply Israel with additional warning in case Sadat acted on his threats. However, this level of protection collapsed on October 6, 1973.

Much has been written and discussed about the "special means." The discussions have focused on the question of whether these "means" were activated on the eve of the war or whether they were never activated at all. The testimony of the head of army intelligence, Eli Zeira, was unequivocal: the "means" were activated and the information that was received was no different than what had been known to the intelligence agency. This may also be concluded from additional testimony. Those who disagree must contend with a very important factor: As part of its plan to disguise the preparations for war in the days preceding its outbreak, the Egyptian army began a large war-simulation training exercise called "Tahrir 41— Liberation of Sinai" that was to continue for six days. The war exercise was not hidden, nor were the communications between the command posts and the participating units. Army intelligence tracked the progress of the exercise and issued a report on it in an orderly fashion. The Egyptian forces understood that the exercise would be completed on October 7, but in fact, as it was winding down, they received direct instructions (which Israeli intelligence did not have the overt ability to intercept) to move over to the war plan.[25] This was confirmed by, for example, the testimony of the Egyptian commander of a helicopter flight squadron who was taken prisoner after his helicopter crashed. He stated that he had been sitting in the cockpit when he received the order for a change in mission and had been directed to land his forces in enemy territory rather than in the training exercise area.[26] In this surprising sequence of events, there is no significance to the question of whether the "special means" operated or not: the large-scale military exercise prevented them from supplying the detection that decision-makers in Israel had expected.

---

[24] The operation was meant to evaluate the Israeli listening devices, improve them, and assess how long they could continue to supply information.

[25] For Egyptian military conduct during the days before the war, see Shazly, 149–59.

[26] Zeira 2004, 145. For the deployment of the Egyptian army during the days before the war, see Shazly, 149–59.

However, in February 1973, just before Ismail arrived in Washington, no one in Israel was expecting such a scenario. In the very few days between the Jabel Ataka operation and the meeting between Kissinger and Ismail in the United States, some of the Yasur helicopters that had flown to the west side of the canal, along with some of the teams who had flown with them, also managed to make a night landing in the Tripoli, Lebanon, area and to fly from there with an IDF force on another daring operation, this time against terrorists operating in Lebanon. This operation was not concealed. The high-level Israeli defense and political echelons' sense of security was at its peak, and this was also reflected by the decision-makers of the American government. This exaggerated sense of security had decisive importance in the way both Jerusalem and Washington related to Ismail's visit and to the secret talks with him.

## "Let This Thing Go Away"

Kissinger had planned to be active in Middle East affairs following the presidential elections in the United States. He prepared Ambassador Rabin, saying, "It is something you should think about. I know you want this thing [the political process] to go away and you see no desire to raise it." He also warned that if it raised the issue for discussion, Israel would be facing a serious problem. Rabin was unimpressed and presented a concise summary of the Israeli position: "We are sure that the present situation is the best." "That is from your point of view," replied Kissinger, who concluded, "I cannot see anything happening further before the first of the year . . . but we should have an informal talk in mid-November [1972]."[27]

In pressuring Israel, Kissinger made use of Nixon's comments supporting Defense Secretary Melvin Laird's suggestion to "take advantage of Sadat's expulsion of the Soviets and move closer to the Arab position."[28] But later Kissinger accepted Israel's recommendation, its position, and its demand to use delaying tactics and to prevent any developments until after the Israeli elections, which were set to take place a year later.

Kissinger was not acting in a vacuum on the local scene. "Very soon we will be very active . . . to see if we can get negotiations started, immediately after the presidential elections," Secretary of State Rogers stated on the television interview program *Meet the Press* on November 7, 1972. In this manner, he returned negotiations in the Middle East to the media discourse and set the threshold of expectations at a high level. In response, Kissinger proposed to the president that he should begin his second term in

---

[27] Meeting between Rabin and Kissinger, October 6, 1972, NA RN, NSC Files, Rabin/Dinitz Box 135.

[28] Kissinger 1982, 202–3.

a level-headed and careful way and suggested that he "ask Secretary Rogers to avoid intimating any particular direction for Middle East diplomacy until you have had a chance to review the situation looking ahead over the next four years."[29]

Neither did Israel always present a unified front. On November 14, 1972, Dayan arrived in Washington to evaluate the atmosphere after the election and was immediately followed by his colleague, Deputy Prime Minister Yigal Allon. During his visit, Allon declared that negotiations should be initiated with the Egyptians on two parallel tracks: one for a partial settlement and the other for a comprehensive settlement.[30] His statement provoked an uproar. The Soviets attributed special importance to it and termed it a "breakthrough." They approached the Americans to "know what the United States was willing to initiate in light of this statement." Later, the office of the head of the Mossad reported to the prime minister that "the approach of the Soviets, as well as the deputy prime minister's discussions here, have caused excitement in the high echelons of government." Kissinger, reacting to the matter at his meeting with Rabin, expressed his hope that Rabin had clarified to the State Department that Allon's statement had no basis.[31]

Even though in November 1972 Israel had for the first time received a focused alert from Marwan about Sadat's intention to launch a military conflict, at the beginning of 1973, the prevailing atmosphere in Israel was that the state of the country had never been better. The government related to the expected initiative and to the threats of war that accompanied it as to an annoyance that had to be gotten rid of or with which they would have to learn to live.

Media reports gave expression to this mood. "At the moment, there is no Arab state ready for peace with significant border changes. Thus, we must plan our lives in accord with the existing situation for a long period," stated Defense Minister Dayan, appearing on Friday evening, January 12, 1973, on the only existing Israeli television channel in those days. Two days later, on Sunday, January 14, 1973, the daily newspaper Ha'aretz reported on differences of opinion between the ministers who were members of the Ministers' Committee for Settlement Matters: whether, as a group of

---

[29] Kissinger to Nixon, November 9, 1972, NA RN, NSC Box 134.

[30] Allon spoke publicly of Israel's need and willness to conduct negotiations in two parallel tracks. Israel hurried to deny that this was its official position and stated that it was ready to conduct negotiations for a comprehensive settlement as long as it was not required to obligate itself to return all territory it had captured in 1967. Davar, December 21, 1972.

[31] Lamed Vav/229, Aleph- 7053/25; Rabin to the Prime Minister's Office, December 22, 1972, Lamed Vav/237, Aleph-7061/5; Freddie Eini, deputy to the head of the Mossad, to the military secretary of the prime minister, December 24, 1972, Taf Aleph/26, ibid.

experts had proposed, to establish a vacation city at Sharm el-Sheikh, with a population of 7,500, and two extensions at Dahab and at Nuweiba (along the eastern coast of Sinai), or alternatively, as proposed by Dr. Ra'anan Weitz (the chair of the Settlement Department of the Jewish Agency), to establish a large city there, Ophira, and another fourteen settlements between the city and Eilat.[32] On the second day of the new year, the newspaper financial column had reported that prices on the Tel Aviv stock exchange had almost doubled in value in 1972, while the volume of trade had increased ten times as much.

The Israeli public, like the political elite, was completely certain of Israel's absolute military superiority. While it was reported from Cairo on the first day of 1973 that the Supreme National Committee for War Matters, assembling under the chairmanship of President Sadat, had granted him authority to use "any means necessary to prepare for total war, with the participation of a section of the armed forces and the Egyptian masses,"[33] Israel on the following day announced its intention to shorten the period of compulsory service in the IDF. On the third day of 1973 *Ha'aretz* reported that, on the previous day, Israeli Air Force (IAF) planes had attacked in Syria; during the operation, two Syrian MiG 21 planes had been shot down. After a few days, the IAF returned to operate in Syria again; they destroyed four radar installations and brought down six Syrian MiGs. The day after, *Ha'aretz* reported that "the inhabitants of Damascus and Latakia had been overwhelmed with fear."[34]

The political issue also received prominent attention in the media. On January 5, *Ha'aretz's* readers were informed that the United States would begin an initiative in the spring for peace in the Middle East. The front-page headline publicized Prime Minister Meir's expected visit to the United States. This trip, it was reported, could expedite American attention to the question of a Middle East settlement. Similar wording was repeated in an article written by political commentator Dan Margalit three days later, in which he reported that observers emphasized that, due to the date of expected elections in Israel, Washington was liable to initiate political activity immediately at the beginning of 1973. On the following day, Margalit wrote about the "fear of an American initiative." After two weeks, Margalit analyzed Israel's situation in *Ha'aretz* and pointed out Israel's sense of ease in its current position. However, he added, "what clouds these comfortable considerations is the unceasing news about the bustle and activity of the State Department."

---

[32] The headlines and reports cited here appeared in *Ha'aretz*.

[33] *Ha'aretz*, January 1, 1973.

[34] *Ha'aretz*, January 4, 1973.

This State Department activity found expression in the front-page headlines of Thursday, January 11: "The United States Expects to Receive New Proposals from Mrs. Meir for a Settlement in the Middle East." The next day, Margalit informed *Ha'aretz* readers that President Nixon had hinted at his desire for Meir to bring new political ideas. A January 21 report that the prime minister of Denmark had transmitted an Egyptian proposal for negotiations to Israel received this reaction from Meir: "Israel is always ready for negotiations. We are waiting."

At that time, Rabin was just completing a five-year term as Israeli ambassador in Washington and was preparing to return to Israel. At a farewell party for him, in a speech which had been defined in advance as an important declaration of a new American policy in the Middle East, Secretary of State Rogers announced that in 1973 the United States would focus its activities on launching an interim settlement as a preliminary stage toward a comprehensive one. In Israel the Liberal-Herut Knesset faction, under the leadership of Menachem Begin, reacted immediately to Rogers's announcement and requested an urgent discussion in the Knesset. About two and a half years before, Begin had led the breakup of the national unity government in reaction to a policy initiative by Rogers.

Rabin, who knew Kissinger's intentions and moves better than anyone else, saw fit to allay Israeli fears. Relying on an update from him, Dan Margalit wrote in *Ha'aretz* that Rabin was of the opinion that those who were spreading confusion about new initiatives were frightening Israel for nothing. Perhaps there would be talk of initiatives for new moves, but Israel did not have to give in to them. The success of Golda Meir's mission to the United States was assured, he declared. The day before, political columnist Yoel Marcus had also ventured that US policy in the Middle East would not change following the end of the Vietnam War, adding that he was not party to the evaluation that Vietnam would be followed by pressure on Israel.[35]

On January 20, on a cold, clear winter day in Washington, Kissinger and his eighty-six-year-old father sat on the podium as President Nixon was sworn in for a second term. The following day, Kissinger, the son, flew off to Paris to initial the ceasefire agreement in Vietnam in the name of the US government on January 23. As he would subsequently testify, this was the climax of all of the suffering and effort he and President Nixon had experienced during the previous four years. Kissinger succeeded in ending an unsuccessful war that had ended in political loss. This was not the end of the Vietnam story, but it provided Kissinger with much more free time in his work schedule. He was aware that he and the president were at a moment of extraordinary possibilities in the Middle

---

[35] *Ha'aretz*, January 29, 1973, and January 31, 1973.

East.[36] Kissinger knew that he would be required to devote much of the time which would now be available to him to the Middle East, but he still had not decided on which direction to take.

## Ismail Would Not Decide

As Nixon's second term began, backstage moves were renewed with regard to the Middle East. These raised Egypt's expectations for opening a secret discussion track with Kissinger at the end of February, but at the same time increased Israel's confidence in its own expectations. Kissinger was not immediately appointed as Secretary of State, but Israeli efforts to block serious moves toward Egyptian-Israeli peace efforts won his continuing support.

On January 24, Kissinger met with Rabin in the Map Room of the White House and told him that the Egyptians were "bombing" him with requests for a meeting.[37] The next day Rabin also met with President Nixon.[38] Immediately afterward, he reported to the prime minister that although the president knew that many wished to have a new initiative in the Middle East, he did not intend to propose such a move. Nixon "will understand even if the prime minister is not able to bring anything new," reported Rabin. Regarding the threats of war, Rabin told the president that, in his view, even Sadat did not believe that he could eject Israel from the Suez Canal.

During the discussion, Rabin told the president, "The most important thing is that the United States and Israel establish a situation in which Egypt does not have a military option. . . . In this way, they will draw the correct conclusions"[39]—in other words, to advance to a solution in accord with Israel's preference for a partial settlement leading only to the reopening of the Suez Canal. If the Egyptians refused, the status quo would remain, with no renewal of hostilities. Nixon's reaction left Rabin with the impression that the White House would indeed choose this line. This impression was reinforced in a telephone conversation between Kissinger and Rabin immediately following Rabin's meeting with the president.

Not all of the American messages were so friendly and considerate. Although Kissinger was still occupied with the Far East, before he left for talks in Peking and Hanoi he renewed his discussion with Rabin on Middle East issues. At that meeting, on February 5, he told Rabin that the United

---

[36] Kissinger 1979, 1474.

[37] Meeting between Rabin and Kissinger, January 24, 1973, NA RN NSC files, Rabin/Dinitz, Box 135; Lamed Vav/314, Rabin to Dinitz, January 25, 1972, Aleph 7069/6, ISA.

[38] Lamed Vav/315, Rabin to Dinitz, January 25, 1973, Aleph-7069. ISA.

[39] Ibid.

States, like "most of the countries in the world, accepted the Egyptian interpretation of [United Nations Resolution] 242, meaning a retreat to the previous international border between Egypt and Palestine." In response, Rabin warned, "Any renewal of attention to a comprehensive settlement entails the danger of a clash between Israel and the United States."[40]

While Kissinger was away, on February 15, Rabin was called to a talk with James Schlesinger, the new head of the CIA, for an update discussion regarding the coming visit of Sadat's emissary, Ismail, to the American capital. Rabin, and through him Prime Minister Meir, learned firsthand about the framing of a secret track. Ismail's arrival in the United States for discussions with Kissinger would be camouflaged by his meetings with Nixon and Rogers in Washington and, on the following day, with United Nations secretary-general Kurt Waldheim in New York. After the public meetings, the secret talks between Ismail and Kissinger would take place on February 25 and 26. When these meetings were completed, Kissinger would take time to meet with Prime Minister Meir and Rabin.[41] A day later, on February 16, Secretary of State Rogers transmitted the date of the official meeting with the president to Ismail—February 23 in Washington. Simultaneously, without Rogers's knowledge, Ismail was updated on the dates and place of his secret meetings with Kissinger.

On February 20, upon Kissinger's return to the United States, the Israeli press renewed its interest in Ismail's visit. "Ismail Will Propose New Ideas to Nixon for a Settlement in Stages," wrote *Ha'aretz*, including a quote from Cairo that had been published in *Al-Gomhuria*: "Perhaps the United States will now understand the extent to which Cairo is willing to advance towards peace." Israeli foreign minister Abba Eban, who was visiting the United States, hurried to calm the Israelis: "There is no special significance to Ismail's visit to the United States. . . . Relations between the United States and Israel are not a matter to be determined by Ismail."[42]

On February 21, two days before the planned visit, the first news arrived that Israeli fighter planes had downed a Libyan passenger plane in Sinai. Out of 113 passengers, 108 had been killed, along with the flight crew. Attention to this bloody incident pushed political moves from the headlines for a few days, but it did not stop their progress, nor did it put an end to the consideration they were receiving behind the scenes.

---

[40] Meeting between Rabin and Kissinger, February 5, 1973, NA RN, NSC, Rabin/Dinitz, Box 135; and Rabin to Dinitz, February 5, 1973, Lamed Vav/334, Aleph-7069/6, ISA.

[41] On Rabin's meeting with Schlesinger, Rabin to Dinitz, February 15, 1973, Lamed Vav/368, Aleph-7046/11, ISA.

[42] *Ha'aretz*, February 20, 1973.

## "How Am I Going to Fill Two Days with Him?"

"Why would Sadat accept such an agreement?" Golda Meir asked Dayan when they met at the Mossad facility at Glilot on February 18 to discuss the position she would present to the American government on her coming visit to Washington.[43] The question followed Dayan's advice for her to propose to the Americans (and, via them, to Egypt) a partial settlement with no prior conditions on Egypt's part, but with the Israeli condition of an end to the state of war. "Perhaps he will not accept it," responded Dayan. "But it is more convenient for him to accept such a settlement than to demand a final settlement for Egypt alone." At this stage, Dayan was assuming (with certainty, it should be noted) that the need to demonstrate solidarity with the other Arab nations would outweigh Egypt's national interests and that Sadat would therefore, perhaps, prefer a partial and unsatisfactory agreement over a comprehensive and sweeping but separate settlement for Egypt with Israel that would return areas of Sinai to Egyptian sovereignty, but leave the issues of Syrian territory and the Palestine question unresolved.

On that very day, Rabin transmitted to Meir his "preliminary thoughts in light of Ismail's expected visit to Washington."[44] Israel ultimately adopted his appraisals and the line of action he proposed, and as a consequence of the coordination and understanding between Rabin and Kissinger, the Americans adopted them as well.

In his telegram, Rabin first praised the success of US policy during the past four years, emphasizing that its policies in the Middle East were now reaping results. He pointed out that "there is not now any pressure on the president to take any political steps in the international arena, or in facing the Soviet Union and China, and he has the upper hand as no other president has had since the end of World War II." When he went on to discuss Egyptian aims, he argued that Egypt had approached the US to examine its political direction, as it had understood that it could not "achieve the goal of pushing Israel back (not even partially) from the Canal line." His recommendation was to transmit secret information to Kissinger—information obtained by the Mossad from its agent Ashraf Marwan and known in Israel. This would "'immunize' Shaul against the possibility that Ismail's purpose was first and foremost tactical, that is, to prevent a commitment by Nixon to continue supplying arms to Israel."

In contrast to Jerusalem's concern about the coming meetings, Rabin summarized his appraisal:

---

[43] Summary of discussion between Meir and Dayan, Aleph-7066/25, ISA.

[44] Rabin to Dinitz, February 18, 1973, Lamed Vav/376, Aleph-7061, ISA.

Considering my acquaintance with President Nixon and with his assistant, Kissinger, I am not worried about the visit. . . . They know that if Ismail has come here, it is because of the resolute position of the United States against the Soviet Union and Egypt and because of the reinforcement of Israel as a factor in thwarting any military initiative in the Middle East. Sadat and Ismail do not belong to the "international league" who may confront Nixon and Kissinger. Moreover, perhaps [Ismail's visit] will even facilitate the prime minister's visit in achieving our political and security objectives.

Indeed, in response to Rabin's proposal to "immunize" Kissinger and Nixon, on the same day, Rabin received a telegram informing him that the head of the Mossad would transmit to him "documents which he was requested to bring to the attention of Shaul [Kissinger] and Robert [Nixon] only."[45]

The coordination and intimacy between Rabin and Kissinger is instructive. On February 21, when Kissinger returned from his visit to China and Vietnam, he immediately phoned Rabin to discuss Ismail's impending visit and admitted, "Well, I have to discuss with you what I have to discuss with him because I don't see how I am going to fill two days with him, and how I can turn him down without simply telling him no." Rabin responded that he had "sensitive and most urgent intelligence material" which the prime minister decided to make known only to him and Nixon. The material provides a full picture of the Egyptian visitor's way of thinking; Rabin requested that Kissinger read the fifteen-page document.[46]

Even before they met the following day, Kissinger and Rabin spoke again by telephone when preliminary information began to arrive about the downing of the Libyan passenger plane over Sinai. Kissinger opened the conversation with a sarcastic comment: "I am glad to hear that your military are just as stupid as ours." Rabin presented the incident as a serious error by Israel; the two referred to the event primarily in terms of the advantage to be gained by Ismail in his meetings and of the burden it would place upon Meir's visit.[47] "So, you like to be a boss of generals, I see," Rabin said to Kissinger, when Kissinger complimented him and offered Rabin a place on his staff when he completed his ambassadorship. "That's my future dream," replied Kissinger.

---

[45] Dinitz to Rabin, Lamed Vav/348 and Lamed Vav/349, Aleph-7061, ISA .

[46] February 21, 1973, Lamed Vav/397, Aleph-7046/11, ISA.

[47] Regarding the first conversation, Rabin to Meir, February 21, 1973, Lamed Vav/397, Aleph-7046/11, ISA; conversation between Kissinger and Rabin at 09:58, February 21, 1973, NA RN, Telcon, Box 18. Regarding the second conversation at 15:40, February 21, 1973, ibid.

## Philosophical Discussions

Following Kissinger's conversation with Rabin, at the end of a telephone discussion between Kissinger and President Nixon, the president also raised the matter of the downed Libyan plane. He termed it a serious incident and asked Kissinger whether he thought the Egyptians would change their plans because of it. His national security advisor's reply was completely negative: he assumed, and justifiably so, that the Egyptians would feel that they had benefitted from the tragic Israeli error so close to their own visit.

On the following day, a day before Ismail's public meetings in Washington, Kissinger tried to find out from Joseph Sisco, Rogers's assistant, whether the State Department intended to propose an initiative during the visit.[48] Kissinger began the conversation with a blunt attack on Sisco and his associates in the State Department, which pushed Sisco into a corner: "I am a goddamn lowly assistant secretary with practically no influence. . . . Henry, get off my back. . . . Henry, I'm with you, I'm your friend, Henry." Later Kissinger stressed that great enthusiasm should not be shown toward the Egyptians. Sisco agreed with him. Kissinger could conclude that the State Department did not intend to present an initiative, but would be satisfied with listening to the visitor. He also portrayed himself as someone who did not know about the schedule of the visit.

"The position which Dr. Kissinger will present is my position. He is speaking with my authority. Let there be no misunderstandings about this matter." Those were the main points that Kissinger requested Nixon emphasize when he received Ismail at the White House the following day.[49] Kissinger himself did not intend to be present at the meeting. In the detailed preparatory memorandum he had submitted to Nixon, he warned that overenthusiasm on the part of the United States would only increase Egyptian illusions. The aim of the United States in the discussions was, according to Kissinger, to prepare the Egyptians for concessions.

On the same day, in the afternoon of February 22, Rabin met with Kissinger.[50] Rabin asked not to discuss the Libyan plane incident or IDF activity in Lebanon, but rather to focus on the most important thing—preparations for the coming meetings. Kissinger updated him on the uncompromising stance Ismail had presented to the British foreign secretary in London, but he also noted that "it was not clear whether Ismail

[48] Telephone conversation between Kissinger and Sisco at 18:30, February 22, 1973, NA RA, HAK, Telcon, Box 18, and FRUS XXV, 59n6.

[49] Working memorandum from Kissinger to the president in preparation for his meeting with Ismail, February 23, 1973, NA RN, NSC Files, Box 658; FRUS XXV, 69–71.

[50] Rabin to Dinitz about his meeting with Kissinger, February 22, 1973, Lamed Vav/415, Aleph-7061, ISA; for the Americans' notes on the meeting, FRUS XXV, 60–66.

wanted to tell the British what he wanted to say to the United States."
The two men went on to analyze the Mossad document transmitted to
Kissinger the previous day. When Rabin began to go into the details of the
document, Kissinger avoided them and turned the discussion to the meetings with Ismail, saying that he would adopt the following position:

> He would tell the visitor that he had just returned from the Far
> East. He was not well versed in the issues of the Middle East and did
> not deal with them on a regular basis. Thus, at this stage, he would
> primarily like to listen. Here he would inform the visitor that he
> was not operating under time pressure. We do not believe in solu-
> tions from one day to the next. In that context, he would tell Ismail
> that the solution to the problem of Vietnam took more than four
> years. . . . Thus, the guest should not fantasize about the chances for
> achieving ready-made solutions.[51]

Rabin reported to Meir that Kissinger had promised him that "in his discussions with Ismail he had no intention of taking any position or commit-
ting himself to anything except for philosophical discussion and a promise
of continuing contacts in the future. Shaul reiterated that nothing would
be done without coordinating with me beforehand." Kissinger ended the
discussion by recommending that Meir avoid telling the president that
reaching a political solution was impossible, but should take advantage of
the fact that Nixon was not knowledgeable about the details. If she presented the "concessions" Israel would make in order to implement a partial
settlement, "Robert would see this as a great achievement."[52]

## The Public Meetings

On February 23, President Nixon received Ismail in the White House for
a historic official meeting that lasted one hour. During the meeting, the
two played the roles Kissinger had staged for them and did not discuss a
political process in depth. Kissinger joined the discussion toward the end.
He heard the president clarify to his guest the two important points
which Ismail was required to hear. First, with regard to advancing of the
political process, Egypt must lower its expectations and place them on
a schedule measured in years: "The press will tend to believe that this
diplomatic activity would bring an early solution. Both sides know that
is not so." The second point was to define the two communication tracks:

---

[51] Ibid.
[52] Ibid.

the public one with the State Department and the secret and significant one with Kissinger.

Ismail did not, of course, know what the president had said to Kissinger before the meeting:

> We've got to take a very strong line with the Israelis. I know that. We've got to take a very strong line with these people.... We're going to meet, and I am going meet with them—we're going to put her—him in this channel with you. I'll do that today. He will understand. The second point is that I'd tell her—we've got to be in a position, Henry, where we cannot let Mrs. Meir come here and take the same hard-nose line about the election. That's all done now. Right now, this is going to be settled.[53]

After the meeting in the White House, Ismail and his entourage lunched with officials at the State Department. During the meal, he presented Rogers with the aim of his visit: "This meeting was an important preliminary step, to persuade the US to change its policy in the Middle East to one which would not be based on what Egypt considers total support for Israel."[54] Of course, he did not mention his secret meetings with Kissinger due to begin two days later. On the following day, Kissinger telephoned Rabin to update him on these meetings. Rabin's report to the prime minister was: "There is, in fact, no progress.... Ismail's attempt to establish a more positive atmosphere succeeded.... Shaul added that nonetheless it should be remembered that Ismail is possibly leaving the real issues for the meeting with him [Kissinger]."[55]

A day later, Sadat's political alternative was put to its first and most important test. The first meeting of the secret track between Ismail and Kissinger took place at a prestigious private residence belonging to Donald Kendall, the CEO of Pepsi-Cola, one of the president's supporters, and an advocate of improving US-Egyptian relations. Kissinger characterized this as his first step as Middle East negotiator. The meeting continued for four hours and forty minutes. On the following day, they met for another five hours and ten minutes.

On the one hand, here was an American president who had been elevated by his political successes and was free from the pressures of competing in another election campaign, as well as a government that was free to

---

[53] NA RN, White House tapes, conversation no. 862-9; FRUS XXV, 67–68.

[54] Meeting between Nixon and Ismail, February 23, 1973; meeting between Rogers and Ismail, February 23, 1973, NA RN, NSC, Box 658; FRUS XXV, 72–78.

[55] Rabin to Dinitz about his telephone conversation with Kissinger, February 24, 1973, Lamed Vav/424, Aleph-7061, ISA.

undertake new missions of peace from a position of strength, navigated by a highly credited advisor in the figure of Kissinger. On the other hand, there was an Egyptian president who had chosen to rely on the United States, who was inviting American support for his initiative, and who was threatening that if his initiative was not accepted, a military eruption would ensue that would undermine the thaw in relations between the Soviet Union and the United States—the pinnacle of Nixon's and Kissinger's political success.

And in the middle, hidden from sight, was the state of Israel, secure in its military, political, and economic power, guided by a leadership facing an election year; a leadership sure of its ability to remove the "threat" of a political process, deter the realization of a military threat; a leadership undeterred by the possible execution of such a threat, due to its confidence in its own military power.

This was the picture that Sunday, February 25, 1973, one month after President Nixon's inauguration for a second term, as Ismail and Kissinger entered the villa in Armonk, New York, north of Manhattan. After ten months of waiting, Sadat had at last found a way to gain Kissinger's attention—but still not his heart.

# 2

# Four Days in February

> *"There is the new Egyptian approach. The president will have to make decisions. The question is, what do you plan to say about negotiations to him tomorrow?"*
> —**Kissinger**

> *"We just will not go along with this!"*
> —**Meir**[1]

The position of national security advisor to the president of the United States is an important and respected one, but no one who held this position before or after Henry Kissinger had such a decisive influence on the management of US foreign policy and on international political change. Kissinger, born in Germany to a Jewish family, immigrated to the United States in boyhood with his family on the eve of World War II. He reached the White House after an academic career as a Harvard University professor, where he taught political science to generations of students, Americans and non-Americans, many of whom later filled central positions in diplomacy and in world politics. Even as an academic, he stood out in his ability to combine academic thought and knowledge with practical politics; Democratic presidents John F. Kennedy and Lyndon B. Johnson often sought his advice.

Towards the beginning of his term as president, in early 1969, Republican president Nixon invited Kissinger, then forty-six years old, to become his national security advisor. Nixon benefitted from this decision. Kissinger

---

[1] Meeting protocol, February 28, 1973, Aleph-7064, ISA.

extracted the United States from the political and military quagmire in which it had become immersed in East Asia and became a central figure in the management of international diplomacy and a salient architect of détente, moderating the conflict between the two superpowers. Simultaneously, he strengthened the status of the United States in the world in general and in contrast to the Soviet Union in particular. In his conduct, Kissinger succeeded in combining the force of military and political power with an impressive ability to manage discreet and personal negotiation.

Until 1973, Kissinger had been deeply involved in only one major event in the Middle East—the 1970 crisis in Jordan (known as "Black September" to the Palestinians), which served as an intimidating lesson both for the Syrians, who had intended to invade northern Jordan, and for their Soviet patrons. This event was also a good example of American-Israeli cooperation, a combination of military deterrence and political wisdom that achieved their joint goal without resorting to military means. Except for this occasion, Kissinger had influenced events in the Middle East primarily as an "advisor" to Israel in its policies of using military power (in the War of Attrition at the Suez Canal) and in opposing the initiatives of the US State Department. This influence greatly contributed to the development of close relations between him and the Israeli ambassador to the United States, Yitzhak Rabin.

At the beginning of 1973, when expectations for political change in the Middle East were at their peak, Kissinger—chosen 1972 Man of the Year by *TIME* magazine, and the future Nobel Peace Prize winner for 1973—was the obvious choice to implement the change. His first test was the scheduled—and secret—meeting with Hafez Ismail. The existence of a track for discussion with the Egyptians was, for him, confirmation of the success of his policies; as noted, it also greatly assisted his strategy vis-à-vis relations with the Soviet Union. In addition, it very well served his personal interest in vying with the secretary of state over management of US foreign policy. Kissinger chose to limit the first meeting with Ismail to getting acquainted (i.e., implying that the prospects for improved bilateral relations were quite good). Both sides knew that the formality would disappear quickly when the real qualities of each were revealed, but neither could predict exactly when this would occur.[2]

## Sunday and Monday: Kissinger's Talks with Ismail[3]

None of the residents of the New York suburb of Armonk could have imagined, in the peace of that Sunday afternoon, that CIA men had organized

---

[2] Kissinger 1982, 214.

[3] Protocol of two days of discussion and Kissinger's report to the president on the discussion on March 6, 1973: NA RN, NSC, HAK, Box 131; Kissinger 1982, 196–216; FRUS XXV, 80–86.

a gathering in an elegant and well-kept home surrounded by natural woodland at the edge of the suburb. Two groups arrived separately at the house. The first group consisted of four Americans: Kissinger, his secretary Bonnie Andrews, and two members of the National Security Council staff, Harold Saunders and Peter Rodman. At the head of the second group, which included five men, the most prominent was a tall, slender, upright figure with thinning grey hair, a person whose character senior statesmen around the world had praised—Hafez Ismail, the national security advisor of President Sadat of Egypt.

As Ismail shook Kissinger's hand at the threshold, he knew that a difficult mission awaited him. In the ten hours of discussions between them, in the formal atmosphere around the large dining room table and in privacy and comfort, sitting in front of the fireplace in the living room, Ismail had to earn his interlocutor's trust, instill credibility as to Sadat's intentions to achieve a peace treaty with Israel, and prove to Kissinger that this could be accomplished. In order to make Kissinger understand that Sadat preferred negotiation to carrying out the threat of combat, he had to promise, even if it was only by declaration, that ultimately Israel would exist, like all of the other states in the region, as an independent country, strong and in a cooperative relationship with other countries. This was almost a reaction, after a twenty-five year delay, to the excited words of David Ben-Gurion as he read the Israeli Declaration of Independence on May 14, 1948.[4]

Sadat's original objective, of course, was not to advance the Zionist vision. His initiative was a tactical move meant to serve Egyptian interests, but to that end, he had to take a step that involved identifying his interests with those of the State of Israel.[5] Ismail's mission was to recruit Kissinger to this goal.

Kissinger did not make things easy for Ismail in these discussions. He listened to him with great interest and at length, but did not present any initiatives, proposals or ideas of his own. He also did not hide his opinion of Egypt's position of weakness in coming to discuss an agreement with Israel; nevertheless, the discussions in Armonk were businesslike from the

---

[4] "We extend our hand to all neighboring states and their peoples in an offer of peace and good neighborliness, and we appeal to them to establish bonds of cooperation and mutual help with the sovereign Jewish people, settled in its own land. The State of Israel is prepared to do its share in a common effort for the advancement of the entire Middle East." *Declaration of the Establishment of the State of Israel*, May 14, 1948, English translation available at http://www.mfa.gov.il/mfa/foreignpolicy/peace/guide/pages/declaration of establishment of state of israel.aspx.

[5] Kissinger also testifies to this and maintains that Sadat's approach to peace had evolved over time. At the beginning, it was only a tactical move, but later, after the war, the peace process became an end in itself for Sadat (Kissinger 1982, 648).

beginning.[6] Kissinger was well prepared for them, much more than the government of Israel could have imagined when they transmitted the secret material to him in order to "prepare" him for the meetings with Ismail and to instruct him on how to deal with Sadat's initiative. In the secret correspondence he had been conducting with Egypt since April 1972, Kissinger had learned of Egypt's aim to "meet in the spirit of goodwill" and he was ready to grant them that meeting willingly.[7]

After getting acquainted by the fireplace, at which time Kissinger introduced his guests to the three people who had accompanied him to the meeting, the group entered the dining room for formal discussions. Kissinger opened the discussion, immediately and smoothly clarifying that this was to be a direct and secret channel of discussion that would take place parallel to and separately from the open channel with the State Department. He was careful to lower Ismail's expectations of rapid progress and explained that his heavy schedule would make it difficult to devote much time to the issue. He stated that he had found the time for this meeting as he did not want to put Ismail off again, but that he had not arrived with well-thought-out ideas, only to hear Ismail's proposals. He therefore suggested that, at this stage, the parties would be satisfied with presenting preliminary thoughts and would later meet to discuss them. He added that, as he thought that a special trip on his part would attract attention, he preferred at this point to set the next meeting for his planned trip to Europe, which was to take place in just three months, or alternatively, they could meet secretly in the United States. In addition, Kissinger informed Ismail that he would be involved in this process only if he identified real intentions to make progress and that, even then, Kissinger would not promise anything that he could not implement. Thus, he did not see any logic at this time in discussing maps. Almost certainly, Kissinger, an artist at negotiation and discussion, was well aware that Ismail had not expected those opening words after waiting almost eight months for this meeting, knowing that Sadat's alternative in case of failure was the probability of war.

At this point, Kissinger stopped talking and offered coffee to his guest. According to the meeting protocol, Ismail preferred tea. After a hint from Kissinger, Ismail introduced the others in his party. He then went on to present the principal points of his proposal. Kissinger, uncharacteristically,

---

[6] A few days later Kissinger told Meir: "In my talks with Ismail, I could apply my usual delaying tactics. Ninety-eight percent of the time he answered my questions and the rest of the time I filled with platitudes." Report of Kissinger's talk with Golda Meir on February 28, 1973, at the home of the Israeli ambassador to the United States. The conversation lasted about two hours. Aleph-7064/8, ISA.

[7] A CIA document regarding secret high-level meetings between the governments of Egypt and the United States regarding peace in the Middle East, January 15, 1973, NA RN, NSC, HAK, Box 131; Kissinger 1979, 1229; FRUS XXV, 4–5.

did not joke with his discussion partner; it seems clear that he appreciated Ismail's style of presentation. Ismail clearly outlined the room for flexibility within which he could progress, but also posed its limits precisely. Kissinger was attentive and focused on identifying the points on which he could base a plan of action. Two days later, he had already used this information to formulate a course of action for progress toward a peace agreement that he tried to present to the Israeli prime minister—but encountered her refusal. Only eight months later, after the war, when the adamant Israeli opposition had abated, could Kissinger begin to implement his program. But then it was already too late for many.

Kissinger identified five key points in Sadat's initiative and presented them to President Nixon after the meeting with Ismail.

**The first point:** Sadat understood that he had to disconnect the negotiations for an agreement between Israel and Egypt from other channels of possible negotiation between Israel and its other Arab neighbors. This had been known to Israel for two years, after it received information from the most secret sources. Israel had considered transmitting this information to President Nixon and Kissinger only, but had chosen not to follow through, fearing that the American administration would pressure Israel to advance separate negotiations with Egypt. Kissinger learned of this decision only now, directly from the Egyptians. It was clear to him that Sadat really meant what he said; he also heard from Ismail how this was to be accomplished without Egypt being considered a traitor in the Arab world.[8]

Sadat viewed the process of trying to reach a comprehensive agreement between Israel and all the other Arab states as an obstacle standing in the way of Egypt's attempt to achieve peace with Israel and initiate relations with the United States. He understood that no progress would be made if he was forced to tie Egyptian negotiations to those between Israel and Syria and between Israel and Jordan and, in addition, to await the decision of who would represent the Palestinians. However, he had difficulty presenting a plan of action that would cut Egypt off from these channels of the conflict. To extract himself from this no-win situation, he proposed a practical formula: Egypt would advance a separate process with Israel, but any agreement it achieved would serve as a basis for peace treaties between Israel and the other countries that would follow. Thus Sadat could present his moves to the other Arab states as groundbreaking and as precedents to agreements in whose framework Israel would retreat from the territory it had conquered in 1967. Simultaneously, Sadat could free himself from his dependence on the restraints of a more comprehensive framework of

---

[8] Sadat's position on this point had already been known to Israel since April 1971 (Rabin 1979, 345–46).

negotiation. In this way he could return Egyptian sovereignty to territory that had been captured, but Israel would not, at the same time, be required to retreat partially or completely from the Golan Heights or the West Bank. Kissinger understood this well and stated later in the process: "This time it is completely clear, the Egyptians are concerned only about themselves and do not tie an agreement with them to the other Arab countries."[9]

Five years later, this wording was anchored in the agreement signed by Sadat and Prime Minister Menachem Begin.

With regard to the Palestinian track, Ismail said, Egypt would accept any understanding achieved between Jordan and the Palestinians on the question of their representation. He declared that the Palestinian problem would be solved by the creation of a state existing alongside the State of Israel, within the international borders of Palestine (the British Mandate borders), or by self-determination for the Palestinians within the framework of the Kingdom of Jordan. The Gaza Strip, he stated, would be accepted by Egypt to be administered temporarily until such time as the future of the Palestinian state was determined. Kissinger asked that Ismail remove any doubts about this matter. He confirmed with Ismail that if problems should arise between King Hussein and the Palestinians, they would not pose a stumbling block to an agreement between Israel and Egypt and Syria and would not prevent their recognition of Israel.

**The second point** Kissinger identified as a key to Sadat's plan: Sadat was aware of Israel's sensitivity about safeguarding its security. Ismail, even at this early stage of negotiations, left an opening for a solution in proposing a continued Israeli presence at key points in Sinai, at Sharm el-Sheikh, and at additional locations, as well as proposing demilitarization.

**The third point** derives from the two previous ones and illustrates Kissinger's rare ability to exploit what would seem to others an impassible obstruction and turn it into the impetus for a breakthrough. Ismail defined the aim of the Israel-Egypt agreement as passage from a state of war to a state of peace—"a full settlement, a final one, an immediate one,"[10] the basis of which would be recognition of the international borders. However, he determined that full normalization of relations, which would include exchanging ambassadors and official trade relations, would be established only after reaching an agreement with the other Arab states. Until then, there would be a "state of peace" (meaning an end to the military conflict), free passage into Israel from

---

[9] Kissinger to Dinitz, June 2, 1973, Aleph-7052/3, ISA.

[10] Protocol of two days of discussion and Kissinger's report to the president on the discussion, March 6, 1973, NA RN, NSC, HAK, Box 131, and Kissinger 1982, 196–216; Kissinger's report to Nixon on the meetings and for their follow-on discussion on February 26, 1973, FRUS XXV, 80–86.

the sea, prevention of guerrilla attacks on Israel, an end to propaganda, and the initiation of contacts leading to normalization. The process would be completed with a solution to the Palestinian refugee problem that would be implemented by the United Nations, but, as noted, there would be no conditions for recognizing Israel. Israel had refused to accept this, maintaining that, in return for giving up the territories it had conquered, it would be receiving less than full peace. Kissinger viewed this as an advantage[11]—Israel would receive a state of peace but would be able to claim that it was receiving less than peace (namely, the lip service Sadat would have to pay to the other Arab states), in order to demand its continued presence in Sinai.

**The fourth point** that Kissinger hastened to adopt was the format of talks proposed by Ismail—US-Egypt discussions at first. The United States, being well acquainted with Israeli positions and needs and representing Israel on the political game field, would reach an understanding with Egypt on the principles of the agreement; only then would Israel be included in the discussion of the issues and their details, with the United States employing its influence on Israel to accept the principles of the agreement.

**The fifth point**, the schedule, was ultimately the one with decisive significance. A number of times during the meeting, Ismail emphasized clearly that Egypt would not wait for the Israeli elections, which were to take place at the end of October. "We think before the first of September we should have the preliminary phase agreed," he stated. "They [Israel] cannot cite their election as something precluding [negotiations] . . . we still are very far from the elections." He later added, "I believe in a few days' time Madame Meir will tell you they have elections this year. But elections don't come up in our calculations. It's enough for us to wait for the American election. They can put to the people the questions of peace and war and we will see what the people have got to say about that."[12] These were just three of Ismail's statements emphasizing Egypt's schedule conditions. Kissinger replied, "They will do that. They will bring it up. But the question is whether we accept it, and we don't. We wouldn't be talking to you if that were true." Here Ismail was careful to be completely clear: The principles of the agreement could be formulated until the end of May. The details for a comprehensive settlement could be discussed

---

[11] Report by Rabin of his of meeting with Kissinger, February 27, 1973, Appendix A, Aleph-7055/8, ISA.

[12] All three statements are quoted from the protocol of two days of discussion between Kissinger and Ismail and Kissinger's report to the president on the discussion, March 6, 1973: NA RN, NSC, HAK, Box 131.

until September 1973 and Israel had to make its partial withdrawal from the Suez Canal by then.[13]

Unlike Meir, who ignored this schedule, Kissinger etched the target date posed by Egypt on his memory. As we shall see, several times in the course of the coming months—and all the more forcefully when he became secretary of state in September, against the backdrop of the Egyptian and Syrian military preparations—Kissinger appealed urgently to Meir to make a move toward some progress in an attempt to moderate the tension, but time after time, he met with her complete refusal.

During the two-day meeting, Ismail and Kissinger also discussed additional aspects of their meetings. One was the fact that secrecy was to be kept regarding this discussion track; as a consequence, there was the question of what would be reported to the Soviets. Kissinger feared that sooner or later the Soviet Union would understand that information was being hidden from them. He concluded, with Ismail, that it would be logical to report their meeting to the Soviets, but not to go into too much detail about it. In this way, he would achieve three objectives: maintaining his credibility vis-à-vis the Soviets; gaining superiority over them as the one who was navigating the process; and delaying Soviet involvement in and pressure for a Middle East settlement with the assertion that he was advancing the issue directly with the Egyptians. Two days later, Kissinger presented these arguments to Prime Minister Meir in order to convince her not to oppose continuing the discussion track with Ismail. In answer to Ismail's question about what Kissinger would tell the British, Kissinger answered that it would be less than what he told the Soviets. In addition, the two men agreed to conceal the secret channel from the State Department and the secretary of state.

Kissinger and Ismail decided not to update Israel on the details of the discussions until they had achieved an agreement on principles. Kissinger had no intention of keeping this part of the agreement. His report to Israel was immediate and included an oral update and transmission of the discussion protocol and the summation documents. Consultation and coordination of positions with Israel were full and absolute.[14]

Kissinger again proposed Camp David as the site for the next meeting: "The facilities for conferences are very good. . . . Very comfortable. Very quiet. I don't know if your associates will be happy there." Ismail responded, "I don't think so. They will want to be in the city near a bar."

---

[13] Discussion between Nixon and Kissinger in the White House, February 26, 1973, 18:31–19:15. NA RN, White House tapes, nos. 413–33; FRUS XXV, 85–86.

[14] Rabin, meeting with Kissinger, February 27, 1973. An American-written "Summary of Conversation" reporting on the meeting between Kissinger and Ismail was included in this report; see also telephone conversation between Kissinger and Rabin, 19:15, February 26, 1973, NA RN, HAK, Telcon, Box 18.

"The next time I will bring two secretaries," Kissinger suggested, and Ismail replied in kind: "No, just a radio. Don't spoil them."

They decided to continue their communication by correspondence and then meet again on April 10 for two days in order to summarize three issues: the stages of recognition of Israel, the various aspects of security matters, and an exact definition of the end of the state of war. Ismail suggested that the third meeting, which was planned for May, take place in Egypt, so that Kissinger could privately summarize the questions which would require Sadat's resolution with the Egyptian president in person.

Ismail did not only serve as a courier. During the two days, he also had lengthy and serious discussions with Kissinger about developments that would change the realities of the Middle East in the long term. Even though, throughout the ten hours of discussions, the possibility of war was not mentioned, it appears that the two were the only ones who realized and internalized the fact that if the discussions did not lead to the hoped-for result and Sadat was called upon to make a military move in order to motivate the negotiations for an Israeli-Egyptian agreement, the fighting would probably take place a short time after September 1973.

Kissinger, with such great experience in negotiations, knew well the gap between opening positions in political discussions and final positions. He also knew how to distinguish the points on which his discussion partner could not compromise. It was on these that he based his estimation that if Sadat's demands for a full withdrawal from Sinai were met, he would be flexible on the other points of disagreement. In the first hours after the two days of meetings, Kissinger formulated a course of action based on what he had heard from Ismail.

The second day of discussions ended in the afternoon and Kissinger hurried to the airport to return to Washington. At 18:30 he was already meeting with the president in the White House, updating him on his meeting and sharing his thoughts with Nixon.[15] "I now see a glimmer of how we might do it," he told Nixon, who was now eager to put pressure on Israel in order to advance the Middle East process. He proposed the president conduct two separate discussions—one for a partial agreement and the other for a comprehensive agreement:

---

[15] Discussion between Nixon and Kissinger in the White House, 18:31–19:15. FRUS XXV, 85-86. The following week, Kissinger transmitted an orderly summary in writing about the meeting and about his conclusions. His recommendation was to allow the State Department to prepare an interim agreement "under his direction" and to discuss the full agreement with the Egyptians in the secret channel. "Summary of my discussions with Ismail," memorandum from Kissinger to Nixon, March 6, 1973, NA RN, NSC, HAK, Box 131; FRUS XXV, 28–84.

> If the Arabs cooperate with us and keep the principals working on it, so that the Israelis can't [unclear] ... then we put the two [channels] together, it would fit right into your summit. It gets the Russians off our back ... and then, by September 1, we have two things going: an interim settlement and direct negotiations ... and it will look lovely, and it will be a tremendous boon.[16]

However, Kissinger opposed the president's inclination to put pressure on Israel by cutting off assistance. "To threaten to cut off aid to Israel is—we could do it, but such action would lead to an uproar," Kissinger responded. He also disagreed with the president's suggestion to mobilize supporters from the Jewish community in the United States to pressure Israel.

At 19:15, immediately after his discussion with the president, he called Rabin, who opened by saying that he had received additional material relating to the opponent's strength.[17] Kissinger customarily used humor in his conversations when he wished to transmit a caustic reaction to his discussion partner. This time, still under the impression of his discussions with Ismail, he responded that Rabin should not be speaking like that: "You are talking about our friends. . . . I tell you, these are friends of ours. They are not an opposing power," he told the Israeli ambassador. Rabin, loyal to his status as an emissary of Israel, hurried to protest Kissinger's rebuke, but internalized the message. He later testified about those days: "Only a blind person could not have seen that a new relationship was being formed between the United States and Egypt, and only someone who had no political sense would not have understood that this relationship would significantly affect relations between the United States and Israel and reflect on the entire range of US positions in the Middle East."[18]

The rest of the telephone conversation between Rabin and Kissinger dealt with coordinating their meeting the following day, Tuesday. Rabin requested to make it earlier as he, the Israeli prime minister, and the heads of the Mossad would be meeting with the heads of the CIA later in the day. But Kissinger said that this was impossible. This time, he did not divulge to Rabin that his guest before noon would be King Hussein of Jordan, who had come to Washington especially to be updated on Kissinger's discussions with Ismail.

---

[16] Ibid.

[17] Telephone conversation between Kissinger and Rabin, 19:15, February 26, 1973.

[18] Rabin 1979, 382.

## Tuesday, February 27, 1973, 11:42, Meeting between Kissinger and Hussein[19]

King Hussein was a comfortable discussion partner on political matters. Bright, courageous, and pleasant, his strength was in his weakness. He could never come with demands or pose conditions in order to receive economic, military, or political assistance. He could only ask for it. But because of his weakness, he received as much as possible. So it was with the United States and so it was with Israel.

In the days preceding the Six-Day War, Hussein had been forced to put himself into Nasser's hands and subordinate his army to Egyptian command. Therefore, he lost control of the West Bank and especially his jurisdiction over East Jerusalem,[20] while Israel earned a convenient partner for secret discussion and quiet cooperation in common areas of interest, both military and civilian. It was enough to remember the events of September 1970. Hussein had not hesitated to kill thousands of Palestinians who threatened his rule and who had been acting against Israel from within Jordan. At the same time, he also expelled another ten thousand, while in the background Israeli army forces were busily planning final preparations to act in northern Jordan in order to stop any advance by the Syrian army. "Look at Hussein—we have a state of peace with him which is almost perfect. I cannot imagine a better state of peace," Meir told Kissinger when she met with him the day after he met with Hussein.

Hussein had arrived in Washington in haste on February 6, 1973 to present an initiative that would prevent a coordinated Egyptian-Syrian military move.[21] A day earlier, and as though according to an unwritten but

---

[19] For details of the discussion: Library of Congress (LOC), Kissinger papers, Box TS32, Geopolitical Files, Middle East, Chronological Files; FRUS XXV, 86–95; Kissinger 1982, 216–20.

[20] At the start of the war, Hussein's hands were tied; he could not accept the Israeli government's request to maintain the calm along the Jordanian border and keep to the armistice line. When an Egyptian commando regiment was stationed in the courtyard of his palace in Amman, Hussein could no longer maintain command of his army. On the first day of the Six-Day War the Jordanian army opened fire on the western sector of divided Jerusalem, attacked targets in Israel from the air, and even fired a number of shells in the direction of Netanya. Later, Arab Legion soldiers captured Armon Hanatziv (the palatial former home of the British High Commissioner) in Jerusalem. Again the Israeli government requested that Hussein withdraw from the Armon and stop the firing; this time, in return, Israel would determine the armistice line to be the permanent border with Jordan. This request did not receive any reaction from Hussein. For the additional letter to Hussein, see Kipnis 2009, 89.

[21] Hussein reached Washington in a state of alarm that a coordinated Egyptian-Syrian military action would take place in the near future. Hussein himself had refused to take part in such a step and was trying to advance political developments that would prevent it. He reported to Kissinger about a meeting between his advisor, Zaid Rifai, with Sadat in Cairo on December 17, 1972. Report from Kissinger, January 2, 1973, LOC, Kissinger Papers, Box CL 168, 1973; telegram from the US Ambassador to Jordan, NA RN, NSC, Country Files, Box 135; FRUS XXV, 37–43.

accepted practice, Kissinger met with Rabin to coordinate positions. In his report about this meeting to the prime minister, Rabin wrote, "I said that it was well known that the prime minister made a great effort in the direction of seeking a possible separate settlement with the youngster [Hussein]."[22] But, he had explained to Kissinger, Hussein's position on peace borders was not acceptable to Israel. That was also true of Jerusalem, about which he wrote that "although the youth agrees to municipal unity, he demands a division into two sovereign separate parts." "I didn't get the impression that Shaul [Kissinger] held out any hope on the subject of Jordan," Rabin summarized, and he was correct.[23]

When Hussein returned to Washington on February 27 and met with Kissinger for an hour (from 11:42 to 12:45), he heard about Sadat's initiative and expressed his opposition to a separate Israeli-Egyptian agreement. After discussing the aid that Jordan would receive from the United States, they returned to a discussion of the Jordanian position paper regarding peace with Israel. Kissinger searched for new ideas he could present to Israel, and Hussein supplied them: an agreement for an Israeli military presence on the Jordan River, leaving intact Israeli settlements which were established in territory captured from Jordan and allowing Israeli residences in places holy to Judaism, such as Hebron and Nablus [Shechem] and the Jewish quarter in the Old City of Jerusalem (but in territory which would remain Jordanian). Hussein proposed that Gaza be joined to the West Bank by an overpass road to be built by the Americans, so that it would be part of Jordan without the need to go through Israeli territory.[24] Hussein and his advisor Zaid Rifai, who had accompanied him to Washington, confirmed that although they were conducting direct contacts with Israel, the ideas they had given to Kissinger had not been presented in such detail to Israel. The presidential advisor did not hide his opinion that the Jordanian plan was fair and stated that he would try to promote it and combine it with the Allon Plan. He also heard Hussein's opinion that no Jordanian or Israeli plan could advance the two sides toward peace—it would have to be an American plan. Kissinger summarized to himself that, with regard to Jordan, there could be no such initiative before October 30, the date of the Israeli elections.[25]

---

[22] Report from Rabin to Meir, February 5, 1973, Lamed Vav/334, Aleph-7061/6, ISA; Meeting protocol, NA RN, NSC, Country Files, Box 135.

[23] Ibid.

[24] The document's exact wording of the Jordanian proposal was as follows: "The Americans will build us an elevated highway so that we can get to Gaza without going through Israel."

[25] Kissinger 1982, 220.

## Tuesday, February 27, 1973, 15:30, Meeting between Kissinger and Rabin[26]

In preparation for a series of political meetings at the end of February, Rabin received the following telegrams from the Prime Minister's Office:

> February 18, 13:00: Under separate cover, the head of the Mossad will transmit to you two documents, one today and the second in two days, which you are requested to bring to the attention of Shaul [Kissinger] and Robert [Nixon] only. As in the past, the head of the Mossad will transmit copies of the documents to his colleagues as well.
>
> February 19, 12:45: In the meantime, it has been decided to delay, repeat, delay, the transfer of the cited documents.
>
> February 25, 11:30: Under separate cover, Zvika [Zvi Zamir, head of the Mossad] will transmit to you, either today or tomorrow, most important additional material, via Efraim [Efraim Halevy, Mossad representative in the United States]. Make sure to bring it to the attention of Shaul and Robert only. Simultaneously, Zvika will transmit the material to his colleagues.

Latent in these telegrams was a sharp disagreement between Prime Minister Meir and Zvika Zamir about whether to share information with the Americans which would expose the existence of a very valuable intelligence source, Ashraf Marwan, a confidant of Sadat.[27]

Zvika Zamir was born in Poland in 1925. His gaunt, almost ascetic, appearance did not testify to his impressive past in military and security affairs. He joined the Palmach (an elite fighting force in pre-state Israel) in 1946 and was imprisoned in Latrun for smuggling Jewish refugees into Israel. During the Israeli War of Independence, he was a commander of the Harel Brigade and thus commanded the difficult battle of the Nebi Daniel convoy on its way to Gush Etzion. He commanded the Sixth Battalion of the Palmach in the Jerusalem-area battles and then served as Givati brigade commander and commander of the Carmeli Brigade in the south during the Sinai campaign. He later headed the Leadership Department of the IDF and ultimately served as head of Southern Command. He served as

---

[26] Meeting between Rabin and Kissinger in the Map Room of the White House, February 27, 1973, NA RN, NSC, HAK, Box 135; FRUS XXV, 96–99; see also Rabin's report, including the American summary of the meeting with Ismail, Aleph-7055/8, ISA. A written report was transmitted to Rabin at 13:00 and the prime minister read it before Rabin met with Kissinger.

[27] Telegrams to Rabin from the Prime Minister's Office, Lamed/348 and Lamed/349, Aleph-7061/6, ISA; also Zamir and Mass 2011, 81.

military attaché in Scandinavia and in Great Britain. Modest, level-headed, and honest, he was appointed head of the Mossad in 1968 and experienced firsthand the German failure to free the athletes kidnapped by terrorists during the Munich Olympics. Since that time he had been committed to planning an Israeli response.

In February 1973, Zamir too was in Washington in order to closely follow the week of Middle East political affairs taking place in the United States. He had submitted to Golda Meir's decision, which was opposed to his own firm opinion, about sharing the information provided by Ashraf Marwan with senior officials of the US government and US intelligence.

The most important material Rabin received from Efraim Halevy to pass on to Nixon and Kissinger included information received from Marwan. Meir insisted on transmitting it since she viewed it as evidence that the Egyptians were leading Kissinger astray and that their initiative was a guise to veil their preparations for war. Kissinger, who did not have time to read the material, asked Rabin to present it to him. The Israeli ambassador presented the report, detailing Egyptian-Soviet coordination as fully as possible, and explained that the document had been prepared by Ismail for Sadat, summarizing his meetings in Moscow. He also presented a letter of commitment from Brezhnev to supply Egypt with advanced MiG 23 fighter planes and ground-to-ground Scud missiles. The letter included a warning from the Soviet Union to Sadat not to initiate a war without coordinating moves with the USSR. The Egyptian document Rabin presented also discussed a political alternative that would require making use of an oil embargo in coordination with other Arab countries. There was also a declaration that the Soviet Union did not oppose the discussions between Ismail and Kissinger.

It appears that Kissinger did not get excited at the material that Rabin was presenting: his only reaction was a sardonic question as to whether Israeli intelligence would also receive everything that he, Kissinger, said to the Soviets? Two days earlier, the White House had received a letter from Brezhnev that informed the Americans about the military steps the Arab states would take, but emphasized what the Israeli material did not detail— that military moves were the alternative in case there were no political developments. As noted above, the Soviet Union feared military moves that would cause difficulties in its relations with the United States, and all estimates were that a military action would end in an additional defeat for Soviet weaponry facing Western arms.[28] Thus Brezhnev stressed the need to

---

[28] The Soviets primarily feared events that might lead to a conflict between the superpowers. Letter to Kissinger from Anatoli Dobrynin, Soviet ambassador to the United States and Kissinger's discussion partner for intimate clarifications about relations

reach a solution to the Middle Eastern conflict in 1973 and clarified to the American government that if the question of Israel's withdrawal from the territories it had conquered in 1967 was solved, the other issues in conflict would be resolved with no difficulty, the independent existence of Israel and its security would be guaranteed, areas of demilitarization would be defined, and Israel would receive free access for its ships through all water passages. Brezhnev added that an agreement would include not only Egypt but also Syria and Jordan.[29]

Two hours before he arrived at the White House for his meeting with Kissinger, Rabin had received for his consideration the gist of what had come up during the two days of discussion between Ismail and Kissinger.[30] Since the Israeli prime minister (who had arrived in Washington the day before) had also had a chance to look at the report, Rabin could update Kissinger on her reaction: "Are they crazy to come with such a proposal to the Americans? . . . It's the toughest Egyptian position we have ever had." Rabin added the prime minister's appraisal: "There is nothing new here." "For me there is something new," replied Kissinger, and he tried to relate his impression of the new ideas in Sadat's initiative. Rabin interrupted him twice. Kissinger went on to discuss the expected meeting between Meir and Nixon.

"Long speeches about how the status quo is the best will not help you. You do what you want, but I am telling you the facts," Kissinger said to Rabin, who was asking to continue the "understandings of December 1971," which had maintained the deadlock until then. The American protocol of the meeting indicates that the two began a private discussion, but does not say what the subject was. We can get more information from Rabin's report: "Shaul [Kissinger] replied that he understood our strategy very well: that is, under the present conditions, to buy time without having any diplomatic activity and to continue to become stronger."

In his report on the discussion, Rabin presented Kissinger's impression of the new ideas in Sadat's initiative, referring to the formula "sovereignty for Egypt in return for security for Israel":

---

between the two powers, January 28, 1973, NA RN, NSC, HAK, Box 70; FRUS XXV, 19–21.

[29] Dispatch from Brezhnev to Nixon, February 25, 1973. In reply to Nixon to Brezhnev, December 18, 1972, NA RN, NSC, HAK, Country Files, Box 135.

[30] It appears that this document was sent on Kissinger's instructions. Rabin met with Kissinger at 15:15 and, as he reported, "most of it was private." In his report he wrote, "The discussion took place after I had already received (at 13:00) a written report of the essence of his discussions with the Egyptian." Report by Rabin of his meeting with Kissinger, February 27, 1973, Appendix A, Aleph-7055/8, ISA.

> The separation between a state of peace and a later state of normal-
> ization of relations at a later stage, provides an opening for Israel
> to present security demands of its own. In Shaul's [Kissinger's]
> opinion, this point exists in the new Egyptian approach, opening
> new horizons. He says that perhaps on this basis we can achieve
> (without sovereignty) the placing of Israeli army units in Sinai in
> different sectors and at different locations and not just in Sharm
> el-Sheikh.[31]

But Rabin also reported that Kissinger emphasized that it would not be
possible to present Israel's demands to change the international border.

Despite these reactions, Kissinger accepted the Israeli position of maintaining the status quo as a fact and decided not to come into conflict on
this point. However, he recommended that "the prime minister not come
to Robert [Nixon] and tell him that there is no need for anything to be
done; that everything is fine and all that he had to do was to give weapons
and money to Israel." He proposed a way to create the false impression of
a positive Israeli approach while delaying the political process. Kissinger
explained to Rabin that, as the president did not know about the problems
of the Middle East in detail, it would be enough for the prime minister to
present him with five concessions regarding a partial settlement so that
"they would seem like new ideas to him." In addition, Kissinger maintained
that his secret track with Ismail would enable the United States to prevent
the Soviet Union from becoming involved in the Middle East. If the United
States could say that it was directing the negotiations with Egypt and that,
with the agreement of Egypt, then "there was no reason at this stage for
parallel talks with the Soviet Union. Shaul [Kissinger] believe[d] that this
was a practical possibility and he was checking with the Egyptian visitor
[Ismail] and in his estimation they could buy time with such a maneuver."[32]
They agreed to continue their discussion the following day.

## The "Understandings of December 1971"

Kissinger and his Israeli discussion partners often mentioned the December
1971 understandings upon which American policy had been based during
1972, so these understandings should be clarified here.

Sadat had declared the first year of his term, 1971, a "year of decision."
As it came to a close, against a backdrop of fear that Sadat would act on
his threat to reopen fire, Meir arrived for discussion with the heads of the
American government in Washington.

---

[31] Ibid.
[32] Ibid.

On December 1, 1971, Meir and Rabin met with Kissinger at the Shoreham Hotel in Washington for an unofficial discussion, as preparation for Meir's meeting with the president the following day at the White House. Because of the importance of the understandings reached at these meetings, Kissinger again met with Meir and Rabin on December 10 at the Waldorf Astoria Hotel in New York to clearly summarize the understandings and to arrange to implement them.[33] Rabin and Kissinger met again on December 24 in order to complete the coordination.[34] The "Understandings of December 1971" were to be valid for two years and became the basis of Israeli–US relations as well as US policy in the Middle East for the following fifteen months. They contradicted US State Department policy and thus constituted additional proof that the Jarring Mission and the Rogers and Sisco initiatives had had no chance of success. Now, in February 1973, considering the new reality, Nixon and Kissinger wanted to revise these understandings while Israel aspired to continue to conform to them.

In the discussions between Meir and Kissinger in Washington in December 1971, it was agreed that the policy of the American government in the Middle East for the next two years would be based on the following understandings:

1. The Rogers Plan, which involved a demand for Israel to withdraw to the international border "which was like a sword over our head,"[35] would not be the basis of discussion between the United States and Israel;

2. The United States would act to prevent an American-Soviet agreement vis-à-vis the Middle East;

3. Israel would be ready to secretly and fundamentally discuss a partial settlement to enable opening the Suez Canal;

---

[33] Meir's discussion with Cardinal (Kissinger's codename in these Israeli correspondences, before he became Shaul, which itself preceded Naftali, another Kissinger nickname) on Wednesday, December 1, 1971, Aleph-4239/3, ISA; report of the meeting between Meir and Nixon, December 2, 1971, Aleph-4239/1, ISA; NA RN, NSC, Country Files, Box 609.

[34] Report on the meeting between Rabin and Kissinger, December 24, 1971, Lamed Vav/416, Aleph-7052/20, ISA.

[35] This was how Prime Minister Meir described the Rogers Plan in her discussion with President Nixon on December 2, 1971. These understandings were added to the working papers in preparation for Meir's visit to Washington in February 1973. They were entitled "Prime Minister's Understandings with 'Robert' [Nixon] and 'Shaul' [Kissinger]," December 10, 1971, Aleph-4239, ISA.

4. The supply of planes from the United States to Israel would continue on the basis of the quantity and rate of supply requested by
Israel (forty-two Phantoms and eighty-two Skyhawks).

To Kissinger, and to him alone, the prime minister also stated that, in the
framework of a partial settlement, Israel would be ready to withdraw to the
Mitla and the Gidi Passes.[36]

Nixon confirmed this agreement at a meeting with Meir, with the addition of the following comment: "I will not squeeze you, but you must conduct diplomatic activity even if it is only so that you will be seen to be doing
it." They also discussed the possibility that, with an end of the "year of decision," Egypt would renew the fighting or create a real threat to reopen fire.
Rabin reported the way Kissinger related to this: "It's fine to buy time, but if
the Egyptians open fire, Israel has to hit them hard. He promised assistance
from the White House." Rabin answered, "There is no doubt that we will hit
them hard if we are attacked. We won't let Egypt choose the rules of the way
and the manner it is fought." Kissinger responded that in that case, which
he did not believe would happen, it would help if Israel waited "more than
two hours" with its retaliation.

The American demand to wait before retaliation in the case of an
Egyptian attack was actually the price it demanded Israel pay for the four
previous understandings. As we shall see, Kissinger's statement that Israel
would have to allow Egypt itself to choose the rules for the initiation and
format of war explains Meir's and Dayan's later conduct on the eve of the
Yom Kippur War.

## Wednesday, February 28, 1973, Morning, Meeting between Kissinger, Meir, and Rabin[37]

That morning, Kissinger arrived at the residence of the Israeli ambassador in Washington for breakfast and an unofficial discussion with the
prime minister and the ambassador that continued for about two hours.
Kissinger's assistant, Peter Rodman, accompanied him; on the Israeli side,
the Americans were joined by Meir, Rabin, and the new ambassador,
Simcha Dinitz.

---

[36] Report on Meir's discussion with Kissinger, December 1, 1971, Aleph-4239/3, ISA.

[37] Israeli protocol of the meeting of February 28, 1973, Aleph-7064/8, ISA. Kissinger
determined the meeting to be private, so there is no official American report. The
meeting continued for two hours and included Kissinger's assistant Peter Rodman,
Simcha Dinitz, and Avner Idan. For the first and last fifteen minutes, Kissinger, Meir,
and Rabin talked alone. There is no documentation for that conversation.

In reply to Rabin's opening question as to why it was necessary to change the Understandings of December 1971, Kissinger explained that the situation had changed and that it was impossible for the United States to avoid becoming involved in the Middle East. He went on without a pause to discuss Sadat's initiative and insisted on the point which, in his (Kissinger's) opinion could be the basis of this step. Sadat had been compelled to distinguish between "a state of peace," which would be the result of an agreement between Israel and Egypt, and "full peace," which would exist only after an agreement with neighboring Arab nations. Meir was suspicious, viewing this as deception, but Kissinger contended that this was not so. He viewed the Egyptian approach as granting Israel the flexibility to leave its forces at Sharm el-Sheikh and at other key points in Sinai for a long intermediate period. Ismail even invited him to develop this subject and to propose a position paper for discussion: "It is possible to get changes in the Egyptian position, but again, I would try only if you and I agree," he said.

In reaction to Meir's protest that the Egyptians were acting as if they had won the war in 1967, Kissinger requested that she return to practicalities and deal with the Egyptian initiative. "The president will have to make decisions. The question is, what do you plan to say about negotiations to him tomorrow?" Meir did not hesitate. "We just will not go along with this!" she replied.[38] At this stage, Kissinger gave up trying to explain his plan (though he did so ten days later to Rabin) and went on to focus on the planned meeting with President Nixon in an attempt to convince Meir to agree to a continuation of his activity in the secret channel with Sadat.

Meir was not convinced. She argued that the United States had gained from its common policy with Israel during the last year; Kissinger agreed with her, but also mentioned that it was this policy that had aroused Egyptian frustration at the political situation and led it to request assistance from the United States. Now, he claimed, since Egypt's change in attitude, the president could not be expected to adopt a policy of inaction. The prime minister refused to accept the need for a change. When she brought up the relations between Israel and Hussein as an example of achieving a "state of peace" without withdrawal, she heard in reply that Hussein was willing to go far in order to reach an agreement based on the Allon Plan, which included Israeli forces remaining in the Jordan Valley and, perhaps, Israeli settlements remaining as well.

Kissinger brought the focus back to the discussion in the Egyptian channel. He explained that it was easier to discuss issues with the Egyptians than with the Russians, and that the Egyptians would insist on a full Israeli

---

[38] The source for all of the quotes is the Israeli protocol of the meeting of February 28, 1973, Aleph-7064/8, ISA.

withdrawal from Sinai but would be flexible about their positions on the other details of the agreement, while the Russians would not. Thus he preferred to talk to Ismail and distance himself from discussions with the Russians, "but again, I will try only if you and I agree." Meir remained entrenched in her position, saying, "I ask you: Should Israel voluntarily put itself in a more difficult, or even a fatal, position?" Kissinger asked what she would say to President Nixon on the following day when he asked her which of the three possibilities open to the United States she preferred: a political standstill, discussions with the Soviets, or discussions with the Egyptians. The prime minister chose to avoid the question and replied in her fashion, "The trouble is that they [the Arabs] do not want us there. Whatever they will sign, tomorrow they will go on trying to get us out." At this point, Kissinger gave up and ended the discussion: "Please let me know by tonight where you stand for tomorrow so that there will be no surprises."

Although the Israelis promised Kissinger that whatever was said at the closed discussions would not be included in a written report, Rabin saw fit to write the most important points of that conversation: "He [Kissinger] clarified to the prime minister what the prevailing atmosphere was in the government, including the highest levels, regarding Israel. The clarification was impressive." He added, "Shaul [Kissinger] again emphasized the question mark about whether it was even desirable to have a visit by the prime minister at this stage." In addition, Rabin reported that Kissinger repeated his proposals regarding how to act at the visit with the president on the following day, so that Israel's negative attitude towards the political process would not be felt. One piece of advice was that, because the president had not yet read the report of Kissinger's meetings with Ismail, the prime minister could refrain from relating to the Egyptian initiative at her meeting with him. Another piece of advice (as previously noted) was that, since the president was not expert in the details of Middle East developments, Meir could present him with positions from the past (December 1971) regarding an interim settlement which were no longer relevant, and they would seem to be a moderation of Israeli positions to the president.

The atmosphere at Meir's other meetings of the day, with the State Department and with the Pentagon, only demonstrated to her that Kissinger had not exaggerated when he described a hostile attitude toward Israel in the other branches of the Nixon administration.[39] That afternoon, the president spoke with Kissinger and argued that Israel should be pressured to advance

---

[39] Meeting of Meir with Secretary of Defense Elliot Richardson and Assistant Secretary of State Peter Rodman, February 28, 1973, Aleph-7055/9 and Aleph-7062/8, ISA.

toward an agreement—it was impossible to force a settlement on Israel, but the US could refuse to supply it with planes. He based his statement on the appraisal of Richard Helms, who had just completed his term as head of the CIA, that Israel had already received more planes than it needed and that it could now strike each one of its enemies and all of them together. Kissinger defended the need to supply Israel with planes so as not make it more difficult for the Israelis to enter a political process, but the president demurred and said that even though that argument had been raised in the past, Israel had received planes but had not advanced the political process.[40]

## Wednesday, February 28, 1973, 19:30, Meeting between Kissinger and Rabin[41]

"I am ready to pack my things and go home, even before the meeting with the president tomorrow morning—if the meeting with him is anything like what I had today from the members of his administration," Meir said to Rabin on their return to Blair House in the early hours of the evening. Rabin indicated that he had never seen Meir so depressed as at the close of the round of meetings that day. In addition to what was said, it had been announced that the US would support a UN resolution condemning Israel for downing the Libyan passenger plane as well as a decision to set up an investigating committee to inquire into the event. Meir was not enthusiastic about Rabin's suggestion to try to formulate an answer to Kissinger that night but, feeling almost helpless, she cooperated with his attempt to do so.[42]

Rabin called Kissinger and requested a private meeting with him; he returned to the White House, where Kissinger told him that "problems of withdrawal and to what point were no long relevant at that moment. The practical problem was how to reach a concrete agreement about the discussion with Robert [Nixon] on the following day." At this stage, Rabin presented the proposal he had formulated with the prime minister:

> Israel would not oppose a continuation of contacts between the United States and the Soviet Union leading to a summit on the basis of the Understandings of December 1971; Israel would not oppose a continuation of contacts with the Egyptian visitor [Ismail]; the United States would not adopt a position on issues which have

---

[40] Discussion between Kissinger and Nixon, 11:07–11:52, February 28, 1973, NA RN, White House Tapes. Conversation No. 865-22; FRUS XXV, 99–101.

[41] Report of the meeting with Kissinger, 19:30, February 28, 1973, at Aleph-7064/8, ISA.

[42] Rabin 1979, 387.

implications for Israel and for a political solution to the Middle Eastern dispute without the agreement of Israel.[43]

Rabin explained to Kissinger that this was the kind of formula that would enable Kissinger to "sell" something to Nixon without entering into too many details in order to receive approval for granting assistance to produce planes (one hundred improved versions of the Mirage) in Israel, as well as a commitment to continue supplying planes (Phantoms and Skyhawks) with a positive approach to the numbers which were submitted by the prime minister.[44] Rabin added that the prime minister would tell the president in detail about Israeli contacts with King Hussein and would describe Israel as attempting to reach agreements with its neighbors.

At the end of the meeting in Kissinger's office, Rabin crossed the street separating the White House and Blair House, received the prime minister's final approval for the understanding which had been formulated, and close to midnight, reported back to Kissinger by telephone.[45] Kissinger had gotten what he had wanted: Israeli agreement to conduct a private discussion channel with Sadat which would serve as a tool in his communications with the Soviets. At the same time, he could lead US policy independently, even in matters concerning the Middle East, without depending on the State Department and without its knowledge. In return, Kissinger was forced to consider Meir's opposition to a comprehensive agreement with Egypt because of the complete withdrawal from Sinai that would result from such an agreement. He would also have to delay advancing the process at least until November, after the elections in Israel. Kissinger was aware of the danger of such conduct in light of Sadat's threat to take military steps. Even though he believed that Sadat would not benefit from a military move, Kissinger remained aware of the possibility that he might carry out his threat.

At 23:30, immediately after completing his conversation with Rabin, Kissinger telephoned the president. They mostly discussed Vietnam matters. Only toward the end of the discussion did Kissinger remind him that they were to meet with Meir and Rabin the following morning and that Kissinger had reached an understanding with them on the issues, which they would conclude at the next day's meeting with the president. Nixon suggested discussing the matter a half hour before the meeting, and added,

---

[43] Rabin's report of his discussion with Kissinger, 19:30, February 28, 1973, Aleph-7064/8, ISA.

[44] Ibid. Quotation marks appear in the source.

[45] Telephone call between Rabin and Kissinger, 23:15, February 28, 1973, NA RN, HAK, Telcon Files, February 27–28, Box 18; telephone conversation between Nixon and Kissinger, 23:30, February 28, 1973, ibid.

"I am going to get her in the right channel. She's not going to just sit there—you're going to talk about this damn thing and she knows." "Oh, yes," Kissinger replied, "she'll be all right. I think—it took some doing but I think she's—okay." He was cut off by the president, who said that he was happy to hear that and ended the conversation.[46]

On the following day, at 09:47, Kissinger met the president, who then heard his advisor's report about Meir's hard feelings after the events of the previous day. During all that time, Meir and Rabin were waiting impatiently for Kissinger's telephone call with confirmation from the president regarding the understanding that would be summarized at the meeting set to take place in a little more than an hour.

## Thursday, March 1, 1973, 11:00, Meeting between Nixon and Meir at the White House[47]

The meeting between Meir and Nixon was set for 11:00 at the White House. Throughout the morning, Rabin tried to reach Kissinger. Only at 10:30 did Kissinger call him from the president's room and transmit Nixon's confirmation of the details of the understanding.[48] With a sense of relief, the prime minister and the ambassador hurried to the White House.

In order to understand the significance of what was said at the meeting with the president, one must first examine the working papers Kissinger placed before the president in preparation for the two meetings, the first with Ismail[49] and the second with Meir.[50] In the memorandum for Meir's visit, Kissinger briefly surveyed the political situation in Israel. He explained that even though Meir often expressed her desire to retire after the coming elections, it was expected that she would continue to serve as prime minister.[51]

---

[46] Telephone conversation between Nixon and Kissinger, 23:30, February 28, 1973.

[47] Discussion between Meir and Nixon in the White House, 11:00, March 1, 1973, Aleph-7038/12, ISA; http://www.fordlibrarymuseum.gov/library/document/memcons/1552563.pdf; NA RN, NSC, Box 1026; FRUS XXV, 105–13.

[48] Telephone conversation with Kissinger, 10:30, March 1, 1973, Aleph-7062/8, ISA; NA RN, White House Tapes, Conversation No. 866-4.

[49] Memorandum from Kissinger to Nixon regarding meeting with Hafez Ismail, February 23, 1973, NA RN, NSC, Country Files, Middle East, Egypt/Ismail, Box 131; FRUS XXV, 69–71.

[50] Memorandum from Kissinger to Nixon regarding meeting with Meir, February 28, 1973, NA RN, NSC, Country Files, Box 135.

[51] The Americans understood Israeli politics well. Ministers and key figures often discussed these matters with them and shared their knowledge and their misgivings. One example of this: A report of a discussion between the ministers Pinchas Sapir, Moshe Kol, and Natan Peled. Telegram from the Tel Aviv Embassy regarding Meir's political plans, February 27, 1973, NA RN, NSC, Country Files, Box 610.

Photo: Moshe Milner, Government Press Office, Israel

*Golda Meir and Richard Nixon at the White House, March 1, 1973*

Kissinger then advised the president that, since no agreement seemed possible until after the Israeli elections, maintaining the status quo was preferable to pressuring Israel, but that impending elections did not have to prevent political initiatives. His recommendation was to establish an official framework that would investigate ways to advance to peace while Kissinger navigated developments and controlled the various discussion tracks. This framework could also integrate the State Department, which would advance an interim settlement proposal with the understanding that it would have the prerogative and the ability to coordinate developments on this track, while Kissinger would advance progress in the discussions for a comprehensive settlement. "So that Mrs. Meir will not later be taken by surprise by the progress toward peace," Kissinger suggested that the president "ask how she feels about our continuing to work on the elements of an overall settlement in the special channel Dr. Kissinger has opened with Egypt and in talks with the Russians. Asking her views about an overall settlement would be a way to press the point that an interim agreement cannot be regarded as a step sufficient in itself, as the Israelis would like it to be."

On other matters that Meir would raise in her talk with the president—aid to Israel, the supply of planes, and approval to produce an Israeli plane—Kissinger detailed the answers that would satisfy the prime minister and advised Nixon to respond to them in the spirit of what he had agreed upon with Rabin.

After reading a memorandum prepared for Ismail's visit a few days earlier, the president had returned it to Kissinger. "This is the time to get moving and they must be told that firmly," he noted on the document. "The time has come to quit pandering to Israel's intransigent position." Elsewhere in the document he added, "Our actions over the past have led them to think we will stand with them regardless of how unreasonable they are."[52] Referring to the possibility that the United States "could stand back and let the two sides reflect further on their position," the president commented in writing, "Kissinger, absolutely not. Rabin must be told this categorically before I see her. I delayed through two elections and this time, I am determined to move off dead center." Responding to Kissinger's statement that "it is difficult to argue that another few months' delay in moving toward a negotiation would be disastrous for US interests," the president underlined most of this sentence and wrote in the margin: "I totally disagree. This thing is getting ready to blow." Nothing of what was written only a week before was expressed in the meeting between the president and the prime minister.[53]

At the beginning of this meeting, the president did not forget to wish Rabin a happy fifty-first birthday, as well as wishing success to Simcha Dinitz, Rabin's replacement, who was also present. After the media people had left the room, the conversation turned to practical matters. Nixon opened by saying, "I'm glad you had a talk with Henry," thus confirming that the meeting actually represented official confirmation for the formulae agreed upon the previous evening. The president made an effort to create a supportive atmosphere. He removed the discussion of the downed Libyan plane from the agenda by saying, "Things like that happen. . . . I have no doubt that you didn't do it intentionally." He went on to focus on the main topics: the supply of arms and the negotiations. Nixon remarked that there was no need to tie the two together, but immediately emphasized the connection: "We supply you with the military and economic assistance which will continue. Israel should be strong enough to defend itself. We also think that it is our and your interest to move on the political side."[54]

As the discussion continued, the two leaders played the roles Kissinger had prepared for them; each of them in turn declaimed the texts he had prepared for them to say. Meir stressed Israel's willingness to conduct negotiations at any time and at any place, and Nixon emphasized the fact that the time had come to implement Kissinger's and his own tactics in

---

[52] Kissinger 1982, 212.

[53] Memorandum from Kissinger to Nixon regarding meeting with Hafez Ismail, February 23, 1973; FRUS XXV, 69–71.

[54] Discussion between Meir and Nixon in the White House, 11:00, March 1, 1973; Aleph-7038/12, ISA; NA RN, NSC, Box 1026; FRUS XXV, 105–13; http://www.fordlibrarymuseum.gov/library/document/memcons/1552563.pdf.

Photo: Moshe Milner, Government Press Office, Israel

*Simcha Dinitz and Yitzhak Rabin in Washington, D.C., February 1, 1973*

the Middle East—two tracks, one public and the other secret. He said that he would not put the prime minister in an impossible situation, from her perspective, and explained that he was aware that she was facing elections. Nixon presented the way to move forward that Kissinger had proposed. In order to allay Meir's suspicions, he explained to her that the moves should be made ambiguously and that "Henry is a master of fuzzy language . . . and the only man who can talk for one and a half hours without saying anything." Kissinger, for his part, saw fit to add that his discussions with the Egyptians would serve as an excuse to postpone receiving the Soviets' detailed position paper.

Even though the president was speaking of a comprehensive settlement, Meir, as Kissinger had advised, went on to speak of the concessions Israel was willing to make for an interim settlement. With help from Kissinger, Meir explained to the president that these concessions had not been publicly stated and that the very act of publicizing them would be considered progress.[55] The concessions to which Meir was referring included withdrawing to the Sinai passes, opening the canal, and allowing a limited number of Egyptian policemen to cross to the east side of the canal. These had solely been intended as information for the president and Kissinger. Kissinger now pointed out to the president that "these proposals have never been formally put." Nixon replied, "Don't tell [the Department of] State the Israeli position [in advance]."

Meir and Dayan had agreed upon these concessions in Israel, knowing that Sadat would not accept an interim settlement that was unconnected to a comprehensive agreement. In other words, these concessions did not constitute a "danger" of setting off real progress in a political process (which Meir opposed); presenting them to the president was meant to "sell" him something in order for him to approve the other Israeli demands.

Nixon summarized the matter by saying that if the United States was the mediator, Israel was in a good position. At this point, as he had been instructed, the president asked the prime minister how she viewed this plan of action. Meir approved it and hurried to propose that they discuss aid issues. As expected, the answers she received were to her satisfaction.[56] "It's very important that nothing be said publicly," Nixon requested, and ended with another request "not to let the Jews incite Congress." He was referring to Israeli support for the US Jewish lobby, which demanded that the United States condition the trade agreement between the United States and the Soviet Union on a change in the Soviet government's attitude toward the emigration of Jews from the Soviet Union. "You can lick anybody except the Soviet Union. We have to keep them out. Let us develop a Soviet policy so we can influence them."

After the meeting, when they were left alone, Nixon asked Kissinger if there was anything significant in the position Meir presented.[57] Kissinger

---

[55] In a telephone conversation between Rabin and Kissinger on March 1, 1973, at 10:30, a half hour before Meir met with Nixon, Kissinger told Rabin that "at a certain stage [of the discussion] Robert [Nixon] would latch onto Meir's statements about a partial settlement." Even before that, Rabin had proposed "selling" the president Israeli concessions regarding a partial settlement, which were not known to him and had not been publicized. 19:30, February 28, 1973, Aleph-7064/8; Rabin's report of the conversation, 10:30, March 1, 1978, Aleph-7062/8, ISA.

[56] After the meeting, Kissinger sent a letter to Rogers and Richardson and updated them that, contradicting Israeli demands, the president had decided to approve at least one hundred improved Mirage planes and to continue the supply of Skyhawks and Phantoms in 1974, without specifying the exact numbers. The decision on the quantity and the rate of supply would be discussed later. Memorandum from Kissinger to Rogers and Schlesinger, March 2, 1973, NA RN, NSC, Country Files, Box 135; FRUS XXV, 116–17.

[57] The meeting between Nixon and Meir ended at 12:39. Nixon and Kissinger talked from 12:44 to 13:06. NA RN, White House Tapes, Conversation No. 866-16; FRUS XXV, 114–16.

presented Israel's willingness to withdraw to the line of the Sinai passes in an interim settlement as "significant," but he also clearly explained the difficulties in making progress. The first, the easier one, was Israel's opposition to Egypt posting soldiers east of the canal and its agreement to place only police officials. The second and more difficult question to resolve was the connection between an interim settlement and a comprehensive one. Here Kissinger was practical. He explained to the president that he would try to get the Egyptians to agree to a version that would include a vague connection between an interim and a comprehensive agreement. This would enable Sisco in the State Department to prepare a proposal for an interim settlement before Kissinger's next meeting with Ismail, which, as noted, was scheduled to take place in another six weeks. He also said that he hoped to get Egypt's ideas for a framework of principles for a comprehensive agreement; if Israel would accept them, "then we're in business." In any case, they could apply pressure on Israel to accept them. "We've got to tell 'em we're not squeezing them and then squeeze 'em," directed President Nixon.[58]

---

[58] Ibid.

# 3

# From Armonk to Golda's Kitchen—
# March–April 1973

*"I know it is an election year for you, and a hard time for a decision.
But I would like some idea of your strategic conception, whether we can
get some heads of agreement that could give us some breathing space—
by, first, getting an interim agreement. . . . Mr. Ambassador, you are in
an odd period of tranquility. You have made your own assessment, but
the reason for the absence of pressure on you now is because I have not
permitted anyone to move. I have told Rabin—you have to be prepared."*

**—Henry Kissinger to Ambassador Dinitz[1]**

With the start of the secret discussions between Kissinger and Ismail, Sadat
felt that a framework for discussion, aiming toward a peace agreement
with Israel, had been created. In Sadat's view, the military alternative would
give momentum toward negotiations if Kissinger and Ismail failed to initiate them. Although Sadat had inaugurated the political channel, progress
depended on Kissinger—specifically, his ability to influence Israel. On
the other hand, Egypt conducted its military activities independently and
unconditionally, directed by the army chiefs with the assistance of Sadat,
who intended to induce the Soviet Union to open its arms depots to the
Egyptian army; to recruit the aid of additional Arab states, particularly
Libya; to persuade the Saudis to activate the oil weapon when the time

---

[1] Kissinger to Dinitz at their meeting on April 11, 1973, in the Map Room of the White
House. NA RN, NSC, Country Files, Box 135.

came; and of course, to coordinate the combined attack with the president of Syria, Hafez al-Assad.

The information accessible to the Israeli intelligence organizations about Egypt's inclinations was limited to activity in the military channel. Their intelligence sources, including the "superspy" Ashraf Marwan, were able to gain information on military preparations only, while other sources who could have supplied the full political information Meir and Dayan required for a general assessment of the situation chose not to do so. Nor did they update Israeli intelligence on the schedule for progress in the political channel, which Sadat had defined and Ismail had clarified to Kissinger: to reach agreement on principles between Egypt and the United States on full peace between Egypt and Israel by the end of spring and, by autumn, to achieve partial implementation and parallel, direct negotiations with Israel on the details of a comprehensive agreement that would be confirmed by the Israeli public in the October elections. This implied ultimatum, which in fact ended when the Yom Kippur War broke out, was completely concealed from the national intelligence appraisal team in Israel but was well known and obvious to Meir and Dayan. They were the only ones among Israeli decision-makers who knew Sadat's deadline for reaching an agreement—September 1973. But Dayan and Meir did not realize the significance of that date for Sadat and for the Egyptians—three years since his appointment as president of Egypt and about a month before the Israeli elections. After three years of disillusionment with the reaction to his peace-seeking intentions and continuing delays in beginning negotiations, Sadat was determined to set a political process in motion, tying Egypt's fate to the support of the United States and returning Sinai to Egyptian sovereignty. He viewed the elections in Israel as a test of the sincerity of Israel's intentions.

In the summer of 1973, Sadat understood that only the military alternative was left to him in order to bring about negotiations.

## The First Steps: March 1973

Discussions completed, Kissinger began to organize his advisory staff to prepare for expeditious action that would include the Middle East. They expected developments that even the energetic national security advisor would have difficulty managing. As James Reston put it, "All Kissinger needs in this situation is for somebody to invent the 48-hour day."[2] Until such an inventor was found, Kissinger intended to go "off for a couple of weeks to rest and to put his mind to the new tasks the president [had] given

---

[2] James Reston, "The Indefatigable Dr. Kissinger Looks to New Worlds to Conquer," *New York Times*, March 8, 1973. Reprinted in *Ha'aretz*, March 9, 1973.

him."[3] However, even before leaving for vacation, he had hurried to formulate his plan, which was intended to advance Sadat's initiative without involving Israel yet. The plan included a schedule of stages:

1. In April Kissinger would meet with Ismail again in the framework of the secret channel to draft the agreement on principles between the United States and Egypt, as proposed by Ismail. In this agreement, the United States would fulfill Egypt's condition by promising, this time via the White House, to act to return Egyptian sovereignty to Sinai up to the international border (excluding the Gaza Strip). The agreement, at this stage, would not be publicized. "What we lose is the commitment by the United States to Egyptian sovereignty," Rabin said immediately upon hearing this. Kissinger responded, "Mr. Ambassador, you will lose something. But you will gain time. You will not be able to maintain a position of doing nothing for the next four years."[4]

2. At the end of June, at a summit meeting in the United States between the leaders of the Soviet Union and the United States, the leaders of the two superpowers would approve the agreement, which would then be publicized. With the announcement of the framework of principles, negotiations between Israel and Egypt would be initiated to achieve a partial Israeli withdrawal and the opening of the Suez Canal. These discussions would continue until the fall.

3. In November, after the Israeli elections, negotiations between Egypt and Israel for a comprehensive settlement would begin, continuing into the following year. According to the principles of the agreement, the Sinai Peninsula would be recognized as an area of Egyptian sovereignty, but temporary security arrangements would be made for an extended period, meaning an Israeli presence in the area.

In this spirit, Kissinger wrote to Ismail on March 9, 1973, that he was making an increased effort to understand the Israeli position in order to

---

[3] Ibid.

[4] This answer, the essence of Kissinger's program, and the schedule he planned were reported to Israel at the meeting between Kissinger and Rabin, March 9, 1973, NA RN, NSC, HAK, Country Files, Box 135. A short time after the beginning of the meeting, Kissinger requested that Rodman, who was the only one present at the beginning of the discussion, leave the room, and most of the discussion in the Map Room took place privately between Kissinger and Rabin. Important details about it are not included in the American protocol and can be understood only from Rabin's report to Meir, 18:00–18:40, March 9, 1973, Aleph-8/7062, ISA.

formulate an agreement on principles according to the outline Ismail had presented.[5] Kissinger received reinforcement for this approach in a report from Eugene Trone, an American intermediary between Kissinger and Ismail who had spoken with Ismail at dinner on February 26 and at the airport on February 27, as Ismail was leaving the United States. Trone's report included the following:

> The key to a compromise, Mr. Ismail said at one point, is the prin-
> ciple of Egyptian sovereignty in Sinai. [He appeared to be studiously
> avoiding the use of the word *territory*.] Sovereignty, he said, is solid
> enough for them to defend to their own people, yet flexible enough
> to accommodate practical arrangements that may be necessary.[6]

Rabin was completing his term as Israeli ambassador to the United States and was due to fly back to Israel on Saturday evening, March 10. The day before, he arrived at the White House to take his leave of Kissinger, who complimented him: "You are one of the few people I will genuinely miss. I don't say this just to be polite." Rabin, embarrassed at the praise, turned the conversation back to political matters: "If you ask me what I worry about, it is the preparation for the summit."

"Let me share my thoughts with you," said Kissinger, but before con-
tinuing, he made sure that Rabin understood that the situation required a political process, even asking, "Does she [Meir] understand it?" Rabin confirmed that the prime minister did. "I have briefed you twice," Kissinger reminded him, and let him look at two pages that one of Ismail's escorts had prepared during the visit to the United States, in which he had summarized Ismail's feelings and thoughts. Rabin was impressed by the signifi-
cant points of the report and communicated this to the prime minister: "The visitor [Ismail] spoke a lot about the new formula which consti-
tuted the central aspect of his discussions with Robert [Nixon] and Shaul [Kissinger], sovereignty in return for security. The visitor reflected a great deal on the possibilities implicit in this formula."

After Rabin had read the document, Kissinger informed him of the action plan he had formulated. It was clear that Rabin understood the importance of his last mission as ambassador. He would be required not only to transmit the details of the plan to Meir but also, and primarily, to report on Kissinger's desire to implement it. Rabin knew that Meir would not rush to accept the information he would present to her, and that he

---

[5] Letter from Kissinger to Ismail, NA RN, NSC, HAK, March 9, 1973, Box 131.

[6] Memorandum from Trone to Kissinger about his conversations with Ismail, after Ismail's meetings with Kissinger. The document is labeled: Shown to Rabin. March 9, 1973, NA RN, NSC, HAK, Country Files, Box 135.

could expect a difficult discussion. He protested to Kissinger, "To come out publicly with principles, say July or August, will be very unpleasant to the prime minister. That is two or three months before our election." (Rabin was referring to the appointed time for publicizing the commitment of the United States to Egypt and recognizing its sovereignty over Sinai, according to Kissinger's plan.) When Kissinger wanted to end discussion of a subject to which his interlocutor objected, he would customarily present the "president's position." This time, he answered the argument about Israeli elections by saying that the president was not influenced by elections in Israel; what interested Nixon was that he, Kissinger, should bring about a solution to the conflict in the Middle East.

This is how Rabin explained Kissinger's plan to Meir:

> Shaul [Kissinger] views the Egyptian readiness, still hesitant, to move from a demand to evacuate territory to a demand to recognize Egyptian sovereignty over Egyptian territory as a significantly important change. Moreover, Shaul sees a possibility to respond to Israeli security needs during the period between signing an agreement between the two sides which will create a state of peace, and the ultimate achievement of normalization between the two states by leaving Israeli military forces at critical points in Sinai, but without harming the principle of Egyptian sovereignty over them. In fact, Shaul foresees the creation of three security areas in Sinai at the stage following the peace agreement: one area which Egyptian forces will control, principally the canal sector; a second area in which Israeli forces will be stationed; and a third area, including most of Sinai, which will be a demilitarized zone serving to separate the two sides. The stage between achieving a peace agreement up to full normalization could be long-lasting and might continue for many years. Of course, Egyptian sovereignty will remain in effect for all of Sinai, except perhaps for adjustments to the former international border. Shaul emphasized that, by this, he means minor changes that are certainly not on the order of what we have presented to him.[7]

Kissinger added an additional and not unimportant element in an attempt to convince Meir: "Shaul repeated that he believed that, with Egypt's agreement, the proposed Egyptian settlement could be separated from any attention to Jordan and/or Syria."

Kissinger summarized all of his expectations for concessions from the prime minister in the question he repeated to Rabin: "Would [Israel] be

---

[7] Telephone conversation between Rabin and Kissinger, 17:15, March 10, 1973, NA RN, HAK, Box 19, Telcon, March 10–14, 1973.

willing to deviate from [its] position of demanding significant border changes in comparison to the international border?"

Rabin promised to return with a prompt answer. The discussion ended on Friday evening at 18:40 Washington time (early Saturday morning in Israel). Rabin waited for a few hours and then called Meir for a telephone discussion. The discussion was long and difficult as Rabin tried, without success, to convince her to accept Kissinger's plan.

On Saturday, at 15:15 Washington time, Rabin telephoned the White House to inform Kissinger of Meir's negative response to his question. The contents of the conversation, as written, may testify somewhat to Rabin's discussion with Meir.

> Rabin: I've tried my best to convey . . . two hours.
>
> Kissinger: One way or the other, this issue is going to get surfaced.
>
> Rabin: Yeah.
>
> Kissinger: Your practical choice is only in what channel.
>
> Rabin: Yeah.
>
> Kissinger: And under whose auspices.
>
> Rabin: I explained that.
>
> Kissinger: And that they should just continue to keep that in mind.
>
> Rabin: I believe that I have tried my best to explain it.[8]

Rabin reported that Kissinger had warned him during the previous day's meeting about what would happen if Israel did not cooperate with his plan. In Rabin's version, Kissinger told him that the president was ready to approve the continued supply of planes to Israel because Kissinger had led him to believe that there would be movement in the political process, but "he would find himself in trouble when, in another month or in three months, he would have to come to Robert and to tell him that he had no solution. He believed that the entire matter would be transferred to the State Department, and then the basis of discussion with the Soviet Union and with Egypt would rest upon the Gromyko Plan."[9]

---

[8] Ibid. According to Rabin, Kissinger warned that if Israel did not cooperate with his plans, the matter would be transferred to the State Department, which was hostile to Israel, and the process would continue with the Soviet Union's draft proposal. See also report of discussion with Kissinger, March 9, 1973, Aleph-7062, ISA.

[9] Rabin's report to Meir, 18:00–18:40, March 9, 1973.

As it later became clear, these warnings did not particularly impress the political echelon in Israel. Mordechai Gazit, who replaced Dinitz as director of the Prime Minister's Office, wrote to Dinitz, who replaced Rabin as ambassador:

> Thanks to the telephone discussion he had with Rabin in accord with the instructions of the prime minister, Shaul [Kissinger] well understands the reservations which became apparent during the first visit. We assume that Shaul will hear Hafez [Ismail]'s reply, respond to it, and throw out some ideas, but that he will emphasize that all of these are ideas for initial investigation and examination and do not obligate the United States, and certainly not Israel. Indeed, Shaul told us that he would not confront us with surprises.[10]

At the end of the discussion, Kissinger understood that there was no further point to this dialogue and moved on to practical matters. He said that he would wait to see what would happen at his meeting with Ismail in April and explained that Israel's decision could wait until the last minute, when Israel would be forced to decide. These proceedings would demand coordination, trust, understanding, and mutual alertness based on close personal relations between Kissinger and whoever would be his contact on the Israeli side. Already, in the course of the previous day's meeting, Kissinger had expressed the fear that Dinitz would not meet these conditions and that Israel would create a different system of contacts in Washington that would bypass the national security advisor. Rabin calmed him, saying: "We have no reason to destroy the only channel of discussion on which we can depend." Kissinger was not calmed: "Yes, but Dayan, for example, thinks that he could work with anyone."

Kissinger continued to feel troubled on this point and expressed the hope that Rabin would continue to be involved in decision-making. He asked whether a request from the United States would help to achieve this. During his term as ambassador, Rabin had not hidden his doubts, when he had them, regarding Meir's political conduct and was aware of her hostility toward anyone who did not agree with her opinions. Meir had also been obliged to hear much praise of Rabin during his time in Washington. Moreover, the success of her visit was in no small measure due to his preparation and his ties in the US government, many of whom admired him greatly. These factors only increased her hostility, which she had difficulty hiding. *Ha'aretz* reported that "in a briefing to the Israeli press, when she

---

[10] Personal letter to Dinitz from Gazit, April 8, 1973, Aleph-7550/4, ISA.

was asked to respond to Nixon's praise of Rabin, she retorted sourly, 'That's one perspective.'"[11]

Thus, Rabin rejected Kissinger's generous offer to request Rabin's continued involvement in negotiations: "Not at the beginning." Kissinger understood Rabin's distress and responded with a quote by Admiral Ernest J. King, a World War II navy commander who, when asked for advice after his retirement, responded: "When they get into trouble, they call for the sons of bitches."

Kissinger did not hide his anger at Meir's negative reply, but his conduct after her refusal indicates that he agreed to make an effort to delay the political process until after the Israeli elections, in the hope that Meir's opposition to his initiative would then weaken. The next two tasks Kissinger set for himself regarding the Middle East were, first, to delay the meeting with Ismail set for April 10, and second, to postpone Soviet pressure to discuss developments in the Middle East, at least until the summit meeting in June. This pressure stemmed from the Soviet Union's desire to prevent the military conflict Sadat was threatening. The Soviet Union, which had cooperated in providing Egypt with military equipment, knew that this threat was real.

Kissinger waited until the last moment to postpone the meeting with Ismail. At this stage, he needed this channel so that he could tell the Soviets, "The Egyptians don't want you in it. As long as we are talking to the Egyptians, we can't get into detailed negotiations with you without total confusion."[12]

## Meir Calms Her Ministers: "Nothing Will Be Done Behind Our Backs"

"We have a great friend in the White House," announced Golda Meir before her return to Israel on March 11. The newspaper headlines of that day had reported that, according to opinion polls, her party would receive fifty-four seats in the Knesset, that Qaddafi had had a nervous

---

[11] "Annoyance for Yitzhak Rabin," *Ha'aretz*, March 12, 1973; also, *Ha'aretz*, March 11, 1973, "Golda Meir Returns from the United States," subtitled "Another Side of the Coin": "Meir rejected an invitation from Israeli Television to participate in a program about Rabin's life which had been filmed in Washington. Her refusal stemmed from emotional reasons more than formal ones. A few days later, in the presence of President Nixon, Mrs. Meir explained that her admiration for the outgoing ambassador was not as great as that of Mr. Nixon." In addition, the article continued, "Mrs. Meir left the clear impression that she was not completely satisfied with the outgoing ambassador, Yitzhak Rabin, and that his political future was not clear at the time."

[12] Kissinger to Rabin at their meeting on March 9. Three days previously, he had made similar comments to the Russian ambassador, Dobrynin. NA RN, NSC, HAK, Box 70.

Photo: Fritz Cohen, Israeli National Photo Collection

*Golda Meir, Yisrael Galili, and Moshe Dayan at Beit Hanassi, May 11, 1970*

breakdown, and that Meir had changed her mind about retiring from politics before the coming elections.[13]

While still in the United States, she had written to Yigal Allon, who had temporarily replaced her in the government while she was away: "A full report of our discussion with the president is being sent with Zvika [Zamir] who will arrive in Israel on Tuesday. The prime minister wishes that the report be shown to you, [Minister without Portfolio Yisrael] Galili, and Dayan only."[14] Allon's report to the government regarding

---

[13] *Ha'aretz*, March 2, 3, and 11. Meir was still weighing her decision regarding whether to continue her political activity after this headline.

[14] From Dinitz to Allon, via Mizrahi, March 2, 1973, Lamed Vav/450, Aleph-7466/4, ISA.

the prime minister's discussion in the United States was very general and was transmitted to the government ministers before Zamir's report reached him.

Upon her return on March 13, the prime minister invited a small group of ministers for a more detailed report.[15] She opened her report with a request:

> I would like to make a request from our friends that the information I supply here about the discussion, particularly with the president, if it is leaked, will make it easily possible to achieve one objective—that they will not talk to us at all. I know that Israelis are willing to climb the barricades for anything, but do not leak this. Not at all.

She updated the ministers on the two objectives of her visit. The first was "to check whether there had been any change in the United States' position, primarily considering the statements that 'this is Middle East month' by members of the American government and with the assumption that after Vietnam they will turn their attention to our area as well." The second was "to clarify actual matters regarding the supply of planes." Most of the comments and questions by the ministers related to the second subject. Regarding the political matter, she added her determination to what they had already read in the newspapers: "There is nothing in what Hussein and Ismail brought up that would provide a basis for a demand that we or the Americans change our positions."[16] This determination did not match Rabin's impressions, which he did not make known to the ministers:

> Kissinger did not try to hide the fact that Ismail's statements pleased him and even I could not deny that the senior Egyptian representative had some interesting things to say.[17]

> The return of full Egyptian sovereignty over Sinai could be combined with the possibility of finding a compromise between full Egyptian sovereignty and the security demands of Israel.[18]

---

[15] In addition to Moshe Dayan and Yisrael Galili, ministers Pinchas Sapir and Shimon Peres participated in the meeting. March 13, 1973, Lamed Gimel/Sheleg, Aleph-7062, ISA.

[16] Rabin 1979, 384; Shlomo Gross (Poless), "Nixon's Compliments to Golda Hinted at the Need for a Settlement," *Ha'aretz*, March 9, 1973.

[17] Rabin 1979, 384.

[18] Ibid.

Rabin also testified that Kissinger told him, "I do not hide my opinion that your [Israel's] territorial demands cannot be achieved in the framework of a political settlement."[19]

Regarding the practical conclusions of the visit, Meir's report reflected reality: "It is clear that [the Americans] will try to be active and to move the sides forward, but there is no demand directed at us. Perhaps Ismail will return to America." She added:

> I was very concerned about what would happen at the summit with Brezhnev, what would happen with Egypt, what the United States' position would be, and I received a renewed promise that nothing will be done behind our backs. We will know and they will talk to us without previously committing themselves to the Russians or to the Egyptians. That has been promised.[20]

Yisrael Galili and Shimon Peres asked to confirm this. Meir repeated and emphasized, "There will be no agreement between them and the Russians at our expense without them speaking to us." There will be no settlement "without our agreement, without our knowledge, behind our backs."

If there were ministers in Golda Meir's "kitchen cabinet" who did not agree with this policy, they did not express it. One minister who viewed the political status quo as dangerous was Yigal Allon, who acted without the knowledge of the prime minister in order to remove the danger.[21] As noted, in November 1972, he had already caused a commotion in the Israeli government and the Soviet Union by announcing that negotiations with Egypt should be opened in two parallel channels, one aimed at a partial settlement and the other at a comprehensive settlement. Now, on March 1, 1973, even before receiving Zamir's report about the discussions in Washington—and, actually, even before the meeting between Nixon and Meir—Allon met in Israel with an American representative, expressed his reservations about Israeli policy, and recommended that the Americans take the initiative and appoint an American emissary to advance developments in the Middle East. It appears that he was implying that Kissinger should take on this role. He explained that if such a step was not taken promptly, it would be even harder to achieve peace, because Israel would start to relate to Sinai as part of the Holy Land.

---

[19] Ibid.

[20] March 13, 1973, Lamed Gimel/Sheleg, Aleph-7062, ISA.

[21] Telegram from the American embassy in Israel to the State Department, Tel Aviv 1677, March 5, 1973. NA RN, NSC, Country Files, Box 658; NA, GR, 59 Pol 27-14 Arab-Isr.

According to his testimony to the Davis Institute, Allon's position on Sinai was a minimal one regarding areas which Israel would demand to hold onto. He believed that Israel's security needs would necessitate control of four points:

> I schematically visualized four arcs which would be essential: . . . one arc would include the area of Pithat Rafiah. . . . The second . . . embracing Auja, el-Hafir, Kuntilla, el-Kysima . . . in the area facing Nitzana. . . . The third arc broadening our hold on Eilat. . . . And the fourth, Sharm el-Sheikh.

Allon did not see the need for territorial contiguity between these areas: "If this is in the framework of peace, there would be no difficulty about crossing, even without another corridor, and if there is no alternative, the sea may also serve for transportation."[22]

The Allon proposal matched Rabin's position and perhaps had even been coordinated with him. The personal closeness of the two graduates of Kadoorie Agricultural School, which had begun in the Palmach (an underground organization that operated under the auspices of the Jewish settlement organization before the establishment of the State of Israel) and continued through the years, found contemporary expression in similar political positions and cooperation.[23] More important—Allon's general position regarding political progress had a common basis with Sadat's initiative and with Kissinger's plan to implement this initiative, which Rabin had heard at their meeting on March 9. However, Allon's opinions had no impact. The political status of his eternal rival, Dayan, was much higher.

In March, the election atmosphere began to be felt and Israel was, for the most part, busy with its own concerns. Decision-makers considered Sadat's moves annoyances to be eliminated. They attempted to rid themselves of this political annoyance through Kissinger and Nixon. Their response to the military annoyance—Sadat's threat of war—was to increase Israel's acquisition of military equipment, schedule additional training, and expand deterrence.

The Meir government had begun its life as a national unity government, with the War of Attrition at the Suez Canal just beginning. Toward summer

---

[22] For Allon's position regarding the security zones necessary for Israel in Sinai, see Aleph-5001/19, ISA, sixth meeting. At the end of 1979, Allon participated in a series of twenty-three meetings at the Davis Institute in Jerusalem to document his memories. More than twenty-five years later, this testimony was approved for publication, but parts of it are still secret.

[23] About two weeks later, Rabin spoke at a gathering of United Jewish Appeal members in Switzerland and stated that the Arab states were interested in having Kissinger mediate a solution to the Middle East conflict. Ha'aretz, March 21, 1973.

1970, the war was at its height and Israel's air superiority, which was expressed on a daily basis in attacks on Egypt, led the Soviets to organize and install a system of ground-to-air missiles at the canal front. The Israeli air force had difficulty dealing with this missile system: attack planes were hit, pilots were killed, and others were taken prisoner. After more than 700 Israeli soldiers had been killed (from the outbreak of the war) and thousands more injured, Israelis awaited an accelerated end to the canal war.

Against this backdrop, the United States advanced what is usually called the Rogers Plan: a proposal for a ceasefire between Israel and Egypt and a renewal of talks between Israel, Egypt, and Jordan for a peace agreement on the basis of UN Security Council Resolution 242. The American initiative included a concealed threat to Israel that if it did not reply positively to the proposal, the United States would stop supplying it with planes. Egypt responded positively to the American proposal; in Israel, as well, a large majority of the political system was inclined to lend support to the ceasefire initiative.[24] Minister Menachem Begin opposed the initiative and led his political camp to dismantle the national unity government.[25]

The Meir government, which responded positively to the United States' proposal on August 7, 1970, ending the War of Attrition, now had to deal with governmental opposition to the political process. In March 1973, half a year before the elections were to take place, this situation greatly affected political discourse in Israel. Considering the political circumstances in 1973, not only did Meir and Dayan refuse to enter a political process, they even chose not to report to the government regarding the possibility of such a process which Sadat's initiative had opened up to Israel. Any internal debate within the government might have been leaked to the opposition and provided an opportunity to attack.[26]

In addition to the conflict between Israeli political blocs, there were internal conflicts in the ruling Labor Party on three levels: first, between camps in the party; second, intergenerational conflict around the issue of who would succeed Meir if and when she retired (that is, would leadership pass on to the younger generation—Moshe Dayan, the defense minister; Yigal Allon, the deputy prime minister; Abba Eban, the foreign minister— or to more mature leadership such as Pinhas Sapir, the finance minister);

---

[24] Syria had not accepted Security Council Resolution 242 and was not a party to political moves.

[25] On July 30, 1970, the official bodies of Gahal (the Hebrew acronym for the Herut-Liberal Bloc) decided by a majority of 116 to 112 to leave the government if it accepted the ceasefire initiative.

[26] Even from a military standpoint, the ceasefire greatly affected the events of October 1973. Israel ended the War of Attrition without the air force finding a way to deal with the confrontation between planes and ground-to-air missiles, and the Egyptians advanced the missile batteries.

third, personal conflicts among the candidates to succeed Meir.[27] In all of these conflicts, Defense Minister Dayan played a central role. Dayan's power stemmed from the strength and the security of his personal status among the general public. Dayan's status to a great extent led him to be uncritical of his own conduct; it moderated public criticism of him as well. His threat, open or implicit, that he would act independently in the political system if his opinions were not accepted carried great weight in the considerations of the Labor Party, in the comments of its leaders, and in the determination of its party platform for the elections.

The question being asked in those days was whether the Labor Party, most of whose members were willing to make wide-ranging concessions for peace agreements, would dare to come out with a "dovish" platform, considering that public opinion was toughening and seemed to be moving toward a position of "not even one inch."[28] In the past, Dayan had submissively and secretly accepted the prime minister's opposition to his proposal to withdraw Israeli forces from the Suez Canal and allow it to be opened. In March 1973, against the backdrop of his party's internal organization for the elections, Dayan became more extreme in his public remarks, demanding that the Labor Party define its settlement map and thus express its position regarding the permanent borders of Israel. In actuality, he forced his opinion on the party, saying, "I prefer the existing situation over a complete or almost complete withdrawal to the previous lines." He added, "By the end of the present decade we will be able to overcome the Arabs if they try to renew the war."[29]

Meir at first opposed Dayan's moves to anchor a map of the future to binding decisions. At a meeting of the Labor Party Secretariat, she stated that the results of her visit to the United States had convinced her that there was no need at present to decide the dispute about the future of the territories vis-à-vis public opinion. She maintained that it was unnecessary to be drawn into a "Jewish war." In this manner, she redirected the internal struggle in the Labor Party between Dayan and his opponents,

---

[27] At the margins of the election campaign but as a significant political development, considering the internal struggle in the ruling party, on March 22 the Labor Party chose the scientist Efraim Katzir (Katchalsky) as its candidate for the presidency. He ran against Yitzhak Navon, who was identified with the Dayan camp (Rafi) in the party.

[28] Ran Kislev, *Ha'aretz*, April 12 and 14, under the headline: "Dayan's Political Poker, Decision in the Struggle about Territories in the Labor Party Delayed."

[29] Dayan said this on March 14, 1973, at a meeting of members of the Moshav faction of the Labor Movement, *Ha'aretz*, March 15, 1973. On March 29, Dayan also met with the kibbutz faction of the Labor Party. He said that this appearance was part of his election campaign, presented his own settlement plan, and thus instigated a sharp debate in the Labor Party with regard to its platform, which culminated in the publication of the Galili document.

most prominently Allon, Sapir, Eban, and Lyova Eliav. But Dayan's position overcame the opposition and Minister Galili was given the task of writing a document that bore his own name but included Dayan's demands.[30]

## In Egypt: "We Will Wait for a Time to See What Results His Statement Will Bring"

Following the meeting between Kissinger and Ismail, during which they agreed to meet again on April 10 to formulate the agreement in principle between the United States and Egypt by May, Sadat continued to operate in two channels, the political and the military. He had to strengthen his status in public opinion to be convincing in his preparation for a military move and, no less important, to use these preparations as an argument to consolidate national forces and freeze activity against the government.

Egypt was not (and still is not) an easy state to lead. Poverty is widespread and the high rate of natural population increase intensifies it. A growing number of students and educated people have difficulty finding suitable employment for their level of education, but know how to demand political freedoms and find outlets for their frustrations. In addition, Sadat had to deal the Muslim Brotherhood movement, a focal point of opposition. He suppressed mass student demonstrations and eliminated a political conspiracy to remove him from power.[31] More than anything, Egypt's stinging defeat by Israel in the Six-Day War and the loss of Sinai in that war hovered in the atmosphere.

On February 27, when Ismail was still in the United States, Sadat had assembled an unusual gathering in Cairo. He invited about 150 senior media figures and opinion-makers in Egypt to a three-hour meeting. Official reports were short and uninformative. At the meeting, Sadat provided a summary of his future activity for 1973. The list of those present and the wording of the report indicate that it was meant for internal consumption.[32] After he had explained to his listeners that the choice was between capitulation and battle, he elaborated about the military track:

---

[30] The Galili document—the written "Oral Law"— reflected the Labor Party's political position, as did the settlement map, which included two-thirds of the Golan, the length of the Jordan Valley, and the Judean Desert, in Israeli hands, as well as east Sinai along the el-Arish Ras-Muhammad line. *Ot*, September 23, 1973.

[31] Shazly 1987, 137–41. For additional information on Egypt's internal problems and their connection to its attitudes to war with Israel, see Shamir 1978 and Maytal 1991, 239.

[32] Special report on Sadat's address to the propaganda and media representatives in Egypt on February 27. April 4, 1973, Mem-Daled 118/4. Based on *Al-Jadid*, Lebanon, March 16, 1973, Aleph-4036/13, ISA; Sadat's address at the meeting with public figures, February 27, 1973, TZK/1755, Egypt, Aleph-7038/3, ISA.

"I am not the right man for capitulation. The decision therefore has been made and it is something which is unavoidable. . . . We will defeat the Zionists in a third war." However, Sadat, who was disappointed that Kissinger had not presented the United States' position on his initiative to Ismail, also spoke of the political track:

> During his discussion with Ismail, President Nixon hinted that he wanted to take the initiative in the direction of peace. We will wait for a time to see what results his statement will bring. I do not wish to predict or to draw conclusions. What interests us is our approach to the battle, and this approach has already been implemented—anyone who does not believe that will be able to see it in the near future.[33]

He summarized his speech by presenting two levels of action:

A. Preparing our armed forces and ourselves, with all of our potential, for an unavoidable battle. . . . We will not lose one moment in this area and everything is being conducted as planned and is based on our acquisition of the most modern equipment.

B. The second level is intensive diplomatic activity, which is completely coordinated with the first level and in its service. This will not end but rather will continue in parallel to the first level; it will go on before, during and after the battle.[34]

Simultaneous to this meeting, Sadat sent the Egyptian minister of war, General Ahmad Ismail Ali, to Moscow for a visit that received wide media coverage. "Ali's job now was to keep the military out of politics," wrote Kissinger to Nixon, updating him on the visit.[35] His explanation was anchored in reality: the military leaders were deeply involved in preparations for battle and were completely excluded from political developments.[36]

---

[33] Ibid.

[34] Ibid.

[35] Memorandum from Kissinger to Nixon, March 12, 1973, NA RN, HAK, Box 131; FRUS XXV, 120.

[36] For example, Shazly, the Egyptian Chief of General Staff, does not mention the political issues at all in his book, as usually accepted in a reliable source regarding the conduct of the military command during the period preceding the war. Shazly 1987.

Nixon received a report of Ali's visit to Moscow from the Soviets as well.[37] The Soviets understood the significance of Egypt's and Syria's requests for equipment well. Brezhnev again warned Nixon that in the absence of progress, Egypt was preparing itself for another round of fighting in an attempt to maintain its status in the Middle East. The Soviets were cooperating with the military preparations, but at the same time, feared their implementation.[38]

On March 26, Sadat gave a speech in Cairo that repeated publicly what he had said a month earlier in the closed forum of media representatives. This time, however, he added a very significant practical step: he changed the composition of his government and chose himself to stand at its head.[39]

After a detailed examination of the speech's content, Kissinger interpreted Sadat's words to President Nixon as statements made to satisfy internal needs with regard to internal agitation against Sadat, which had reached its peak in January, as well as a reaction to criticism in the Arab world for his contacts with the United States while the US continued to supply arms to Israel.[40] Regarding the double meaning in Sadat's words, Kissinger summarized:

> Sadat has been giving considerable thought to what Ismail was told in Washington. He remains skeptical, but appears realistic about what he can expect from the US. Finally, he seems to be considering the idea that the concept of restoring Egyptian sovereignty might allow for some arrangements that address Israel's security concerns. It would seem premature to judge that he has rejected the possibilities inherent in this concept.[41]

---

[37] Brezhnev to Nixon, March 14, 1973 NA RN, NSC, Box 131; discussions between Dobrynin and Kissinger, NA RN, HAK, Telcon, March 10–14 and 15–27, 1973; FRUS XXV, 118.

[38] Regarding the complex position of the Soviet Union in the area at that time: Telegram from Freddy Eini, aide to Zamir, to Meir, March 27, 1973, following the meeting between Mordechai Gazit, director-general of the Prime Minister's Office, and Yevgeny Primakov and Yuri Kotov, Soviet representatives, Aleph-7061/6, ISA.

[39] Sadat's speech at a joint meeting of the Central Committee of the Egyptian People's Assembly, March 26, 1973, Aleph-7038/3, ISA; excerpts from Sadat's speech, March 26, 1973, NA RN, NSC, Country Files, M.E. Box 132; NA GR 59 POL 27 Arab-Isr., Cairo 909, March 27, 1973.

[40] Memorandum from Kissinger to Nixon regarding Sadat's March 26 speech, March 30, 1973, NA RN, NSC, Saunders Files, Box 1171; FRUS XXV, 123–24.

[41] On March 1, the *Washington Post* published an article by James Hoagland analyzing Sadat's February speech, arguing that it appeared that a military attack on Israel was not Egypt's immediate policy, that Sadat did not use the term "war" but rather "a battle of all of the nations," that the diplomatic campaign was not just a performance but rather expressed his intention to give precedence to a peaceful solution, and that if negotiations were started, this approach would receive wide support among the population.

## The Secret Channel—
## From Doing Business to Dragging Feet

"I will be talking intensively with the Israelis in an effort to develop an understanding of their position as it might relate to possible heads of agreement in the plan you outlined," Kissinger updated Ismail. It was March 9. Kissinger had met with Rabin earlier that day and had not as yet received Meir's negative reply to his proposal.[42] In his letter to Ismail, Kissinger also referred to the murder of the American diplomats in Khartoum at the beginning of the month and protested against the use of terror for political purposes. Three weeks later, Kissinger would make use of this murder as a pretext to postpone his meeting with Ismail.

In his reply of March 20, Ismail protested Kissinger's use of the special communications channel between them for issues unrelated to political negotiations.[43] Regarding the political process itself, he wrote, "We have taken note that Dr. Kissinger has started talks with the Israelis and that he intends to conduct further talks with them." At the same time, he added that he expected to exchange ideas that would enable quick progress at the coming meeting. Ismail objected to the public revelation that the United States had decided to continue supplying Israel with equipment; he pointed out that this course of action had, in the past, led to the failure of talks. In addition, he emphasized that Egypt understood that it was again expected to make concessions, with the assumption that these would perhaps lead Israel to cooperate in the political process.

Having accepted Israel's opposition to advancing the process, and with the Israeli ambassador (who could offer him direct contact with Meir) absent from Washington, Kissinger determined to delay the negotiations and to use the communications channel with Ismail as a means of lessening Soviet pressure to make progress toward a settlement and preventing Egyptian military moves for as long as discussions were going on.

The continuation of the communications between Kissinger and Ismail must be examined on the basis of what Kissinger told Ambassador Dinitz at their first meeting:

> Regarding Egypt, as we know, an additional meeting with Hafez Ismail was set to take place on April 10. In the interim, there was Khartoum, and Shaul [Kissinger] announced to the Egyptians

---

[42] Regarding the effect of the diplomats' murder, Kissinger wrote to Ismail, "You cannot imagine how difficult it is here to deal with the impression that many Arab governments make calculated use of terror as a political instrument against the United States." NA RN, NSC, HAK, Box 31.

[43] Ibid.; FRUS XXV, 121–22.

that, considering what had happened, it was impossible to continue developments as planned. . . . In any case, the ball is now in Egypt's court. Shaul is certain that they will request another meeting, and he will agree, but in the meanwhile, another few weeks will go by and the summit [between Brezhnev and Nixon, which was planned for the middle of June] will be approaching and so it seems that we will get through the summer without any unnecessary pressures. However, he thinks that the moment will come when we must relate to the practical problems and thus we must prepare. . . . He will not set any practical discussion on issues involving us without full coordination with us and agreement on our part. He does not at the moment expect any quick political progress but, in his opinion, we [Israel] must be ready for the possibility of political negotiations if and when they are renewed. He, on his part, of course, will continue with his foot-dragging and will not speed up the pace of developments.[44]

From Kissinger's answer to Ismail on March 22, it becomes clear that, indeed, he transferred the ball into Ismail's court.[45] Kissinger wrote that he was still waiting to receive a detailed reply from Egypt regarding the issues which had been brought up at the first meeting, as well as the suggestion of a suitable date for the next meeting. After Sadat's speech on March 26, Kissinger saw fit to send an additional letter.[46] Alongside his report to the prime minister, Dinitz added, "Again Shaul is the initiator." It appears that Kissinger understood that the Egyptians were suspicious of his intentions and wanted to regain their trust by writing a placatory letter.

Ismail's reply arrived about a week later, on April 7.[47] Even though, at that stage, the preparations for war had reached an advanced point, the letter indicates an effort to return the channel to practical matters. Ismail ended with a request that Kissinger propose a date for a meeting between them that month, April, in a neutral country. In the meantime, Sadat had

[44] Report on meeting between Dinitz and Kissinger, 12:00, March 30, 1973, Lamed Vav/555, Aleph-7052/1, ISA. Quotation marks in original. At this meeting, Dinitz also updated Kissinger on the meetings between Gazit, Primakov, and Kotov, in which the Soviets investigated the possibility of being involved in a political process and reestablishing official representation of the Soviet Union in Israel, although they opposed establishing Israeli representation in Moscow. Further information on the Soviets' attempts is in Gazit's report of the meeting on March 24, 1973, Aleph-7045/13, ISA, as well as the American protocol of the meeting on March 30, 1973, NA RN, NSC, HAK, Box 135; FRUS XXV, 125–29.

[45] NA RN, NSC, HAK, Box 135; report from Dinitz to Meir, April 12, 1973, Lamed Vav/606, Aleph-7052/1, ISA.

[46] Letter from Kissinger to Ismail, March 30, 1973, NA RN, NSC, HAK, Box 135.

[47] NA RN, NSC, HAK, Box 131.

decided to recruit the Saudis to his effort to urge Kissinger on. He informed them of the secret channel that had been initiated. They immediately took action and warned the United States of the possibility of a renewal of fire between Egypt and Israel.[48]

Kissinger responded to Ismail's letter on April 11.[49] His reply criticized Egypt for revealing the secret channel's existence to the Saudis and threatened to cease his involvement in it if the rules of secrecy were not maintained as had been determined. But he also gave a detailed reply that included the United States' desire to conclude an agreement on principles (Kissinger used Ismail's term, "heads of agreement") based on UN Security Council Resolution 242. He also suggested a date for a meeting— May 9, a postponement of a month from the original date which had been set.

Dinitz reported on this letter to Meir's office, which replied that "this matter is not clear to us." They knew that Kissinger had postponed the planned meeting using the excuse of the events in Khartoum. "Have the Egyptians applied to him since then?"

"The application is new," affirmed Dinitz.[50]

## April: Military Tension Rising and Falling

By the end of March, about a month after the meetings between Ismail and Kissinger, Sadat understood that the meeting set for April 10 would not take place and the weight of the military option increased. The message was transmitted by the senior editor of *Newsweek*, Arnaud de Borchgrave, who had been waiting in Cairo for three weeks to conduct an interview with Sadat.[51] The headline of the interview that followed read: "The Battle Is Now Inevitable." In the interview, Sadat expressed complete disappointment with the reaction of the United States to his initiative. "If Hafez [Ismail] had conducted discussions with Golda Meir, the results would have been less ridiculous," said Sadat, referring to the United States' mediation, and added, "Yes, I want a final peace agreement with Israel, but there was no response from the US or Israel except to supply Israel with more Phantoms."

---

[48] Report from Joseph Greene, principal officer of the United States Interests Section in Egypt, to Secretary of State Rogers on his discussion with the Saudi ambassador on April 4 in Cairo, April 6, 1973, Cairo 1024, NA GR 59 Pol 27-14 Arab-Isr.

[49] NA RN, NSC, HAK, Box 131; FRUS XXV, 140–42.

[50] Gazit to Dinitz, Lamed Vav/529, and reply, Dinitz to Gazit, Lamed Vav/600, both April 9, 1973, Aleph-4996/1, ISA.

[51] Greene was the US diplomatic representative in Cairo. He reported on the interview on March 30. The interview was published on April 9, 1973, in *Newsweek*. NA GR 59 Pol 27 Arab-Isr.; Cairo 950, March 30, 1973; see also Aleph-7062/18, Aleph-7066/11, and Aleph-7038/3, ISA.

"The time has come for a shock," Sadat said to the reporter, who added his own impression that the Egyptian president "did not close the door on a diplomatic settlement but insisted that unless there was peace based on justice, there will be nightmares, and everybody will lose." The president repeated his distinction between an agreement on Sharm el-Sheikh, which would grant Israel the security it desired, and returning Egyptian sovereignty to Sinai. "We must remind the world that Israel still occupies our country and we are prepared to die by the thousands for national liberation," he said.

About a week after this interview, the *Newsweek* reporter arrived in Israel and asked to meet with the prime minister to update her on what he had heard from Sadat that was not meant for publication. He was politely refused.[52] Immediately after *Newsweek* published the interview, Sadat left for a two-day visit to Libyan president Moammar Qaddafi, his neighbor in Tripoli. Qaddafi had prevented the transfer to Egypt of Mirage planes and parts purchased from France, claiming that Sadat was not serious in his intention to do battle with Israel. Sadat's visit was meant to convince Qaddafi of the seriousness of his intentions.[53] During the visit, an official source in Cairo reported that Egypt would not initiate a wide-scale action against Israel and that it would continue to conduct a dialogue with the United States despite the narrowing possibilities for a settlement.[54]

Upon his return from Libya, Sadat assembled his government, requested approval for a military action against Israel, and received it by a majority. Sadat told the government he now headed that there was no other way except for battle and that "even though the United States has the power to lead to a solution of the dispute, it does not want to."[55] He added, "This stage of the general conflict means taking up arms to defend our rights and to return our land, and it requires general mobilization for the campaign by everyone in our homeland." The same week, *Ha'aretz* published reports about his visits to Egyptian army units at the canal. However, Sadat simultaneously took a very meaningful step in order to strengthen Egypt's link with the United States when he appointed Hafez Ismail, his partner in the secret political moves, as

---

[52] Medzini 2008, 522.

[53] El-Saadany 1994, 102.

[54] The official source was quoted by foreign journalists and appeared in *Ha'aretz*, April 4, 1973.

[55] Sadat's words at the government meeting of April 5, 1973 (Meytal 1991, 263). Based on Ismail's memoirs, Ismail 1987, 268; Stein 2003, 95. Stein relies on interviews with el-Gamasy and Ismail. Other researchers rely on el-Gamasy's testimony, but he, like other members of the government, did not know about the political discussion channel.

director of the Prime Minister's Office, in addition to his services as national security advisor.

The headline of the article by Zeev Schiff, military correspondent for *Ha'aretz*, referred to Sadat's actions: "Sadat Threatens: Israel Has the Ability to Establish Facts Across the Canal." The article continued: "The reactions of authorities [in Israel] can be summarized as follows: There is no reason to get excited. These declarations are no different than previous ones and they are meant, first and foremost, for internal consumption and to put pressure on the superpowers." In contrast, the correspondent of the *Sunday Times* reported from Cairo that "Sadat will gamble on a limited attack to break the ice in the Middle East."[56]

## Operation "Spring of Youth" in Israel

At the height of the increasing Egyptian threats, one of the most complex and successful Israeli commando raids reached its practical stage. Agents of the Mossad began preparations for an operation in Beirut, Lebanon, that later became known as Operation Spring of Youth.[57] During the early hours of the morning of April 10, after landing from the sea on the Beirut coast, the Israelis attacked a number of points in the heart of the city.

In an exclusive neighborhood in the northwest of the city, Ramlat al-Baida, three PLO leaders were surprised and killed: Muhammad Abu Yusuf Najjar, a leader of the Black September Organization (BSO) and one of the planners of the massacre of Israeli athletes at the Munich Olympics; Kamal Adwan, the BSO's head of special operations; and Kamal Nasser, Arafat's spokesman. Sayeret Matkal, an elite special operations force, was entrusted with carrying out the mission, while the commander of the force, Ehud Brog (Barak), and two of his fighters, Amiram Levine and Loni Rafaeli, participated dressed as women. Another force of paratroopers, led by Amnon Lipkin, blew up the building where the commander of the Popular Front for the Liberation of Palestine (PFLP) was staying. In addition, two other targets in Beirut and another north of Sidon were attacked by the paratroopers and Flotilla 13, the navy commando unit. Dozens of terrorists (in the Israeli view, or combatants, as viewed by the Palestinians), from a number of organizations, were killed. Intelligence material taken from the terrorists' apartments and at other points enabled the arrest of terrorists from areas under Israel control. Hagi Ma'ayan and Avida Shor, members of

---

[56] This series of reports appeared in *Ha'aretz*, April 2–9, 1973. The *Sunday Times* report was reprinted in *Ha'aretz*.

[57] For a description of the preparations for the operation: Zamir and Mass 2011, 73; about the operation itself, Caspit and Kfir 1998, 118–31.

the elite paratrooper unit who had participated in the force that blew up the PFLP headquarters, were killed in the daring operation in the heart of Beirut. The Egyptians reacted to the operation by stating that its aim had been "to implant the feeling in the hearts of the Arabs that Israel was the region's ruling power."[58]

Indeed, the sense of power was intoxicating for the Israeli general public and for its leaders. The day the commanders and the force returned from Beirut to the port of Haifa, Defense Minister Dayan proclaimed from the peak of Masada, "We will establish a new Israel, with wide borders, not like in 1948."[59] At the beginning of April, at an assembly of paratroopers in Jerusalem, Dayan had stated, "It seems to me that we are at the opening of a peak phase in the 'return to Zion.'" At Masada he went a step further in his appraisal: "At this time we are blessed with conditions which I doubt that our nation has ever seen in the past, certainly not in the 'return to Zion' period."[60]

Six years later, on April 16, 1979 (twenty days after signing the peace treaty with Egypt), Dayan would proclaim:

> Perhaps in the Golan, as well, Israel will face the same question which it faced regarding Sharm el-Sheikh: that is, whether to keep Sharm or whether to prefer peace without Sharm. Perhaps such a question will arise regarding the Golan and we will have to decide what Israel prefers—the Golan Heights without peace with Syria, or peace with Syria without the settlements in the Golan Heights.

How far this statement is from the speech he made at Masada about the new Israel and its wider borders![61]

## Meanwhile, in the Not-Secret-Enough Channel

Apart from the practical difficulties between Egypt and the United States, the secret channel also suffered from other disturbances. At the beginning of April, with the publication of Sadat's *Newsweek* interview and following the discussions with the Saudis, Joseph Greene, the principal officer of the United States Interests Section in Egypt, who was operating as a representative of the State Department, had discovered that there was a parallel channel of communication between the White House and Sadat via the

---

[58] *Ha'aretz*, April 12, 1973.

[59] Ibid.

[60] Ibid.

[61] Dayan's talk at a visit to the Jordan Valley, *Davar*, April 17, 1979. For addition information on this topic, see Kipnis 2006, 248–50.

CIA.[62] "Hence I am perplexed about what to say to whom in the government of Egypt, and, for that matter, how to report and analyze for the US government what is or is not going on in Egypt," he wrote to the State Department.[63] Greene completed his scathing telegram with the question, "How I can perform that function when the government of Egypt clearly knows that I am unaware of both the form and content of a parallel channel through my own establishment?"

By prior agreement between the president and Kissinger, the secret channel between Kissinger and Sadat via Ismail had been kept hidden from Secretary of State Rogers and from the State Department. Now the president was forced to patch up the rift.[64] At a joint meeting with Kissinger and Sisco, Nixon explained to the State Department representative his role in a double game—to create the appearance of an open channel and to enable Kissinger to conduct negotiations through a secret channel. "We all know the Israelis are just impossible," said Nixon, explaining the use of these tactics. "We're getting closer to their election, too, Mr. President," Sisco said, trying to defend Israel. The president reacted: "Well, yeah, but they're always close to an election. Then they'll be closer to ours. See, that's always the excuse they've taken."[65]

Following the State Department clarification, and possibly as a result, Abba Eban, the Israeli foreign minister, also tried to deal with the matter. He turned to the American ambassador in Israel with a request to receive "additional and tangible clarifications" about these political developments, about which he too had known nothing. The request was passed on to the State Department, which transmitted it to Kissinger. Dinitz reported that Kissinger responded by telling him that such requests "endanger his [Kissinger's] handling of the matter" and requesting that the prime minister "let the matter drop."[66]

---

[62] He learned about the details from Kamal Adham, advisor to King Faisal of Saudi Arabia, from his telegram titled "The Egyptian-American Dialogue Regarding the Middle East," NA GR 59 Pol 14-27 Arab-Isr., April 6, 1973, 1023. On April 6 Kissinger even asked Dinitz not to react to a State Department pronouncement regarding the Sadat interview in *Newsweek*, "because what we know is more than what those in the State Department who will issue the pronouncement know." Telephone conversation between Kissinger and Dinitz, Lamed Vav/593, ISA; also the record of the discussion, NA RN, HAK, Telcon, April 2–6, 1973.

[63] Telegram from Greene regarding communication between the US and Egyptian governments, April 2, 1973, NA RN, NSC, Country Files, Cairo 978, Box 658.

[64] Conversation between Nixon and Kissinger in the Oval Office, February 21, 1973, NA RN, White House Tapes, Conversation No. 860-15; FRUS XXV, 55–59.

[65] Meeting between Nixon, Kissinger, and Sisco in the Oval Office, April 13, 1973, NA RN, White House Tapes, Conversation No. 895-24; FRUS XXV, 144–48.

[66] Dinitz to Meir, April 9, 1973, Lamed Vav/597, Aleph-7045/2, ISA.

The prime minister promptly took care of the difficulty. Mordechai Gazit, the director-general of the Prime Minister's Office, wrote a personal letter to Dinitz:

> Dear Simcha,
>
> A few comments for organizing communication: The prime minister is inclined to leave the distribution of Shaul's [Kissinger's] material as it has been. . . . The prime minister will talk to the foreign minister and explain the decision to him.[67]

However, from then on, Kissinger had to include the State Department in his communications with Ismail, and Sisco coordinated replies to Greene in Cairo and to the ambassador in Tel Aviv regarding the Middle East with Kissinger. In his book *Years of Upheaval*, Kissinger explained the limitations of his ability to maneuver as stemming from the exposure of the secret channel. However, there is no doubt that during this period, Kissinger was the only person deciding the foreign policy of the United States, even in matters of the Middle East. Although the Secretary of State submitted his letter of resignation only four months later, he was already on his way out in April. Kissinger acted to achieve this move and Israel was happy to assist.

If Kissinger did not already have enough problems in his difficulties with the State Department, he also had to deal with the wariness of Meir, who expressed doubt about the credibility of his updates regarding his contacts with Ismail. "Henry, the Israelis will give you a very hard time on that one," Sisco said to Kissinger when they spoke on the telephone about the leaked details.[68] Indeed, Meir expressed her suspicions harshly in her reaction to news of the continuing contacts between Ismail and Kissinger.

Kissinger's and Dinitz's awareness of Meir's suspicions was already evident in their April 11 discussion in the White House, most of which was devoted to exchanging messages with Ismail. Part of the discussion took place privately. Forty minutes after it ended, Dinitz reported to Meir regarding, at least, everything related to the letter to Ismail. He wrote in a placating tone by telegram: "Shaul showed us the documents. . . . An additional meeting will take place between Shaul and Hafez in Europe around

---

[67] Top secret, personal, Gazit to Dinitz, April 8, 1973, Aleph-7550/4, ISA. Later, Meir agreed with Eban that he would receive communications telegrams for perusal but that they were not to be passed on the people in his office. Personal letter from Gazit to Dinitz, April 15, 1973.

[68] Telephone conversation between Sisco and Kissinger, 20:02, April 9, 1973, NA RN, HAK, Telcon, April 7–11, 1973. Sisco, the assistant secretary of state, coordinated with Kissinger on the State Department's reaction to the leaked reports about his contacts with Ismail, while hiding this coordination from the State Department.

May 10. Shaul still must reply to Hafez's last request and we will probably meet tomorrow for him to show me his answer."[69]

Dinitz was meeting with Kissinger secretly. The need for an intermediary between the White House and the Prime Minister's Office in Jerusalem with regard to the secret channel made it necessary for Kissinger to summon Dinitz even before he had been sworn in as ambassador and before, as was accepted procedure, he had met with the secretary of state. Dinitz would arrive at the eastern entrance of the East Wing of the White House, which was used by maintenance and service people, not by diplomats and visitors; this side entrance led directly to the wings, far from the eyes of the media. He was accompanied to the Map Room by Alexander Haig, Kissinger's assistant as head of the National Security Council, where they waited for Kissinger. This practice continued for several months, until Kissinger's appointment as secretary of state in September 1973.[70]

The April 11 meeting was only the second working meeting of the two. The two men had not yet developed a personal relationship, and Kissinger was careful to be businesslike in his conversations. He told Dinitz what he had already emphasized to Rabin—his wishes, his plan, and his schedule for advancing the plan, on the basis of what he had heard from Ismail and in consideration of Israel's difficulty in publicly discussing a comprehensive peace agreement before the elections. "I must draw your attention to the fact that it does not mean that this [postponement] can be done indefinitely. I have been stringing along the Russians for 18 months and the Egyptians for 10 months," he informed Dinitz.[71] He warned that if, during his next meeting with Ismail, there was no progress, "the Egyptians would open fire, even though it was clear to them that they could not achieve any advantage by doing it, and at the same time, they would focus on pressure using the oil issue."[72] They would take this step even if their military inferiority was clear to them.

He clarified that Israel must not err in thinking that, because of the Watergate affair, which was gaining momentum, the president would not be able to put pressure on Israel and warned that the United States was liable to pressure Israel to accept its political dictates even if there was no change in the Egyptian position, as Israel expected.

---

[69] Dinitz to Meir, 19:30, April 11, 1973, Lamed Vav/605, Aleph-7052/1, ISA; NA RN, NSC, Country Files, Box 135. On the following day, Dinitz reported in detail on the private conversation. April 12, 1973, Lamed Vav/608, Aleph-7052/1, ISA.

[70] Dinitz 2003, 69. Dinitz never finished editing his book, which was never published. The manuscript was given to me by his wife Vivian and his daughter Tamar, and I would like to express my thanks here.

[71] NA RN, NSC, Country Files, Box 135.

[72] Dinitz to Gazit, April 12, 1973, Lamed Vav/606, Aleph-7052/1, ISA.

Kissinger saw fit to repeat his warnings again and again and, as a consequence, to request credit for his program:

> I know it is an election year for you, and a hard time for a decision. But I would like some idea of your strategic conception, whether we can get some heads of agreement that could give us some breathing space—by, first, getting an interim agreement. . . . Mr. Ambassador, you are in an odd period of tranquility. You have made your own assessment, but the reason for the absence of pressure on you now is because I have not permitted anyone to move. I have told Rabin— you have to be prepared.[73]

Kissinger presented Dinitz with his evaluations, speaking as an advisor to Israel and as someone who was concerned about its interests. In retrospect, it ultimately became clear, of course, that Kissinger was right in his appraisals and in the need to act according to them. However, first and foremost, Kissinger was at this time acting in accord with American interests—as the United States could be the only superpower to lead to a breakthrough in the Middle East, thus avoiding a war that could renew Egypt's dependence on the Soviet Union and return Soviet influence to the region. It also did not hurt that the line of action Kissinger had chosen suited the promotion of his personal status in the internal government power structure.

In his discussion with Dinitz, Kissinger was extremely focused and asked for Israel's approach on three points: first, the Israeli idea of how to begin the political process; second, how Israel thought it should continue; and third, an interim solution that would break through the current deadlock. Kissinger, in a formulation Dinitz chose to transmit to the prime minister, "would ascribe great importance to receiving from us a number of general principles for his coming meeting with Hafez in May. . . . The only thing that he requests is that we give him ammunition in order to continue to delay the matter, as he has done up to now, both before the summit and afterward."

On the next day, Dinitz returned to the White House so that Peter Rodman, Kissinger's assistant, could, as promised, show him the letter Kissinger meant to send to Ismail.[74] In accord with Meir's directions, Dinitz asked Rodman to delay sending the letter so that Meir could transmit her comments. He followed the instructions he had received from the Prime Minister's Office stating that "when Shaul [Kissinger] shows you the wording of his answer to Hafez, tell him that you want to transmit

---

[73] NA RN, NSC, Country Files, Box 135.
[74] 15:00, April 12, 1973, Lamed Vav/609, Aleph-7052/1, ISA.

it to the prime minister, and for her eyes only prepare an outline of the intermediate reply so that she can make her comments on that basis."[75] Kissinger lost his patience and reacted angrily that it had been "an arrangement of a meeting, and that was all. . . . You must know that, following your request to enable the prime minister to make her comments, I ordered our intermediary in Cairo to delay the draft until this morning. It will just be lying there until then, but it cannot be delayed further." The reason for the urgency in transmitting the reply testifies to the military tension Sadat had raised in order to press for political progress. Kissinger estimated to Dinitz that the chances of Sadat opening fire were fifty-fifty. He said that if Egypt began a military action, "we can say that we did everything we could and we will not be responsible if the ceasefire is breached or if it collapses." Dinitz relayed this in a telephone conversation to the Prime Minister's Office late that night.[76] Gazit, who wrote down the contents of the conversation, added in the margin, "At one point in the conversation, Simcha [Dinitz] said that he had the feeling that Shaul and his friends were more worried than we were at the possibility that Egypt would take hostile action."

Meir's reply arrived the following morning: "As Shaul's letter is already waiting in Cairo and he is of the opinion that the matter is urgent, the prime minister does not see fit to enter into an argument about the wording of the letter." Its tone was both worried—"We too have received information about Egyptian preparations to open fire in the near future"—and practical—"The prime minister requests to ask Shaul whether this information has also reached them."[77] This wording replaced a different draft version in which Meir complained that she had not been given an opportunity to consider and react to the correspondence between Kissinger and Ismail. That draft still expressed an attempt to dictate to Kissinger his reply to Ismail.

After two days, Gazit updated Dinitz about Israeli suspicions regarding Kissinger and about the line of action Meir wished to adopt:

> Her opinion is that despite the legitimate questions which I present here, she considers that Shaul has proven himself "above and beyond" and we should not now reproach him. She is also of the opinion that, at the beginning, you should earn his trust and thus we should avoid quibbling with him, If, heaven forbid, it becomes

---

[75] Gazit to Dinitz, 12:45, April 12, 1973, Vav Lamed/536, Aleph-4996/1, ISA.

[76] Telephone conversation between Dinitz and the Prime Minister's Office, 02:10, April 13, 1973, Aleph-7052/1, ISA.

[77] To Dinitz, for his eyes only, April 12, 1973, Vav Lamed/536, ISA; 18:00, April 13, 1973, Vav Lamed/539, Aleph-4996/1, ISA.

clear to us that we have no alternative but to have a confrontation with him, we will not recoil from doing so.[78]

In accord with Meir's demands, Kissinger's answering letter to Ismail, in which he proposed a date for a meeting, was delayed in Cairo. The designated date for the meeting, April 10, had passed without an alternative date being set. Sadat adopted the quickest means to expedite the matter—spreading a war alert rumor[79]—while aiming at another milestone in the process, the summit meeting in June. Ashraf Marwan reported quickly to his contacts and, on April 11, transmitted detailed information to Israel that the Egyptians were planning to open fire in May.[80] The Israelis also received intelligence reports from other sources that did not correlate with the actual preparations for war in Egypt. Apparently, only two weeks later, Sadat met with Assad to begin coordinating plans that would be ready toward autumn.

Military intelligence chief Eli Zeira later used this fact in his argument that Marwan was actually a double agent who knowingly misled Israel. Zeira raised the possibility that this warning served Sadat as a trial balloon to test Israel's reaction to an approaching war threat and determine how it would prepare for such an eventuality.[81]

Israel had to react to targeted threats of a war that could break out as early as the following month. Israeli decision-makers reacted with gravity to Egypt's acquisition of armament but agreed, at this stage at least, that

---

[78] Gazit to Dinitz, April 15, 1973, Aleph-7550/4, ISA. Dinitz answered this letter from Gazit as follows: "I tell you that I completely accept the prime minister's approach. Our main goal is to maintain trust in the Shaul channel. Of course, the trust must be mutual." But Dinitz continued by defending Kissinger's conduct: "Regarding his contacts with the mischief-maker: Just to remind you, he does not need our approval to maintain these contacts." Dinitz to Gazit (handwritten), April 25, 1973, Aleph-7550/4, ISA.

[79] "Between the end of January and the second week of April 1973, no concrete warning of war reached Israel" (Bar-Yosef 2001, 168). It appears that the warnings were Sadat's tool to urge Kissinger to advance the political process and that Sadat had no real intention of opening fire.

[80] See also Braun 1992, 27; Bar-Yosef 2001, 168. In another written source, Bar-Yosef (2010, 193) wrote that Marwan transmitted the report using a special two-way radio supplied to him by the Mossad. A year later, a corrected version to this book was published (Bar-Yosef 2011), in which the story of the radio was eliminated. In fact, Marwan did have a two-way radio, but he did not use it. On April 5, Sadat assembled a new government with himself at its head and decided that there was no alternative but to open a military campaign. The warning Marwan provided was based on Sadat's request to Minister of Defense Ismail following the government decision, in which he "asked General Ismail to examine the possibility of breaching the ceasefire and, at the same time, to assemble the National Defense Council and present the matter, while increasing the intensity of our diplomatic attack." Gamasy 1994, based on Ismail 1987, 267–69.

[81] Author's personal discussion with Zeira, September 19, 2011.

Sadat's moves were made "to improve his cards and his chances to put political pressure on Israel and on the United States, and at the same time, to improve his internal status. . . . We do not distinguish any special activity in the region of the canal."[82] The Israelis knew that Egypt was still far from completing its rearmament.[83] Defense Minister Dayan's appraisal was most important:

> In my estimation, Egypt is on track toward a return to war, whether this is being done consciously or unconsciously. I think that at least until the discussion in the Security Council and the summit meeting between Nixon and Brezhnev, the Egyptians will only threaten.[84]

Ismail finally received the message containing Kissinger's suggested time for the meeting on April 12. In reply, he confirmed May 9 as the date the two would meet.[85] Simultaneous to this determination, the immediate threat of military action evaporated. But in Israel, a small group of decision-makers would need to have a comprehensive discussion about expected military developments as quickly as possible.

## In Golda's Kitchen:
## Going to War, Not to a Political Agreement

Meir, Dayan, and Galili were the only ministerial participants in an informal discussion on April 18 at Meir's home.[86] They determined that Israel preferred to accept a coming war with Egypt, apparently in the near future, over a political agreement with Egypt mediated by the United States. This agreement, as noted, would have stipulated that Israel retreat to the international border between Israel and Egypt; in order to ensure its security, it

---

[82] Telegram 234 from GHQ Intelligence to the Embassy in Washington, April 15, 1973, Aleph-7066/4, ISA. The telegram included a detailed report by Aryeh Shalev, head of the military intelligence research department on Egyptian armament.

[83] The pilots designated to establish a squadron of MiG 23s were going to be sent for training in the Soviet Union in May or June. The Scud rocket division was planned to arrive in Egypt and begin deployment only in August, in addition to 200 modern armored personnel carriers (APCs), Sager rocket launchers, a division of SAM 6 ground-to-air missiles, and 180 mm field guns (Shazly 1987, 144).

[84] As stated at the cabinet meeting, April 24, 1973 (Braun 1992, 23).

[85] Letter from Kissinger and reply from Ismail, NA RN, NSC, HAK, Box 131; for the Kissinger letter to Ismail, FRUS XXV, 140–42.

[86] Bartov 2002, 257–62; Bar-Yosef 2001, 172; Arbel and Ne'eman 2005, 162–65. Regarding the meeting and its participants, see telegram from Gazit to Dinitz, April 19, 1973, Vav Lamed/649, Aleph-7045/2, ISA. Zvi Zamir, Eli Zeira, and Avner Shalev, who participated in the meeting, are permitted to read the minutes. They have confirmed that the material quoted by Bartov consists of exact quotes from the minutes of the meeting.

would be permitted to maintain a presence at key points in Sinai (including Sharm el-Sheikh).

From the protocol of the discussion, it is clear that the three ministers decided without sharing information about these political developments, the details of the alternatives, and the significant security implications of each alternative with the heads of the intelligence and defense establishments. Despite Galili's reservations, they decided not to share this information with the other members of the government or not to conduct the discussion this would have required.

Photo: Ministry of Defense, Israeli National Photo Collection

*Zvi Zamir in IDF senior staff photo, January 1961*

When they made this decision, the three ministers knew that the war would take place in the coming months, at a time determined by the Egyptians. They also had good reason to believe that Israel would not act in advance of Egyptian moves by carrying out a preventive attack or by calling up an increased number of reservists to heighten tension before war broke out. Kissinger's words—"You will have to wait more than two hours"—were engraved in their consciousness. It is possible that Minister Galili only found out after the war about this informal obligation to the United States government, the price for its agreement not to force Israel into an agreement and to continue to supply it with planes.[87]

On Monday, September 12, 2011, I held a discussion with Zvi Zamir. The cameras and microphones of the Israeli television network Channel One recorded our conversation for the program *Mabat Sheni* (Second Look), which reexamined the Yom Kippur War. Itay Landsberg, the program's editor, sat with us and participated in the discussion from time to time. Zamir's book, *With Open Eyes*, which he had written with all his heart, was about to be published. I had already read it and knew that his discussion of 1973 focused on intelligence aspects. Zamir gave his answer as to "why it had happened" by discussing the failure of military intelligence appraisals regarding the likelihood that war would break out, as well as

---

[87] This is what Minister Yisrael Galili told Arnan Azaryahu (Sini), his close assistant and confidant, in a long series of discussions conducted at Azaryahu's home in Kibbutz Yiron between June 2004 and August 2008.

the fact that the military and political systems had blindly followed military intelligence evaluations. But I wanted to clarify the important question to which Zamir had not referred, not even in his book: Why had a war broken out? I knew that the answer to this question could not come from a discussion of the intelligence and the military realms.

I opened the discussion by saying:

> You were there, in "Golda's kitchen," in the most intimate circle of decision-making. To a certain extent, you were there as an observer from the sidelines. The role of the Mossad, which you headed for five years, was limited "only" to special projects and to assembling information and data, not to research and evaluation. You were there because of your personality and due to the great respect Golda Meir had for you, and not just because it was required by your job description.[88]

I asked that we try to look together at the political developments of 1973: he as someone who had seen and experienced them at close range and in real time and I as a historian researching the period.

However, as I tried to share with him the account that had become apparent to me during my research, it became clear that the former head of the Mossad had only known about it in the most general terms. He had not been privy to the details of what had taken place in the channel between Kissinger and Ismail, nor those of the most secret channel between Kissinger and Meir via Rabin and Dinitz.[89] The first to distinguish this, with its full import, was Landsberg, looking on from the sidelines. Time after time, he asked Zamir whether he was acquainted with the documents and if he had known the political consequences that could be concluded from them. Again and again Zamir answered in the negative. This was not because his memory had betrayed him. His memory was excellent. Nor did he answer like a court witness, exempting himself with an "I don't know." That was not Zamir's character.[90]

---

[88] *Mabat Sheni* (Second Look), Channel One, Israeli Television, October 9, 2011.

[89] Unlike the channel between Kissinger and Sadat, which was conducted via the CIA, the contacts between Kissinger and Meir were transmitted by the ambassadors: first Rabin, then Dinitz. Communication consisted of personal meetings and telephone conversations between Kissinger and the ambassadors and dispatches to and from the Prime Minister's Office.

[90] After reading the Hebrew version of the book, Zamir told me that only after he had read all of the details had he realized the importance of my emphasizing to him that they (Elazar and the heads of GHQ military intelligence and the Mossad) had not known the details of the secret political channel and the extent to which this had harmed the decisions taken in Israel. Recorded on my telephone answering machine, September 26, 2012.

Conducting research is prolonged in nature and is developed step by step. It is rare that the picture becomes clear in a flash of merging sources. This time, though, it had happened. Zamir's answers completely correlated to what retired general Eli Zeira, who had been chief of military intelligence in 1973, had told me. He too had not been acquainted with the documents I had shown him, nor had he known of their content. In addition, as far as can be ascertained, David "Dado" Elazar, who had been chief of general staff, also received the most general report of these political developments.[91] I now integrated his testimony and the picture I had already received with a document whose importance has already been known to researchers of the period. The protocols of the meeting mentioned above, on April 18, 1973, in "Golda's kitchen," now completed a clear and solidly based description that was astounding in its significance.

For this dramatic meeting, in addition to Dayan and Galili, the prime minister had invited Elazar and his office director Avner Shalev, Zamir, and Zeira. Also present at the meeting was the director-general of Meir's office, Mordechai Gazit. A stenographer took notes of everything that was said. Those present were well acquainted with the targeted warnings Israel had received from a number of sources, foremost of which was the information Ashraf Marwan transmitted, which cited the middle of May as the time planned for war. Several dates had been mentioned, but May 15 was the most prominent among them. All of those present also were aware of the accelerated armament in Egypt.

At the beginning of the meeting, Dayan asked the three intelligence and defense representatives to present their appraisals regarding the possibility of Egypt initiating war. Each of the three replied at length. "There were no fundamental differences among them," determined the Agranat Commission, which comprehensively investigated their evaluations.[92] After they had finished, Meir and Dayan related their own reports.

Following this part of the meeting the ministers continued the discussion; Dado, Zamir, and Zeira remained in the room as listeners but did not take

---

[91] Avner Shalev, the head of the Office of the Chief of General Staff in 1973, testified to this in a telephone conversation I had with him.

[92] Agranat Commission Report, Additional Partial Report, Substantiations and Implications, 1974, vol. 1, 167.

part in the discussion, as Zamir and Zeira testified and as the protocol noted. Meir, Dayan, and Galili did not reveal the details of what was transpiring in the Kissinger-Ismail channel or the Kissinger to Dinitz and Rabin to Meir channel. They already knew that the second meeting between Kissinger and Ismail, which was supposed to have taken place originally on April 10, had been postponed and would possibly take place on May 9. (In reality, it was again delayed and took place on May 20). Meir certainly knew that, in accord with her demand, Kissinger intended to continue to procrastinate in dealing with Sadat's initiative.[93]

What Galili said at that meeting speaks for itself:

> This whole system [Egypt's preparations and threats of war] stems from the fact that we don't agree to withdraw to the former line. In theory, if we accept what Hafez [Ismail] said. . . . The point of departure starts with this, that they are ready for peace and for a series of agreements and international guarantees and so on—all that on the condition that we make a full withdrawal to the former line.[94]

He proposed bringing the matter up for discussion in the government "because I feel that this requires a new mandate—that on our side, there is no agreement about returning to the former line and beginning negotiations on the basis of our response to a demand to return to the former line." Government debate was necessary so that there would not be, in his words, "complaints in case [war] should take place."

Dayan and Meir agreed with Galili when he suggested "a new mandate from the government, that on our side, there was no agreement to return to the former lines on any of the borders, but certainly not on the border between us and the Egyptians." But they disagreed when he added, "It would also be possible to avoid this whole calamity if we are ready to enter into a series of discussions on the basis of a return to the former border."

Dayan's reservations were clear. He was ready to inform the cabinet ministers about the likelihood of war ("in very minor tones," in his words), but he opposed any discussion of examining the political alternative:

> But really, in very minor tones . . . we have to say that there is a possibility [of war]. The newspapers are all writing about it, the Egyptians are saying it, and the Americans are saying it, and Zvika [Zamir] says that the Arabs are now taking it more seriously. Yisrael

---

[93] Revealed in Bartov 2002, 257–62. The following long quotes come from the same pages in Bartov.

[94] Bartov 2002, 260–61.

[Galili], I would not suggest that it should be raised in the government in this context, whether we are ready even to go to war in order to avoid having to return to the Green Line. I don't think that question is being raised at the moment. . . . I understand that we may go to war and that we are concerned about that, and it's impossible for the government not to know something about that. . . . If it develops into a discussion like that, so be it, but in my opinion, we must raise it in the government as information. No one will guarantee us that the Egyptians won't proceed to that.[95]

Meir added her support to Dayan's opinion with regard to how to portray the military situation to the members of the government. She said nothing about presenting a political alternative: "We cannot enter into war if the government isn't in the picture." She added, "The government has to know, and if it doesn't, why do we need a government at all?" To that, Dayan responded sarcastically, "That's a good question, in and of itself. That's a matter which is worth discussing."

From the discussion between Meir, Dayan, and Galili, it is clear that it was not at all completely self-evident that the government had to be informed of the military situation and of the worry that war was about to break out in the near future. They finally decided to inform the ministers, although Dayan demurred and said that it should be done ambiguously. Galili thought that members of the government should be informed that a proposal for a political move to prevent the war also existed and thus wanted to involve them in the responsibility for rejecting such a move. Dayan disagreed. The prime minister ignored this point.

Meir referred to another aspect, stating that it would be advisable to ask the United States to try to prevent a war, but at the same time added, "What is important, whatever happens, is not to create the impression that we have become alarmed, and so they understand that that is not the point. We are quite sure of ourselves, but we do not want it to happen."

Dayan was firmer: "We should not request their guarantee that it will not happen . . . because you know our friends there. They will make sure, first of all, that it is at our expense." He was referring to the fear that the Americans would take advantage of Israeli concern in order to advance their own political developments.

Meir, as in many other cases, aligned herself with Dayan: "I propose that we tell them everything: There is information about it. On the ground there is still nothing. We are quite strong. We will remain in contact with them."

---

[95] Bartov 2002, 261.

Throughout the discussion, Galili was the one asking the difficult questions, which sometimes left the impression that the whole discussion, which seemed to be an annoyance to Meir and Dayan, was being held because Galili had requested it. This time he raised the forbidden question: Do we want war? He chose to present it in this way: "When Dado was speaking, he made a very significant statement. He said, 'If it [war] happens, let it happen.' But in his opinion, this necessitates that our behavior lead to a 'meaningful resolution.' Those are very intriguing words."

Here Meir decided to use the censor's scissors: "In all these serial novels, at this moment, we are stopping the tape." But Galili insisted on receiving an answer. "If so, I say, just before stopping the tape, that we need an authorized explanation to decipher this thing." Meir agreed to reveal her position more fully, while presenting it as derived from the conduct of the chief of staff, who no one would think was acting on his own: "He [Dado] said that they [the General Staff] are planning and preparing things. For the protocol, I announce that I do not want war. That will certainly surprise you." Dayan sounded amused: "I have suspected you of that for a long time."

Meir, who made a clear distinction between what would be accomplished but not appear in the protocol and what *would* appear, added what the stenographer wrote down:

> On Friday I visited the Shor family [whose son Avida had been killed a week earlier in Operation Spring of Youth]. . . . His mother is all broken up about it and she told me, "I always said that I wasn't at all worried. I didn't fear for his life because he was holy. . . . I was sure that nothing could harm him."[96]

The prime minister spoke sincerely; she almost certainly did not want a war. She spoke from the depths of her heart, but her eyes were wide shut and she consistently and decisively refused to take the necessary steps to avoid one.

---

96 Ibid.

# 4

# To Paris and Back—May 1973

*"I don't share Israeli optimism about the low probability of war being renewed and I don't believe that you can continue to stay calm and comfortable without moving."*

**—Kissinger to Dinitz**[1]

"The prime minister has determined that, although we are sure of victory, it is in our greatest interest to prevent a war, as far as it is in our power," Gazit, Meir's office director-general, telegraphed Dinitz, the Israeli ambassador in Washington, on the day after the "kitchen cabinet" meeting at the prime minister's home.[2] Gazit explained to Dinitz that the three ministers had chosen to employ deterrence measures in order to prevent war, while Israel would increase its state of alert "without publicity." The report reflected Israeli policy, which was intended to reduce the fear created by the threat of hostilities so that it would not be used by Kissinger as an excuse to advance a political process. What Gazit did not mention at all was the possibility of preventing war by negotiations to reach an agreement, an alternative that Dayan and Meir refused to discuss in any wider forum.

With regard to the United States, Dinitz was informed that "we will transmit the main points of information and emphasize that: a. we estimate that there is a low probability of renewal of the fighting by Sadat; b. we are completely certain of our strength." However, "you are not requested

---

[1] Report to the Prime Minister's Office about the meeting between Kissinger and Dinitz, May 13, 1973, Lamed Vav/672, Aleph-7052/1, ISA.

[2] Gazit to Dinitz, 13:00, April 19, 1973, Lamed Vav/649, Aleph-7045/2, ISA.

to act on this matter at present. In a few days we will send you a summary of information to be transmitted via Efraim [Halevy] to his friends, and through you, to Shaul [Kissinger]."[3]

## The First Warning from Hussein—"From Time to Time 'Charles' Has a Tendency to Exaggerate"

The exchanges between Kissinger and Ismail continued fitfully, to the relief of the Israeli side. By April 18 Kissinger had still not received confirmation of the meeting date he had suggested. Dinitz was happy to report this to Meir: "He [Kissinger] doesn't intend to approach him again and the lack of a reply until now almost makes it impossible to conduct the meeting on May 9 or 10. On his part, he is happy about the lack of response. He will keep me posted."[4]

Dinitz and Kissinger met on April 18. Most of the conversation did not relate to the contacts with Ismail, but rather centered on the president's anger at the US pro-Israel lobby's attempts to ensure the failure of the trade agreement with the Soviet Union. Kissinger threatened that Nixon was liable to cancel the supply of planes to Israel if there was a conflict with senators about the trade agreement. Dinitz reported to the prime minister what Kissinger had told him at the meeting, which had concluded with a private talk: "The president's mood is agitated. . . . His mood is also affected by other things, like Watergate. He does not like Jews. We will need him in the future, as well. We must not break his rules."[5]

Only on April 23 did Ismail confirm the May 10 meeting date in a letter to Kissinger. On the following day, when Dinitz again met with Kissinger, he came to understand how justified Egypt's complaints were regarding the United States' support of Israel and the level of coordination between the two states. Kissinger let Dinitz read the letter from Ismail and explained that he intended to delay the process until after the coming summit between Nixon and Brezhnev. Kissinger was planning to devote May 9 and 10 to meetings in Moscow in preparation for the summit, which was to take place in June.[6] Based on intelligence updates from the beginning of April, Kissinger informed Dinitz of his assessment that the atmosphere of war the Egyptians were creating was artificial, meant to serve internal political

---

[3] Ibid.

[4] April 19, 1973, Lamed Vav/635, Aleph-7052/1, ISA; Lamed Vav/632, ibid.; Lamed Vav/631, Aleph-7061/6, ISA; NA RN, NSV, HAK, Country Files, Box 135.

[5] Dinitz to Gazit, April 18, 1973, Lamed Vav/632, Aleph-7052/1, ISA; Aleph-7061/6.

[6] Telephone conversation between Dobrynin and Kissinger, April 24, 1973, Aleph-7052/1, ISA; NA RN, HAK, Telcon, Box 19.

needs, and should not be taken seriously. Kissinger assumed that there was no danger that the Egyptians would open fire in the coming weeks.[7]

Dinitz reported to the prime minister:

> Shaul [Kissinger] said that he does not intend to enter into negotiations on the basis of this document [of principles to settle the conflict in the Middle East, agreed upon by Nixon and Brezhnev at a summit meeting in May 1972]. In his opinion, he must carry out the meeting [with Ismail], but he will postpone it until about May 18 in order to bring it closer to the summit. . . . He believes that he must have another meeting. . . . If he refuses to go, they [Egypt] will accuse him of breaking off contact and that will make it difficult for them [Kissinger and Nixon] at the summit. His aim is to get through the summit. After his meeting with them [the Egyptians, on May 18] he will postpone his reply to them for two weeks and thus we will get through the summit.[8]

Despite these statements, Kissinger was still hoping to prepare the groundwork for later negotiations; he asked Dinitz to clarify the Israeli position "because he only wanted to be ready to understand our thought processes."[9]

Two months previously, Kissinger had still been worried that it would be difficult for him to develop a relationship with Dinitz as he had with Rabin. Indeed, the new ambassador could not take Rabin's place as an authority on security and political matters, but he turned out to be a reliable and trustworthy partner who transmitted messages accurately, both in language and in spirit, between Kissinger and Meir. When Meir and her office expressed doubts as to what extent they could trust Kissinger, Dinitz replied, "Our principal objective is to maintain our trust in the 'Shaul channel.' . . . The level of trust he has demonstrated up to now, and his willingness to share his information with us is no less than it was in the past, and in some cases is even greater." Dinitz did not hesitate to give examples of this.[10]

The trust was mutual. Before Kissinger left for Moscow, he met again with Dinitz for the fifth time that month. The Israeli ambassador gave Kissinger detailed information from the Mossad about Egypt's and Syria's preparations for war. The intended (and incorrect) date for attack had been transmitted by

---

[7] Dinitz to Gazit on his discussion with Kissinger, April 18, 1973, Lamed Vav/632, Aleph-7045/2, ISA.

[8] April 24, 1973, Lamed Vav/643, Aleph-7052, ISA; NA RN, NSC, HAK, Country Files, Box 135.

[9] Ibid.

[10] Personal letter handwritten by Dinitz to Gazit, April 25, 1973, Aleph-7550/4, ISA.

the Egyptian Mossad agent Ashraf Marwan, and the details of the attack had been received from King Hussein himself.[11] The king, in contrast to Marwan, did not stipulate an appointed date and thus did not fail in his prediction. Dinitz reported to Meir after his discussion with Kissinger:

> I read aloud to him [Kissinger] Charles's [Hussein's] message to the prime minister. . . . I finished with the questions: What was his appraisal? Had Charles transmitted similar information to them? And, in his opinion, would Iraqi and Syrian forces enter Jordanian territory to open another front against Israel? . . . I told him that, from time to time, perhaps Charles had a tendency to exaggerate in the severity of his reports, but this time there was general confirmation from other reliable sources as well.[12]

King Hussein not only sent a message to the prime minister, but also took the trouble to go to Tel Aviv in order to meet with Meir and Dayan on May 9.[13] The king later told the Americans that this time, unlike in the past, Dayan had treated him cordially. Most of the meeting was taken up by the expectation of war. Meir and Dayan agreed with Hussein about the probability that Egypt and Syria would initiate hostilities, but they did not expect that this would take place in the near future. Their estimation ignored the warning they had received from Marwan and even contradicted the "intelligence assessment," which determined that, from a military standpoint, Egypt was still not ready for war. Meir's and Dayan's appraisal was based on a political consideration—the Egyptians would wait for the results of the Kissinger-Ismail meeting and the Nixon-Brezhnev summit meeting. The prime minister even added her prediction that the Soviets had no interest in a war and would use their influence to restrain the Egyptians and Syrians. Dayan and Meir were relying on updated intelligence reports, according to which Syrian forces had been withdrawn from the border, but Hussein maintained that his sources in Syria had reported that this had been done for purposes of reorganization.

A short time after the meeting, Hussein transmitted a detailed report to the Americans about the Egyptian-Syrian attack plan.[14] He clarified that

---

[11] Meeting between Dinitz and Kissinger, 18:30, May 3, 1973, NA RN, NSC, HAK, Box 135. With regard to the information received from Jordan, the head of Jordanian intelligence was an additional senior source who transmitted information to the Mossad. He was the source who transmitted the Syrian war plans to the Mossad.

[12] Dinitz to Gazit, May 3, 1973, Lamed Vav/655, Aleph-7052/1, ISA.

[13] Memorandum from Saunders to Kissinger, May 25, 1973, NA RN, NSC Files, Box 618.

[14] Memorandum from Saunders to Kissinger about information received from King Hussein, May 17, 1973, NA RN, NSC, Box 757. The CIA confirmed most of the details

Jordan was not preparing to place its forces under joint Arab command and that Jordan would not participate in a war unless there was a threat to its territory. The CIA, which had also received this information directly from the Mossad, estimated that Egypt meant for its threats of war to increase pressure before the Nixon-Brezhnev summit meeting and that fighting would not be renewed before the end of June.[15] In Israel, there was more worry about the coming summit between the superpowers than about the meeting between Kissinger and Ismail; the Israelis were relying on Kissinger's cooperation and his virtuoso ability to delay his Egyptian interlocutor and lead him astray.[16]

*King Hussein and President Nixon, December 1970*

Photo: Robert L. Knudson, NARA

## Egyptian Conduct: If They Threaten, They Don't Fire

Indeed, the Egyptians had no intention of going to war in the spring.[17]

Researchers of the period busy themselves discussing whether the Egyptians intended to attack at the beginning of May. They search for intelligence and military signs pointing in one direction or another, but in vain.

---

Hussein supplied. In his reply to the king, Kissinger avoided detailing the diplomatic moves that the United States would make in response to the information.

[15] Memorandum from CIA director James Schlesinger to Kissinger, May 5, 1973, NA RN, NSC Files, Box 647. Schlesinger assumed that the Soviets would limit the Syrians, while the Egyptians would not take a military step until the conclusion of the discussions about Israel in the General Assembly. In effect, he estimated that fighting would not be renewed during the coming six weeks.

[16] Gazit to Dinitz, urgent, April 22, 1973,Vav Lamed/643, Aleph-4996/1, ISA; Dinitz to Gazit, April 24, 1973, Lamed Vav/643, Aleph-7052/1, ISA; meeting between Kissinger and Dinitz, April 24, 1973, NA RN, NSC, HAK, Box 135.

[17] Seale (1993, 196) writes that, at the Sadat-Assad meeting in April, they agreed only on the principal guidelines of the war. As a result, Assad traveled to Moscow at the beginning of May to request equipment he was lacking for war, primarily planes and air defense systems.

Indeed, the very fact that the wide media coverage of these events was creating an atmosphere of approaching war testifies that Sadat did not intend to attack Israel in the spring. An investigation of his political conduct only adds more strength to this fact.

*Ha'aretz* reported that on April 21, the Egyptian National Assembly met and heard an announcement from the government, whose members had, over three days, discussed "the plan for a total conflict with Israel." [18] The announcement also provided an explanation of the need for a military conflict: "The government of the United States supports the policies of Israel and continues to strengthen Israeli potential, along with its vacillating recognition of our rights to sovereignty over our land."[19]

"A Conference of Threats" was the headline of a *Ha'aretz* article describing a conference of sixteen Arab chiefs of staff, meeting in Cairo to coordinate the war effort against Israel.[20] Only the chiefs of staff of Morocco and Tunisia were absent. "Some Progress Was Made in the War Effort," *Ha'aretz* reported.[21] "The Artillery Will Not Be Silent for a Long Time to Come," predicted Musa Sabri, editor of the Egyptian daily newspaper *Al-Akhbar*, as the conference drew to a close.[22] The Lebanese Druze leader Kamal Jumblatt joined in creating the warlike atmosphere; after a discussion with Sadat he stated, "President Sadat is determined to carry out military action against Israel in the near future. Sadat feels that internal circumstances in Egypt, Israel's stance, and the international situation all necessitate going down the path to war." The Egyptian media published articles about the Egyptian army's winter training, which had ended in March, noting that "they particularly trained for crossing water barriers, including a model similar to the Suez Canal, and for gaining control of the opposite bank of the canal in order to establish a bridgehead for additional forces."[23]

This is not the way a nation behaves when it is preparing to attack immediately and by surprise. Perhaps this is the way a government conducts itself when it wants to create the impression that it is going to do so, both for internal and external reasons.[24]

---

[18] The following reports appeared in *Ha'aretz* between April 19 and 30, 1973.

[19] The complete version of the announcement can be found in Aleph-7027/12, ISA.

[20] Oded Zarai, "A Conference of Threats," *Ha'aretz*, April 24, 1973.

[21] Ibid.

[22] Ibid.

[23] *Ha'aretz*, April 27, 1973.

[24] Egyptian Chief of Staff Shazly testified that only in August were the possible dates for war determined as either September 7–10 or October 5–10 (Shazly 1987, 146–47); the chief of the Operations Branch, General Mohamed Abdel Ghani el-Gamasy, stated that

The actual preparations in the military were conducted simultaneously and secretly, and necessitated a target date which was further away. At Burj al-Arab, west of Alexandria, Sadat and Assad met on April 23 and 24 to discuss the details of war coordination. In order to recruit the Syrians into his plans, Sadat had to deceive them by camouflaging his approach. Returning Sinai to the Egyptians by political means would, perhaps, make it necessary for Egypt to adopt a war plan with limited objectives. Thus Sadat presented the Syrians with military aims that neither he nor the Egyptian army leaders had considered—capturing the mountain passes in order to advance into eastern Sinai. The two armies were not yet ready for war; the two presidents determined that the heads of the army together, in the framework of what was termed the Supreme Cooperative Council of the Armed Forces, would formulate a war plan in the coming months and propose dates to implement it.[25]

Immediately following the meeting between Sadat and Assad, Marwan reported that, in coordination with the Syrians, the start of the war had been delayed until the end of May or the beginning of June. A month later, on May 25, Marwan reported to his handlers that Sadat had decided to postpone the war for at least two months, without specifying the date.[26]

Directly after the date for the meeting between Kissinger and Ismail had been determined, the threat of immediate war was eliminated. The United Nations remained the place where Egypt could continue to apply political pressure. Indeed, Egypt attempted to pass a resolution to censure Israel for its action in Lebanon (Operation Spring of Youth) in order to test the United States with the dilemma of whether to veto it. President Nixon vigorously ordered the US representative to refrain from issuing a veto.[27]

At this stage, both the Egyptians and the Americans understood that the special discussion channel would not lead to a political process in the immediate future. They now turned their attention to the summit meeting at the end of June, and the two sides estimated that an additional meeting before that would not aid in advancing negotiations. However, both the

---

as of April, the date of the war had not yet been determined but he was "convinced that a war between Israel and Egypt would break out within six months" (Stein 2003, 95).

[25] Shazly 1987, 26; Seale 1993, 201; Bar-Yosef 2001, 222; Maoz 1988, 97–98; Arbel and Ne'eman 2006, 166.

[26] The explanations Marwan gave Israel for these delays were that in April, the Syrians were not ready for war; in May, the delay was so that Egypt could receive the aerial defense systems (SA 6). For additional information, see Shazly 1987, 144.

[27] Exchange of telegrams between Jerusalem, the embassy in Washington and the Israeli delegation to the United Nations in New York between April 16 and 18, 1973, Aleph-7066/4, ISA; also Kissinger's intervention, principally to deal with the State Department, April 20, 1973, Lamed Vav/639, Aleph-7066/4, ISA; telephone conversation between Nixon and Kissinger, April 21, 1973, NA RN, Telcon, Box 19.

United States and Egypt still acted to implement the meeting, both in order to gain time and so that neither would be blamed for causing the discussions to fail.

In those days, Cairo was a model of political calm in comparison to Washington (in the shadow of the Watergate affair) and Jerusalem (in the shadow of Golda Meir's indecision about whether to continue in office after the elections). In Israel the picture quickly became clear: "Around Independence Day Golda Meir will announce her willingness to stand at the head of the Ma'arach [political party] list in the coming elections and form the government. A small number of ministers already know this," Dan Margalit and Matti Golan reported in *Ha'aretz*. In contrast, in Washington, matters were becoming more and more complicated. In his report to the prime minister, Dinitz was informed enough to know that Nixon "is moving around like a caged lion and is about to make decisions with far-reaching consequences. . . . The president has secluded himself and does not want to see anyone." Nixon asked Secretary of State Rogers for help in reorganizing the White House team. Dinitz reported, "Our friend Shaul [Kissinger] is, of course, worried about the whole matter. . . . When the boat rocks, even he feels unstable. The government in general and the White House in particular are almost completely paralyzed. . . .The newspapers are talking about a crisis of trust which has never been seen before in this century."[28] At the beginning of May 1973, Rogers was already on his way to resigning his post as secretary of state. Kissinger was aware of this and was acting to help it come about.[29] He even discussed it with Dinitz.

In the heat of events, the meeting between Kissinger and Ismail was again postponed, this time to May 18. The desire to maintain secrecy about the meeting necessitated that Kissinger "disappear" for a day or two while in Europe. In order to determine the new place and time, he had to choose between Madrid and Paris. The new place and time were determined— Kissinger and Ismail would meet Paris on May 20.[30]

Kissinger reported to Dinitz that, in contrast to the meeting in February, he now felt a lack of interest on the part of the Egyptians and added, "This

---

[28] Dinitz to Gazit, April 25, 1973, Lamed Vav/646, Aleph-7061/6, ISA.

[29] Scowcroft to Kissinger, May 8, 1973. Haig had spoken to the president about changing positions in the government—replacing the secretary of state, appointing Schlesinger as defense secretary, and appointing Casey in his place as the head of the CIA. The president intended to implement these changes only after the summit in June. NA RN, HAK, Trip, Box 39.

[30] The Israeli Foreign Ministry knew the place and time of the meeting even before Dinitz's report; he asked Gazit to find the source of the leak. Dinitz to Gazit, May 3, 1973, Lamed Vav/655, Aleph-7052/1, ISA; HAK to 013, May 6, 1973, NA RN, HAK, Trip, Box 39; May 13, 1973, Lamed Vav/665, ISA.

whole exercise is barren and nothing can come of it. It seems as though they think there is no chance of political progress." "I asked Shaul whether this slowness bothered him," wrote Dinitz to the prime minister:

> Shaul said that the opposite was true. He is not urging them on and as far as he's concerned, that's fine. But from time to time, he asks himself the question of whether there won't come a time when we have to initiate something. . . . We have to think about what to do in the future because the present standstill is not good. After all, he has been dragging it out for two years and he doesn't know how long he will be able to continue doing so. As he has said to me and to my predecessor a number of times, pressures are liable to develop which will demand movement. But, he added, not now.[31]

"Not now." What did this mean? One interpretation—not before the summit; a second interpretation—not before the elections in Israel; a third interpretation—not before Kissinger was appointed secretary of state; a fourth interpretation—as long as there was no actual threat of renewal of war. A reasonable possibility is that all of the interpretations are correct.

## The Meeting in Moscow— What Is Amusing Kissinger and Brezhnev?

In spring 1973, two central issues were at the focus of US foreign policy: stabilizing the ceasefire in Vietnam and signing a trade agreement with the Soviet Union. The trade agreement was actually a camouflage for moves to save the Soviet superpower from going hungry. The Soviet Union was forced to accept this situation, but acted to reduce its effects. With regard to the Middle East, it hoped that Egypt's attempt to grant Kissinger control over political affairs would fail. Simultaneously, it secretly increased its efforts to gain Israel's authorization to be involved in Middle East politics.[32]

The main barrier to approval of the trade agreement was the demand by a large, vocal, and influential group of US senators to condition the agreement on human rights improvements in the Soviet Union, particularly with regard to the rights of Jews there. This proposed condition won great support from

---

[31] Dinitz to Gazit, May 3, 1973, Lamed Vav/655, Aleph-7052/1, ISA.

[32] Initiated by the Soviets, a number of secret meetings took place in Geneva between Mordechai Gazit, the and Soviet representatives Yevgeny Primakov and Yuri Kotov. Gazit's report to Meir about the discussions, March 23 and 24, 1973, Aleph-7045/13, ISA; directive to Dinitz to inform Kissinger of those meetings, Lamed Vav/475, March 24, 1973, Aleph-4996/1, ISA; reports of the meetings to the United States, NA RN, Country Files, M.E., HAK, Box 135.

the pro-Israel lobby in the United States, which was acting with quiet encouragement from the Israeli government. Nixon and Kissinger did not hide their anger. They argued in vain that quiet diplomacy with the Soviets would lead to Jews emigrating from the Soviet Union in unprecedented numbers, mainly via Vienna. Israel was in no hurry to lose this important political bargaining chip. Kissinger's departure for Moscow during the second week in May, and his meeting with General Secretary Leonid Brezhnev and Foreign Minister Andrei Gromyko, was intended to complete the trade agreement between the two states. The White House and the Israeli government applied mutual pressure: the United States forcefully demanded that Israel aid in removing congressional opposition to the trade agreement; in return, it would support Israel's call for a practical freeze in Middle East political moves. As Nixon was occupied with Watergate matters, only Kissinger remained to lead the developments in Moscow.[33]

"Let's turn to an easy question now—the Middle East,"[34] suggested Brezhnev when he and Kissinger had some time off from their meetings on other subjects. Indeed, the Middle East was on the margins of the discussions; this discussion took place in a light atmosphere as the two sides challenged each other in jokes that hinted at their attitudes toward the subject.

Kissinger, who estimated that the Egyptians would initiate a war in which they would be defeated, opened with a story about a crab who asked the camel to let him cross the Suez Canal on his back and pinched him strongly in the middle of the crossing. Minutes before they both drowned, the camel asked the crab why he had done so. The crab replied, "You forgot that this is the Middle East."

Brezhnev, perhaps in order to gain time to think of a proper response, riposted with another version of the same story, this time about a scorpion and a frog. Here Brezhnev was agreeing with Kissinger that Egypt might initiate a war that would be disastrous for it, but that would also cause damage to the Soviet Union, its benefactor.

Kissinger, who felt that the Egyptians were liable to be prisoners of their own threats of war, did not let the matter drop. This time he told a joke about an Arab who was lying down in his tent when his rest was disturbed by the noise of children outside. To make them go away, he told them that the neighboring village was giving out free grapes. Immediately after the children left for the neighboring village, the Arab said to himself, "You idiot, what are you doing here if they are giving

---

[33] Quandt 2001, 100–101.

[34] The account that follows is based on the protocol of the meeting between Brezhnev and Kissinger, at the Politburo vacation home in Zavidovo, May 7, 1973, NA RN, NSC, HAK, Box 75.

out free grapes?" And he too got up and joined those who were going to the neighboring village.

With Kissinger's encouragement, Brezhnev did not remain silent. His next joke returned to the trade agreement and the obstacles the pro-Israel lobby had posed to its confirmation. He told of two Jews, one of whom asked the other, "Abraham, why are you not going to Israel? You applied for a permit and everything seemed to be settled." "Some goddamn fool wrote an anonymous letter about me, alleging that I am not a Jew," answered Abraham, according to the General Secretary of the Soviet Union. And so it continued...

Essentially, Kissinger and Brezhnev agreed that the central common goal was to prevent a war—in particular, that war should not break out before the summit meeting. Both knew that after the meeting the war might occur and that they could not prevent it except by a political agreement. Neither side was ready to do what was necessary in order to pressure Egypt and Israel to advance a political settlement. Kissinger "updated" the Soviet leader with regard to Egyptian preparations for war and "was updated" in return about the Israelis being equipped with attack planes. The Soviets, on their part, transmitted a statement of principles that contained nothing new, but, as will be seen, it enabled Kissinger to wave it in front of the Israelis as a worse alternative that awaited them if they did not cooperate with him.

Kissinger also proposed a practical summary of the discussion: to wait until after his meeting with Ismail. The main goal of the meeting, as he tried to explain, was to stop the Egyptians from making military moves. In a report to the president on his discussions, Kissinger wrote that "Brezhnev has several times stressed his concern that a conflict may break out before, during or shortly after this visit [to the US]."[35]

## "Shaulson Will Be Disappointed"

Kissinger returned from Moscow and began preparations to leave for Paris on Vietnam-related matters, while simultaneously planning for his meeting there with Ismail. In Washington, Israeli foreign minister Abba Eban was waiting to meet him. Before their discussion Dinitz asked Kissinger to compartmentalize Eban—Dinitz's official supervisor—from being involved in the discussion channel with Ismail.[36] "I made sure to tell Shaul that the foreign minister has not been included

[35] Ibid; Kissinger to Nixon via Scowcroft, May 8, 1973, HAKTO 194, NA RN, NSC, HAK, Trip, Box 32, 19A.

[36] Protocol of the meeting between Kissinger and Eban, May 12, 1973, NA RN, NSC, HAK, Box 135.

Photo: Moshe Milner, Israeli National Photo Collection

*Moshe Dayan, Shimshon Shapira, Golda Meir, Yigal Allon, and Yisrael Galili at the government table in the Knesset in Jerusalem, February 9, 1971*

in the secret contacts with Hafez [Ismail] and the various appraisals [intelligence information] that we have transmitted to them," he wrote, to the prime minister's relief, after reporting that Kissinger had agreed to his request to meet with Eban.[37]

In Israel, the smallest possible group of "Golda's Kitchen" was preparing for Kissinger's trip to Paris. "We hope to send you a few thoughts sometime soon, some 'provisions for the road' so to speak, for Shaul, leading up to his meeting," they informed Dinitz on May 10.[38] Surprisingly, they asked the ambassador, as a preliminary, to clarify whether, in past discussions regarding a partial settlement at the canal, Israel had agreed that it would be valid for two years only. Dinitz, who checked and confirmed this, wondered—to a great extent justifiably—in his answer to Gazit: "As all this seems completely theoretical to me, could you explain to me why you are interested in this point?"[39] But before this could be clarified, Dinitz informed Jerusalem that "I have been invited to a meeting with Shaul tomorrow, May 13, at 09:30. I know that he will want to

---

[37] Dinitz to Gazit, May 11, 1973, Lamed Vav/664 and Lamed Vav/665, Aleph-7052/1, ISA.

[38] Gazit to Dinitz, May 10, 1973, Vav Lamed/568, Aleph-7052, ISA.

[39] Dinitz to Gazit, May 17, 1973, Lamed Vav/684, Aleph-7052, ISA.

talk about his trip and the meeting with Hafez. Let me know urgently whether there are instructions for this discussion."[40]

Until that moment, Israel had not actually dealt with the new political situation created since Ismail had presented Kissinger with Sadat's initiative in Armonk; the Israelis had not even taken the trouble to answer Kissinger's repeated requests to "give me something." This time, in reply to his request, Dinitz received a long list from the prime minister, including instructions, questions, and requests for clarifications and explanations. Had the Israeli "fixation" on political and military thinking finally cracked?

The first series of instructions was accompanied by a clarification letter, the importance of which goes far beyond the contents of the instructions themselves. The letter read:

> In addition to the above, it is important that you know that we do not assume that we have any special "supplies" (or any new "supplies") to give to Shaulson [Kissinger] in preparation for his meeting. So we have telegraphed you that if *he does not* request "supplies," don't initiate communication of the "supplies" which we have transmitted to you. You will surely note that we take into account the possibility that Shaulson will be disappointed when he hears what you have to say and that he will protest that we are obstructing him and the like. We would not want that to happen and we are depending on you to find the proper way and the right "arguments" to transmit our opinions without leading to an explosion, as long as he insists on receiving "ideas" from us.[41]

This reaction, in which Defense Minister Dayan was a central partner, derived from the fact that Israel did not have anything to offer. The Israeli political echelon was aware that if it had no choice and was forced to present a position, it would propose "ideas" for the sake of appearances. This was also the reason for clarifying whether Israel had in the past agreed that the partial settlement at the canal would be only be valid for two years. Meir's instructions indicated that if Israel was forced to present ideas, it would recycle the idea of a partial settlement, which was not relevant, but would agree to set its validity for a longer or unlimited period of time, knowing that the Egyptians would reject this. She also told Dinitz to bring to Kissinger's attention alone that the prime minister would not agree to the idea of "sovereignty in return

---

[40] Dinitz to Gazit, May 12, 1973 Lamed Vav/668, Aleph-7052/1, ISA.

[41] An accompanying letter added to Vav Lamed/570, 08:00 Israeli time, May 13, 1973, ISA. Again listed in Vav Lamed/573, Aleph-7052/1, May 13, 1973, ISA: "As background to our understanding Vav Lamed/570, I add the following." Emphasis and quotation marks in original.

for security" and was not willing to recognize Egyptian sovereignty over all of Sinai. Israel had indeed undertaken that, in a partial settlement, the line of withdrawal would not be final, but it requested to clarify that "our position is that substantial changes will be necessary, that is to say, a change in sovereignty." In addition, Meir called to Dinitz's attention that "we have not been offered simultaneous negotiation on both a partial and a comprehensive settlement, and we, for our part, do not agree to that."[42]

Dinitz received his instructions and hurried to the White House to hear Kissinger warn that, in Moscow, Brezhnev had decisively asserted that the chances for a renewal of fighting in the Middle East were great, despite the Soviet Union's moderating influence over Egypt and Syria. He had also stated that the Soviet Union could not allow itself a war in the area either before or after the summit.[43] "I don't share Israeli optimism about the low probability of the war being renewed and I don't believe that you can continue to stay calm and comfortable without moving," warned Kissinger, who chose to emphasize that "thanks to me there has been a standstill for twenty months and that is above and beyond what can be imagined. . . . Now it is going to end." His more severe assessment of Sadat's motives could have also been based on the CIA's appraisal, which stated that it "now believe[d] that Sadat is serious and that to consider that he is bluffing is unrealistic."[44] However, at the same time, he received a memorandum from Saunders which determined that "Sadat doesn't really want to break the deadlock by force."[45]

During the meeting, Kissinger transmitted to Dinitz the US-Soviet statement of principles regarding the Middle East from May 28, 1972, about which Israel had not known before this discussion, as well as the "statement of principles for a Middle East settlement" that the Soviets had given him in Moscow only a week earlier, on May 7. Kissinger knew that Israel would reject these documents, so he said that there was no need to relate them at present—they could wait until the summit which would take place on June 18. On the other hand, he requested that, before he left for Paris—in other words, within two days—the prime minister give him her analysis and comments with regard to Egypt's position. Kissinger complained that

---

[42] Ibid.

[43] Dinitz to Meir about meeting with Kissinger, May 13, 1973, Lamed Vav/670, Lamed Vav 672, and Lamed Vav 673, Aleph-7052/1; Lamed Vav/674 and Lamed Vav/675, Aleph-7052/2, ISA; protocol of the open discussion, NA RN, NSC, HAK, Box 135.

[44] Central Intelligence Agency, *Nixon and the Role of Intelligence in the 1973 Arab-Israeli War* (Washington, D.C.: Central Intelligence Agency, 2013), 41. May 14, 1973. Available at https://www.cia.gov/library/publications/historical-collection-publications/arab-israeli-war/nixon-arab-isaeli-war.pdf.

[45] Ibid.

"he was going to see Hafez for two days and wondered what they would talk about for such a lengthy period" and added that he wanted to continue to gain time, but had no new proposals.[46] "If you could just give me some statement of your position on the connection between the interim and the overall. Can you give me some formal statement?" Kissinger pleaded with Dinitz and did not hesitate to stress again that time would not work in Israel's favor. At that point in the discussion, Kissinger reached the crux of the issue: "Why couldn't you take it in the form of security zones instead of annexation? Sovereignty would remain in Egyptian hands but you would be there in practice."[47]

Dinitz remained loyal to his instructions and did not propose anything. "When a discussion begins everything can be discussed, but without prior conditions. . . . We won't deceive Egypt by saying that we will not demand any change in the border," he answered, almost contradicting himself.[48]

Kissinger was not satisfied with knowing what Israel would not demand. He wanted information about what Israel would accept: that is, what were its territorial demands for a full peace agreement? In his discussion with Dinitz, he focused on important points that he had not seen fit to discuss with Eban a day earlier. The conversation with Dinitz was as follows:

> Kissinger: My estimate of what you want [as a final border] is a straight line west of el-Arish.
>
> Dinitz: It might not be a straight line . . . but in general terms you are right. . . . In strategic terms we need sufficient depth to make it secure. But three-quarters of Sinai would go back.
>
> Kissinger: Why couldn't you take it in the form of a security zone instead of annexation?
>
> Dinitz: On the borders, it entails a change in sovereignty [annexation]. That was a government decision.[49]

Again Kissinger despaired of receiving Israeli approval to advance his plan. Following the discussion, Dinitz reported to the prime minister that "he ended the discussion by saying that he would check with Ismail as to what could be done. At least he would make sure that Ismail did not leave in

---

[46] This and the following are direct quotes from Dinitz's dispatch to the prime minister (ibid.); Dinitz to Gazit regarding his meeting with Kissinger, May 13, 1973, Lamed Vav 672, Aleph-7052/1, ISA.

[47] Ibid.

[48] Ibid.

[49] American minutes of the discussion between Kissinger and Dinitz on May 13, 1973, NA RN, NSC, HAK, Box 135.

despair from the meeting with him in order to avoid reaching the point that contact would be severed." In a strictly private conversation with Dinitz, Kissinger also added information about Watergate and about possible changes in the US government that might work to the detriment of Israel. In addition, he advised Israel to accept the proposal for a compromise on the pace of airplane supply, even if it wanted planes to be sent at a faster pace.[50]

Dinitz opened his report to the prime minister about this private conversation with a request: "From the private conversation with Shaul on May 13. Please make sure to strictly compartmentalize this telegram."

1. He [Kissinger] began to talk about Watergate and the attempts to entangle him in the affair. He is innocent, but there are those, of course, who are interested in involving him. And this is connected to two areas: One of the people who was working with him left his office and was lent to Haldeman. Shaul had no control over him or knowledge of his deeds. The second "accusation" is that he saw intelligence material about the leaks, which was obtained by secretly listening in on newspaper reporters. Shaul argues that even though he naturally receives intelligence information, his job does not include clarifying how this material is obtained.

2. Regarding John Connelly, Kissinger said that Connelly's present position as presidential advisor was "a partial and undefined role," but as a result, he would try to delve into various areas and the danger was that one would be in the Middle East because of his oil interests. He repeated that he [Connelly] was no friend. . . . Shaul stated that it wouldn't be a bad idea if they [Israeli emissaries] would apply pressure in order to neutralize him, and we decided on possible activity.

3. Shaul said that Schlesinger's appointment to the Defense Department would benefit us. He [Schlesinger] was open and intelligent and although he [Kissinger] did not know Schlesinger's specific views of the Middle East, he was a great improvement in comparison to Richardson.[51]

---

[50] Report by Dinitz to Meir on his private discussion with Kissinger on May 13, 1973, 20:30, May 14, 1973, Lamed Vav/677, Aleph-7052/2, ISA. Dinitz recommended accepting the compromise on aircraft supply; perhaps this was Kissinger's aim in transmitting the information about possible changes in the government. On the following day, Dinitz received confirmation to end the matter of the supply of planes as he had recommended. Telegram from Gazit to Dinitz, May 15, 1973, Vav Lamed/578, Aleph-4996/1, ISA.

[51] Dinitz to Gazit regarding his meeting with Kissinger, May 13, 1973, Lamed Vav/677, Aleph-7052/2, ISA.

Kissinger's threats indeed worked, to a certain extent. On the day following the meeting, Jerusalem reacted with new instructions. The letter to Dinitz began:

> At earlier stages in the contacts between Shaul and Hafez, it seemed certain that benefit could be had in gaining time. Now, considering the reports, it seems that the development is liable to be dangerous—whether moving toward a split between Shaul and Hafez or whether due to negative content from the standpoint of Israel. . . . We are aware of the danger that the matter will be transferred to the care of the State Department. . . . It is important that Shaul acts to prevent a split with Egypt. Even if a split does occur, it is preferable that this does not happen before the summit.[52]

However, in contrast to what Kissinger asked for and expected to receive, Israel did not reevaluate its position. No new directives were forthcoming from Jerusalem that could supply Kissinger with something to hold onto. The only change was tactical. Instead of not presenting Kissinger with any "ideas" to advance, Israel would provide him with something so that he could maintain direct contact with Sadat, but would not give him a shred of information to connect between an interim settlement and a comprehensive one:

> As Shaul asked if we could possibly give him a formula to connect between an interim and a comprehensive settlement, the prime minister suggests that he propose a formula as if it was his initiative. It could be in accord with what the prime minister raised on December 10, 1971, in a discussion with him. As an introduction to the proposal, it could be said that, in order to achieve peace according to Resolution 242, we agree to a settlement regarding the Suez Canal.[53]

Also included were Meir's reasons for opposing a simultaneous discussion of a final settlement, along with an interim one, on the opening of the Suez Canal. Meir again ignored Kissinger's question: Why did Israel insist on annexing territory? Why was it not satisfied with holding onto strategic points and security areas whose sovereignty would remain in Egyptian hands even though, in practice, Israel would maintain its presence?

The great fear in Jerusalem was that, at the meeting with Ismail, Kissinger would try to achieve the outline of an agreement. Gazit wrote to Dinitz:

---

[52] Gazit to Dinitz, May 15, 1973, Vav Lamed/580, Aleph-7052/2, ISA.
[53] Ibid.

Does he intend, already at his next meeting with Pohazy Hafez Ismail [the name used is a play on the Hebrew word for "reckless"], that this will be a subject for active attention, according to what was said in [Kissinger's] letter to [Ismail] on April 12, 1973? . . . How does that correspond with his promise to us that he would not make any proposal to Pohazy and his friends before getting our approval?[54]

Israel was entrenched in its refusal to deal with a comprehensive settlement or to give Kissinger a green light to reach an understanding on principles with Ismail. Israel remained insistent even when Kissinger clarified that he intended to make an effort to continue the discussion toward a comprehensive settlement for a long period of time. The developments and changes in the Israelis' attitude during the time Kissinger was preparing for his meeting with Ismail were manipulative only—tactics for additional postponement. Examining them helps us to understand why Kissinger defined the war that broke out five months later as "the culmination of a failure of *political* analysis on the part of its victims."[55]

## Kissinger's Distress: "I Think We Ought to Waste Time So That There's No Blowup"

In Washington, Kissinger and his staff were carefully planning the meeting with Ismail. Kissinger had asked Hal Saunders, a member of the National Security Council, to assemble all of the material necessary to conduct a wide-ranging investigation of the Middle East issue. On May 15 the documents had been supplied, including: an analysis of the US-Soviet understandings of May 1972 and suggestions for changes; comments on the May 1973 Soviet document; a document of principles for an agreement that, for each clause, presented the Israeli position, the Egyptian position, and proposals for bridging them; and a eight-page document containing discussion points on each of the issues expected to be brought up at the meeting.[56] The seventh and last clause of the latter document—"the conduct of negotiations," in reaction to Ismail's proposal to formulate heads of agreement—recommended telling him: "We are still in the process of exploring whether it is possible to develop such principles or what they might look like if we can develop them. We want to reserve this judgment a bit longer." This concluding sentence expresses the reality of the situation: in the absence of Israeli

---

[54] Gazit to Dinitz, undated but apparently from May 15 or 16, 1973, referring to discussion in preparation for Kissinger's trip to Paris, Aleph-7066/25, ISA.

[55] Kissinger 1982, 459.

[56] Strategy with Ismail, Saunders to Kissinger, May 15, 1973, NA RN, NSC, Box 132.

willingness to cooperate with Kissinger's bid to advance negotiations, Kissinger had no choice but to take the risk and to continue to adopt delaying tactics.

Before he left for France, Kissinger met with Nixon in the Oval Office of the White House. Kissinger explained the aim of the meeting immediately, and the essence of his conversation with the president was as follows:

> Kissinger: I think we ought to waste time so that there's no blowup until the summit. . . . I've been talking to the Israelis. I think they're moving a little, but not enough. But after I come back from talking to Ismail, Mr. President, we might review that situation.
>
> Nixon: Yes, yes. We don't want a war in the Middle East this summer on our conscience.
>
> Kissinger: No, no, no! There's a chance that that will happen, simply because of the Arab lack of logic.[57]

Kissinger shared his thoughts with the president on how to set the process in motion and bring Israel to simultaneously discuss an interim settlement and a comprehensive settlement and added, "If that would work, we could buy ourselves a year." "That'd be great," responded the president, who, from that point on, ceased focusing on the subject and did not react to Kissinger when he pointed out that the Russians had, in principle, agreed with Kissinger's approach.[58]

The intelligence appraisal in Washington that Sadat's threats, which had been intended to put political pressure on Israel, were liable to get out of control became stronger. The general evaluation was that it was unreasonable to expect a military confrontation in the coming weeks but that "the danger probably will rise if [the] Middle East debates in the UN Security Council (early June) and Nixon-Brezhnev summit (late June) pass without any results Sadat considers useful. The US and the USSR have some, but limited, leverage in the situation."[59]

## Kissinger and Ismail—Last Tango in Paris

On May 19, Kissinger met in Paris with Le Duc Tho, representing North Vietnam, for discussions on an end to the war. *Ha'aretz* reported that the meeting took place in a friendly atmosphere and went on for four hours

---

[57] NA RN, White House Tapes, Conversation No. 919-3.
[58] Ibid.
[59] National Intelligence Estimate, May 17, 1973, NA RN, NSC files, Box H-91.

and twenty minutes, and that the American and North Vietnamese delegations continued their discussion on the following day, but that Kissinger
and Le Duc Tho were not present at the discussions for the first time since
negotiations had begun a few years previously.[60]

Ismail, as well, had found his way to Paris. Disguised as a trip to meet
French president Georges Pompidou and foreign minister Michel Jobert
for political discussions, Ismail arrived in the French capital on May 16.[61]
On Sunday, May 20, between 10:15 and 15:20, he and Kissinger met south
of Paris in an ancient house in Moulin St. Fargeau, near the town of
Rochefort. Kissinger could not hide his wonder at the enchanting country
simplicity of the house, whose American owners had invested large sums
of money in its renovation and maintenance.[62]

As a political "supervisor" representing the State Department, Alfred
R. Atherton, assistant secretary for Near Eastern affairs, accompanied
Kissinger, who was forced into trickery in order to maintain the secrecy
of the discussions. After the official discussion and lunch, Kissinger and
Ismail went out into the pastoral garden and the caressing spring sun and
continued their conversation privately.

After listening to Ismail's doubts that the United States intended to
apply the full force of its weight in order to achieve a peace agreement,
Kissinger explained that the United States had no interest in leaving Israel
in Sinai; it was interested in leading to an agreement, but progress toward
this agreement would have to be made in stages—"step by step"—and
with a slower schedule than the Egyptians expected. An interim agreement
could not be achieved before 1974, and a comprehensive one only a year
later. He said this even though he knew that the significance of his words
might lead to great disappointment for the Egyptians or to an increase in
the danger of an armed conflict, and might even end the communications
channel between them. However, he left an opening for another round. He
proposed to Ismail that Egypt and the United States exchange the agreement on principles for a general declaration, by the United States only,
regarding a peace agreement in the Middle East. "The issue now is whether
Sadat can accept the step-by-step approach with assurance of persistent
White House involvement. Ismail frankly said he could not commit himself. He would have to talk with Sadat," Kissinger later reported to President
Nixon. Kissinger also asked for Egypt's reaction to his interpretation of the

---

[60] *Ha'aretz*, May 20, 1973.

[61] Paris 13632, May 17, 1973, NA, Pol 27-14 Arab-Isr.; Paris 13857, May 18, 1973.

[62] Protocol of the talks: NA RN, NSC, HAK, Box 132; more detailed report to Nixon,
June 2, 1973, NA RN, NSC, HAK, Box 132.

concept of security arrangements as meaning an Israeli military presence in Sinai under Egyptian sovereignty.[63]

The results of the discussion were summarized in the report Kissinger transmitted in a short telegram at the end of the five-hour meeting. He reported that the official discussion had been less useful than the previous meeting, and that "the principal result of the meeting was [Ismail's] agreement that in the meantime there would be no Egyptian military action to disturb the US-Soviet summit. We agreed to have another meeting after your talks with Brezhnev."[64]

After Kissinger left, Ismail remained alone in the garden, his head in his hands. His sadness and despondency were visible to the few who saw him, one of whom was an American intelligence agent. There is no doubt that Sadat's advisor well understood the significance of the delay in the political process. Kissinger received the following report from the CIA. He transmitted it to Dinitz who passed it on to Meir: "Hafez reported . . . that despite this, it was worthwhile to maintain contact with Shaul as, even if hostilities are renewed on the Egyptian front, it will be good for Egypt to have direct contact with the White House, in order to influence its direction."[65]

Egypt and Syria continued to prepare for war. The top Israeli leadership, which was very well aware of this, also prepared for the expected conflict, both immediately and during the following months. At General Staff discussions led by Dayan in Tel Aviv on May 21, one day after Ismail's meeting with Kissinger, it was decided to prepare for a war that would break out in the coming months.

[63] Ibid.

[64] Regarding Kissinger's report to Nixon, see "Memo for the President" from Scowcroft, May 21, 1973, NA RN, NSC, HAK, Box 132. Scowcroft transmitted the text he had received from Kissinger a day earlier to the president, May 20, 1973.

In his book, Kissinger (1982, 227) defined a "useful discussion" as diplomatic language meaning one which did not produce practical results. An examination of the thirty-one pages of protocol for the meeting cannot add anything to an understanding of the situation. Kissinger himself testified that what was said at the official meeting was worthless, as Kissinger and Ismail discussed the important things in the two rounds of discussion while walking in the garden. Despite that, in most writing about the events of 1973, the protocol of the official meeting takes a central place, if not the only one, and is presented as an important political event. Kissinger's summary for Nixon of the meeting with Ismail, dated June 2, 1973, can be found at http://www.gwu.edu/~nsarchiv/NSAEBB/NSAEBB98/octwar-02b.pdf.

[65] Dinitz to Meir on a number of additional matters from the private discussion with Kissinger on July 3 in San Clemente, among them a report from the CIA on Ismail's reaction to the meeting with Kissinger in Paris on May 20, July 4, 1973, Lamed Vav/766, Aleph-7046/9, ISA.

# 5

# Dayan: Gentlemen, Please Prepare for War—June–August 1973

*"I must add and greatly emphasize: Throughout the years of my government's term of office, we have not wasted nor have we rejected any possibility of serious contact between us and our neighbors regarding peace and the way to achieve it. . . . I hereby state to the Knesset: We have agreed to any proposal which has had any measure of reasonable seriousness, even if it had little chance. . . . For as long as this government remains in office, [it] will initiate and will accept open or confidential contacts, guided by the effort to expedite peace."*

**—Prime Minister Golda Meir, speaking from the Knesset podium, July 25, 1973**[1]

"Gentlemen, please prepare for war." With this instruction to the IDF, Moshe Dayan ended a series of discussions with the defense leadership that had begun immediately after the meeting at the prime minister's home on April 18. These discussions were later expressed practically in an IDF plan for war prepared under the code name "Blue-White."[2] The plan included establishing new armored units and armored infantry units; obtaining a new supply of tanks, artillery, and military bridging equipment; bringing

---

[1] Golda Meir, speech to the Knesset, 457th session of the Seventh Knesset, July 25, 1973, 4275.

[2] Bartov 1978, 241–70; Braun 1992, 23.

forward and adding reserve exercises to serve as a replacement for large-reserve mobilization; and camouflaging such a step.

As Meir, Dayan, and Galili had agreed, other government ministers received no report regarding the political developments in process—not about Sadat's initiative, not about the diplomatic alternative to initiation of hostilities, and not about Kissinger's request to promote this alternative. In addition, in private discussions Dayan and Meir did not refer to the political alternative at all, but only dealt with questions of how to relate to the possibility of war. "I think that is what they are planning," Meir said. Dayan added, "The Egyptians are on the road to war. Sadat has taken that road and at some point he will reach it."[3]

Despite focused warnings from Marwan and others about the initiation of hostilities in May, the minister of defense, the head of military intelligence, and the head of the Mossad all correctly evaluated that the probability of war breaking out was low at that time.[4] On April 17, at a meeting of Northern Command officers taking place at Kibbutz Yifat, Dayan stated that the period in which the Arabs had hoped to achieve their aims by political means had ended, and now they were planning to renew the fighting in order to change the existing situation. He initiated three conferences with IDF officers in each command. The birth of "Blue-White" took place on April 20, when Dayan requested that the army chief of staff "determine a schedule for . . . [an operational] program . . . just in case it is needed."[5] Chief of Staff David Elazar was not surprised by these instructions. A day earlier, in an evaluation of the situation, he had already determined that war preparations were necessary on two fronts to deal with the possibility of an Egyptian attempt to cross the Suez Canal and a Syrian attack on the Golan Heights. He also determined that this should be done even if the probability of hostilities breaking out was low.

Members of the government heard a report about war warnings and about the IDF's preparatory steps on April 24. Dayan, Elazar, and Zeira all argued that the threat of war was intended to precede the Nixon-Brezhnev summit and the debate about the Middle East in the General Assembly of

---

[3] Braun 1992, 24. The exchange took place on April 27, as Dayan and Meir were examining King Hussein's warning about Egypt's and Syria's intentions to go to war.

[4] "There was no difference of opinion between the Mossad and military intelligence regarding the chances of war breaking out," Dayan said in reply to a direct question on the subject by Knesset member General (ret.) Moshe Carmel in discussions of the Knesset Foreign Affairs and Defense Committee (Braun 1992, 30). The Agranat Commission also determined that Zamir was more skeptical than Zeira regarding the low probability of war in May: "But fundamental differences of opinion did not exist between them" (Agranat Commission Report, Additional Partial Report, Explanations and Completions, 1974, First Volume, 167).

[5] Braun 1992, 21.

the United Nations. However, Dayan, who was the only one of the senior defense figures receiving full political and military information, took a clearer position: "Egypt, in my opinion, is on a path leading to war, whether this is being done consciously or unconsciously." He surmised that after the summit and the debate in the General Assembly, both in June, "they will attempt to open hostilities. . . . I conclude that we must be ready for Syria to open fire."[6]

On May 9, the day after Israeli Independence Day and a few days after Golda Meir quietly and modestly celebrated her seventy-fifth birthday with her family and friends, Meir went down to army headquarters in Tel Aviv. In the presence of Dayan, Zeira, and senior officers, she was shown IDF deployment plans for a war to be initiated by Egypt and Syria in the coming months. The plans were based on complete information gathered by intelligence with regard to the organization of Egyptian and Syrian army forces and how they would be deployed if war broke out. The chief of staff pointed out that this plan took into account a warning period of forty-eight hours, as well as considering the political necessity of avoiding calling the reserves early or initiating a preliminary preventive attack, and explained that the holding action would be accomplished by regular army forces. "The invaders will be taken care of by Arik [Ariel Sharon] and the tanks," Dayan added, clarifying that the air force would be busy destroying rockets and planes. Only after they could count on freedom of action in the air would ground forces cross the canal to the west side.[7]

On May 14, the general staff met, with Dayan participating, for a discussion of the war objectives. They continued the discussion a week later, on May 21. Immediately after the first general staff meeting ended, Dayan, together with Elazar and Zeira, also met with past chiefs of staff and told them that Egypt and Syria intended "not to capture Europe, and not to take Sinai, nor the territories, but to set the political machine in motion. Their aim was not really to gain ultimate achievements but perhaps to create a different situation."[8] He made similar comments at a meeting of Central Command officers, arguing that Egypt's and Syria's preparations "tell us that they really want to threaten us. If they can achieve their aims only by the threat of war, so be it. If not, then they will renew the fighting."[9]

At the end of the general staff discussion on May 21, Dayan summarized as follows:

---

[6] Ibid.

[7] Ibid., 21.

[8] Ibid., 27.

[9] Ibid.

In my role as minister of defense, I would like to summarize with the following eight points:

1. Take into consideration that there will be a renewal of hostilities during the second half of this summer.

2. The war will be renewed on the initiative of, or with a clear attack by, Egypt and Syria.

3. In the war . . . Egypt and Syria will participate and Jordan will not. . . .

4. Considering what I said about Egypt and Syria beginning the war. . . we should take into account preparing for a preventive blow or a preliminary attack in the framework of renewal of their war. . . .

5. If the Arabs renew the war, the IDF must now prepare a response that will lead them to a crushing defeat.

6. We must make preparations to cross the borders of these two states, both on the Egyptian and Syrian sides.

7. That the war will continue for a short time. . . . It is possible that the war could continue for some days and then there will be a Russian-American intervention that will necessitate a ceasefire.

8. Regarding oil: As there is liable to be a situation in which, as a result of international conditions, the Arabs will try to pressure the West with a halt in the oil supply . . . we must be less dependent on oil from the Persian Gulf. In other words, we must enlarge the oil fields in our possession, like the Morgan fields or others.[10]

Dayan analyzed the situation accurately. He did not need an intelligence appraisal about the probability of war. He had better information than the intelligence organizations did to formulate his own evaluation; he integrated military data with intelligence information that military intelligence did not have. Researchers who have not included this aspect of Dayan's judgment and his evaluation of the circumstances in their investigations err when they determine that "Dayan tended to rely on Zeira's intelligence evaluations."[11] As evidence for this conclusion, on April 13, in a discussion in his office, Dayan told Zeira, "I disagree with you. They will be ready to open fire with five or six divisions and Sadat will sleep well if twenty thousand of his soldiers are killed. In his thinking, that's also a way of moving things forward."[12] Dayan's estimation of the situation at this stage was correct and, as noted above, it required that the IDF prepare for war "during the second half of this summer."[13] His instructions to General Command

---

[10] Ibid., 25.

[11] For example, Bar-Yosef 2011, 20.

[12] Braun 1992, 19.

[13] Ibid., 29.

were clear. Elazar even referred to them and confirmed that IDF planning "completely correlated with this summation."[14]

The following day Dayan, who agreed with Zeira about the low probability of war in the coming weeks, explained his evaluation for the members of the Foreign Affairs and Defense Committee:

> I am more stringent than the head of military intelligence. Not actually about timing. . . . I take a harder line than he does in view of the process. They are not releasing soldiers, nor are they decreasing the size of their army, and they are maintaining a state of constant tension, leading up to war. . . . And they are liable to experience a situation in which they will have difficulty in putting a stop to that . . . . Today I must tell myself, and you, and the army, that when the entire army is called up and making preparations and bringing in armaments from the Soviet Union and so on, and mobilizing in other places, that leads to a renewal of the fighting in one way or another. . . . We must take into consideration that, during the coming six months, the possibility of Egypt and Syria opening fire exists.[15]

Was Dayan surprised on October 6 at 14:00? Was Elazar surprised? We will discuss these questions in due course.

At this stage, one thing cannot be doubted: Dayan prevented any discussion in any political or military framework of what Israel would prefer, an agreement in accord with Kissinger's outline—based on and as a continuation of Sadat's initiative—or war, which he himself estimated would break out "during the coming six months."[16] The only person who attempted to move Dayan in the direction of the political track was the assistant head of General Staff, General Yisrael Tal. Without knowing about the alternative, during a General Staff discussion on May 21, Tal said to Dayan:

> The evaluation of the military situation [regarding the objectives of the war] derives from national objectives . . . a total war—no matter who delivers the first blow, who wins, and what the scope of the victory, its chances of promoting our national objectives are minimal, if not nonexistent. And in contrast, there are many dangers: great human and material losses, negative effects on Israeli society itself, an undermining of the present line, and a worsening of our international status. In this situation, our goals should be both an effort

---

[14] Ibid.

[15] As reported at a meeting of the Foreign Affairs and Defense Committee dated May 22, 1973 (Braun 1992, 29).

[16] Ibid.

to prevent the war with political activity, which is not in the IDF's realm of responsibility, and military deterrence to the enemy's use of force.[17]

In his reply to General Tal, Dayan hastened to direct his response to the military aspect of the question. "When you ask whether Israel wants war, it is correct that Israel does not want war. . . . But the question today is what we do if the Arabs make war against us. And what, in our view, the desired results of such a war are."[18] What Dayan had prevented his listeners in the General Staff from hearing—an examination of the political alternative— he did by himself. On his own initiative, he signaled to the United States with regard to the possibility of a peace agreement between Israel and both Jordan and Egypt. He intended that his position, which he secretly transmitted to the Americans via his close associate Gad Yaacobi, would give Sadat's initiative a fitting response—emphasizing that these measures would be taken only after the Israeli elections.[19]

Dayan's position as it was transmitted to the Americans can be summarized as follows: In Sinai, under Egyptian sovereignty, there would be no military presence and in the central sector, the mountains, an Israeli-Egyptian warning station would be set up. The airports would be run by third-party states. Dayan preferred a permanent Israeli military presence at Sharm el-Sheikh, but if the negotiations were positive, he would be willing to accept a demilitarized Sharm. There would be tiny border changes in northern Sinai up to the Rafiah junction and in the Eilat area. To that end, Dayan was willing to consider land transfers. Regarding annexing areas in Sinai, Dayan maintained, via Yaacobi, that the "oral law" of the Labor Party allowed for settlements over the international border that would be under Israeli administration but not Israeli sovereignty—a distinction he made clearly, making it understood that he was willing to compromise on this basis.

The American ambassador's report on Dayan's proposal ended with the conclusion that Dayan was presenting variable positions in accord with the changing political situation. In the words of the report:

---

[17] Bartov 2002, 284, quoting General Tal at a discussion in the General Staff in May, based on the protocol of the meetings.

[18] Braun 1992, 26.

[19] Regarding Jordan, Dayan's proposal was much more complex and was based on the assumption that a peace treaty with Jordan would only be signed twenty years later. Dayan erred only by one year: the peace agreement with Jordan was signed in 1994, twenty-one years later. Tel Aviv 3903, May 18, 1973, Telegram from Zurhellen, deputy US ambassador to Israel, in Tel Aviv, regarding Dayan's thoughts about the possibility of a peace agreement with Jordan and Egypt (NA, GR, 59 Pol 14–27 Arab-Isr.).

He can shock the public with new ideas, when troubled by bellicose talk out of Cairo (or by us, when probing for an Israeli conciliatory gesture toward Egypt), he can take very tough line re Sinai. If the negotiating process between Israel and Egypt should ever get under way, Dayan would probably number among advocates of a hard opening position but might be prepared eventually to move farther than some Israeli leaders to achieve a successful outcome.[20]

This message was passed on to the Americans at the very time Dayan was stirring up emotions within his party by demanding a wide-ranging settlement plan, including settlements in Sinai and the Golan. Meir opposed this, but was forced to accept his demand in order to prevent Dayan from acting on his threat to resign if it was not fulfilled. In any case, the report was transmitted from the US embassy in Tel Aviv to the State Department; it is doubtful whether Kissinger knew about it.

## On the Way to the Summit

In Egypt, the disappointing results of the second secret meeting between Kissinger and Ismail fanned the flames of possible war just before Brezhnev arrived in the United States. On May 23, *Ha'aretz* announced: "Sadat again speaks about a military action regardless of the cost. The objective—to clarify to the world that Egypt has a problem and that its demands are just." Five days later, additional information appeared in *Ha'aretz*, relying on a report from the Beirut newspaper *An-Nahar*: "The army has been moved from the Cairo area to the Suez Canal front. Sadat has finally become convinced that war is the solution. He is conducting secret meetings with the Supreme Command." At that time, Marwan also reported to his handlers regarding the massive movement of troops to the canal.[21]

A report published on June 15 in *Ha'aretz*, relying on the Cairo newspaper *Al-Ahram*, related that Sadat had visited Damascus and discussed the renewal of hostilities. The newspaper also saw fit to communicate that the visit had been secret and had continued for two days. This secret visit was also publicly reported by *An-Nahar* in Beirut. Its senior correspondent, Fouad Matar, also added that the war against Israel would begin in a concentrated air attack and include special actions.

Marwan, who met with his handlers from June 14 to 16, reported that Assad and Sadat had agreed to initiate the war in late September or early October. Was this information trustworthy? It might sarcastically be said that not a month had gone by without warning of an impending

---

[20] Ibid.
[21] Bar-Yosef 1992, 196.

war—this time September and October were having their turn. However, in actual fact, this was the first time the heads of the Egyptian and Syrian armies had met to determine possible dates for opening fire. Those had centered on early September or early October, but did not include late September. In the military channel, Egypt and Syria were preparing for war according to a schedule that fit the time limit Sadat had dictated to the United States for achieving an agreement. Assad and Sadat met a number of times in Egypt and Syria; reports of these meetings did not always reach Israeli intelligence.[22]

At the end of May 1973, Kissinger celebrated his fiftieth birthday. After Dinitz presented him with a congratulatory letter from Prime Minister Meir at their June 2 meeting, Kissinger asked the ambassador whether he wanted to hear about the meeting with Ismail: "It won't take more than five minutes." From this conversation, Meir found out that Kissinger was intending to take advantage of his request for an answer from Ismail with regard to the defense arrangements in Sinai. This would show the Soviets that his secret dialogue with the Egyptians was continuing and serve as an excuse to postpone Soviet pressure to publicize common principles for a Middle East settlement at the coming summit meeting.[23] As Dinitz put it in his report to Gazit:

> With regard to the summit, [Kissinger] said that he hopes we may get out of this without a comprehensive discussion of Middle East affairs. If he succeeds in continuing to sabotage the technical preparations, the chances that the two leaders will be able to summarize new formulas will be minimized. At the moment, he is postponing Dobrynin [the Soviet ambassador in Washington, Kissinger's contact person to the Soviet leadership, and liaison for the arrangement of the summit] with the argument that he is waiting to hear from Hafez. If he receives a reply from Hafez, we will have another talk about how to continue.[24]

---

[22] In May, Assad paid a secret visit to Egypt. For a report of this visit without details, see Arbel and Ne'eman 2005, 178. Bar-Yosef, who wrote in depth about Israeli intelligence in general and Marwan in particular, did not cite this visit. Sadat's visit to Damascus in the middle of June has not been reported at all in the research literature dealing with Egyptian and Syrian preparations for war.

[23] Protocol of the meeting between Dinitz and Kissinger in the White House, Saturday, June 2, 1973, NA RN, NSC files, HAK Box 135.

[24] Report from Dinitz to Meir about the meeting. Dinitz to Gazit, Lamed Vav/703, June 2, 1973, ISA.

However, despite the pessimistic atmosphere, Kissinger emphasized to Dinitz that "this time it is completely clear, at any rate, that the Egyptians are concerned only with themselves and don't tie an agreement with them to the other Arab states."[25]

In the meantime, Ismail also understood that Kissinger was using the discussion channel between them in order to gain time and avoid Soviet pressure. At the very hour Kissinger and Dinitz were meeting in Washington, Ismail, in Cairo, was transmitting to Kissinger his reactions to their meeting in Paris.[26] In diplomatic yet resolute and clear language, he clarified to Kissinger that Egypt expected an agreement on principles from the United States, not a non-binding American declaration. He also informed Kissinger that Egypt had requested that the Soviet Union renew its involvement in the process, and that it would resume the discussion of Middle East matters at the coming summit on the basis of the May 1972 Soviet proposal. Regarding the discussion channel between him and Kissinger, Ismail's answer was sharp and unmistakable—they would talk after the summit if the results created suitable conditions for continued discussion.

In a personal discussion with State Department representative Joseph Greene in Cairo, Ismail stated that, for Egypt, a state of no peace and no war was worse than war, even if it was clear to the Egyptians that they would be defeated in a military engagement. On the basis of similar declarations, Secretary of State Rogers received a memorandum from Department of State intelligence stating that the probability of war in the autumn was high.[27] Because of the problematic relations between Kissinger and the State Department, Kissinger remained unaware of this memorandum. It is also doubtful that he was updated on Greene's report from Cairo citing Sadat's frustration at the United States' attitude toward his initiative.[28] The fact that Ismail had invited Greene—a representative of the State Department, which had been compartmentalized from the existence of the secret channel—for a discussion that was personal, not official, was a clear message to Kissinger about Ismail's disappointment with the results of the discussions between them.

---

[25] Ibid.

[26] Ismail to Kissinger, June 2, 1973, NA RN, NSC Files, HAK, Box 132.

[27] Central Intelligence Agency, *Nixon and the Role of Intelligence in the 1973 Arab-Israeli War*, 42; Memorandum to the Acting Secretary from INR, Ray Cline, "Growing Risk of Egyptian Resumption of Hostilities with Israel," May 31, 1973.

[28] Memorandum to Secretary of State Rogers, May 31, 1973, FRUS XXV, 199; NA, GR 59, Cairo 1619, June 2, 1973, Pol 27 Arab-Isr.; report from Greene, NA, GR 59, Cairo 1689, June 8, 1973, Pol 27-14 Arab-Isr.

Despite this, Kissinger continued to try to maintain contact. It was important for him to present the impression at the summit that the channel was entirely under his control and that of the United States. During the next few days of early June, he sent Ismail two dispatches and requested his agreement for the United States to propose a version of a joint declaration at the summit that would enable the initiation of negotiations. Ismail, who was in no hurry to break off communications, responded immediately.[29] In his reply, he explained that Egypt could relate to a proposal only after studying its wording. Kissinger did not reply until July 7—two weeks after the summit had ended!

At this point, Washington was devoting serious attention to the superpower summit, which would open about a week later. Intense preparatory discussions only began on June 14, after Kissinger returned from discussions on Vietnam.

## By the Wayside

At their meeting on Saturday, June 2, Dinitz told Kissinger, "Your friend Yigal Allon will be coming. . . . He would like to see you at my house on a personal basis." Kissinger proposed a joint breakfast on June 12 at 08:00 in Washington. "That's a week before the summit and there is a chance that I will be free," he added.

In the absence of written correspondence, we cannot know what Deputy Prime Minister Allon wanted to discuss privately such a short time before the summit. But Allon's intentions can be understood indirectly from the exchange of messages between Dinitz and the office of the prime minister, which included reports about coordinating Allon's meeting.[30] On June 12, Dinitz was informed that "since Shaul is having thoughts about parallel or simultaneous negotiations, it is important that you inform him that we oppose parallel negotiations for a comprehensive settlement and an agreement about the canal at the same time, and that goes for the idea of discussions by two teams from each side as well." Referring to these instructions, Dinitz replied on the following day: "The breakfast between Yigal and Shaul did not take place as Shaul has not yet returned from Paris. . . . I will return to the idea of parallel discussions when I meet with him on his return."[31]

---

[29] Ismail to Kissinger, June 10, 1973, NA RN, NSC, HAK, Box 132; FRUS XXV, 202–3.

[30] Gazit to Dinitz, Vav Lamed/611, Aleph-4996/2, ISA; Dinitz to Gazit, Lamed Vav/725, ISA.

[31] Dinitz to Gazit, June 13, 1973, Lamed Vav/725; Gazit to Dinitz, Vav Lamed/611, Aleph-4996/2, ISA.

Allon had been promoting the idea of parallel talks on a partial agreement between Israel and Egypt and then on a comprehensive agreement. Cynics might say that this was his way of creating an oppositional position to Dayan's. "Allon's counterblow" was the term *Ha'aretz* used.[32] However, it was important to Allon that this meeting take place; he left for London in the hope of meeting Kissinger there. "I felt sorry for Yigal when he left," former Mossad chief Zamir testified.[33] It is possible that coordinating the failure of Allon's personal meeting with Kissinger was Golda Meir's way of thwarting his initiative while avoiding another clash between him and Dayan. As noted, Allon was the only senior minister who thought political steps should be taken before the elections.

Immediately after Kissinger returned to Washington, he spoke to Dinitz by telephone and said, "I am really sorry that I missed Yigal Allon. Is he still in the area? Those idiots here did not tell you to ask him to wait."[34] In his report to the prime minister, Dinitz was more gentle, but added that "in addition, he asked [me] to let Rabin know that he was sorry that he had missed him." This makes it clear that not only did Allon intend to speak to Kissinger, perhaps in order to propose a political initiative personally, but Rabin did as well.[35] Rabin, ex-ambassador to Washington and former chief of military staff, had returned to Israel and begun his "basic training" in Israeli politics; the prime minister had declined to take advantage of his military and political experience and connections in the American government. He and Allon were troubled by Meir's and Dayan's stubbornness in maintaining the standstill, but remained distanced from the focus of decision-making.

The prime minister received two items of good news from Kissinger at the beginning of June. The first was a detailed report of his meeting with Ismail in Paris. The second, no less welcome, was transmitted by dispatch from Dinitz:

> Robert had offered him the position of Secretary of State to replace Rogers. . . . It was intended that he would continue to administer the two roles. . . . He told me that this would be the first time in

---

[32] *Ha'aretz*, June 4, 1973.

[33] Author's discussion with Zamir, February 19, 2012.

[34] Telephone conversation between Kissinger and Dinitz, June 14, 1973, NA RN, HAK, Telcon Box 20.

[35] Lamed Vav/726, June 14, 1973, 11:00, Aleph-7052/3, ISA.

American history that the Secretary of State would be Jewish and that this would help us, as he would be able to delay initiatives of the State Department even before they found their way to the White House. . . . There is a possibility that he will request my assistance on the Hill [i.e., in Congress] to have his appointment approved.[36]

Meir and Dayan knew well that for the past half year Kissinger had been solely navigating US policy in the Middle East; now this would be official. No less important was the fact that Kissinger wanted Meir's assistance in the political "give and take" so that his appointment would be confirmed by Congress. Three days later, Meir informed Dinitz that "she was committed to recommending Shaul [Kissinger] and to activating her friends on [Capitol] Hill."[37]

But not all of the news was as encouraging for the prime minister. The leaders of the European countries, concerned about the danger of war in the Middle East, had something to say to Nixon before he began his series of meetings with the Soviets. British prime minister Edward Heath sent him a long and resolute letter that he stated also represented the views of French president Georges Pompidou and German chancellor Willy Brandt.[38] In the letter, he excitedly called on the president, as Dinitz put it, "to use all of his influence to bring the Israelis to a change in their inflexible stance and to induce them to agree to declare their willingness to retreat to the international border with Egypt." Kissinger passed on a copy of the letter to Meir in order to soften Israel's position and to prepare her for the developments he intended to set in motion.

A number of days earlier, Chancellor Willy Brandt had visited Israel. In a private conversation, Meir had told him "that he could tell Sadat that he, Brandt, was convinced that we really want peace, that we do not want all of Sinai or most of Sinai." It appears that Brandt understood Meir's political language very well that she was willing to discuss peace with no preliminary conditions, except that Sadat would agree to give up Egyptian sovereignty on large sections of Sinai. The letter from the European heads of state to President Nixon also served to clarify to Meir that Brandt too had received the impression that her inflexible position was an obstacle to negotiation. Nixon acted accordingly. He avoided acceding to Meir's request to speak to

---

[36] Lamed Vav/704 and Lamed Vav/705, June 2, 1973, Aleph-7052/3, ISA.

[37] Vav Lamed/602, June 5, 1973, 20:00, Aleph-4996/2, ISA.

[38] Heath to Nixon, June 14, 1973, NA RN, Pres. Cor. U.K., Box 764; Dinitz's report to Meir, Lamed Vav/730, June 15, 1973, Aleph-7052/3, ISA.

Sadat personally and sent a junior official, who transmitted Meir's message as an emissary and did not try to mediate.[39]

Like the British, French, and Germans, the Soviets, who knew something about the Egyptian preparations for military action, were interested in preventing an armed clash in the Middle East. They transmitted messages to Israel regarding the escalating danger and the pressing need for an agreement via the Russian journalist Victor Louis. Louis had traveled to Israel to attend the International Press Institute conference, met with Gazit, director of the Prime Minister's Office, and reported that, in Moscow, "there was fear that after the summit, perhaps due to Egyptian disappointment with its results, they would take extreme steps and drag the Soviets with them. This worries certain circles in Moscow who would not want such a development." He added that "the Soviet Union was interested in persuading Egypt to enter discussions with Israel. The impression is that Egypt is ready to be coerced into going in that direction."[40]

At the same time, since Kissinger knew that he was about to be appointed secretary of state, he began to prepare the groundwork for the moves he would initiate after the summit—if necessary, only after elections in Israel, but before that if possible. "The one area where Soviet policy seems most uncertain and confused is the Middle East," began the memorandum he wrote to prepare the president for the summit discussions.[41] In it, Kissinger estimated that Sadat and Ismail were still considering his proposal to conduct a peace process that would advance step by step on the basis of general principles he would propose to the Soviet Union as an understanding at the summit talks. He also assumed that the Soviets would allow him to direct developments as long as their image and respect as a superpower involved in the decision were maintained.

"Sadat continues to hold out the resumption of hostilities as his only choice if there is no diplomatic movement on a basis he considers acceptable. . . . The objective of a negotiation between Egypt and Israel is to find a way of reconciling Egyptian sovereignty in the Sinai with security arrangements that will help lessen the danger of another war," Kissinger clarified in the memorandum, explaining that this would happen only if the two sides compromised on their position. Israel would in the end reconcile itself to the diplomatic process, accepting full Egyptian sovereignty over Sinai,

---

[39] Discussion points between Meir and Brandt, June 19, 1973, Aleph-370/5, ISA; Ambassador Lothar Lahn to Gazit, report of mission to Cairo, July 3, 1973, Aleph-4239/15, ISA.

[40] Vav Lamed/617, June 14, 1973, Aleph-7053/3, ISA; Gazit to Dinitz, Vav Lamed/621, June 15, 1973, Aleph-7053/3, ISA.

[41] Kissinger to Nixon, June 14, 1973, NA RN, NSC, HAK, Country Files, Europe, USSR, Box 75; FRUS XXV, 204–7.

while Egypt would begin negotiations with no advance Israeli commitment on such recognition. The objective Kissinger posed to the president was to convince the Soviets at the summit to accept his approach for a graduated process based on the mutual document of principles upon which they had already agreed in May 1972 in Moscow and which had, until now, not been publicized.[42] Kissinger hoped to make slight changes, to give it binding status by publicizing it as a summary of the summit talks, and to add a joint declaration regarding the superpowers' opposition to military action, which would deter Egypt from that initiative.

## "Let Them Talk about Any Subject in the World Except Us"

On June 14, Kissinger returned to Washington from Europe after taking an additional step toward an agreement in East Asia. "Now I can take my old time to settle the Arab-Israeli dispute. Can you start by going back to your 1967 borders? We'll have another settlement. And then settle with the Palestinians," he told the Israeli ambassador in a telephone call on the morning immediately after his return, in reply to a polite "How are you?" Dinitz did not appreciate Kissinger's humor and replied ironically, "And then forty-seven [i.e., the 1947 borders]."[43]

After they clarified the missed opportunities for the meetings with Allon and Rabin (or the deliberate obstruction of those meetings), they went on to discuss the approaching summit. They focused on choosing between two possibilities: the first, agreeing to a previously decided understanding between Kissinger and the Soviet foreign minister, Gromyko, on a joint document of principles, the contents of which would not be popular with Israel; or the second, to gamble. In other words, the second alternative was to reach the meeting with no preliminary understanding and to leave the issue to Nixon and Brezhnev. In that case, either the summit would end well from Israel's standpoint, with no understanding—"the document which we don't like will disappear," as Dinitz put it—or it would end badly, "if this remains in the hands of Brezhnev and the president."[44]

---

[42] The document hinted that possible border adjustments between Israel and Egypt, with regard to the situation existing on June 4, 1967, would amount to not returning the Gaza Strip to Egypt. Meeting between Rabin and Kissinger, March 9, 1973, NA RN, NSC Files, HAK, Box 75.

[43] Telephone conversation between Kissinger and Dinitz, June 14, 1973, 09:20, NA RN, HAK, Telcon Box 20.

[44] Ibid. Kissinger immediately responded to Dinitz: "It will not disappear" (Dinitz to Gazit, Lamed Vav/726, June 14, 1973, Aleph-7052/3, ISA).

Kissinger asked that the prime minister inform him by the next morning what Israel would prefer. He did not hide that, in his view, it was preferable to reach a preliminary understanding with Gromyko and said that the choice of a preliminary understanding did not obligate Israel to accept the document's principles, only to agree to a negotiation process.[45]

The answer was returned immediately. From her sick bed, Meir directed Dinitz to prevent Kissinger from reaching an agreement with Gromyko based on the May 1972 understandings:

> We completely oppose the '72 document and if it is approved, we will consider it extremely harmful. . . . In our view, it is essential that there will be no document. We depend on you to find the proper way to convince Shaul to find ways to avoid the document. . . . There is no reason at present to reach a crossroads between us and them, which is liable to occur if this document or one like it is approved. The prime minister requests that Shaul do everything he can to disengage from this document.[46]

That evening, the three members of the prime minister's "kitchen cabinet," Meir, Dayan, and Galili, met to discuss Israel's preparation for the summit. The next day, Dinitz received updated instructions:

> You should tell Shaul [Kissinger] that, as you have already clarified to him, Israel entirely rejects the document. But in an attempt to respond to his request for comments and in the case that he nevertheless enters into negotiations on this document (not in our name or on our behalf) . . . we prefer that it is based on [UN Resolution] 242, to which we agreed at the time.[47]

Those present in the Prime Minister's Office did not feel calm. An hour later, they sent Dinitz an additional message that contained nothing new—only a last effort to bolster him two hours before his meeting with Kissinger. The new message said, "Tell Shaul that the prime minister has

---

[45] Reports from Dinitz about his telephone conversation, Lamed Vav/726, June 14, 1973, 11:00; Lamed Vav/728, June 14, 1973, 15:45, Aleph-7052/3, ISA.

[46] Gazit to Dinitz, Vav Lamed/618, June 14, 1973, 20:00, Aleph-4996/2, ISA. At the time, Meir was ill, and it was reported that she had cancelled all of her meetings. However, as may be understood from the messages transmitted, she continued to conduct secret dealings with Kissinger and manage everything connected with the coming summit meeting in the United States.

[47] Gazit to Dinitz, Vav Lamed/620, June 15, 1973, 12:30, Aleph-4996/2; Dinitz to Gazit, Lamed Vav/728, Aleph-7052/3, ISA. Regarding the forum that summarized the instructions, Gazit to Dinitz, Vav Lamed/622, June 15, 1973, 16:00, Aleph-4996/2, ISA. Dinitz also received Israel's detailed comments on each item of the document.

been reinforced in her opinion that she must ask him to do everything he can so that no mutual document is composed. Shaul's attempt to formulate a new document only proves to us how dangerous this matter is. We continue to reject the need for an understanding between the big ones [superpowers]."[48]

Kissinger and Dinitz met on Friday, June 15, at 11:05 Washington time, in the Map Room of the White House. After polite greetings, Kissinger, without pausing to discuss the political issue, opened with: "We have received a letter from Heath which I wanted to discuss with you because it applies great British pressure on you to return to the international lines. This is part of the international situation now." Dinitz was surprised at the speed with which Kissinger, ignoring the accepted opening sentences, went straight to the point. Kissinger seemed to be making use of Heath's letter, representing the French and the Germans as well, to soften up the Israeli position to force Israel to relate realistically to the political situation and refer to the May 1972 document, which they had rejected out of hand. Perhaps Kissinger also wanted to hint at Israel's dependence on him. The Israeli ambassador had to stop for a moment to organize his response and apologized, explaining that he had received the last update from the prime minister only twenty minutes before and was not properly ready to present what he had to say.[49]

Kissinger dropped the subject for a moment, perhaps giving Dinitz time to collect his thoughts, and asked, "Is the foreign minister in the picture?" It is doubtful that Dinitz was aware at the time of the significance of his immediate reply: "No, not at all. Just the prime minister. Maybe on some aspects of defense, she brings Dayan in, and Allon on general matters."[50] For many years Dinitz had closely and loyally accompanied Golda Meir in her work. It appears that, in his answer, he intended to elevate her status. But, for good or bad, he had accorded her the major responsibility for decision-making.

The pause Kissinger granted Dinitz enabled him to focus on the instructions he had received from the prime minister. After discussing the Soviet attitude to the situation and the implications of the Watergate affair on attitudes in Washington, Kissinger and Dinitz returned to discuss the document Kissinger thought could provide the basis for a summation of the Middle East discussion at the summit meeting and enable the initiation of negotiations. Dinitz presented the Israelis' reservations at length; Kissinger

---

[48] Gazit to Dinitz, Vav Lamed/628, June 15, 1973, 17:00, Aleph-4669/2, ISA.

[49] Protocol of the meeting, NA RN, NSC Files, HAK, Box 135; noted in FRUS XXV, 208n2 regarding the private conversation: Dinitz to Gazit, Lamed Vav/352, June 15, 1973, 17:00, Aleph-7052/3, ISA.

[50] NA RN, NSC, HAK, Box 135.

made sure that he understood the prime minister's points well. When they reached the border issue and Dinitz stated that "the 1967 boundaries certainly weren't secure and recognized," Kissinger, constantly alert, responded with alacrity, "They certainly weren't recognized. But it is rather hard to maintain from the outcome of the 1967 war that they weren't secure."

In summary, Kissinger noted Meir's request that the United States do everything in its power to reject the document, acknowledging that Israel did not accept the document or permit the United States to discuss it in Israel's name. The report that Golda Meir heard about the private and personal discussion between Kissinger and Dinitz was meant to calm her:

> He will not raise the subject at all on his part. He will try to avoid any discussion of the matter, but there is the possibility that Brezhnev will take Nixon aside and tell him "We must bring the Israelis to withdraw to the borders of 1967" and the president will shake his head or agree, and then Rogers and Gromyko will be instructed to deal with the matter. In such a case, Kissinger would have to intervene in order to salvage the situation. It would be best if he were to use the ammunition he has [referring to Israeli arguments against the May 1972 document]. He repeated that he would never say that he had received the arguments from us or give the impression that there was any agreement on our side. . . . He said that he would want to be in contact with me during the summit. He said that if they raised any of their considerations, he would want to let me know. He repeated that he would try to push aside the entire subject of the Middle East as much as he could but that his problem was that all the other issues were actually settled and that he was racking his brain trying to think of what they would talk about. I told him to let them talk about any subject in the world except for us.[51]

When they finished, Kissinger gave Dinitz a copy of Heath's letter and showed him the last letter from Ismail—but only let him have a close look.[52] That night, a telegram arrived at Meir's office in which Dinitz reported on the June 10 dispatch from Ismail to Kissinger. "I have written it down from memory since Shaul only let me read it," apologized Dinitz. The crux of the message was that the Egyptians understood that, until now, Kissinger had led them astray. Dinitz's report to Meir stated

---

[51] Dinitz to Gazit about his private conversation with Kissinger, which lasted twenty minutes. Lamed Vav/732, June 15, 1973, Aleph-7052/3, ISA.

[52] Dinitz to Gazit, Lamed Vav/731, June 15, 1973, 16:00, Aleph-7052/3, ISA; FRUS XXV, 202–3.

that Ismail had informed Kissinger that the US position and its intentions were

> in fact a retreat from its position as Egypt had understood it at the
> time of Hafez's discussions with Kissinger. The government of Egypt
> considered that Kissinger was aiming for heads of agreement whose
> fundamental principle was how to lead to a total Israeli withdrawal
> to the 1967 borders. Now Egypt was no longer sure about United
> States intentions and viewed its present policy as a retreat.[53]

Dinitz also reported to the prime minister on Ismail's ironic reference to
Kissinger's formula for a linkage between a partial and a comprehensive
settlement. "The Israelis have said these things publicly without [our]
having to 'convince' them." At the end of his letter Ismail clarified what
Sadat was expecting from Kissinger so that Egypt could decide on its
continuing path:

> Due to the ambiguity that envelops the American position, Mr.
> Ismail will appreciate it if Dr. Kissinger clarifies what he exactly
> means by "principles of a general nature which would permit the
> parties to start a process of negotiation," which Dr. Kissinger pro-
> poses to discuss with the Soviet side. This will enable the Egyptian
> side to state its point of view in a precise manner.[54]

The opening ceremony of the summit was planned for Monday afternoon,
June 18, in the White House garden. Brezhnev, who was not accustomed
to long flights, had arrived in Washington on Saturday in order to rest
at Camp David and prepare properly for the discussions. The preparations included informal talks with Kissinger. According to the program,
Brezhnev and his entourage were supposed to move to Blair House, close to
the White House, and working meetings would be held until Friday. Then
the leaders would fly to San Clemente, California, where they would spend
the weekend in additional discussion. On Monday, June 25, Brezhnev was
due to leave the United States.

A few minutes before leaving for the White House garden to officially
welcome the Soviet leader, Kissinger telephoned Dinitz and asked him to

---

[53] Ibid.

[54] Dinitz to Gazit, Lamed Vav/731, June 15, 1973, Aleph-7052/3, ISA. Ismail to Kissinger, FRUS XXV, 202–3.

update Golda Meir with another calming message: "The Middle East issue will certainly not be raised before Wednesday and it is very possible that a situation will develop in which we will not have to discuss the 1972 document at all. He will keep me in the picture, and in the meantime asks that we contact Peter Rodman in order to get the paper Shaul has prepared based on our last conversation."[55]

"Mrs. Golda Meir announced yesterday to the Labor Party that she was ready to continue as prime minister for an additional term," read the report that day in *Ha'aretz*. What remained concealed from the public, and from political figures, was the fact that she was receiving a series of radiation treatments at Hadassah hospital, pretending to visit a sick friend. "It's very exhausting, sometimes to death," Meir said, sharing her secret with her close friend Yaacov Hazan, the leader of the Mapam Party. "I will get over it," she added, and so she did. She continued to function as usual.[56]

It is easy to underestimate Meir's and Dayan's sense of security at the time. The two felt in complete control of Israel's political conduct. Now their interest in mitigating the war atmosphere had increased in importance, although they knew that war was likely to break out. They understood that admitting to a rise in tension might increase pressure on Israel by the United States and Soviet Union to participate in a political process. This they wanted to avoid, or at least to evade as long as they could, until after the elections if possible.

## The Last Minute of the Summit: "Brezhnev Was Seized with an All-Consuming Desire to Discuss the Middle East"

As Kissinger had predicted, during the first days of the summit, the subject of the Middle East did not come up. "Egypt is disappointed with the summit talks in Washington and is indirectly expressing its anger at the Soviet leaders, who prefer to deepen their bilateral relations with the United States, neglecting Arab interests," *Ha'aretz* reported after the meetings began.[57] The main headline stated: "Agreements between Nixon and Brezhnev are Expected in the Realms of the Atom, Culture, and

---

[55] Dinitz to Gazit, Lamed Vav/739, June 18, 1973, 12:00, Aleph-7052/3, ISA; Dinitz to Gazit, Lamed Vav/740, June 18, 1973, 12:00, Aleph-7052/3, ISA. "This is Shaul's attempt to prepare an outline for himself based on the 1972 paper, considering our last conversation. The following is the complete paper." In an additional telegram at 16:30, Dinitz transmitted his comments for the new version and requested instructions for future attention, if this was needed.

[56] Medzini 2008, 530.

[57] *Ha'aretz*, June 19, 1973.

Photo: CIA

*Brezhnev and Nixon*

Agriculture."[58] Regarding Middle East affairs, two days later, the newspaper stated, citing "observers" in Jerusalem: "The two states are likely to agree only on general formulas, such as the formula that was decided on during the previous summer, indicating the need to avoid a conflict between the two blocs in the area."[59] *Al-Gomhuria* in Cairo agreed: "We should not expect that the superpowers will in the visible future undertake any steps to change the Middle East situation. The Arabs have no alternative but to find a solution themselves—and the solution is that what was taken by force will be returned by force."[60]

The summit talks expressed wide-ranging preliminary agreements between the two superpowers; the matter of the Middle East was, from their standpoint, a nuisance. Publishing a document setting forth understandings between them on the topic would have created a problem for the United States. On the other hand, if the two superpowers did not formulate a common approach, there was the danger of renewed military conflict in the area. A non-binding reference to the issue was liable to cloud the secret communications track between Kissinger and Sadat, as well as between the Soviet Union and both Egypt and Syria.

Kissinger conducted a series of telephone conversations on June 19 with the Soviet ambassador to the United States, Anatoly Dobrynin, and

---

[58] Ibid.
[59] *Ha'aretz*, June 21, 1973.
[60] *Ha'aretz*, June 27, 1973.

the president regarding this issue. Twenty-five minutes in, Rodman, who served as the contact person between Dinitz and Kissinger during the summit, telephoned with "a request from Kissinger for our reaction to the paper he had left with us the night before," according to Dinitz.[61] After half an hour, Jerusalem sent Dinitz a familiar response: "Tell Shaul that the prime minister has reinforced her opinion that she must request that Kissinger do everything in his power to prevent the formulation of a common document."[62] Dinitz met with Rodman and precisely relayed Meir's words for him to pass on to Kissinger.[63] On June 21, Dinitz had reported, "General Scowcroft rang a moment ago and advised that Shaul had asked him to report that, in the discussion of the Middle East, the issue of a common paper had not arisen."[64] On Friday morning, June 22, the two delegations flew to San Clemente as planned.

Only in the late morning hours of June 23, the last day of discussions, did Kissinger and Gromyko begin to discuss the Middle East for the first time. As expected, they did not reach an agreement. "The meeting concluded with the understanding that Dr. Kissinger would revise the principles and bring a copy to the afternoon meeting," Saunders summarized in his meeting memorandum.[65]

This additional meeting between Gromyko and Kissinger in order to formulate a summation document did not occur. Instead, that afternoon, there was a relaxed cocktail party by the pool, followed by supper.[66] Brezhnev, who was going to leave the following morning for Washington and from there, after a day of rest, to Europe, requested to have dinner earlier. Afterward he returned to his residence at the site of the meetings, as did Kissinger. The president went to bed. The danger had seemingly passed.

A telephone call at 22:00 California time informed Kissinger that the Soviets had thought up something unexpected for the last minutes of the week-long summit. A Secret Service man announced to Kissinger that the Soviet guest wanted to have an unplanned meeting with the

---

[61] Dinitz to Gazit, Lamed Vav/743, June 19, 1973, 09:30, Aleph-7052/3, ISA.

[62] Gazit to Dinitz, Vav Lamed/628, June 19, 1973, 17:00 (Israeli time), Aleph-7052/3, ISA.

[63] NA RN, NSC, HAK, Box 135; FRUS XXV, 208–11.

[64] Lamed Vav/747, June 21, 1973, Aleph-7052/3, ISA.

[65] NA RN, NSC, HAK, Box 75; FRUS XXV, 211–18; Saunders sent Kissinger an updated version of the Israeli-Arab agreement principles, taking into consideration the comments of Israel in three versions: Dinitz's proposal; the tiny correction made as a result; and, for comparison, the optimal version from the US standpoint. Saunders to Kissinger, June 21, 1973, NA RN, NSC, HAK, Box 136.

[66] Kissinger 1982, 294–301.

president and to do it urgently—immediately. A quarter of an hour later, Kissinger woke Nixon. "His initial grogginess was replaced by immediate alertness when I told him what was afoot," Kissinger later described the moment. A quick conversation between Kissinger and Gromyko clarified that "Brezhnev had been seized with an all-consuming desire to discuss the Middle East." At 22:45, Nixon and Kissinger sat down with Brezhnev and Gromyko.[67] The Americans then heard the Soviet leader's most significant reference to any of the issues that had come up during the entire week of discussions. Brezhnev demanded that the United States and the Soviet Union agree, then and there, on a Middle East accord that would be based on full Israeli withdrawal from the Occupied Territories in return for an end to the fighting, with a full peace dependent on negotiations to take place afterwards with the Palestinians, and that the superpowers would guarantee the fulfillment of the agreement. He warned of what could be expected to take place in the Middle East if no agreement was reached based on those conditions.

The Soviets would have known that there was no chance of reaching such an agreement in the few remaining hours. It was certainly impossible to reach any understanding with all of the tracks of the Middle East dispute. Thus Brezhnev had waived the options of outlining a document or publishing a statement in advance, but was ready to accept a "gentlemen's agreement." "I can assure you that nothing will go beyond this room. But if we agree on Israeli withdrawals, then everything will fall into place," he said. Brezhnev was determined to solve the Middle East dispute that summer. He was so resolute in his presentation that Dobrynin asked the translator to slightly censor Brezhnev's remarks. Kissinger received the impression that the Soviets were expressing frustration rather than a conviction that Brezhnev's proposal would be accepted.

Kissinger and Nixon stood firmly against this demand. It was already clear to them that negotiations could not begin before the Israeli elections. Nor could Nixon put pressure on Israel at the peak of the Watergate hearings. Brezhnev's statements referred in general to all of the sides in the dispute; there was no chance of including all of them in one document. Nixon was alert, combative, and decisive; he brought the discussion to an end, saying, "We can't settle this tonight. . . . We don't owe anything to the Israelis. That means I am interested in a settlement. . . . That will be our project this year. The Middle East is the most urgent place."[68] He added that an agreement of the kind Brezhnev was pressuring him to accept at that moment would only eliminate all possibility of a political process.

---

[67] NA RN, NSC, HAK, Box 75; FRUS XXV, 220–24.

[68] Ibid.

It appears that Brezhnev was actually making an effort to avoid a war; like the Americans, he predicted that any war would end in the defeat of the Arabs. However, Kissinger evaluated the situation differently. In his appraisal, an agreement such as the one Brezhnev was demanding would have eliminated the United States' and Kissinger's exclusive ability to control developments and would have returned the Soviet Union to a position of power, able to grant the Arabs' wishes. "He did not vouchsafe to us how so revolutionary a scheme as a peace imposed by the United States and the Soviet Union on the Middle East could be kept secret if it were to be implemented," was Kissinger's cynical and scornful reaction to the proposal.[69] He added, "Twenty-four hours after renouncing the threat of force in the agreement on the prevention of nuclear war, Brezhnev was in effect menacing us with a Middle East war unless we accepted his terms."

But another point of view can be suggested that Kissinger did not consider at the time: a comprehensive peace based on the 1967 lines, implemented over a long period of time, suited both the American position and Sadat's initiative. A quiet understanding on this point between the two superpowers was likely to enable the Soviet Union to throw all of its weight behind pressuring the Arabs to prevent the coming war, even at the price of Arab dissatisfaction. In such a reality, Kissinger could put his plans into action after the Israeli elections and then do likewise with other states. The supremacy of the United States on the diplomatic level, which rested on Israeli military superiority, would have been maintained. But that did not happen.

The summation of the summit talks was three thousand words long, of which only eighty-nine referred to the Middle East. The summit discussions did not lead to a breakthrough. Sadat would have had difficulty surviving another "year of decision" without taking steps, either political or military, to return Sinai to Egyptian sovereignty. The hope of an impending move had come to nothing. Anyone with enough information to analyze the political situation knew that the Middle East was marching toward conflagration, but at the end of June no one yet knew the exact date. Sadat and Assad had not yet agreed on it.

## "We Came Out Well"

There was one official body that had not lost hope of motivating a political process to avoid a military conflict. For more than four years, Secretary of State Rogers and Sisco, his assistant for Middle Eastern affairs, had been initiating attempts to reach an agreement; decision-makers in Israel

---

[69] Kissinger 1982, 298.

therefore loathed these two "enemies" of the status quo. The two had not been kept in the picture during the Nixon-Brezhnev summit discussions and in the preceding months, they had not been included in the limited circle of those involved in Middle East issues. Now, after the summit failed to make any progress, they made an additional effort.

On June 28, Rogers transmitted a memorandum prepared by Sisco to the president, entitled "The Next Steps in the Middle East."[70] It contained a proposal to open secret talks between Israel and Egypt immediately, under the auspices of the United States, on the basis of the understanding that, while Resolution 242 did not demand Israel's full withdrawal, neither did it reject such a withdrawal. The reason for the pressing need for this initiative was clear—the evaluation that Sadat would not give up his efforts to pressure the United States to cease backing the continued standstill, and would therefore either renew the fighting or activate the oil weapon against the United States and the West.

Nixon sent his prompt and decisive reaction to the initiative to the State Department via Alexander Haig, White House chief of staff, the following day. This step actually indicated Kissinger's awareness of Rogers's approaching resignation and his own impending succession to that office.

> The President did not want the Secretary to proceed with the initiative outlined in this memorandum. . . . The President was awaiting a response from Brezhnev following the discussion he had with Brezhnev last week on the Middle East and does not wish anything else to be done on this subject until a response from Brezhnev has been received.[71]

Nixon, then deeply engaged in the Watergate scandal, remained in San Clemente to plan his next moves. Kissinger remained with him and continued his involvement in the pressing Middle East issue from there. One day after the difficult late-night discussion with Brezhnev in San Clemente, Kissinger transmitted an amended document of understanding to the Soviets.[72] The document was even further from the Israeli position; in fact, from a territorial standpoint, it was no different than what Rogers and Sisco had presented in their proposal of June 28. The significant difference between their proposal and Kissinger's was its urgency. While the State Department wanted immediate negotiations,

---

[70] Rogers's memorandum, June 28, 1973; FRUS XXV, 227–30; Nixon's directive, June 29, 1973, NA RN, NSC, HAK, Box 70.

[71] NA, RG, 59 Pol 27-14 Arab-Isr.; FRUS XXV, 229n4.

[72] Kissinger to Dobrynin, June 24, 1973, NA RN, NSC, HAK, Box 70; FRUS XXV, 225–26.

Kissinger only wanted to lay the groundwork for negotiations to begin after the Israeli elections; his document was intended only to enable him to continue his contacts with Ismail.

During the week after the summit, Kissinger continued to deal with foreign affairs from San Clemente. In addition to Nixon's difficulty coping with the Watergate scandal, he also became ill with pneumonia and had to rest for a few days. Kissinger updated him on foreign affairs by telephone; the Middle East was not mentioned in these conversations.[73] Kissinger also often spoke to Dobrynin in Washington, discussing in particular the contacts Kissinger was developing with the Chinese, but nothing was said about the Middle East. The only subject discussed in relation to Israel was the list of Jewish prisoners in the Soviet Union; the United States was working with Israel to obtain their freedom.

In the Prime Minister's Office there was, of course, great satisfaction at the results of the summit. Dinitz received this message:

> We feel that Robert's [Nixon's] achievement was important. Egypt has reacted with disappointment and with anger, and that is positive and must lead to greater restraint. The [Egyptian] grievance is not directed to the United States, but rather to the Soviet Union, and there is an atmosphere of tension in Egyptian-Soviet relations. . . . We estimate that the possibility of renewal of the fighting has remained low.[74]

This time Meir's evaluation of the probability of war was based on a political—rather than an intelligence—analysis of the situation.

Dinitz flew to the West Coast in order to meet with Kissinger in San Clemente, be updated on the summit discussions, and coordinate the next moves with him. The two met on July 3. Kissinger asked to begin the meeting in private.[75] After expressing condolences on the murder of Joe Alon, the Israeli air attaché in Washington, and hearing from Dinitz that Israel

---

[73] Telephone conversations between Nixon and Kissinger, July 13, 14, and 18, 1973, NA RN, HAK, Telcon Box 21.

[74] Gazit to Dinitz, Vav Lamed/640, July 2, 1973, Aleph-4996/2, ISA.

[75] Regarding the private conversation, Lamed Vav/762, July 3, 1973, 23:45, Aleph-7046/9, ISA. In an additional dispatch on the same date and time (Lamed Vav/763), the document that Kissinger had proposed to the Soviets was also transmitted. Another dispatch was sent that night, July 4, 1973, 01:30. At the official discussion, which continued for an hour and a quarter, Scowcroft and Shalev were present in addition to Dinitz and Kissinger. For its contents, see Lamed Vav/764, July 4, 1973, Aleph-7046/9, ISA. In the Prime Minister's Office's summary of Dinitz's report, Gazit to Dinitz, Vav Lamed/656, July 11, 1973, Aleph-4996/2, ISA; full protocol of the discussion, Ford Library, NS Advisor, Box 2, available at http://www.fordlibrarymuseum.gov/library/document/memcons/1552592.pdf.

had no further details on the case, Kissinger told Dinitz about Rogers and Sisco's initiative. Dinitz later reported to the prime minister that

> he, Shaul, had succeeded in dealing with it for the meanwhile, to give himself time to talk to us and to receive our reaction to the initiative.... That he did not explicitly reject the idea that the June 4 lines would be the secure and recognized final border between Israel and Egypt.... That in our private conversation, he wanted to make sure that we would not fall into Sisco's trap of formulae.... The State Department also did not know that he was transmitting this information to us. He requested that we keep this in deepest secrecy, but of course, he would like to have our reactions for the record, as well as the comments of the prime minister.[76]

Dinitz responded, "If so, why bring up the subject at all?" Kissinger answered that he agreed with Dinitz, but wasn't sure that he would be able thwart the initiative. It should be remembered, however, that the president had already ordered the State Department to stop the initiative five days earlier.

With regard to the summit itself, Kissinger told Dinitz that "there had been a difficult struggle with the Russians and, in his opinion, we had come out of it well. After a long struggle, he had managed to kill Paper 72 [the May 1972 US-Soviet agreement] and not to reach an agreement on any new paper, although we gave them a proposal that they will certainly not accept.... But we are not as good as we would like. In any case, the whole matter is a trick."[77]

At the end of the meeting, Kissinger again asked to talk to the Israeli ambassador in private. The discussion was longer, continuing for forty-five minutes, and Kissinger did not miss the opportunity to persuade Israel not to cooperate with the State Department, terming its proposal as dangerous to Israel. This was meant to prepare Israel for the moves Kissinger would initiate on the basis of the conditions he defined as "not as good for Israel as we would like." Kissinger also did not hide that he had already proposed conditions such as these to the Soviets the day after the end of the summit—he had even suggested discussing them in proximity talks, on different floors of the hotel or in separate hotels. With regard to the details of the document, Dinitz reacted, "A version like this one will never be agreed to. I will not be able to accept a document which says that the 1967 lines are not rejected." In an attempt to calm the prime minister, Kissinger said that although the United States was including the possibility of a complete

---

[76] Dinitz to Gazit, Lamed Vav/762, July 3, 1973, 23:45, Aleph-7046/9, ISA.

[77] Ibid.

Israeli withdrawal, the discussion would be under his control and in coordination with Meir. Kissinger well knew that now in particular, three months before the elections, Israel was not interested in any moves at all.

In the context of the channel with Ismail, Dinitz reported to the prime minister on what he had heard from Kissinger:

> A long time has passed and he still hasn't replied, and an answer must be sent. He does not want to detail the "outline of an agreement" or to present any sort of paper. All he intends to do in his reply is to propose an additional meeting. It cannot take place before September. That will again make things easier for him in his contacts with the Russians, as he will be able to play one against the other and again, to gain time.[78]

In Jerusalem, in the Prime Minister's Office, there was an atmosphere of relief: the summit had been successfully completed without any political developments. Meir's sense of security and the feeling that the chances of initiating negotiations had been minimized led her to update the foreign minister with regard to the political conduct of the country. She "confirmed that we would prepare a short summary of two issues which the holiday of the first fruits [referring to the foreign minister, Abba Eban] had not been party to: 1. Fohezy [Hafez Ismail]; 2. The summit/Shaul, and would update him. I am thinking of a concise summary, as the minute details which were telegraphed at the time are no longer important," Gazit wrote to Dinitz on July 8.[79] He added that, even in the future, they would have to hide developments from the foreign minister. "The reason is clear: leaks flourish in the garden of first fruits (on a peak day—as many as three a day)."

Deputy Prime Minister Yigal Allon was at that time hospitalized and had been ordered to rest for a long period. He too was distanced from developments. And Dayan? Except for Galili, he was the only minister who was fully informed as to the secret political developments. Already in June, he had begun to scatter calming public messages even though—or perhaps because—the disappointing results (for Egypt) of the meeting between

---

[78] Ibid.

[79] Personal letter, Gazit to Dinitz, July 8, 1973, Aleph-7550/4, ISA. However, Gazit added, "With regard to Fohezy, you can simply say that one more meeting took place (does he know about the one in February), and that were the essential points and now another meeting is scheduled to take place in two months. The problem will still remain without solution, even after preparing this summary. The question is what should be done with the telegrams immediately after their arrival. On this matter, the prime minister's position is clear and unequivocal. That is to say, since the new summary with Robert/Shaul at the time of her last visit, the prime minister has determined to do less."

Kissinger and Ismail were already known in Israel.[80] These messages became even stronger toward the end of the month, following the feeble decisions at the end of the summit.

It appears that the success in postponing negotiations led Dayan to change his appraisal regarding the coming war. In May, he had estimated that Egypt's disappointment would lead to war; now his complacency was incomprehensible to many. (In fact, it ultimately gave rise to a "conspiracy theory" that maintained, without any basis in fact, that Dayan and Kissinger had planned a surprise Egyptian attack that would partially succeed and create better conditions for a political process.[81] A few of those who supported the argument of collusion—based solely on imagination— added the murder of Joe Alon to their weird theory. (They asserted that he had been murdered because he had found out about the details of the conspiracy and it was suspected that he would make the information known.) On July 6, Dayan and Elazar, in the continuing atmosphere of complacency, decided to shorten the term of compulsory army service, effective April 1974. "We must announce this to the public and to the nation," Dayan was careful to tell Elazar when they agreed.[82] "A preplanned total war with all of the Arab states on all of the fronts—this does not seem to be on the horizon in the near future. If it does happen—we will schedule another lecture and I will explain why it did. At the moment, it doesn't seem to be in the offing," Dayan confidently boasted later in the month at a closed conference of Ministry of Defense workers, at which he had analyzed the political-security situation.[83]

Dayan was preparing his listeners for another battle—for the coming political pressure and for a conflict with the United States, "whose motives for supporting us unconditionally will lessen with the changes in the relations between the superpowers and with the decline of the Soviet Union in the area. The superpowers do not want a conflict between them and do not want war; thus, we can expect political pressure on Israel."[84]

At the end of July, the Americans vetoed a proposal to condemn Israel in the Security Council. In an interview with *TIME*, Dayan stated that "for the

---

[80] In discussion of the defense budget, he had made known that a declaration of military alert was too far-reaching (Bartov 1978, 272; Braun 1992, 80). Two days earlier, he had stated in an open lecture that in the next ten years, Israel would be able to maintain its military superiority, deterring the Arabs from action (NA, GR 59 Pol 14-27 Arab-Isr.).

[81] Arbel and Na'aman 2005, under the heading "Insanity with No Atonement."

[82] Braun 1992, 31–32. The report of the decision was brought up at the Foreign Relations and Defense Committee on August 10.

[83] Dayan's speech to staff B of the defense system at the Habima Theater in Tel Aviv, July 17, 1973, Aleph-7068/15, ISA.

[84] Ibid.

next ten years, the borders will remain frozen along the existing lines—but during this time, a major war will not break out."[85] Dayan's appraisal of the situation continued to change as time went by, leading him to recognize that, shortly after the Israeli elections, Kissinger would initiate a political process based on Sadat's initiative, which would rest on recognition of Egyptian sovereignty over Sinai. This new evaluation of the situation led Dayan to do two things. First, he formulated a position that suited the principles of Sadat's and Kissinger's plans and signaled to the Americans that he was ready to lead such a course of action. Second, he became overconfident, an attitude that continued until the outbreak of the war and that was based on his opinion that it was illogical for Sadat to open fire because in the near future it would be possible to return Sinai to Egypt without a war.

## "Who Would You Like to Be My Assistant for Middle Eastern Affairs?"

Kissinger and Dinitz met again on July 20. At this meeting, Kissinger gave the Israeli ambassador a copy of the messages he and Ismail had exchanged, as well as an update on Ismail's visit to Moscow.[86] In the private part of the conversation, Kissinger saw fit to demonstrate the benefit Israel could gain by cooperating, and Dinitz transmitted Kissinger's proposal:

1. The Sisco initiative [memorandum from Rogers to the president of 28 June 1973]: Shaul stated that he had succeeded in killing the matter and that he hoped that it would not be resurrected;

2. The Russian paper [the May 1972 Soviet document]: He repeated that, as he had expected, the issue had been buried and the Russian paper had managed to enable them to escape from the summit, gain time, and kill the previous paper;

3. Hafez: Shaul was very interested in hearing what we knew about his visit to Moscow.[87]

The wording of the third item may testify that Kissinger knew that the most closely guarded secrets of the Egyptian-Soviet relationship were known to Israeli intelligence. With regard to his planned meeting with Ismail, Kissinger admitted to his Israeli interlocutor that he had nothing concrete to discuss with the Egyptian, but "it is good that the meeting is

---

[85] Dayan, interview in TIME, July 30, 1973. As reported in Ha'aretz, July 24, 1973.
[86] Dinitz to Gazit, Lamed Vav/813, July 20, 1973, Aleph-7046/9, ISA.
[87] Ibid.

Photo: Marion S. Trikosko, US Library of Congress

*Henry Kissinger, March 1976*

on the horizon because this is another way of buying time. . . . It will take at least a month until a meeting with Assad is arranged," Dinitz reported, quoting Kissinger.

At the same time, Dinitz related, "Shaul surprised me and asked who I would like to have as assistant to the secretary for Middle Eastern affairs in place of Sisco."[88] The sense of security such an expression of interest created should not be minimized, not to mention the additional mission Kissinger requested: "Shaul completed this part of our discussion with the

---

[88] Dinitz to Gazit, Lamed Vav/812, July 20, 1973, Aleph-7045/9. ISA. Dinitz proposed Alfred A. (Roy) Atherton; Kissinger reacted positively but said that he had been favorably impressed by L. Dean Brown, then the ambassador to Jordan, with whom he had cooperated when dealing with the crisis in Jordan in September 1970.

comment that if and when his appointment was publicized, it would be very beneficial if a number of senators expressed positive public reactions, but at the moment, it was still too early and he would let me know so that I could help with this matter."[89]

The activity in the Kissinger-Ismail channel had, as mentioned, come to a halt at the beginning of June, when Ismail had clarified that contacts could continue if the results of the summit created the right conditions. In any case, Kissinger's interest in maintaining the relationship had only intensified. On July 7, he wrote to Ismail and proposed meeting again secretly in Spain. "The US side would be pleased to arrange secure transportation for Mr. Ismail to a meeting site, as discussed between Mr. Ismail and Mr. Trone in Paris," Kissinger offered in his message.[90] Four days later, Ismail replied that he was leaving for Moscow, would return to Cairo on July 14, and expected to receive by then a suggested date from Kissinger for their meeting.[91]

Sadat understood that the secret moves he had tried to promote in the Ismail-Kissinger talks had failed, and his hopes that the summit discussions might lead to political developments had also been dashed. In order to continue his preparations for war, he had to strengthen ties with the Soviet Union. "Hafez Ismail went to Moscow because there was no other way except to talk with the Soviet side about an international discussion, which Brezhnev said would continue for twenty or thirty years," explained the Egyptian president.[92]

Brezhnev reported to Kissinger and Nixon regarding his July 13 talks with Ismail in Moscow:

> They [the Egyptians] came to the conclusion that Israel and the US do not intend to modify their long-held position on the settlement and specifically so, with respect to the troop withdrawal. . . . The US government would not move ahead in its approach to the problem of Middle East settlement and continued to pursue a one-sided pro-Israeli position which, to a great extent, prevents a settlement of the Arab/Israeli conflict on a just basis.[93]

---

[89] Ibid.

[90] Kissinger to Ismail, July 7, 1973. The message was sent on July 9. NA RN, NSC, HAK, Box 135.

[91] Ismail to Kissinger, July 11,1973, NA RN, NSC, HAK, Box 135.

[92] Sadat's speech to the Central Committee of the National Assembly, July 16, 1973. Report of the speech in Communication 585, transmitted to the embassy in Washington, July 17, 1973, Aleph-5256, ISA.

[93] Dobrynin orally transmitted a message from Brezhnev to Kissinger on July 19, 1973, regarding his meeting with Ismail on July 13 in Moscow (NA RN, NSC, HAK, Box 135).

Brezhnev said that he had told Ismail that "we haven't heard a firm statement from the Americans to the effect that the US supported the demand for total withdrawal of Israeli forces from all of the Arab territories occupied in 1967."[94] In response Ismail had warned, "The situation in the Middle East is very complicated and fraught with danger of serious explosion [sic]." He added that the Egyptians had lost their belief in achieving an agreement by diplomatic means, but that they would still try to achieve that possibility in the Security Council discussions that were soon to begin.[95]

Kissinger transmitted Brezhnev's report to the president along with Brezhnev's repeated warnings that fighting in the Middle East was likely to break out at any minute and that it would harm the international community as well as relations between the United States and the Soviet Union. He informed the president of the details of the Soviet report on July 21 and wrote to him, "I will probably see Ismail again sometime next month."[96]

The public Egyptian diplomatic effort was conducted in Security Council deliberations. A proposal to condemn Israel was still on the agenda, and Egypt intended to present Israel as refusing peace and the United States as backing Israel. Sadat said, in an address to the Central Committee of the National Assembly in Egypt on July 16:

> The United States attempted and is still attempting, even at this moment, to again delay the meeting of the Security Council, as it understands that it and Israel are in a position of weakness and they both sense their isolation. It is very intensively working to postpone the meeting of the Security Council until after August or September in an effort to avoid a situation in which it is liable to be forced to use its veto or to expose itself, especially in the view of the Arab nation. We have not gone to the Security Council in the expectation of gaining a solution that will bring peace. We have gone in order to present the world, and especially the superpowers, with their responsibility.[97]

---

[94] Ibid.

[95] Kissinger to Nixon, July 21, 1973, NA RN, NSC, HAK, Box 68; FRUS XXV, 243–44. Richard W. Smith, the representative of the US Interests Section located in the Spanish Embassy in Cairo, had already predicted that Sadat would now choose to apply coordinated Arab pressure on the United States while taking advantage of the oil weapon. Cairo, 1990, July 3, 1973, Smith to Rogers, NA RN, Country Files, Box 658.

[96] Ibid.

[97] Memorandum from Executive Secretary of the Department of State Theodore Eliot to Kissinger summarizing the United States' misgivings regarding the proposed Security Council resolution. NA, RG, 59 Pol 27-14 Arab-Isr.; and FRUS XXV, 245-47; also Shalev-Rodman meeting, 25 July NA RN, NSC Files, HAK, Box 135; also Shalev to Gazit, Lamed Vav/824, Aleph-7046/4 ISA.

As expected, the anti-Israel proposal passed in the United Nations and was vetoed by the United States.

The editor of the newspaper *Ma'ariv*, Arieh Dissenchik, and his political correspondent Shmuel Segev, with the assistance of the Israeli embassy, were able to arrange a meeting in Washington with senior members of the American government to determine the atmosphere in Washington. The embassy reported on this interview to Jerusalem:

> In a discussion with [Harold] Saunders (a member of the National Security Council and Kissinger's assistant) in the White House, he told them [Dissenchik and Segev] that he did not expect any political activity in the coming months. The Egyptians were aware that elections were approaching in Israel. The Americans viewed the visit of [Kurt] Waldheim [the secretary-general of the United Nations, who was about to set out for discussions in the Middle East], as a good way to fill the vacuum until after the Israeli elections. . . . The American dialogue with the Egyptians was very perfunctory and the US did not even have a man in Cairo at that point (Greene had resigned).[98]

At this stage, all Egyptian public political activity was frozen. In Washington, as in Jerusalem, this was considered an unavoidable acceptance of a situation that would exist until after the Israeli elections. Discussions between Kissinger and Dobrynin did not deal with the Middle East, nor did Kissinger's discussions with the president, who was deeply occupied with Watergate.

In August, Israeli diplomatic activity was reduced to dealing with a campaign by the American oil companies intended to divert United States policy in the Middle East from its all-embracing support for Israel. In those days, at the margins of the Egyptian channel, Kissinger received two proposals to open a discussion channel with the Palestinians. One of these was received via the Moroccans. The second came from Richard Helms, the former head of the CIA and, at the time, ambassador to Iran. On August 3, he met with Kissinger and reported on his reliable contact with Arafat's right-hand man.[99] The message he transmitted was that the Fatah organization recognized the existence of Israel in fact and as a basis for the existence of a democratic state of Jews, Muslims, and Christians, and that

---

[98] Telegram 363 from the embassy in Washington to the Foreign Ministry in Jerusalem, July 31, 1973, Aleph-7075/11, ISA.

[99] Discussion in Kissinger's office. The other participants were Richard Helms and Harold Saunders. July 23, 1973, NA RN, NSC Files Box 1027; Dinitz to Gazit, Lamed Vav/849, August 14, 1973, Aleph-4996/2, ISA.

it would consider the possibility of establishing a Palestinian national state in place of the Hashemite kingdom. Kissinger requested that a positive response to the exchange of communications via this channel be transmitted to the Palestinians.[100]

At the margins of the diplomatic track, the secretary-general of the United Nations, Kurt Waldheim, arrived for a tour of the Middle East and met with Meir in Jerusalem on August 30. At the opening of their conversation, he stated, "I have no illusions that we can perform miracles. . . . I don't have any program with me for a solution in the Middle East." During his visit, Waldheim proposed using the United Nations Charter as a formula to enable a breakthrough in the process.[101] Dinitz reported Kissinger's reaction to Waldheim's mission: "Naftali [Kissinger's new alias] said that we shouldn't attach any importance to his mission, and that Waldheim himself was a fool; in essence, what was important was not to get entangled with him in initiatives or in any moves whatsoever."[102] Waldheim's visit served Meir as another futile move to pass the time until the elections. For Sadat, the visit served as another futile move to create a calm atmosphere in the area until the approaching war.

In August, public expressions concerning renewal of the fighting diminished in Egypt. Newspaper readers in Israel could easily distinguish this; on August 6, Marwan's report from Egypt confirmed it.[103] The preparations and coordination for the war had entered high gear, but this activity now disappeared from Israeli intelligence bodies and from their sources. Against this backdrop, on August 12, the Israelis decided to end the "Blue-White" army alert.

A few days before, an exceptional incident took place in the skies over the Middle East, an event that disturbed the relaxed August atmosphere. On Friday, August 10, Israeli military intelligence received a message, from a reliable source, that George Habash, the leader of the Popular Front for the Liberation of Palestine, was planning to leave Beirut that evening en route to Baghdad on Iraqi Airlines Flight 006 to attend a terrorist conference.[104] Zeira, who had received the information, promptly descended to the floor below and presented it to Elazar, the army chief of

[100] When they returned to discuss this subject ten days later, Kissinger proposed a version of a written message. Helms preferred that the message be transmitted orally and not in writing. NA RN, NSC Files Box 1027; FRUS XXV, 248.

[101] Protocol of the meeting, Aleph-7027/9. ISA; Gazit to Dinitz on the Meir-Waldheim meeting, Vav Lamed/706, September 2,1973, Aleph-4996/2, ISA.

[102] Dinitz to Gazit on his meeting with Kissinger, Lamed Vav/883, September 10, 1973, Aleph-4996/2, ISA.

[103] Braun 1992, 11.

[104] Zeira 2004, 66; author's personal interview with Zeira.

staff. "We will intercept him," Elazar responded without hesitation, and he continued to hold this opinion even after a four-way meeting with his deputy, Yisrael Tal; Zeira; and the new commander of the air force, General Benny Peled, despite Tal's and Zeira's strong opposition to the move. Elazar requested Dayan's approval. Dayan, even after summoning Zeira and hearing all of his reasons for opposing the action, recommended implementation to the prime minister.

Military intelligence prepared to carry out the mission and augmented its tracking and bugging devices in Beirut, while the General Staff Commando Unit (Sayeret Matcal) received orders to prepare for action and report to the Ramat David Air Force Base, where the air force prepared a squadron of Mirage airplanes to intercept the Iraqi passenger plane. In the evening, Dayan joined the tactical command at the air force base. However, a technical malfunction in the Iraqi plane caused a flight delay, and a Lebanese plane was leased to replace it. The plane, which took off late as newly numbered Flight 1006, was intercepted by Israeli Air Force planes and obeyed their orders to land on the runway of Ramat David. Immediately after it landed, the commando unit burst into the plane, meeting no opposition. They ordered the seventy-four passengers and seven crew members to leave the plane for identification. George Habash was not on the plane. It was later discovered that he had cancelled his flight.

Two days later, Dayan publicly accepted responsibility for the failed hijacking attempt. Meir stated that the decision to intercept the plane had been made at the most senior level, and that she had been a part of it. After a few days, a source close to George Habash made it known that the Soviet Union had hinted to Habash about the intended hijacking, but he had come to the Beirut airport to continue playing the game to its climax. The Security Council voted to condemn Israel, this time with the support of the United States. Most of the Lebanese government supported expelling Habash and Arafat from Lebanon. The source who had transmitted the information about Habash's movements stopped functioning.

After his discussion with Kissinger about the hijacked plane, Dinitz reported to the prime minister:

> Naftali told me that, as far as he was concerned, there was no need to explain, as he was of the opinion that we were correct in our action and he was only sorry that Habash and his colleagues were not on the plane. . . . He asked if they [Habash's colleagues] had suspected that we were planning to act. . . . He let me understand

that Edward [Nixon's new alias] had no complaint against us regarding the plane.[105]

## Six Guests in the Officers' Club in Alexandria

The deeper the diplomatic activity sank into its summer sleep, the busier the armies of Israel, Egypt, and Syria were in their preparations for war. Israeli preparations included gathering information about what was going on in the Egyptian and Syrian armies and estimating the timing of the war.

Three agencies were dealing with these questions, only two of which had been officially assigned to that role. The first was the Mossad, which at that time was the information-gathering agency for the prime minister, the defense minister, the army chief of staff, and military intelligence. The Mossad did not concentrate full information in its own hands and was not required to formulate an intelligence appraisal, but Zvi Zamir, the head of the Mossad, was requested to do this on the basis of his close acquaintance with the information he transmitted and its sources, in particular Ashraf Marwan. His status in the narrowest forum of policy makers rested to no small degree on Meir's great respect for him and the fact that she viewed him, like Elazar, as a close associate who could balance the weight of Dayan.

The second body, the IDF, was the only organization required to compile the military intelligence gathered by various means and to supply decision-makers with its evaluations. This responsibility rested on the head of military intelligence, Eli Zeira, and above him, the chief of staff, David Elazar. As we have seen, toward the summer, despite focused alerts, including one from Marwan in April about a pending war in mid-May, military intelligence estimated that the probability of war breaking out in the near future was low. The head of the Mossad, as the Agranat Commission later determined, did not fundamentally disagree with this analysis. At the time, both were correct.

Above military intelligence and the head of the Mossad was the third agent—the political one. In practice, this consisted of three people: Golda Meir, Moshe Dayan, and Yisrael Galili. Only they were exposed to the full range of information: to the direct raw material supplied by the Mossad, the army intelligence supplied by the military intelligence organization, political information such as Dinitz's reports, and the steps they themselves took in their capacity as decision-makers.

---

[105] Dinitz to Gazit, Lamed Vav/883, August 14, 1973, Aleph-4996/2, ISA; Dinitz to Gazit on his private discussion with Kissinger, Lamed Vav/849 and Lamed Vav/850, August 14, 1973.

In this upper circle, Dayan was the dominant figure, both in his official capacity as defense minister, coordinating the political system with its subordinate military system, and also due to his personality, public status, and weight in the political system, which increased in the months leading up to the elections.[106]

Meir's various duties and limited expertise in military and defense matters required that Galili be included in this small team. Yisrael Galili was a member of Kibbutz Na'an and had been chief of the national command of the Haganah, the central organized defensive arm of the Jewish population during the pre-state period. His wisdom and conduct had earned him great respect in the political arena; he was a close associate of the prime minister and was available for this task. He received all of the information meant for Meir and, with the help of his assistant, Arnan "Sini" Azaryahu, aided her in learning the material and forming opinions about it. To a great extent, Galili represented a counterweight to Dayan's dominance in Meir's political decision-making.

While in April Dayan had accepted Zeira's and Zamir's appraisal of the low probability for a war in May, by the end of May he had integrated information from various sources that was not available to others and this made it possible for him to reject their evaluation of military intelligence. Based on this integrated information, along with details of activity in the secret channel and the rejection of Sadat's initiative, Dayan knew enough by the beginning of summer to correctly evaluate the high probability of war during the coming six months and to predict Egypt's political goals and military means to achieve them. "My evaluation is different from [Zeira's]. They [the Egyptians] think that they will achieve something and they are ready to pay for it," Dayan told the Knesset Foreign Affairs and Defense Committee on May 22, continuing, "I think that their goal in renewing the war is to achieve political gains. . . . The Egyptians assume that . . . when the fighting ends, they will succeed in gaining a foothold on the east bank of the canal. . . . They see it as a total failure that all they have managed to do is to create a war mood in order to serve the political situation, and they think that they will achieve only small military achievements at a great and heavy cost, but to them it is worth it."[107]

---

[106] As Pinchas Sapir had warned, "Dayan is liable to leave and form an independent party list. He is likely to gain 12 to 15 Knesset seats taken from the Ma'arach [Labor Alignment party]" (Nakdimon 1982, 45); "There is a reasonable chance that Dayan will leave the party and serve in a government led by Gahal [Herut-Liberal bloc] which will be formed by Menachem Begin" (Medzini 2008, 520).

[107] Braun 1992, 29. The military intelligence organization also predicted that the aim of an Egyptian war would be to motivate political development, but believed Egypt would go to war only when it had the ability to attack deep into Israel to deter Israel

At the beginning of June, Dayan repeated his appraisal that the war was expected "during the next six months." He also personally verified that the air force was aware that it would be required to assist in interception in an area defended by surface-to-air missiles.[108] He also visited Southern Command and asked about the roller bridge that would be needed to cross the canal to the west bank; Command General Ariel Sharon reassured him that the bridge was well made and reliable.[109]

On the military level, Israel was preparing in accord with the "Blue-White" program in May, based on Dayan's instructions to be ready for a war whose timing and conditions would be dictated by Egypt and Syria, without Jordan. The IDF prepared to react to an attack with short warning by planning a holding action to be carried out by regular army forces. Preparation for this reaction to a surprise attack was based on the "Dovecote" plan and was meant to be conducted by regular forces only.[110] The transition to attack mode would take place after approximately two days, and only after the arrival of reserve forces to the battle arena. To this end, in the framework of "Blue-White," the order of battle of the armored corps, armored infantry, and artillery, were re-equipped and reinforced by establishing new units. Simultaneously, the IDF expanded its training program for both regular and reserve units. When the war actually did break out, the price of this acceleration was felt sharply by reserve fighters, whose emergency storerooms lacked the necessary ammunition and equipment for the fighting.

During the summer months Egypt's readiness for war improved significantly. The Egyptian chief of staff, Saad el-Din el-Shazly, later recalled of August 1973, "We were as ready for battle as we could ever be."[111] A month previously, when Hafez Ismail told him about his trip to Moscow and asked Shazly to update him on the extent of Egypt's cooperation with the Soviet Union for arms and supplies, Shazly had responded that he had no complaints about the Soviets and that they had fulfilled all of their promises according to schedule.

In July, after the summit talks and the American veto in the Security Council, Sadat completely revised his public references to the situation.

---

from attacking deep into Egypt, as it had done during the War of Attrition (Shalev 2006, 63). This analysis relies on military intelligence documents from June 1971 and February 1972.

[108] As he stated to the air force commander on May 22, 1973 (Braun 1992, 30).

[109] As reported to the Economics Committee in Jerusalem on June 1, 1973; Sharon's words to the air force commander on May 22, 1973; Sharon's words on a visit to Southern Command along with the chief of staff and the head of the command, June 4, 1973; Braun 1992, 30.

[110] Bar-Yosef 2001, 188.

[111] Shazly 1987, 144–45.

He no longer called for negotiations and threatened war if no political process was forthcoming. Now that Sadat knew that in the coming months he would fire the opening shot of the war, he sent clear messages of friendship to the Soviet Union while trying to hide his satisfaction at its military support for his preparations. The *Ha'aretz* Arab affairs reporter who covered Sadat's speech on the twenty-first anniversary of the Egyptian revolution was aware of Sadat's difficulty in transmitting this message: "Speaking slowly and haltingly, as if seeking the right words, he declared that the Soviet Union was the only country standing alongside the Arabs, and it was not possible for Egypt to lose a friend like that." But in the same speech, Sadat also took care to say that "Egypt is not satisfied with Soviet military aid."[112]

Syria's improvement in military readiness was even greater and was accompanied by aggressive statements against Israel that led to unusual Syrian deployment near the front. Egypt's and Syria's moves to equip themselves were not hidden to Israeli intelligence. On August 10, Zeira reported on Egypt's moves to the Knesset Foreign Affairs and Defense Committee. On August 20, he also reported on Syrian moves in a discussion with the army general staff.

At the end of August, an incoming report about a division of Scud missiles being organized in Egypt was the subject of a discussion between Elazar and Dayan.[113] Among the passengers on a Soviet liner from Latakia, Syria, to the port of Alexandria, Egypt, on August 21 were six men using forged passports. Their civilian dress concealed their status as senior figures in the Syrian army, led by the minister of defense, Mustafa Tlass; the army chief of staff, Yusuf Shakkur; and the head of Syrian intelligence, Hikmat Shihabi. The six stayed at the Officers' Club in central Alexandria; in the early evening hours of that day, they were driven to the Egyptian Naval Headquarters at Ras el-Tin, for the first (and only) meeting of the Joint Supreme Council of the Armed Forces.

As noted, at the end of April, presidents Sadat and Assad had determined that this joint forum would coordinate the preparations for war. The senior military figures on the Egyptian side were the war minister, Ahmad Ismail; the chief of staff, Shazly; the commander of the air force, Hosni Mubarak; and the head of the operations branch, Mohamed Abdel Ghani el-Gamasy. After two days of discussions, they agreed that the two armies were ready to open a coordinated attack. This was the first time they had discussed an opening date for the war, and they decided that "two possibilities in the coming months, September 7–11 or October 5–10, would

---

[112] *Ha'aretz*, "Sadat Is Not Satisfied with the Soviet Aid," July 24, 1973.
[113] Braun 1992, 33.

be suitable for the beginning of the battle."[114] The senior officers waited for Sadat and Assad to make their final determination between these two alternatives and asked to receive their decision fifteen days beforehand.

These dates were not coincidental. Anyone who is involved in night activity is well aware of the contribution of moonlight to natural lighting conditions. In the days before night vision equipment, the phase of the moon was a central factor in planning military action. The timing of the war's opening was determined in accord with the dates when moonlight would enable the attacking armies to operate by night as well as day on the first days, before the Israeli reserve forces could reach the front.[115]

The Israeli intelligence agents did not know the content of this meeting; Marwan reported on its taking place, but not on its content. The Egyptian war plan determined at the meeting was to breach the Mitla and Gidi passes, a distance of forty-eight kilometers from the canal—but, as mentioned previously, the Egyptians had no intention of implementing this objective.

On August 23, even before the members of the forum had completed their discussions, Sadat left for Saudi Arabia, accompanied by Marwan, his contact person in Saudi Arabia and Qatar who had played a central role in preparing the two visits.[116] Sadat met with King Faisal and reported to him that the war would begin in the very near future. He received the king's encouragement and coordinated the "oil war" with him. He did not give an exact date for the beginning of the war; he planned to discuss this with Assad four days later.[117] From Saudi Arabia, Sadat continued to Qatar with Marwan in tow. At the end of his meeting with the Emir Khalifa, the two signed a mutual declaration that all Arab resources would be mobilized to put an end to Zionist aggression. For the Gulf state of Qatar, this meant oil.

On Saturday, August 25, Sadat went on to Syria and met with Assad in Blodan, west of Damascus. The two waited for the arrival of the Egyptian air force commander Mubarak and the Syrian defense minister Tlass, who updated them the following evening about the decisions of the army chiefs in Alexandria. The discussions between the

---

[114] Heikal 1975, 1–5; Shazly 1987, 146–47.

[115] The nights between the nine days after the new moon and the full moon was were best for light. Before that, the light would be too weak; after that, the moonrise would be too late after the sunset. The nights of September 7–11 and October 5–10 fit, from the standpoint of lighting needs. The influence of the tides is not felt in the Suez Canal, even though this is erroneously cited in some sources as influencing the determination of the war date.

[116] See details in the appendix dealing with Marwan.

[117] Regarding this meeting, see Robinson 1988, 136.

two presidents went on late into the night. They stopped to rest and returned to meet in the morning. They separated without agreeing on a date—thus, in practice, rejecting the September dates. The October dates now remained the only alternative.[118]

Marwan did not accompany the president to Syria, but, as Sadat had instructed, flew to Cairo for an urgent meeting with President Qaddafi of Libya, who had made a surprise visit. After meeting with Qaddafi, Marwan left for Damascus to fill Sadat in on their discussion.

News of Sadat's journey, his visits to Saudi Arabia, Qatar, and Damascus, and the fact that Marwan had accompanied him was reported in the newspapers.[119] What was known about these in Israel? Marwan reported on the discussion between Sadat and Assad to his contact and the head of the Mossad on September 2, when they met in Rome. (This meeting is discussed in detail in the appendix.) In his report, Marwan stated that Sadat had asked Assad to join him in a war that would take place at the end of 1973.[120] This was the most exact advance notice that Marwan could transmit to Israel until fourteen hours before the war broke out.

Sadat also hid the coming war from members of his own government. He had a few partners in this secret. One of them was Egyptian journalist Mohamed Hassanein Heikal; Sadat informed Heikal about the approaching war on his return from Damascus, and Heikal joined Sadat's efforts to camouflage war preparations.[121] At the end of August, US Senator Joe Biden visited Cairo and met with Heikal. On August 31, Biden arrived in Jerusalem and was received by Meir. He told her that, of all of the people that he had met, "there was not one who denied the complete military superiority of Israel, and thus maintained that Egypt could not go to war against Israel at this time."[122] It appears that this was what Sadat wanted to transmit to the people around him. This was Marwan's impression as well, and he hurried to report it to Israel.

---

[118] Heikal 1975, 4–5; Shazly 1987, 146–47; Gamasy 1994; Seale 1993, 197. Seale asserts that the two did not reach an agreement because Sadat wanted to attack earlier while Assad preferred the later October alternative.

[119] *Ha'aretz*, August 28, 1973.

[120] For the fact that he reported on a war that would break out only at the end of the year, see also Braun 1992, 68; Bar-Yosef 2011, 218.

[121] Report from Smith, the American representative in Cairo, about the information the Soviets held about the opening date of the war, Cairo 3242, October 26, 1973. During those days, Heikal published an article supporting King Hussein, who claimed to represent the Palestinian struggle. Ehud Yaari, in an analytical article, attributed this to Sadat's desire to strengthen the eastern front (*Davar*, September 4, 1973).

[122] Report to Dinitz on Meir's meeting with Senator Joe Biden, September 2, 1973, Aleph-7072/21, ISA.

On the last day of August, the newspaper headlines announced that the settlers who had come to live at the center of Pithat Rafiah (in northwestern Sinai, in Egyptian territory captured in June 1967) were the pioneers for a city of a quarter of a million residents. They reported that negotiations to establish the Likud (a unified right-wing political party) had failed, as the Gahal party had rejected Ariel Sharon's proposal.

August ended. In Egypt and in Syria the preparations for war were complete and the military tension increased as the army waited for final confirmation of the war's exact date and, fifteen days before that, the exact date on which they would begin the final stage of preparations. In Israel, as well, "Blue-White" military preparations had also been completed, but the longer the waiting for an Egyptian-Syrian war initiative continued, the more the military tension in Israel relaxed.

# 6

# Dayan's Political Conception— September 1973

> *"That horse is dead and now it is important*
> *to design a new common strategy."*
> **—Kissinger to Dinitz, September 30, 1973**[1]

An outwardly relaxed political atmosphere prevailed during September 1973 and the first days of October. This served the needs and aims of all of the decision-makers: Sadat, Assad, Meir, Dayan, and Kissinger. However, under the mantle of quiet and calm, very significant developments were taking place in Israel with only the participation of Defense Minister Dayan, Prime Minister Meir, and her trusted ally, Minister Galili.

Election day in Israel (October 30) was drawing near. The political system was sizzling, with the various parties immersed in organizing their campaigns. Decision-makers in Israel were, for the most part, preoccupied with their own concerns. The opposition was busy exhausting political negotiations on the initiative of Ariel Sharon that were intended to unite them into one bloc—the Likud. In the government party, the Ma'arach (Labor bloc), Galili published a document bearing his name and expressing settlement policy in the occupied territories, a move Dayan had forced on party leaders by threatening to resign. The document, which aroused a storm in the Labor movement, also included establishing a city, Yamit, in the northern Sinai Pithat Rafiah region, that would include a large port. The Secretariat of the Labor Party approved this on September 4, but only

---

[1] Lamed Vav/934, Dinitz to Gazit, September 30, 1973, Aleph-4996/2, ISA.

78 of 161 secretariat members voted for it. Most of the others abstained from participating in the vote as a sign of protest. Treasury Minister Pinchas Sapir publicly refused to commit himself to implementing the decision. The strongest opposition came from Lyova Eliav, who attacked the Meir government's deadlock policy. "We and our children will have to repay the debt for the dead end into which our policies have pushed us, into which you are directing our futures," Eliav's supporters responded, referring to the approval of the "Galili document."[2]

Never had Israel's situation seemed better and more secure. Military tension would have done harm to this general evaluation. It might also have invited international pressure to open negotiations immediately, with public discussions taking place on the eve of elections and under the threat of renewed fighting.[3] An increased military threat, which would have required mobilizing the reserves and conducting elections in an atmosphere of impending war, would also have played into the hands of the opposition. Meir and Dayan well remembered the political implications of the military alert in the summer of 1967, Eshkol's replacement with Dayan, then in the opposition, as defense minister; and Begin's addition to the decision-making forum.

The events visible to the public and to most of the decision-makers reinforced this atmosphere of complacency. Israel's success in demonstrating both an impressive intelligence achievement by preventing a powerful terrorist attack at the beginning of September and, later that month, its display of total airpower superiority over Syria contributed to the illusion that the Egyptians and Syrians would not dare to create a military conflict now—and that, if they did, they would be defeated. The Egyptian and Syrian armies' increased build-up that month, which was a direct result of their war preparations, was attributed in Israel to the tension stemming from the September 13 air battle over northern Syria and Syria's fears of Israeli initiatives.

Ironically, Israeli decision-makers' efforts to create the illusion of a relaxed security atmosphere and minimize manifestations of an approaching military conflict suited the aims of their counterparts in Egypt and Syria, who had great interest in muffling the drums of war and creating a camouflage under which their military preparations could be completed. Thus each side, in its own way and for its own reasons, contributed to this illusion, avoiding moves that might disrupt it

---

[2] *Davar*, September 25, 1973. Open letter sent to Galili by Avraham Shapira of Kibbutz Yizrael. Shapira was the editor of *Shdemot*, the journal of the younger generation in the settlement movement, and one of the editors of *Siah Lohamim* (*The Seventh Day*), a collection of soldiers' reminiscences after the Six-Day War.

[3] Kissinger 1980, 464.

and adopting restrained behavior in a situation that would usually have involved increasing tension.

There was another reason for the calm. In September, Dayan privately reached an evaluation of the situation that proved to be incorrect. Based on the messages transmitted to him, he concluded that Sadat was aware that in the near future, immediately after the Israeli elections, he would get what he wanted and would enter negotiations leading to an Israeli withdrawal from Sinai. Dayan had a good basis for believing this: already, in May, Kissinger had presented Egypt with a negotiation schedule according to which an interim agreement would be reached in 1974, and a comprehensive one a year later. Under these conditions, Dayan concluded that, in any case, Sadat had no real reason to go to war.[4] On September 10, the day Sadat and Assad met in Cairo to decide on the date the war would begin, Dayan was basing his position on his assessment that "there is reason to believe that the Arab states will now prefer another political round rather than a military one." He expected Kissinger to launch a new diplomatic initiative in November or December, and indicated that, in this context, "such an initiative should not be received coldly or with reservations by the Israelis."[5] This "conception" is what led to the terrible failure of the Yom Kippur War. It was this understanding of the situation—and not necessarily what is known as the "intelligence conception"—which focused responsibility on the military level.

Researchers, like the Agranat Commission and the Israeli intelligence chiefs before them, have not extensively considered the political events that took place during this period, and have focused comprehensively and deeply on the military and intelligence aspects of the conflict in their research and writings. There have been disputes among researchers, but on one central aspect they have all agreed: The mistaken "intelligence assessment" led to the surprise; the "greatest of Israeli disasters" was the result of an intelligence failure that led to an erroneous and inflexible belief that Egypt would not go to war with Israel until it had closed the gap in its air inferiority and gained the ability to act as Israel could, penetrating deep into enemy territory. According to past research, this fixation on the part of military intelligence is what prompted Israeli decision-makers to push aside all signs of the impending war.

---

[4] Dan Margalit, in an op-ed column, quoted Dayan: *Ha'aretz*, September 11, 1973. Similar information was published on the same day in *Ma'ariv*. The US ambassador in Israel reported Dayan's words to the State Department in Washington. Tel Aviv 7122, September 11, 1973, available at http://aad.archives.gov/aad/createpdf?rid=68658&dt=2472&dl=1345.

[5] Ibid.

The argument blaming the military intelligence organization is twofold. First, it should have concluded from the accumulating information that Egypt's conditions for initiating war had changed. Second, other signs of impending war should have received more weight in appraising the probability of war. However, researchers of the period and the war developed an interpretation in which the intelligence was to blame—they formulated a "conception" of the failure, but did not update the information on which they based this assessment, which was purely military in nature.

The "military conception," which involved strict adherence to the intelligence evaluation of Egypt's conditions for initiating war, was presented by Eli Zeira. In retrospect, Zeira maintained that it was strictly modeled on documented information received from Ashraf Marwan, information which had been investigated and found to be authentic.[6] Dayan, who had received the raw intelligence data, stated as well:

> This "conception" was not the invention of some crazy genius in the military intelligence organization, or of the intelligence chief or the Minister of Defense. It was formulated by us on the basis of very solid intelligence information. . . . I can say with complete confidence that any intelligence service in the world, and every minister of defense or military chief of staff who had received this material and had known how it had been acquired, would have come to the same conclusions.[7]

On the other hand, Aryeh Shalev, the former head of research in the military intelligence organization, whom the Agranat Commission also branded as responsible for the mistaken appraisal, wrote, "It is true that there was an intelligence failure. There was an error on the strategic level, an inability to foresee Sadat's decision. This was due to the absence of a basic understanding that would have enabled a correct outline of his map of interests and conditions for initiating a war, a map which was changing and about which Israeli intelligence knew nothing."[8]

Indeed, the process of deploying a large number of Egyptian and Syrian forces to the front was obvious to the intelligence organizations and military system, and information about its development was reported to the small high-level political-security elite and, first and foremost, to Meir and Dayan. But except for Meir, Dayan, and Galili, none of the decision-makers knew of the secret political developments. Not even

---

[6] Zeira 2004, 116.

[7] Bergman and Meltzer 2003, 182.

[8] Shalev 2007, 57.

the army chief of staff, the chiefs of military intelligence, or the Mossad were told the details. So, for example, the intelligence officials and the army did not know what Meir, Dayan, and Galili knew: that Sadat had chosen September as the concluding date for negotiations for a comprehensive agreement and had even emphasized that this should be done before the Israeli elections. This important factor was not considered in the intelligence appraisal.

This strict compartmentalization in everything concerned with political contacts placed a heavy responsibility on Meir, Dayan, and Galili, to whom Kissinger was referring when he determined: "Policy makers in Jerusalem and in Washington did not lack information. The mistake was in the conclusions they drew from this information."[9] Kissinger included himself in that group.

In Egypt Sadat already despaired of his initiative, made at the beginning of the year, to achieve an agreement by September. On August 13, Kissinger again attempted to set a political process in motion to prevent Israel from having to announce before the elections that it was ready to accept Egyptian sovereignty over all of Sinai. Under the patronage of the Shah of Iran, the Iranian ambassador in Washington, Ardeshir Zahedi, was requested to meet with Hafez Ismail in Geneva to try to convince him to advance an agreement using the "step-by-step" approach.[10] The Egyptians reacted positively to the approach, but expressed doubt about the United States' ability to implement it. Zahedi reported the results of his mission to Kissinger on September 15 in the White House: "Egypt is ready to accept that a full withdrawal will take place step by step." But with regard to recognizing Egyptian sovereignty over Sinai, Zahedi added, "Egypt wants all of the salami on the table and then to slice it. The Egyptians are not ready for the salami to be kept outside the room with an additional slice brought to them each time."[11]

Sadat had announced time after time, for three years, that this would be "a decisive year." In his understanding, only the military alternative was left to him in order to start negotiations that would result in the return of Egyptian sovereignty over Sinai; he could no longer retreat from this decision. On the political level, Egypt was now strictly focused on its efforts to prepare for the United Nations General

---

[9] Kissinger 1980, 460.

[10] "It's only between His Majesty and myself. No one else on our side is involved." Iranian initiative meeting between Zahedi and Kissinger, August 15, 1973, NA RN, NSC, HAK, Box 132.

[11] Meeting between Kissinger and Zahedi in Kissinger's office on September 15, 1973, during which Zahedi reported on his meeting with the Egyptians. Ibid.

Assembly meeting at the end of the month: directing a pan-Arab diplomatic campaign to present Israel as making every effort to maintain the stagnation, refusing to negotiate, and endangering international political security. The use of an Arab oil embargo, instigated by Sadat, was intended to present Israel's refusal to reach a peace agreement as threatening the economies of the developed countries.[12] In Washington, diplomatic interest centered on the oil crisis. Sadat's moves achieved two goals: to prepare world public opinion to understand and accept Egypt's military action and, simultaneously, to minimize Israel's alertness for a sudden military attack and convince it that Egypt would be satisfied with the oil embargo.

On a parallel track, the military one, Egypt and Syria were completing their preparations for the coming war as secretly as possible. All that was left for Sadat and Assad to do was to determine the day and hour they would start the attack. Any other military event connected to the Middle East that might occur was liable to prevent or delay the opening of the war, which had already been determined to begin on one of five days after October 5.

In Washington, Kissinger was preoccupied with the debate over his appointment as secretary of state and thus limited his public involvement in political affairs until after his official appointment on September 22. Dinitz, the person in intimate contact with Kissinger and Meir, took advantage of this break and flew to Israel for consultations in preparation for the expected American initiative after Kissinger's appointment. He was absent from the American capital for ten days. When he returned, he was forced to wait another week before he could meet with Kissinger, who was busy during his first days as secretary of state organizing his staff, dealing with the UN General Assembly discussions, and holding meetings to prepare the groundwork for a political process. Dinitz and Kissinger were only able to have their working meeting on Sunday, September 30. During that discussion, Dinitz heard Kissinger's views on the new period that was about to begin in the Middle East. He had just managed to report this information to Meir when he was called back to Israel following the death of his father. He only returned to Washington after the war had broken out.

## "Terrorists Plotted to Bring Down an El Al Plane in Rome Using Russian Rockets"

A photograph of the prestigious *Queen Elizabeth* ocean liner docking in Ashdod harbor was displayed on the front page of *Ha'aretz* on April 22,

---

[12] In addition to statements from Saudi Arabia and the other Persian Gulf states about the use of the oil embargo, on September 1, 1973, Libya nationalized 51 percent of all foreign oil companies operating in the country.

next to the main headline. The article stated that, on its way to Israel, the liner had sailed along the coast of North Africa, passing through the territorial waters of Algeria and Tunisia, but instead of continuing along the Libyan coast had deviated from its route in the direction of Sicily. Exceptional security measures on the ship were also reported during its journey. The location of the picture and the coverage of the cruise were not without significance; however, the tourists on the ship, who arrived in Israel to celebrate its twenty-fifth Independence Day, did not know that they owed their lives to the president of Egypt, Anwar Sadat.

Moammar Qaddafi, the young ruler of Libya, aspired to take revenge for Israel's downing a Libyan plane over Sinai two months earlier.[13] He had ordered the commander of an Egyptian submarine to sink the passenger liner on its way to Israel, but this plan was foiled on the order of the Egyptian president.[14]

The event took place a day or two before Sadat was to meet with Assad to agree upon their common plan to initiate a war with Israel. Sadat did not want a terrorist event to disrupt their preparations for war or to transform Israel's image, which he had made such a great effort to mold, from aggressor and conqueror to victim and sufferer. He also considered that it would quickly become known that an Egyptian submarine had carried out the terrorist act. It later became clear that someone had made an effort to warn the relevant Israeli security bodies of the plan to attack the ship.[15] Ashraf Marwan, Sadat's representative responsible for Egyptian-Libyan ties, left for Libya after the attack was thwarted and returned to Cairo on April 23, 1973.[16]

Qaddafi's desire for revenge had this time remained unsatisfied. But at the beginning of September, while preoccupied with coordinating war plans, Sadat had to deal with yet another initiative by the Libyan ruler.

The next drama took place among the beautiful treasures of Rome. As the front page of *Ha'aretz* reported: "Rome, September 5. A commando unit of five Arabs, who were arrested this morning, intended to bring down an El Al plane with two Soviet-made rocket launchers, according to an announcement made by Roman police." Even in the stormy circumstances of the Middle East, this

---

[13] El-Saadany 1994, 104.

[14] Bar-Yosef 2010, 210–11.

[15] Irregular security arrangements during the voyage testify to the advance information about plans to attack an Israeli ship. The shop was accompanied by British battleships and fighter planes. There was also an unexpected change in the route taken along the North African coast. Transportation minister Shimon Peres also made an unexpected visit to the ship, which anchored in Ashdod. *Davar*, April 22, 1973.

[16] Cairo 1230, report from US Interests Section in Cairo, April 25, 1973. No longer available online; copy in author's possession.

was an unusual event with exceptional significance. This time, the newspaper report represented a story that, had it been written as a detective novel, would have been considered the product of a fertile imagination.

Downing an Israeli passenger plane with all of its passengers and crew would have been a "mega-terror attack" that would necessarily have involved a decisive Israeli reaction, creating a new reality in the Middle East. There is no doubt that this would also have shuffled all of Sadat's and Assad's plans to initiate the war. That was why Sadat prevented the attack. The intended victims, the flight passengers, also owed their lives to President Sadat. However, the real story, which follows, leaves the reader with question marks—and the possible answers completely contradict one another.

On August 23, as mentioned above, Ashraf Marwan accompanied President Sadat on his trips to Saudi Arabia and Qatar; Sadat then continued on to Damascus to discuss the date for the start of the war against Israel. Marwan did not continue on to Damascus but returned to Egypt, where a new mission awaited him. He immediately left for Rome. Zvi Zamir, the head of the Mossad, relates that at the end of August 1973, he received an urgent request from Marwan to come to Rome in order to meet with him.[17] Marwan informed Zamir that the Libyans had requested Egypt's help in bringing down an El Al plane that would be leaving the international airport in Rome headed for New York and that, to that end the Egyptians had sent a number of the newest Strela anti-aircraft missiles under Egyptian diplomatic post. These were personal "shoulder-fired" missiles made by the Soviet Union that could target a plane by the heat of its engines.

A few days earlier, Marwan had seen to it that two boxes, each 6 by 2 by 5 feet, were sent to Rome in the cargo section of an Egypt Air flight, addressed to Mona Nasser, daughter of the late, respected president of Egypt and Marwan's wife, who was on her way to London. These had been picked up at the Rome airport and loaded into a station wagon that had carried them to the Academy of Egyptian Art, where they awaited Marwan, who transferred them personally to the terrorists.[18] The commander of the small group, Amin al-Hindi, was to receive the boxes. In order to camouflage their unusual cargo, al-Hindi and his men bought carpets from a nearby store, wrapped the missiles in them, and transmitted them to a hiding place in an apartment.

Mossad operatives under the direct command of Zamir, who remained in Rome, identified the terrorist group, found the car in which the missiles had been transported, and followed it to the house, which was south of the airport, along the plane route. On Zamir's orders, the El Al workers delayed

---

[17] Zamir and Mass 2011, 143.
[18] El-Saadany 1994, 105–106.

the plane's takeoff. Zamir personally met the head of the Italian security service, who hurried with his men to the apartment from which the terrorists intended to act and found six missiles wrapped in carpets. The man who was in the apartment was arrested; the Mossad operatives directed the Italian security men to the hotel where the rest of the terrorist group was staying. They too were arrested and the El Al plane was approved for takeoff. Roman newspaper reports credited the Mossad for informing Italian security services about the group.

The way the attack had been prevented—on Marwan's initiative and as a result of his intimate relations with Sadat—lent additional support to Israeli decision-makers' sense of security that they would learn of anything happening in Sadat's close surroundings. Paradoxically, in the coming month, this damaged their judgment when they had to evaluate the clear, increasingly accumulating signs of war.

Did Sadat know that Marwan would prevent the attack in Rome by transmitting the information to Israel? Those in the intelligence community who believed that Marwan was a double agent used by Sadat in order to trick Israel, and that he was Sadat's messenger in his contacts with the Mossad, would answer positively. Others believe in an alternative explanation. Didn't Marwan suspect that it would become clear that Israel had prevented the attack and that Sadat would suspect him of passing on the information? Those who believe he was a double agent would answer that he had no fear that this would happen. Those who believe otherwise would reply that he was concerned but willing to take the risk.[19]

But whether Marwan was acting on his own initiative or under Sadat's directive, this almost led to Egypt's incrimination in an attempt at a massive terror attack. Five days after the attack was thwarted, Dinitz transmitted the following request from Kissinger:

> In our discussion today, Naftali asked whether we were ready to provide him with the numbers of the missiles seized in Rome, so that he could transmit them to Dobrynin and demand that he investigate who had provided the terrorists with these weapons. He is scheduled to meet with Dobrynin on Thursday. Please telegraph.[20]

---

[19] Zamir especially feared this. When he met with Marwan a few hours before the war, he saw fit to precede the discussion of the coming war by clarifying the danger to Marwan's safety following the affair in Rome. Zamir and Mass, 2011, 148; also five interviews which took place between September 21, 2010, and February 19, 2012. Questions about the elite agent Marwan are discussed in the appendix.

[20] Dinitz to Gazit, Lamed Vav/886, September 10, 1973, Aleph-4996/2, ISA.

Previously, Dinitz had called to the attention of acting secretary of state Kenneth Rush that the Soviet Union had supplied these missiles to only three countries: Egypt, Iraq, and Syria. At this stage, he did not update Kissinger about who was behind the successful frustration of the attempted attack.

Zamir reported the story to the prime minister with Dayan, Galili, and Allon present. Upon completing the report, Zamir called attention to Dayan's impatient behavior during the meeting as "typical of the atmosphere during meetings in which Dayan reported on events that had occurred post factum," stressing the lack of trust Dayan had created in the smallest group of decision-makers who shared state secrets and determined Israel's fate.[21]

## "What Is Moshe Dayan Cooking Up?"

Dayan's conflicting and inconsistent appraisals have, in retrospect, made it difficult for historians to understand his part in the surprise of the Yom Kippur War. This is made even more difficult by the fact that in some cases, the minister of defense made firm statements in public without his listeners necessarily understanding the full significance of his words or what he was basing them on, while he took other steps as a "lone wolf," almost completely compartmentalizing others.

By May, Dayan had already rejected the "military assessment," which maintained that Egypt would not go to war before developing the ability to react to belligerence by attacking deep in Israeli territory. Dayan was then wise enough to determine that Sadat would make the decision go to war even without this ability, since his aim was political rather than military. Dayan explained that it would even be sufficient for Sadat to "take a step onto the east bank of the canal"; he therefore instructed the army to be prepared for war during the second half of 1973. Despite this display of insight, Dayan later began to sound much calmer about the possibility of war. This placating approach was not only intended for political consumption; Dayan continued to express calm until the morning of the war. How can this be explained?

Perhaps the solution to the apparent contradiction actually lies in Dayan's developing political analysis. Dayan had transmitted a secret message outlining his political ideas to the United States in June, and by September he began talking about his positions publicly. At that time, he saw fit to widely express his opinion that Israel should take far-reaching political steps after the elections. He also had a discussion with the air force commander, Benny Peled, at the beginning of September about "the

---

[21] Zamir and Mass 2011, 150.

need to prepare for political pressures 'with teeth.'"[22] "If a war does not take place," he stated a day later, "and I hope that it will not, political activity will increase, because the situation cannot remain static. In essence, if there is no military struggle, there will doubtless be a political struggle. . . . In this struggle, we may reach a point that will not only involve words but will also be expressed in practical moves."[23]

A week later, on September 10, as mentioned, Dayan expressed his expectation that Sadat would prefer "another political rather than a military round" to take place in another two or three months. "Israel is facing another round of political confrontation with the Arabs. It is unavoidable," he said.[24] Three days later, Dayan was already speaking of the need for an Israeli initiative. On September 14, leading up to the High Holy Days in Israel, he spoke of the "not-so-holy days anticipated for Israel after the elections, because, in the political arena, it will be necessary for the government to make some proposals to the Americans, some leads for unraveling the entanglement in the Middle East."[25] Yosef Harif, *Ma'ariv's* political correspondent, wondered in an article after a talk with Dayan: "What is Moshe Dayan cooking up?" The article detailed that Dayan had surprised everyone "with his suggestion to 'offer something' in order to assist Dr. Kissinger in renewing the American initiative . . . the intention to divide Sinai without Israel demanding to expropriate any territory from Egyptian sovereignty."[26]

There is no room for doubt. Dayan was presenting new political ideas and a novel political approach for action in line with the principles of Sadat's initiative, which had already been presented to Kissinger in February 1973—sovereignty over Sinai for Egypt and security for Israel. Moreover, Dayan had adopted the program Kissinger had proposed

---

[22] Quoted at a meeting of newspaper editors on September 5, 1973; Braun 1992, 34.

[23] Ibid.

[24] *Ha'aretz*, September 11, 1973. Similar comments appeared in *Davar* on the same day.

[25] *Ma'ariv*, September 14, 1973. Similar comments appeared in *Ha'aretz* on the same day.

[26] Ibid. *Ma'ariv* reported Dayan's planned departure for the United States after the elections, as well as a statement by Dinitz about expected American pressure on Israel in order to motivate a political process on September 13. The US embassy reported this to Washington on September 11. See Tel Aviv 7122 regarding Dayan's position on new diplomatic activity in the Middle East: "Arab states would prefer new diplomatic round to renewed fighting." This document is available at http://aad.archives.gov/aad/createpdf?rid=68658&dt=2472&dl=1345. See Tel Aviv 7276 regarding Dayan's position on new diplomatic activity in the Middle East, available at http://aad.archives.gov/aad/createpdf?dt=2472&rid=63576&dl=1345. The US embassy made sure to verify Harif's report; Harif confirmed again that what he had written was what Dayan had actually said. Tel Aviv 7411, September 20, 1973, available at http://aad.archives.gov/aad/createpdf?dt=2472&rid=73742&dl=1345.

to Israel on March 9, which he had repeated on additional occasions during that year. Like Kissinger, Dayan's plan was based on the same idea Ismail had proposed—determining an intermediate period during which a "state of peace" would prevail between Israel and Egypt, but not yet full peace.

In contrast to Dayan's past proposals regarding a partial settlement, he was now agreeing to base negotiations on Israel's recognition of Egyptian sovereignty over Sinai, while for a long intermediate period Egypt would agree to an Israeli presence at key points. As Harif, writing in *Ma'ariv*, put it: "As some of his colleagues understand . . . it [the basis for an agreement] is to partition Sinai for as long as possible (there is talk of twenty years) without claiming sovereignty over any part of Sinai and merely to exercise control—without affecting Egyptian sovereign rights over the limited area needed by Israel for security purposes."[27]

If, up to now, Dayan had outlined Israel's security borders based on the assumption that it would not be possible to achieve peace, now he was referring to anticipated territorial steps leading to a peace agreement. No less important, Dayan was publicizing his ideas during the days leading up to the elections and declaring that, immediately after the elections, he would leave for the United States to discuss the political situation. He was not presenting a fully realized plan for a comprehensive settlement with Egypt, but he was defining his framework of principles and proposing progress in stages. This was exactly what Kissinger had previously put forward—and it was identical to the political process Kissinger would begin to implement together with Sadat two months later, after the war. What was the reason for Dayan's change of heart?

In the Meir-Dayan-Galili triangle, the only cabinet members who knew about the secret deliberations between Egypt and Kissinger, Dayan was the first to internalize that Kissinger, as secretary of state, was set on leading a peace process in the Middle East directly after the Israeli elections at the end of October. Dayan also well understood that Sadat's ultimate goal was a peace agreement between Israel and Egypt under the auspices of the United States. He only assumed that, considering the timing, Sadat would not go to war before giving the political process another opportunity to take place. He also believed, like Kissinger, that Sadat would wait for the results of the American peace initiative, which was about to begin. The intelligence information passed on to him before the war gave him ample evidence to strengthen this attitude.

It was clear to Golda Meir and to Dayan that Israel would not conduct negotiations before the elections. On October 4, two days before the

---

[27] *Ma'ariv*, September 14, 1973.

war broke out, Kenneth Keating, US ambassador to Israel, reported to Washington: "Dayan's interest, according to [journalist Yosef] Harif, was to give the US administration indications of fresh Israeli ideas to draw Egypt into negotiations with Israel. He thought it would not be surprising if Mrs. Meir went to Washington in December or January." Keating added that "no negotiating position could be accepted by the government of Israel if Dayan did not give his seal of approval."[28]

Dayan and Meir were well acquainted with the high-quality source of information close to Sadat who was able to warn Israel weeks and months in advance about Sadat's intentions. They were tempted to believe that they could be sure of receiving a war warning forty-eight hours in advance, which would enable them to take diplomatic steps to prevent it. If the military tension increased to the point of the danger of war, Kissinger would act on the political level to prevent it.[29] This was Dayan's "political conception." He did not take the trouble to write it down, but it determined his actions and he kept to it until the moment war broke out.

## "The Americans Are Talking a Lot about the Need for Progress"

In mid-September, Ambassador Dinitz took advantage of Kissinger's confirmation hearings to return to Israel for consultations. On the evening of September 10, before he left for Israel, he met with Kissinger in the White House. Kissinger told him that the pressure from Washington to come up with new political steps would increase and that it was important for Israel to appear to have initiated proposals for progress.[30] Kissinger expressed optimism regarding the political process with Egypt. "Egypt is already willing to make a separate peace," he said and added, "It is extraordinary that the Egyptians have

---

[28] Tel Aviv 7699, October 4, 1973, available at http://aad.archives.gov/aad/createpdf?dt=2472&rid=81407&dl=1345.

[29] Kissinger's impression of Dayan was revealed at the beginning of 1975 in a discussion with President Ford, at a time when the political process between Israel and Egypt had become bogged down: "If he were prime minister, we would be all set. . . . If it hadn't been for [the events of] 1973, he would have replaced Golda. He has great imagination and courage. But he's mercurial and wild—like the others in their domestic politics. He said to me last fall [about a year after the Yom Kippur War] that Israel had to do whatever was necessary in the Sinai to get Egypt off its back." Working meeting of President Ford and Kissinger with Max Fisher, an American Jewish leader. Available at http://www.fordlibrarymuseum.gov/library/document/0314/1552941.pdf.

[30] Regarding the meeting, NA RN, NSC, HAK, Box 135; Shalev to Gazit, Lamed Vav/887, September 10, 1973, Aleph-4996/2, ISA; regarding the private conversation, Dinitz to Gazit, Lamed Vav/885, September 10, 1973, Aleph-4996/2, ISA.

not leaked my negotiations with Ismail. It shows they have not given up yet on my approach."[31]

When they remained alone, Kissinger requested that Dinitz "explain again and again to the prime minister that, in a reasonable period after elections, we will have to respond to the question of how to continue the game without giving up any card which is vital to us."[32] After Dinitz left for Israel, his deputy notified him that it had been leaked to the media that, at their meeting, Kissinger had hinted that "a change in US policy toward Israel should be expected."[33]

The ambassador took the hint and, on his way to Israel, emphasized to the media that "his contacts in the US government repeatedly stressed that the situation under no condition could remain at a standstill and that there would have to be intense efforts to find a solution. Dinitz added, "It is clear that Professor Kissinger intends to initiate a new diplomatic offensive in the Middle East after the Israeli election."[34] He continued along these lines at a cabinet meeting: "The Americans are talking a lot about the need for progress in political initiatives, and they expect Israel to be the one to make this progress."[35] Dayan was planning to leave for the United States on December 8, after the new Israeli government was installed, "to investigate various proposals that would lead to a practical and not just a political thaw in the freeze."[36]

These public pronouncements by both Dayan and Dinitz echoed the atmosphere in Washington, which was preparing for a new and unusual era in US foreign affairs in which the White House national security advisor would also be serving as the secretary of state. The new atmosphere in Washington was anchored in a document written by Bill Quandt, one of Kissinger's close aides in the National Security Council, who in his report predicted that progress would take place when Sadat proposed that Israel recognize Egyptian sovereignty over all of Sinai. The disengagement would continue for ten to fifteen years and would leave an opening for bargaining over limited areas that would remain under Israeli authority. During this period, Quandt expected differences of opinion in the

---

[31] NA RN, NSC, HAK, Box 135.

[32] Ibid.

[33] Shalev to Gazit, Lamed Vav/893, September 12, 1973, Aleph-4996/2, ISA.

[34] *Ma'ariv*, September 13, 1973.

[35] *Ha'aretz*, September 17, 1973.

[36] *Ma'ariv*, September 13, 1973; see the front-page headline in *Ha'aretz*, September 17, 1973. At the end of the month, when Dinitz met with Kissinger, he updated him that Dayan would arrive on December 8. Dinitz to Gazit, Lamed Vav/934, September 30, 1973, Aleph-4996/2, ISA.

*US president Richard Nixon greets Syrian president Hafez al-Assad in Damascus, June 1974*

viewpoints of the United States and Israel.[37] In his Senate testimony during his confirmation hearings, Kissinger called for negotiations in the Middle East: "Israel and the Arabs must be ready to carry out difficult decisions resulting from the agreement."[38]

## A Three-Way Summit in Cairo

Sadat could not read Dayan's thoughts and did not know of his hints. For him, Dayan's announcement of the construction of a port in Egyptian territorial waters (Yamit) was evidence of his intentions. That is what he told the Egyptian journalist Mohamed Hassanein Heikal on September 10, when he informed Heikal that he intended to go to war in the coming month.[39] On that same day, Kissinger and Dinitz met in Washington. Simultaneously, President Assad and King Hussein arrived in Egypt to confer with Sadat. Hussein was visiting Egypt "for the first time after years of ostracism" since Sadat had risen to power three years earlier, according to Arab affairs reporter Ehud Yaari's description in *Davar* newspaper, in an article on the rehabilitation of the "Eastern front."

---

[37] Quandt, "Developments in the Middle East and Chances for an Arab-Israeli Agreement." September 24, 1973, NA RN, NSC, Harold Saunders Files, Box 1173.

[38] Nahum Barnea, *Davar*, September 12, 1973.

[39] Heikal 1975, 12.

Hussein was not present at all of Sadat's and Assad's discussions at this three-way summit meeting, which had only one real intention—to coordinate the coming war. He was not present, for example, at the September 12 meeting during which Sadat and Assad determined that the war would begin on October 6. Like Assad and the Israeli intelligence services, Hussein also did not know that the military objectives of the Egyptian war plans were limited.[40] But what the Jordanian king did hear was enough to agitate him. Two weeks later, after he received detailed information from his intelligence sources regarding Syrian preparations for war, he arrived in Israel and personally warned the prime minister of the approaching war for the second time.

Hussein had clarified to his interlocutors in Cairo that he would not participate in the war. He had not forgotten the loss he had suffered in the war of 1967, as well as what he had gained from cooperating with Israel and the United States in September 1970. There was an additional reason for his refusal this time: joining the "Eastern front" would involve a demand to give safe passage to PLO fighters via Jordan so that they could join the battle against Israel, a demand Jordan rejected out of hand.

A joint announcement broadcast on Radio Cairo during the visit stated:

> In line with the interests of the one nation to which we all belong, in line with conducting the fateful conflict against the enemy, and as a result of the contacts between Cairo, Damascus, and Amman, it was agreed that the three leaders of the confrontation states would meet for discussions. At this meeting, all of the problems involving the three states were discussed, as well as the problems and preparations for the crucial struggle. It was agreed to continue discussions and contacts in order to carry out the solutions proposed, which are now being evaluated.[41]

The front-page headline of *Ha'aretz* read: "Cairo Summit with No Agreement." On the same day, Egypt and Jordan also announced the renewal of diplomatic relations between them.[42]

At the same time, Israel received reports from a reliable source that Sadat was interested in three more years of quiet. On the other hand, at the beginning of September, Marwan had transmitted information that "Sadat was continuing to talk about war, but this time had indicated that

---

[40] Stein 2003, 43, based on an interview with Zaid al-Rifai, the prime minister of Jordan at the time, who accompanied Hussein to the talks.

[41] Israeli Foreign Ministry report to the embassy in Washington, Het/955, September 13, 1973, Aleph-7072/21, ISA.

[42] *Ha'aretz*, September 13, 1973.

he was referring to a time toward the end of 1973."[43] This updated the previous warning he had transmitted in July, in which he mentioned that the war was to begin at the end of September or the beginning of October and emphasized that "in his opinion, the timing was not serious and . . . this date would pass like all of the other dates in the past." When Marwan transmitted a war warning he usually added his own reservations, indicating that it was doubtful whether Sadat would actualize his threats. He did so again the day before the war broke out, when he met with his handlers and the head of the Mossad in London.

Assad and Sadat kept the opening date they had determined to themselves for another few days. On September 22, the two leaders informed their defense ministers and the commanders-in-chief of their armies. This was exactly two weeks before the date of attack, as the ministers and commanders had requested.[44] In Egypt and in Syria, the fourteen-day countdown had begun.

## September 13: Thirteen MiGs

In early September Syria began to reinforce its troops at the front and put its army on increased alert. One explanation for this—which was accepted in Israel—was Assad's trip to the meeting of non-aligned nations in Algiers during the second week of September; he would continue from there to Cairo. One day after Sadat and Assad determined the date of the outbreak of the war, before it was passed on to the military commanders-in-chief, another unusual event took place, this time in the skies over Syria.

On Wednesday September 13, two Israeli Air Force Mirage jets set out on a sortie to obtain oblique photographs of Syrian forces in the Damascus, Homs, and Hama areas. They crossed the Syrian coast eastward, executed a wide leftward circle at an altitude of 40,000 feet, and left north of Tartus.[45] Simultaneously, as bait, four Phantom jets left on a reconnaissance flight, starting at low altitude over the sea until they reached a point opposite Tripoli in Lebanon; from there they continued in the direction of the Syrian coast. At 13:15 Israeli time, they too climbed to an altitude of 40,000 feet, flew six miles westward to the Syrian coast, then circled from a point south of the city of Tartus until the Latakia region, close to the Turkish border, where they turned westward and returned toward Israel. An additional quartet of Phantoms and a quartet of Mirages accompanied them over the sea at ten miles and twenty-five miles west of the coast. They turned

[43] Braun 1992, 35, 68; Bar-Yosef 2010, 208; Shalev 2007, 108.

[44] Shazly 1987, 149.

[45] A detailed report of the battle sent to General Motta Gur, the military attaché in Washington, September 16, 1973, Aleph-7075/12, ISA.

upward for two or three minutes, following the bait planes, and climbed to 25,000 feet. An additional patrol, the third group of Mirages, was on guard, flying over the sea in the Nahariya area.

The Syrians launched a MiG 21 quartet from the Hama airbase and another quartet of MiG 21s from Qusayr, directing them westward. Immediately afterward, another two MiG 21 quartets launched from these airbases; they too flew toward the sea and toward the two Israel quartets that remained opposite the Syrian coast. The MiG pilots ejected their detachable tanks and readied their weapons systems, a sign of preparation for an air battle.

The battle developed over the sea, south of Tartus. It continued for six or seven minutes during which the Mirage quartet patrolling the Nahariya area joined the Israeli force. In total, twelve Israeli planes participated in the battle (four Phantoms and eight Mirages) against sixteen Syrian MiG 21s. As the battle began, a Syrian MiG was downed; as it continued, eight more went down. An Israeli Mirage that had completed the battle was damaged by a missile about fifteen seconds after it started on its way south. As its motor caught fire, the pilot shut it down and, at an altitude of 7,000 feet, bailed out and parachuted into the sea opposite the Syrian coast.

The MiGs continued to patrol along the Syrian coast from the border of Lebanon north to Latakia. They knew that an Israeli plane had been hit, but not that the pilot had bailed out. A Syrian helicopter was directed to the area where the plane had gone down, but due to fog, it returned to the coast. On the way back, it picked up a Syrian pilot who had ejected over dry land.

Another Israeli Phantom quartet was sent to search for the Israeli pilot, identified him using his radio, flew upward to encounter a quartet of Syrian MiGs, and brought all four of them down. At this point, the Syrians directed all of their planes eastward, where they continued to patrol east of the coastline.

An Israeli CH53 Yasur helicopter had accompanied the photographing mission and was present at the battle in the patrol lane above the Nahariya area. It was carrying a medical staff and divers ready to rescue pilots and treat them, if circumstances demanded. When the captain heard the report that the Israeli pilot had bailed out, he turned north to the area of the bailout, but received orders to return to base at Ramat David in order to refuel. Although he protested, explaining that he had enough fuel to fly to the area and remain there for a time, the commander of the force ordered him to return and refuel. While the helicopter was refueling at Ramat David, "Zurik" Lev, the commander of the base, approached the helicopter crew and told them that the pilot who had bailed out was from the Mirage squadron under his command. He requested what was clear to all—that they return the pilot to the base. The helicopter took off toward the area and found the pilot in good condition in the water, next to an uninflated lifeboat. They rescued him and he continued to track events, standing behind the pilot in the Yasur. After completing this mission, the helicopter pilots were free to search for and rescue a Syrian pilot who they had heard was on the sea in his lifeboat. He was treated by the medical staff on the helicopter as it flew southward.

The Israeli Mirage pilot was, as promised, flown to his base in the Jezreel Valley, where his friends were waiting for him with a bottle of champagne and his mother had been brought from their home in Kibbutz Geva. The party was cut off when the order came to fly to Tel Aviv. The captain of the rescue helicopter and the rescued pilot of the Mirage were pulled out of the helicopter immediately on landing and taken to Sokolov House, home of the Israel Journalists Association, and told their stories—still in their flight overalls, with reporters facing them and television and newspaper cameras behind them. At the time, this was an unusual media event. "A Record for the Air Force in Battle," *Ha'aretz* called it the following morning.[46]

The political and security systems had good reasons for highlighting this event, which demonstrated the military superiority of Israel. No one wanted a war to break out a month and a half before the elections; the air battle sent a deterrent message to Syria about advancing the forces it had already stationed at the front another step forward. Israel regarded aerial superiority as a central component of its deterrence strategy. "Is there a connection between the battle and Assad's return from Cairo?" American intelligence representatives asked the head of the air force intelligence department Fursman, when he reported on the battle. He replied that there was no connection; it seems he was right. A day earlier, Assad and Sadat had finalized October 6 as the day the war would begin, but the air battle had no connection to this decision.[47]

## In Israel: "To Prepare the Army for a Period of Calm"

Israel's sense of confidence in its air and military abilities peaked after the events of September 13; at the same time, it prepared for a retaliatory reaction from Syria. To a great extent, this event also made it difficult to judge Syria's and Egypt's war preparations as they were being made, since the Israelis incorrectly perceived Syria's defeat in the aerial battle as the reason for its unexpected increase in troop concentration at the front. This was at

[46] *Ha'aretz*, September 14, 1973.

[47] Military intelligence report to the military attaché in Washington, General Mordechai Gur, about the update communicated to US intelligence services on the air battle. Gimel/5833, September 16, 1973, Aleph-7075/12.

the end of the summer, a period when, in the past, the Syrians had usually moved troops to the rear.

In his Rosh Hashanah (Jewish New Year) interviews, the army commander-in-chief noted that the Arab militaries were arming, but predicted increased calm: "We should shorten the period of army service ... we must match army conditions to the period of calm, and we will do this in many areas." Regarding a possible war, he stated, "We can prevent it; we can deter the enemy from war only by constantly maintaining a force that cannot be defeated on the battlefield."[48]

Immediately after the air battle with Syria, Dayan and the army general staff held far-ranging strategic discussions; only at the margins of these talks did they deal with the rising military tension. The first discussion took place on September 17, the second one week later, and the third on October 1.

Zeira, the head of military intelligence, opened the first discussion, as usual, with a summary of the present situation. He argued that Egypt had become concerned following the aerial battle and placed its air force on high alert.[49] In the long run, Zeira estimated, Egypt's and Syria's rearmament could harm Israel's deterrent power, but "despite this additional weaponry, I do not think that the Arab states will feel that they can overpower the IDF, capture Sinai, and defeat us in a large military operation.... I think that if we don't want a war of attrition to begin and certainly not a large war, we must find ways to maintain our deterrent power.... The Arabs will be very much affected by military incidents and small wars between now and 1978."[50]

Elazar directed the remainder of the discussion toward long-term military planning.

On September 21, Zamir met with the prime minister for a routine update, during which he reported to her about the operational actions of the Mossad. As usual, Yisrael Lior, Meir's military secretary, was present. At the end of the report, Zamir added,

> You know that we have received information about 300-kilometer-range missiles, the Scuds. We have verification.... Yesterday, we also received questions from [here a word appears which has not been released for publication, but from the contents of the document it can be understood that the missing word was Americans] on this

---

[48] Bartov 1978, 288.

[49] Braun 1992, 38–41. Regarding the discussion in the General Staff on September 17 and 24, 1973, see Bartov 1978, 290–94.

[50] Ibid.

subject. It appears that they too know something about this. It's the Scud, which they consider a medium-range missile. Between 100 and 300 kilometers. It has a chemical and nuclear head.[51]

This apparently meant that it had the ability to carry a chemical or nuclear warhead, not that the Scuds were actually equipped with such warheads.

After the war, Lior testified before the Agranat Commission, which investigated the failures of the war, that Zamir's and the prime minister's attitudes regarding this information was how to report it to the Americans in order to demand similar weaponry—Lance missiles. The investigative commission tried to determine whether Zamir and Meir had also evaluated how this intelligence information affected their assessment of the probability of war. Yigael Yadin, a former chief of staff and a member of the commission, put it this way:

> What is the intelligence significance in the fact that the Egyptian have Scuds, in light of our assumption that the Egyptians are always looking for weapons to be used against us? Deep ones. And that's one of the reasons that prevented them from going into war against us. I am referring to an intelligence "follow-up" to war.[52]

Despite the fact that he was asked about this time after time, Lior could not testify that Zamir and Meir had viewed the information as a sign of imminent war.

On September 22, as noted, the heads of the different sectors of the Egyptian and Syrian general staff received the order to initiate war on October 6. This of course, required deploying troops on both fronts. The troop movements were camouflaged as training, but were too obvious to be ignored. Israeli aerial photographs taken that morning made it clear that the Syrian army was already stationed in full emergency formation. Israeli military intelligence analysis of the Syrian deployment was as follows: "Despite the defensive character of the present emergency deployment, it should be remembered that, if the Syrians still want to have the last word after the downing of their planes by an Israeli strike, which is in our estimation improbable, the present deployment makes it easier for them."[53]

---

[51] Testimony by Yisrael Lior, military secretary, to the Agranat Commission, December 6, 1973, available at http://www.archives.mod.gov.il/Pages/Exhibitions/Agranat2/IsraelLior/7/mywebalbum/index.html.

[52] Ibid.

[53] Braun 1992, 39.

The second discussion in the general staff took place on September 24, two days before Rosh Hashanah. The only one who indicated awareness of the immediate danger of possible hostilities was the head of Northern Command, General Yitzhak Hofi. He did not actually refer to imminent war, but viewed the situation through the prism of his obligation to respond to the military force facing him. Hofi feared a limited strike by the Syrians against a settlement or two in the Golan Heights, and considered Syria more dangerous to Israel than Egypt. Israel had conquered the Golan Heights in 1967 in order to distance Syrian fire from the northern settlements, but the establishment of Golan settlements again brought Israeli settlements close to the front. The threat to the several hundred residents of the sixteen young Golan settlements had become a compelling factor in Israeli military planning.[54]

Dayan related seriously to the possibility Hofi raised and responded,

> The situation is very serious because, in theory, Syria could allow itself to strike against us, even if afterward it lost the war in the long run. . . . It could take the risk that we will bomb Damascus. . . . That one morning they could, without us knowing, send in tanks and take two or three settlements, or even more, in the Golan.[55]

Turning to Chief of Staff Elazar, Dayan said, "If I were in your place I would follow this scenario. I wouldn't take a Rosh Hashanah vacation—not even a break. Either you and the General Staff prove that Hofi's and my evaluation is mistaken, or find a practical solution to the possibility that the Syrians might actually do that."[56] In his reply, Elazar ignored the possibility of a Syrian sneak attack Hofi and Dayan had mentioned. He referred only to the possibility of total war: "If the question is one of war, in my opinion, this deployment does not change the air force's ability to finish Syria off in a day and a half." Bartov, who has written at length about this discussion, summarized: "Even though, in the second round [of talks], different evaluations were voiced with regard to what was needed in the long run—for the coming years—not even one person related to the coming days or months, and around the table, there was no sense of an approaching war. In all of the appraisals of the situation, there was no hint of fundamental disagreement."[57]

---

[54] For additional information about Golan Heights settlement, see Kipnis 2013.

[55] Braun 1992, 38.

[56] Ibid.

[57] Bartov 1978, 39.

Zvi Zamir was also present. The Agranat Commission later determined his position during the discussion as follows:

> During the days before the outbreak of war, he supported the military intelligence appraisal. And this is what he said in the general staff discussion on September 24, 1973: "Let's say that even under existing political circumstances as we may predict them, although with regard to the existing forces the danger of total war with the Arab countries is great, war is not expected in the near future. If we make assumptions about their inclinations, I will have to assume that if we are dealing with an appraisal for the coming year, their inclination is, in fact, not to go to war."[58]

There is no doubt that, more than anyone else, Zamir was basing his opinion on the information received from Marwan up to that point.

On September 23, after a short meeting with King Faisal of Saudi Arabia in Tabuk, on the Saudi-Jordanian border, King Hussein of Jordan requested an urgent meeting with the prime minister in Israel. Two days later, on the afternoon of September 25, the Mossad was still waiting for "an answer from the neighbors" regarding his arrival.[59] In the meanwhile, reports were starting to come in about Egyptian troops being deployed to the front. That evening an Israeli helicopter flew the Jordanian king to Tel Aviv, together with his prime minister, Zaid Rifai, and the head of his military intelligence (who was acting as an agent for the Mossad).[60] From there, they were taken to Herzliya to meet with Meir and Director-General Gazit. Hussein had not been included in the secret Egyptian-Syrian coordination. His intelligence sources were focused on what was occurring in Syria, particularly its military deployment and how this affected the Jordanian border; he expressed as much in his discussion with the prime minister.[61] He felt that Assad and Sadat would not tolerate a situation of no peace and no war, and he agreed with them. He stated that he was not willing to join a military action and that he hoped to direct a process to prevent war.

With respect to military information, Hussein stated that, according to plan, the Syrian army was preparing for an attack under the cover of a training exercise. "Does this have any significance or not? No one knows.

---

[58] Agranat Commission Report, Additional Partial Report, Explanations and Additions, Vol. I, 167.

[59] Gazit to Dinitz on the subject of Zvika, Vav Lamed/738, September 25, 1973, 14:00, Aleph-4996/2, ISA.

[60] Arbel and Neeman 2005, 190.

[61] For the discussion and the updated discussion regarding this meeting, see Shlaim 2009, 315–18; Shalev 2007, 108–18.

But I have my own doubts. In any case, no one can know for sure. We can only relate to facts." At this point, Golda Meir asked, "Is it possible that the Syrians will start something without the full cooperation of the Egyptians?" Hussein replied, "I don't believe so. I think they will cooperate."[62]

There were many hidden witnesses listening in on this conversation. The meeting was filmed and transmitted by closed circuit to another room where three intelligence officers, among them the head of the Jordanian sector of Israeli military intelligence, who cannot be named here, and Meir's military secretary Israel Lior. At the same time, Zamir was meeting with the Jordanian head of intelligence. Zamir directed most of the discussion toward the subject of moves against terrorist organizations, then the focus of his attention, not toward warnings of impending war. Some time later, the Jordanian complained that Zamir had not taken his war warning seriously enough but had been occupied with other concerns.

The content of the discussion was also distributed to others. At midnight, immediately following the conclusion of the meeting, Prime Minister Meir telephoned Dayan and updated him.

Among those who had heard the discussion with Hussein, there was general agreement that nothing new had been added to the defense elite's military information that they had not already received from Israeli military intelligence reports. Zamir also noticed that Hussein had chosen to emphasize that the political stagnation would lead to a military conflict, but had not given a date or remarked on cooperation between the Egyptians and Syrians.[63] "I would almost say that I hope that there will be a war; in any case, a war will not take place," Elazar said, referring to the king's comments.[64] The king's information was later integrated into the military intelligence reports. No one disagreed, although an intelligence report mentioned it in a later (October 3) consultation meeting between Meir, Dayan, and Elazar that the king had personally doubted Syria's intentions to initiate hostilities in the short term. (This consultation will be discussed comprehensively in the next chapter.)

However, only Meir and Dayan could weigh the severity of the king's warning, considering everything else that they knew but had kept from the evaluative bodies and other decision-makers—that is, the political aspects of the situation. The best person to testify to that was Mordechai

---

[62] Ibid.

[63] Shlaim 2009, 316.

[64] Statements by Zamir and Elazar during the two meetings on the morning of September 26 (Shlaim 2009, 316; Braun 1992, 40; Bar-Yosef 2001, 248). Elazar had received a personal report from Yaakov Stern, head of the Operations Department of the General Staff, one of the officers who heard the conversation between Meir and Hussein.

Gazit, and so he did. Gazit was almost the only party to the secret dealings between Kissinger and Meir and was with her during her meeting with Hussein. Later, he saw fit to emphasize, from what the king had said, that Sadat's and Assad's intentions were to break the ice of inaction, and deploying the army was an expression of this intent. He maintained that Hussein had doubted that the troop deployment meant that war was imminent; he had hoped that the political developments would prevent war.[65] Another witness who had heard the discussion, the head of the Jordanian branch of Israeli military intelligence, testified that Hussein "had given a warning from which I had understood that an attack would take place very soon if there was no significant political progress."[66]

Hussein's account, which he provided ten days before the outbreak of the war, supported Dayan's sense of the situation—that an expeditious political move would prevent war. This led him to assume that, despite the threatening troop deployment, Egypt would not go to war before giving Kissinger the opportunity to lead such a move immediately after the Israeli elections. An additional possibility was that, as he had done in the spring, Sadat was again using increased war tension to advance the political track.

On the morning of September 26, the day before Rosh Hashanah, two discussions took place about the situation in reaction to pressure by Hofi, the head of Northern Command. Hofi had been greatly affected by the appraisal of Avi Yaari, the head of the Syrian section of Israeli military intelligence, with regard to the significance of the Syrian troop deployments. The information King Hussein had given Meir a day earlier also hovered in the background. In the first discussion, with the participation of Elazar, his deputy Israel Tal, Zeira, air force commander Benny Peled, and Hofi, it was decided to upgrade Israel's state of alert during the holiday and add reinforcements of 175mm artillery batteries and two tank companies from the seventh division. "We will have 100 tanks against 800 Syrians. That's enough," Elazar declared. After the holiday, the tank crews returned to Beersheba and on Yom Kippur Eve were again flown to the Golan to meet the Syrians face to face.

About forty-five minutes later, at 09:00, the second discussion began; this time Dayan also participated. The participants again assumed that they were not facing a flare-up with Egypt. Thus Elazar stated, "I would not make any warlike preparations in order to prevent hostilities in the Golan Heights." Dayan did not disagree with him, but chose own his way to deal with the tension. He traveled to the Golan on Rosh Hashanah Eve, and the

---

[65] Shalev 2007, 110, quoting from a letter from Gazit to the editor of *Ha'aretz*, January 10, 1998.

[66] Ibid., 109, relying on Gen. Shlomo Gazit, *Mabat Malam 34*, 7–8.

Golan residents met with him at 15:00 in Kibbutz Ein Zivan. Dayan invited the media, including an American television crew. His objective was to publicly intimidate the Syrians in the presence of the Golan residents with a step that would create an impact. He thought that it would be enough to proclaim that Israel knew about the Syrian troop deployment and was ready to respond in order to deter Syria from attacking. Elazar had opposed this move, saying, "Dayan invited the television people and I said that it would spoil the holiday. We could have raised the level of alertness without ruining the holiday."[67] Dayan later chose to avoid this type of behavior on the day before the start of the war, when he needed to deter Egypt.

## Why Did They Advance the Zero Hour?

The long weekend of Rosh Hashanah passed calmly for the Israeli public and for the army. However, Elazar and his family found their holiday at faraway Sharm el-Sheikh interrupted by an event that took place far from the Middle East: terrorists hijacked a train carrying immigrants from the Soviet Union from Czechoslovakia to a transit center at Schoenau Castle in Austria. After negotiating with Austrian chancellor Bruno Kreisky, the terrorists released the hostages; in return, Kreisky decided to close the immigrant transit center. On the next day, September 30, life returned to normal and Meir left for Strasbourg to participate in a session of the European Council.

In the meanwhile, Egypt continued preparations under the cover of a military exercise, announcing a mobilization exercise on September 27—the first day of Rosh Hashanah and nine days before "D-Day" for Egypt and Syria. This was the twenty-third mobilization exercise in nine months. This time, the recruits were informed that they would be released on October 7. On September 30, there was an additional mobilization and on October 4, the release of the first group was announced. However, in reality, only 20,000 conscripts were released.[68]

In contrast, September 28, the third anniversary of Nasser's death, was marked with restraint and with a minimum of warlike proclamations in Egypt. Sadat's speech might have calmed Israeli decision-makers and citizens. The September 30 *Ma'ariv* headline read: "In a Speech Mostly Devoted to Internal Issues, Sadat Left an Opening for Contacts with the United States and Even a Visit From Kissinger." The article continued: "He hinted that his country was interested in a continuation of its dialogue with Washington and does not rule out a new initiative from the American

---

[67] Nakdimon 1982, 55; Bartov 2002, 311.
[68] Shazly 1987, 150.

*Meir and Dayan speaking with soldiers on the Golan Heights, November 21, 1973*

Photo: Ron Frenkel, Israeli National Photo Collection

secretary of state." The speech went on in a tone that would not arouse concern: "I was surprised when I heard that Kissinger wanted to understand Egyptian views.... I want to tell you that he knows our positions very well." Sadat referred to war at the end of the speech: "You have noted, of course, that I have not spoken about the war up to now. We have been satiated with words. I want to say only one thing: I will not promise anything and I will not go into detail."[69]

Immediately afterward, on October 1, the "exercise" began and was to continue for about a week. A real exercise did not take place. It was just a cover-up for war preparations, including deploying artillery along the canal and moving and assembling bridging equipment at the crossing points. The fighting-force commanders still did not know that they

---

[69] Oded Granot, *Ma'ariv*, September 30, 1973.

would receive orders to cross the canal. Before the beginning of the exercise, a few senior officers were included in the secret, including the commanders of the second and third armies. Israeli intelligence sources reported on the exercise and simultaneously transmitted information about the mobilization and the movement of forces to the canal. From observation points and from the canal front, information also kept flowing in regarding the war preparations. Zeira and the intelligence evaluators understood these to be part of the exercise: "The advance of forces and additional preparations being carried out or will be carried out in the coming days, such as completing fortifications, mobilizing civilian fishing craft, and investigating the operational fitness of the units, could theoretically be seen as signs of alert, but are actually only connected to the exercise."[70] This information gap created growing tension in the reporting and evaluating chain of Israeli intelligence but did not raise doubts among policymakers.[71] They remained imprisoned in their confidence that Sadat would not go to war before allowing Kissinger to fully exhaust the political track after the Israeli elections.

On the other hand, Soviet representatives in Egypt were aware of both the Egyptian and the Syrian military preparations; it was impossible to hide from them that an unusual event was about to take place. On September 22, Vladimir Vinogradov, the Soviet ambassador to Egypt, met with Sadat. According to Marwan, Sadat told Vinogradov on September 29 that Egypt would soon break the ceasefire.[72] On October 2, Vinogradov reported to the Soviet Union that the Egyptians were expecting an Israeli attack. This cover story remained intact even the next day; only on October 4, the day the information was passed on to the Egyptian army brigade commanders, did the Soviets learn that a war would break out two days later. They quickly prepared to airlift their people out of Egypt and Syria.[73]

In Syria, there were difficulties in maintaining the schedule. On Wednesday, October 3, Egyptian defense minister Ahmad Ismael flew to Damascus for a few hours in order to reject Syria's demand to postpone

---

[70] Bar-Yosef 2001, 251, relying on the military intelligence document dated September 30.

[71] Ibid., 251–66.

[72] Heikal testified that Sadat avoided reporting to the Soviets about the war and its timing; the report that Egypt would soon break the ceasefire was transmitted to Vinogradov on October 1 at 19:30 (Heikal 1975, 15).

[73] An official report was issued regarding the meetings between Vinogradov and Sadat on September 22 and October 3 (but not their contents) (*Ha'aretz*, October 4, 1973). Arbel and Neeman argue that the report to the Soviets was transmitted only to the Russian ambassador in Damascus and that only after the evacuation decision was made did the Soviet ambassador report this to Sadat, even informing him that Moscow accepted the decision with understanding and would stand behind Egypt (Arbel and Neeman 2005, 230).

the attack for forty-eight hours.[74] At this opportunity, the Egyptians suggested to Syria that they advance the zero hour to 14:00. They presented the advance as advantageous to Syria—a compromise between better initial conditions for Egypt and for Syria. Attacking toward nightfall would be more favorable to Egypt with regard to the angle of the sun, since Egyptian troops would be attacking eastward, but this did not suit the Syrians, who would attack westward. The low, setting sun would make things more difficult for the Israeli ground and air defense, which would be facing westward on the canal front, but would make the fighting more difficult for the Syrian planes and ground forces, also facing westward.[75]

However, Egypt's real consideration in advancing the zero hour was perhaps different. Two months after the war (and many years before the Israeli intelligence community questioned the reliability of Ashraf Marwan), Mohamed Hassanein Heikal, one of those who shared Sadat's secret, testified that "the hour was brought forward by the high military command because, on the evening of October 4, Israel had received information about the zero hour."[76] It would appear that Marwan did not know about this last-minute change, as he had left Egypt that very day. This is the explanation given by those who believe that Marwan did not intend to deceive Israel. Zeira would later argue that Marwan knew very well about the change but led Israel astray on purpose with regard to the zero hour.

Heikal's comment requires serious consideration. How did he know, two months after the outbreak of the war, about the warnings Israel had received on the evening of October 4? Even more surprisingly, the Egyptians had proposed the change in the zero hour on October 3. How did they know even then, as Heikal has testified, that Israel would receive information about the impending war that evening? We will discuss this question in the appendix dealing with Ashraf Marwan.

On October 2, in Cairo, President Sadat also received a visit from Abdul Salem Jaloud, the prime minister of Libya. A picture of him conferring with Sadat and Marwan appeared on the following day in *Ha'aretz*. The newspaper, of course, could not report on the contents of the discussion. Sadat avoided providing information about the approaching war to the Libyan prime minister, but asked him to expedite the arrival of the military equipment that Libya was due to supply to Egypt. Heikal, who was also with them, reported that Sadat had told Jaloud, "What I was talking about

---

[74] It is possible that, at this opportunity, the two sides coordinated the announcement that would be made at the beginning of the attack—that it was in response to an Israeli attack at the Gulf of Suez (Shazly 1987, 151).

[75] Heikal 1975, 22.

[76] Mohamed Hassanein Heikal in *Al-Ahram*, December 7, 1973, which appeared in *Ha'aretz* on December 9, 1973.

[the military equipment] must get here as quickly as possible, that is, within hours. Don't be late."[77]

The following night, October 3, Marwan left Egypt to organize the assembly of the Egyptian naval fleet and the squadron of Egypt Air planes. He later testified that he did not know the timing of the first attack of the war, but he did know that, thirty-six hours before it began, he would have to transfer Egyptian naval craft to Libya and that, twenty-four hours in advance, he would have to transfer the planes. Later he maintained that he thus concluded that the war was planned for the coming days.[78]

The next day, October 4, Marwan left Libya for Paris, where he reported to his handlers "that there were many chemicals"—that is, that there was much talk about the impending war. He asked to meet with Zamir in London the following evening. On Wednesday, October 4, in the evening hours, while Marwan was in Paris, the Egyptian minister of aviation ordered the director of Egypt Air to cancel all flights and to hide its planes outside Egypt. On the following morning, the order was remanded in fear that such activity would give away the secret of the war.[79] Between the telephone call from Paris and the meeting the following evening in London, Marwan verified the war information and gathered additional data about it, including when it would break out—or at least that is how he explained the additional delay in transmitting his war warning to Zamir. In fact, Marwan gave his only accurate warning extremely late; he claimed that he had found out about the opening attack only by chance. Even the preliminary report he transmitted to his handlers and Zamir did not seem urgent enough. His behavior led Zeira and others to claim that Marwan had been a double agent who had deceived Israeli intelligence, actually acting as an emissary of Sadat.

On Friday afternoon, October 5—Yom Kippur Eve—while Zamir and Marwan's handler were waiting in London to meet with him, the Egyptian chief of staff, Shazly, was standing on the shore of the Suez Canal with the commander of the Egyptian Second Army, watching the Israeli military post of Purkan, opposite Ismailia. It was enveloped in Yom Kippur quiet.

Far from the Suez Canal, in Tel Aviv and Jerusalem, the High Holy Days were busy ones for the political and military elites, who seemed overwhelmed with the information flowing in. Before examining in detail and adding to all that has been revealed in the research and the

---

[77] Heikal 1975, 14.

[78] Marwan's contact person communicated this information. He was with Zamir at the decisive meeting in London on the night of October 5.

[79] Shazly 1987, 155. Bar-Yosef 2011, 232–34, presented a different version of how Marwan found out that this time there would actually be war.

literature about the six days that preceded this one,[80] it is important to return for a moment to Washington and investigate what Kissinger was doing at this time.

## "But We Were Going to Put Pressure on Them"

On Saturday, September 22, the day the commanders of the Egyptian and Syrian armies received the order to start preparing for October 6, Henry Kissinger, in the White House, placed his right hand on a Bible held by his mother and swore to uphold the Constitution of the United States against all of its enemies abroad and at home. Five hundred people were present at his swearing-in ceremony as secretary of state, applauded the first Jew in the United States ever to be appointed to this position, and heard him promise to work for sustainable peace throughout the world. President Nixon also spoke during the ceremony, stating that he and the new secretary of state would work together to ensure that they would not miss the historic opportunity to achieve such peace.

Kissinger was aware of Sadat's target date for the end of negotiations and a subsequent increase of tension. Immediately upon his appointment, he acted to create the feeling that a real political process would begin in the near future. Kissinger knew Dayan's positions met his expectations for Israel. As far as he knew, these would be a good basis for a framework agreement that would meet Sadat's expectations as well.

The political schedule determined that Kissinger would devote his first days in his new position to the debates in the United Nations General Assembly. These were usually a platform for talks rather than deeds. Even during his confirmation hearings, Kissinger had spoken of his intent to demand that Israel and the Arab states make difficult decisions. Now, on September 24, after his official appointment, he would devote his first promised General Assembly speech to adopt a balanced policy in the

---

[80] At the end of 2012 and into 2013, the Israeli State Archives and Defense Ministry Archives released a large number of documents for publication that had not been accessible to researchers in the past. Bartov 1978 and Braun 1992 have provided us with most of the details, the former in defense of Elazar and the latter in defense of Dayan. Other researchers have summarized their findings and added to them, but only minimally. In essence, they have all tried to explain the gap between the information about the clear and obvious signs of war and the defense elite's weak response to these signs. Each of the researchers has his or her own ideas about who bears the main responsibility for this failure: Bar-Yosef (2001) emphasized the role of military intelligence; Arbel and Neeman (2005) blamed Dayan for knowingly leading the nation to war; Zeira (2004) has defended the position of military intelligence and particularly his own position, with the central argument that Ashraf Marwan actually was acting as an emissary of Sadat in order to trick Israel; Shalev (2007) has attempted to explain events from his own viewpoint as the former head of the research department of military intelligence.

Middle East in order to bring about an agreement. When he had completed his speech, he was free to go back to work.

On the same day, Bill Quandt submitted the previously mentioned position paper to Kissinger. It opened: "Developments within the Middle East over the past two months may well have increased the prospects for movement towards an overall Arab-Israeli settlement."[81] Quandt based his evaluation *inter alia* on the following points:

- Sadat had lessened his extreme statements about war and was more interested in diplomatic and economic steps to solve Egypt's problems;

- Sadat's foreign minister Mohammed el-Zayyat was hinting at a moderate line for an agreement with Israel;

- in Israel there was a sense that the status quo was not receiving uniform sympathy, particularly in light of the threat of an oil crisis; and

- Israel understood that now the United States would be serious about according the Middle East preferential status.

The paper also stated: "Dayan, among others, seems to feel that Israeli interests would be well served by putting forward new positions concerning Egypt that would shift US attention from trying to elicit Israeli flexibility to persuading the Egyptians to enter negotiations."[82]

On the following day, in an unusual gesture, Kissinger hosted foreign ministers of Arab states. He later met separately with Zayyat. "Kissinger announced that he would not begin a new initiative in the area before the elections for the Knesset. . . . For now and until after the elections, we will have to be satisfied with listening to words, and only that," reported the Egyptian newspaper *Al-Ahram*. Dinitz reported to Meir that before the meeting with Zayyat, Kissinger had asked Hafez Ismail "what he could say to Zayyat and to what extent the foreign minister was in the picture" and received the reply that he could speak to him freely.[83] And that is what Kissinger did.

---

[81] Quandt 1973, NA RN, NSC Files, Harold Saunders Files, Box 1173. Quandt asserted in a conversation with the author that Dayan did not have a personal discussion channel with Washington and that information about him was based on reports from the US Embassy in Israel.

[82] Ibid.

[83] Reported by Kissinger to Dinitz when they met a few days later, Dinitz to Gazit, Lamed Vav/934, September 30, 1973, Aleph-4996/2, ISA. Kissinger thus understood that, in contrast to Israeli foreign minister Abba Eban, Zayyat was included in what was occurring in the secret discussion channel.

A week before the war, on September 28, Nixon and Kissinger met in the White House with the Russian foreign minister, Gromyko, who warned: "We feel the possibility could not be excluded that we could all wake up one day and find there is a real conflagration in the area. That has to be kept in mind. Is it worth the risk? A serious effort has to be made for a solution because a solution will not just fall down from the sky." Nixon promised that Kissinger would consider the matter to be pressing and would, for this reason, leave for Moscow in November or December in order to aim for progress on the issue.[84] When Kissinger talked by telephone with Dobrynin one day after the outbreak of war, he declared: "You know yourself we are perfectly prepared to ask Israel after it is over to make accelerated diplomatic moves."[85]

On October 5, one day before the war broke out, Kissinger and Zayyat met again. "Zayyat and I . . . discussed how to begin negotiations for Middle East peace, which the US intended to pursue immediately following Israel's parliamentary elections scheduled for October 30," Kissinger later recalled.[86]

The next day, about an hour before the battles began, Kissinger and Zayyat talked again by telephone. The discussion was short and to the point, and dealt with the war both already knew was about to erupt in the coming minutes. When they spoke again that evening, after the battles had broken out, a disappointed Kissinger concluded, "I thought we had done rather well in our discussions yesterday [about the peace process to start in January] in establishing a basis of some mutual confidence, and I look forward to seeing you down here and resuming our discussions in November."[87] When quoting the conversation, Kissinger saw fit to add in parentheses what had not been said: that the peace process would begin in January. In an additional conversation, Kissinger again promised to keep his word "even if the Israelis are gaining territories."[88] Kissinger received the impression that Zayyat had not led him astray and that, just before the war, he had not hidden the fact that it was about to break out. The Egyptian foreign minister had left Cairo about two weeks before and could not have known about Sadat's decision to initiate the war. The secret of D-Day had been strictly maintained. The members of Sadat's cabinet found out about the war only one day before it erupted.[89]

---

[84] NA RN, NSC, HAK Box 71.

[85] In a telephone conversation with Dobrynin, October 7 (Kissinger 2003, 98).

[86] Kissinger 1982, 453.

[87] Kissinger 1982, 453; Kissinger 2003, 76; minutes of the discussion with Zayyat, October 6, 1973, 20:48, NA RN, HAK, Telcon. Chron. Files 1973, October 6.

[88] Telephone conversation with Zayyat, October 8, 1973, 13:45, Kissinger 2003, 129.

[89] Telegram sent by Smith, head of the US Interests Section in Cairo, regarding Sadat's reports to the Soviets and his own people about the opening date of the war. Cairo 3243, October 26, 1973, NA RN, NSC, Box 1175; FRUS XXV, 347–48.

The extent to which the political process was on the agenda can also be determined in retrospect by additional events during the war. One day after the war broke out, Hafez Ismail renewed contact with Kissinger.[90] In his message, he wrote that if Israel was willing to retreat from the territories it conquered in 1967, Egypt would be ready to call a conference to discuss a peace agreement. Kissinger viewed the very fact that Sadat had turned to him at a time when, more than at any other, he needed the support of the Soviet Union to be a great risk for the Egyptian president. He understood that "what was significant was the fact of the message, not its content. Sadat was inviting the United States to take charge of the peace process."[91] In the wording of Sadat's message, Kissinger saw an opening position only, not intended to "push Syria into leaving the common struggle or to lead the Soviet Union into decreasing its supply of weapons."[92]

In his reply to Ismail, Kissinger wrote that even before the outbreak of hostilities, he had informed Zayyat of his intentions and his willingness to seriously and expeditiously investigate with Israel and Egypt how to reach a peace agreement. "This offer still stands," he added.[93]

So only a few hours after the beginning of the war, when only a few had paid its price, Sadat proposed to stop and discuss his initiative for a peace agreement. Dayan was ready to accept a ceasefire. This time, he explained his stance in terms of military considerations: "We do not have to initiate a ceasefire. If there is one, we will not be sorry." However, Golda Meir demanded that Israeli forces must return to their original prewar positions: "Can't Kissinger mobilize another two or three countries to call for a ceasefire and 'let them go back to their places'?" she complained. "If we analyze the situation well, and considering the little support we have, they will tell us: 'If that is what you want, it would be better for you to withdraw to a place which does not give you any reason for war.'"[94]

On the second day of the war, Kissinger continued to clarify possibilities for political steps using the secret track (via the CIA). This time, Ismail had already narrowed his reference to Israeli withdrawal and the return

---

[90] Ismail to Kissinger, received via the "back channel," October 7, 1973, NA RN, NSC, HAK, Box 132; Kissinger's reply to Ismail, October 8. In this reply, Kissinger mentioned the message from Sadat via Iran; the message from Ismail, October 9; and Kissinger's reply of the same day (FRUS XXV, 347–48).

[91] Kissinger 2003, 110.

[92] Ibid.

[93] NA RN, NSC, Box 132; FRUS XXV, 367–68.

[94] Discussions between Dayan and Meir in the Prime Minister's Office, October 7, 1973, at 09:10 and 14:50, available at http://www.archives.gov.il/ArchiveGov_Eng/general/YomKippurWar

of Egyptian territory to include only Egyptian sovereignty: he demanded Israel retreat to the international border only in Sinai.

Simultaneously, Sadat applied to the United States twenty-four hours after the war began via the Shah of Iran, who transmitted the message to President Nixon that Sadat was ready to stop the fighting immediately if Israel would withdraw from all of the territory it had conquered in 1967. In that case, Egypt would agree that the territory evacuated would remain under international control—under the auspices of the superpowers, the United Nations, or another force to be determined. In addition, Sadat was ready for international control of freedom of navigation. In his reply to Ismail, Kissinger stated that the United States was willing to do everything possible in this context. In order to stress the seriousness of his intentions, Kissinger passed on a copy of his reply to Zayyat, who was in New York, and expressed his readiness to continue discussions between the two. Kissinger and Ismail continued to exchange messages for the duration of the war, but neither believed that it was still possible to initiate negotiations before a ceasefire was agreed upon. Only afterward did they coordinate their efforts to this end.[95]

Kissinger's sincerity in his efforts to achieve a settlement between Israel and Egypt can be viewed in his conduct and President Nixon's during the war. At the beginning of the war, when it was thought that Israel would easily defeat Egypt, Nixon was concerned that this might make it difficult for him to put pressure on Israel to reach an agreement. "They'll cut the Egyptians off. Poor dumb Egyptians, getting across the Canal and all the bridges will be blown up. They'll cut them all off—thirty or forty thousand of them. Go over and destroy the SAM sites. The Syrians will probably go rushing back across now," predicted Nixon.[96] Thus, Kissinger made certain that the airlift to Israel would not be accelerated.

On the fifth day of the war, when it became clear that Israel was having difficulty on the canal front, Kissinger and Nixon discussed what final result of the war would be most desirable for the United States and what to do in order to achieve it. Kissinger mentioned that, before the war, he had been putting out feelers for negotiations to begin after the Israeli elections, but now that the situation had changed, Israel should not be made to lose its security. Otherwise, it would be impossible to pressure it to reach a peace agreement.[97] Later, on October 14, Kissinger told the president, "Incidentally, should the Israelis clobber the Egyptians, that will turn out

---

[95] Kissinger 2003, 112–13, 260–61.

[96] Telephone conversation between Nixon and Kissinger on October 8, 1973 (Kissinger 2003, 138–41).

[97] Protocol of a working meeting in the Cabinet Room of the White House on October 10, 1973, Ford Library, NSA, Box 2.

to be a pretty good position. . . . The Egyptians are demanding a return to the '67 borders. . . . That has to come as a result of the subsequent negotiations that follow the war." Nixon replied, "We've got to squeeze the Israelis when this is over. . . . We've got to squeeze them goddamn hard. And that's the way it is going to be done." Kissinger answered, "Well, we were going to squeeze them. We were going to start a diplomacy in November, right after the Israeli [elections]. . . . And we have made all of the preparations for that."[98]

## "An Election Season Is Not a Convenient Time for Serious Discussion"

Considering Kissinger's conduct on the Egyptian track, we will now examine the parallel contacts on the Israeli side. With perfect timing, on September 23, Kissinger's first day of work in his upgraded position, Dinitz returned to the Israeli embassy in Washington and promptly clarified with the prime minister how to deal with Kissinger's new initiative. "Before my discussion with Naftali [Kissinger], which will apparently take place this week in New York or in Washington, I am raising the essentials of what I want to tell him on the various subjects. Due to the sensitivity of the issues, I request the comments of the prime minister and/or her approval for my presentation," Dinitz requested in his telegram to Jerusalem that day.[99]

However, the meeting with Kissinger was postponed. He was occupied with completing the organization of his staff, with the General Assembly session taking place in New York, and with diplomatic meetings with the representatives gathered there, including, as noted, the Egyptian and Soviet foreign ministers. Kissinger had already clarified his intentions to Israel; now Dinitz was forced to wait to coordinate a meeting with him, while using the time to "review" the points he would present at this meeting.

Dinitz's consultations with Israel took place with the recognition that Kissinger "considered that in due course, after the formation of the government, we would conduct consultations for the purpose of reaching an agreement on political steps."[100]

Neither Dayan nor Meir related seriously to Sadat's schedule for reaching an agreement or his emphasis that this had to be done before the Israeli elections. In addition to their full confidence that Egypt would be defeated

---

[98] Telephone conversation between Nixon and Kissinger on October 14, Kissinger 2003, 249–53.

[99] Dinitz to Gazit, Lamed Vav/918, September 23, 1973, Aleph-4966/2, ISA.

[100] Dinitz to Gazit, Lamed Vav/918, September 23, 1973, Aleph-4996/2, ISA.

in a military conflict—and that it would not therefore be worthwhile for Sadat to initiate one—there was the fact that Kissinger had now presented a political horizon for negotiations and was using pressure in order to advance these negotiations immediately following the elections. But, in contrast to Dayan's political creativity in sending up a personal trial balloon in the direction of the Americans and the Egyptians, Meir's policies remained frozen. Her orientation was not to deal with the issue at all until the elections and, even afterward, to move only slowly. These tactics were aimed at tying Kissinger to his promises in the past, when he was only the national security advisor: "to share his thoughts with us openly" and not to force a settlement Israel was not ready to accept.

In Dinitz's request that Golda Meir approve of the version agreed upon during consultations in Jerusalem, which he would transmit to Kissinger, the ambassador detailed a number of clauses that related to the political aspect. Three important ones were as follows:

> Clause 4: We have not closed our ears or our thoughts regarding attempts to find a way to achieve progress and to make efforts to move ahead and break the stalemate. Now, at the height of an election campaign, we cannot conduct investigations and inquiries, but after the new government is formed, the prime minister will initiate internal clarifications directed toward considering how it will be possible to at least attempt progress. We would be interested, of course, in sharing our thoughts with him and perhaps in working on common interests.

> Clause 5: At the beginning of the year, in January or February, the prime minister will be ready to come for discussions with him [Kissinger] and Edward [Nixon], if he [Kissinger] feels that this is necessary. These discussions will be oriented toward developing a common strategy, to use his words, as we have done in the past, which will enable us to advance toward a solution or at least to get through the coming period with understanding between our two countries.

> Clause 6: In the meanwhile, the prime minister requests that Kissinger help us to avoid the impression of tension or changes in our relationship. Such an atmosphere will not be positive from any standpoint. It is also important for us to get through the General Assembly session [set to continue into October] without using that arena to aggravate the struggle in the Middle East. The United States can help in this by not letting the Arabs think it will put pressure on Israel because of the energy crisis or for any other reason. It is also

important that the United Nations arena not serve as a platform for throwing out initiatives or thoughts in that direction.[101]

Two days later, ten days before the war, Dinitz received the prime minister's reactions to his telegram:

> The approach you have taken seems correct to us, but instead of clauses four and five, tell him: "As you know, we are not of the opinion that the present situation is the ideal one. But an election season is not a convenient time for serious discussion. After the election and the composition of the new government, we will discuss matters with you as in the past and we will consult together about what can be done. It is very important for us to arrive at a joint course of action as we have done in the past. This will allow us to pass through the coming period with maximum understanding between our two countries. We consider this to be very vital."[102]

Considering the corrected and more concise version, it appears that Meir did not want any political clarification, not even behind the scenes. She refused to commit herself to going to Washington at the beginning of 1974 in order to discuss the possibility of a constructive process. Dinitz saw fit to comment on that omission: "I refer your attention to the fact that this [corrected version] eliminates my reference to the willingness of the prime minister to come for talks at the beginning of the year. In my opinion, it is important to raise this possibility now in order to demonstrate our readiness for discussions with them and in order to give him [Kissinger] the power to buy time."[103]

Would a different reply from the prime minister have halted the wheels of war at this stage? No one can answer that. But anyone who speculates about this question might also take additional information into account. Along with Ashraf Marwan's various warnings about the timing of the war, he added reservations as to whether Sadat would actually carry out his threats. Marwan often repeated that Sadat could stop his war preparations at any moment. He also mentioned this at the "fateful meeting" in London, just a few hours before the start of the war. Zamir also testified to this: "During the conversation Marwan added his own reservation: 'I must tell you that if different political or military conditions exist, if there are important and decisive political or military changes, Sadat can stop all of

---

[101] Dinitz to Gazit Lamed Vav/918, September 23, 1973, Aleph-4996/2, ISA.

[102] Gazit to Dinitz, Vav Lamed/738, September 25, 1973, Aleph-4996/2, ISA.

[103] Dinitz to Gazit, Lamed Vav/922, September 25, 1973, referring to ibid.

this.' He did not know how to concretely detail what conditions were being referred to."[104] (This meeting will be further discussed later, in the appendix.) We will principally investigate what occurred there to strengthen Dayan's "political conception," leading him, even a very few hours before the war and despite the full information set before him, to predict that the Egyptians would not attack.

To Meir's dissatisfaction, immediately upon Kissinger's appointment as secretary of state, the political character of his appointment for Israel began to be revealed in the media. "Kissinger Will Demand an Initiative from Israel to Break the Stalemate in the Dispute," *Ma'ariv* announced. The article went on to state that this would be done in private conversations, not public declarations, and that "almost everyone agrees that this unwise stalemate should not be allowed to continue."[105] Uri Porat, the correspondent for *Yedioth Aharonoth* in London, quoted details published in the London *Times* regarding Kissinger's program for a settlement, transmitted to the Saudis for them to pass on to Egypt, Jordan, and Syria. He reported that King Faisal had accepted the program as a suitable basis for negotiations with Israel.

On the following day, *Ha'aretz's* front page read: "The United States Will Demand Territorial Flexibility from Israel." The article cited "the most reliable observers in Washington" as its sources. Following the war, the term became "a senior source in the secretary of state's plane." Likewise, the readers of *Al-Ahram* learned of a relative improvement in relations between the United States and Egypt.

The readers of *Davar* could take advantage of the two days of Rosh Hashanah and the Sabbath that immediately followed to give an in-depth reading to an article by the first head of Northern Command, ex-minister Moshe Carmel, who wrote:

> The deep stalemate in the Israeli-Arab dispute, which has continued for more than three years, is apparently nearing its end. At the beginning of the coming year, we may expect political-diplomatic activity that will disturb the calm around us, moving the Middle

---

[104] Zamir and Mass 2011, 148; Egyptian general Taha Magdub, the Egyptian counterpart of the Israeli deputy chief of staff, in discussions of the Military Committee of the Geneva Conference, which was negotiating a separation of forces agreement between Israel and Egypt after the war, provided similar information. This was in response to General Herzl Shafir's question as to what would have happened if Israel had reacted differently to the Egyptian military deployment preceding the war. The Egyptian general responded that Sadat could have stopped the attack even at the last moment (lecture by Shafir at a conference at Efal on December 2, 2010, dealing with the separation of forces agreement).

[105] Philip Ben, *Ma'ariv*, September 23, 1973.

East out of its paralysis and arousing strong debate about the methods of its solution. . . . Henry Kissinger's reputation as a daring and talented activist and as someone who has attained impressive diplomatic achievements . . . will not allow him to rest on his laurels in our area, defined as sensitive, complicated, and dangerous at this point in time.[106]

Golda Meir and Dayan were acting with the clear knowledge that the pressure would begin within slightly more than a month's time, and they were preparing for it. Meir was not moving ahead quickly and Dayan, characteristically, aimed for surprise with an initiative of his own. As far as both of them could judge, Sadat should have had an interest in waiting.

In Washington, on Saturday, September 29, Dinitz still had not succeeded in talking to Kissinger. During these days the tension rose to new heights. But it was the closure of the immigrant transit camp in Vienna, not the tension on the Syrian border, that led Dinitz to attempt urgently to contact the White House. On the following morning, Sunday—an uncommon time for a diplomatic discussion—he was asked to come to the State Department to meet with Kissinger. Kissinger "apologized for summoning me on Sunday and said that he had wanted to see me since I returned, but that this was the first free hour he had had. . . . He was principally interested in knowing about my discussions in Israel and also how we would plan the coming period together," Dinitz reported.[107] Kissinger indicated that he had taken advantage of his first weekend in Washington to read intelligence reports. As noted, two days earlier, on September 28, he and the president had heard Gromyko's evaluation that a flare-up in the Middle East could happen at any time. Kissinger had promptly invited Dinitz "in order to investigate our plans to begin negotiations in the Middle East before the end of the year."[108] At the meeting, Dinitz did not mention anything about the tense security situation in the north to Kissinger. Such an admission, he knew, would likely lead to an immediate diplomatic initiative by Kissinger. (Dayan's evaluation had affected the mood among senior representatives of Israel: "You know our friends there. They will be worried, first of all, at our expense," Dayan had said in Golda Meir's "kitchen" in April.) "I talked about how important it was that during this [election]

---

[106] Moshe Carmel, *Davar*, September 26, 1973. Moshe Carmel was an ex-Israeli government minister. On June 19, 1967, he was the only minister of the unity government not to support the government decision to propose a peace agreement to Egypt and Syria on the basis of the international borders.

[107] Dinitz to Gazit, Lamed Vav/934, September 30, 1973, Aleph-4996/2, ISA.

[108] Kissinger 1982, 463.

period nothing would be done which would create the impression of tension or of conflict" between the United States and Israel, reported Dinitz. True to his instructions, he also did not raise the subject of the security tension in their private conversation.[109] An intelligence report from the CIA and one from State Department intelligence, both of which included information about the deployment of Syrian forces in the Golan Heights, were on Kissinger's desk,[110] but it appears that he had not yet looked at them. In any case, he did not ask about the security tension either.

Kissinger updated the ambassador about his meeting with the Arab foreign ministers, in which "he had led them to admit that they did not intend to make real peace with Israel, even after complete Israeli withdrawal, and that they did not intend to establish diplomatic relations or exchange ambassadors with Israel, and that even after an Israeli withdrawal, the Palestinian problem would remain open," Dinitz reported.[111]

Dinitz read the written version of the message Meir had asked him to transmit to Kissinger: "After the election and the composition of the new government, we will discuss matters with you as in the past and we will consult together on what can be done." From what he said, it appears that Meir had retreated from her decision and accepted Dinitz's suggestion to visit to the United States at the beginning of 1974. "An excellent idea," Kissinger reacted. Dinitz added that Kissinger then said that "when he formulated a common strategy with us two years ago, he totally kept his word and neither of us has been the loser for it. But that horse is dead and now it is important to design a new common strategy."[112] Kissinger also gave Israel a target date for accepting his proposals to advance the political process—January 10, 1974.

The prime minister did not manage to reply to Kissinger's entreaties. After her speech on October 1 at the European Council in Strasbourg, she continued on to Vienna to meet with Chancellor Kreisky. She only returned to Israel on October 3, heading straight into discussions about the developments at the Suez Canal and on the Golan Heights.

[109] Dinitz to Gazit on his private discussion with Kissinger on September 30, 1973, Lamed Vav/937, Aleph-4996/2, ISA. In this discussion, the two also dealt with the commercial treaty with the Soviets, filling positions in the State Department and White House, and compartmentalizing the Israeli foreign minister, who had arrived for the UN General Assembly session and with whom Kissinger was scheduled to meet.

[110] Central Intelligence Agency 2013, 46.

[111] Ibid.

[112] Dinitz to Gazit, September 30, 1973, Aleph-4996/2, ISA.

# 7

# Six Days Before the War—
# Who Was Responsible?

*"I completely accept the conception that there is a difference
between Egypt and Syria. . . . To cross the canal, the Egyptians
can and will be farther from their base and what will it give
them in the end? On the other hand, the situation
is completely different with the Syrians."*

**—Golda Meir to Dayan about his "political conception"[1]**

Dayan's central and, in most cases, exclusive role in decision-making led
Israel to act in accord with his perception of the political and security situation in the days preceding the war. His importance greatly exceeded his
official position as minister of defense. As former chief of staff in wartime
and as defense minister during the Six-Day War and the War of Attrition,
he was the supreme security authority, both officially and unofficially. He
analyzed intelligence information and the military situation as well as the
head of military intelligence and the chief of staff. He had the skills, the
experience and, even more important, an outline of the political situation
that other military personnel and intelligence bodies lacked. His undis-
puted public status gave his conduct additional validity; this was also true
of his status in the political system, especially in the various camps of his
own party. All of these factors led the prime minister and other ministers
to accept his positions, determinations, and demands, even if Dayan chose
not to insist on them.

---

[1] Nakdimon 1982, 71.

Dayan did not frequently include other decision-makers in his considerations; whenever possible, he avoided sharing his appraisals of the situation with others. This was not based simply in the need to maintain secrecy: Dayan's character led him to behave this way. His close associates usually served as messengers to convey his positions rather than interlocutors with whom to evaluate these positions.

The events of the six days preceding the war required Dayan to deviate from his habits and reveal a bit more of his line of thought and his analyses. He was receiving large amounts of the intelligence information flowing into Israel as well as military intelligence assessments of this information. As in the past, he did not adopt military intelligence positions that conflicted with his own analysis regarding both the Syrians and Egyptians. So, for example, he completely rejected an intelligence analysis that maintained that there was only a low probability of a Syrian attack. Although Dayan thought that Egypt would not attack, he based his considerations on an evaluation of the political state of affairs rather than on an analysis of the military intelligence situation, as did the military intelligence organization.

Until the moment the war broke out, Dayan retained his mistaken belief that Sadat would not initiate war before affording another opportunity for a political process and would wait for an American peace initiative after the Israeli elections. This evaluation was reinforced by the fact that, in two of the warnings received on the eve of the war, King Hussein's (on September 25) and Ashraf Marwan's (on October 5), there was one important shared element that lent support to Dayan's political assessment: both had qualified their warnings, stating that an attack might be avoided at the last minute if there was a political development.

Dayan's viewpoint, which Prime Minister Meir shared, dominated Israel's decision-making during those fateful days to a greater extent than the mistaken military intelligence assessment. Thus, only if we add political considerations can we properly investigate the dramatic events of the six days preceding the outbreak of war and fully and convincingly explain the Israeli decision-makers' apparently puzzling conduct, considering the information available to them and the obvious threat it contained. This does not lessen the intelligence and military failure to evaluate the situation correctly or faulty preparation for the impending war, but it directs a great share of the blame to Golda Meir—and especially to Moshe Dayan.

## Sunday, September 30: In Israel No One Is Talking and No One Is Telling Kissinger

The reports of the unusual deployment of Syrian and Egyptian troops at the front began to reach Israel immediately after September 22, the date the Syrian and Egyptian army chiefs of staff received orders to launch the attack on October 6. Although this military movement greatly occupied Dayan in the days preceding Rosh Hashanah, he did not see fit to invite the prime minister to discussions regarding the irregular deployment. When Hussein hastily arrived in Israel to meet Meir on the night of September 25, Dayan only requested that she ask Hussein about the meaning of Syria's moves. He did not demand to participate in the meeting—or perhaps was not invited to participate. Meir, for her part, updated Dayan only by telephone on what she had heard from the king.[2] The absence of a security authority from the Meir-Hussein meeting was striking. The most senior security figure present at the time was Zamir, the head of the Mossad. Although, during his discussion with the head of Jordanian intelligence, Zamir had received Syria's war plans in addition to a warning about the imminent war, he focused his interest on another issue: namely, Palestinian terror. In retrospect, King Hussein and the head of Jordanian intelligence complained that the Israelis had not given their warning the attention it deserved. From then on the war warnings were left to Dayan, who was the supreme security authority in actuality, even in the eyes of the prime minister.

On the political level, it remained important to Israel to hide the tension in the area as much as possible, lest it move Secretary of State Kissinger to take unwanted steps. This affected Ambassador Dinitz's conduct during his meeting with Kissinger on September 30. They met for the first time in Kissinger's State Department office. When they finished at 17:30, Dinitz hurried to the embassy to report to the Prime Minister's Office. Kissinger continued to go over the material that had piled up in his office during his absence. A report discussing Syrian military intentions was bothering him; he had just spent an hour and a half in an intimate discussion with Dinitz, the Israeli ambassador and the prime minister's confidant, and nothing had been said about the military tension in the area.[3] The only thing Dinitz had mentioned about military affairs was to point out that the "Arabs are being strengthened, both from Soviet and Western sources"[4]—and even that

---

[2] Hever 1987, 17; Arbel and Neeman 2005, 189.

[3] Report from Ray Cline, director, Bureau of Central Intelligence, State Department, September 30, 1973, NA RN, NSC, Box 1173; FRUS XXV, 278–79.

[4] Dinitz to Gazit, Lamed Vav/934, September 30, 1973, Aleph-4996/2, ISA.

was only as background to Israeli requests for weaponry from the United States. Dinitz had been acting on Meir's precise instructions, which had not included anything about reports of unusual military deployment.[5]

At 19:45 (early Monday morning, October 1, in Israel), Lawrence Eagleburger, Kissinger's assistant, telephoned Dinitz on Kissinger's behalf and requested that the ambassador urgently clarify the significance of the information about Syrian moves.[6] After consulting with a representative of the Mossad, Dinitz replied that Israel was investigating the matter. Dinitz reported to Meir that Kissinger had told him "to notify him about any development at any hour of the day or night."[7] The next day, Dinitz transmitted an intelligence assessment to Kissinger: "Our people are now studying the situation based on some reports that have reached them. The present evaluation is that from the beginning of September, the Syrian forces have been taking up their emergency positions in a defensive posture."[8]

Israel already knew the information about which Kissinger had asked Dinitz. It included a detailed program for a Syrian attack that was to begin at the end of September—that very day. This information had not necessarily rocked Israel to its foundations; it was primarily based on Hussein's warning. During that period, Israeli intelligence surpassed the CIA in its ability to gather high-quality information on matters concerning Egypt and Syria. Considering this information, Zeira wrote that morning that Israel had the attack plan and it was no different than the one military intelligence had acquired several months before, in May, except for the new addition that all of the preparations had to be completed by the end of September.[9]

After the three-day vacation opening the new year in Israel, on Sunday, September 30, the military tension appeared to relax. Even the tank crews of the Seventh Brigade, who had been flown to the Golan on the eve of the holiday, were returned to their base near Beersheba. On that day, military intelligence distributed an intelligence compilation that cited a comprehensive exercise beginning in Egypt, intended to practice crossing the canal and capturing areas

---

[5] Dinitz to Gazit, Lamed Vav/918, September 23, 1973; Gazit to Dinitz, Vav Lamed/738, September 25, 1973; Dinitz to Gazit, Lamed Vav/924, September 25, 1973; Dinitz's reports of the meeting, Lamed Vav/934, September 30, 1973, and Lamed Vav/937, October 1, 1973; all at Aleph-4996/2, ISA.

[6] Dinitz to Gazit, Lamed Vav/935, September 30, 1973, Aleph-4996/2, ISA.

[7] Ibid.

[8] Ibid.; Dinitz to Meir's military secretary Lior, Lamed Vav/941, October 1, 1973, 15:00, ISA.

[9] Researchers of the events of that day rely on Braun 1992, 44–45, which was based on his private notes, and Bartov 2002, 313–16.

in Sinai. This was how Israel explained the high alert in the Egyptian military and the expected troop movements on the west side of the canal.

At the end of the day, army leaders had some free time to discuss the military situation. At 18:00 Israeli time they held a consultation in Chief of Staff Elazar's office about the Syrian front. The participants were Elazar; his deputy, Yisrael Tal; Eli Zeira, the head of military intelligence; Aryeh Shalev, the head of the military intelligence research department; Yitzhak Hofi, the head of Northern Command; and Benny Peled, commander of the air force. Zeira predicted that Syria would not go to war; Peled said that the only change that had taken place, from his point of view, was the arrangement of surface-to-air missiles and the alignment of the Syrian Air Force. Thus, he clarified that if Syria attacked in the evening, the Israeli Air Force "will be able to destroy all thirty-four missile batteries in two sorties lasting an hour and forty minutes to two hours. If the attack takes place in the morning I will need four to six hours to prepare the attack."[10] Israeli ground forces would have to block the Syrian troops during those hours without the Israeli air force's assistance.

Tal objected to Peled's appraisal that the standing army could block the Syrian forces and asked to reinforce the Golan troops with an additional regular army brigade and to call up reserve forces. Elazar disagreed with this objection. Later, in a discussion he requested with Zeira, Tal disagreed with Zeira's evaluation that the probability of a Syrian attack was low. But Zeira continued to argue that Syria would not attack without Egypt. In that, he was correct, but his failure was in his assessment of Egypt's intentions.

In Northern Command, where Syria's preparations were both obvious and tangible, the attitude towards the alert was different. The fact that preparations were not evident in Egypt did not calm them. "I don't need any more warning signs. All of the attack elements that they need, they already have. According to combat doctrine, all they need is the order to move immediately. For me, the signs are all there," stated Hagai Mann, the intelligence officer of Northern Command.[11] In the end, Elazar partially accepted Hofi's demand and it was decided to reinforce the artillery deployment with an additional regular unit and to increase the number of tanks and crews in the Golan Heights by leaving a reserve battalion force that had been called up for an exercise; later, they added a regular force from the seventh brigade as well.

Meir was out of the country at the time and her deputy, Yigal Allon, was serving in her place. Dayan avoided holding consultations or discussions

---

[10] Bartov 2002, 313.

[11] Gordon 2008, 170.

among government ministers to consider the information about the Syrian army's deployment.

In 1937, Yigal Allon, a member of the group that settled Kibbutz Ginossar that year, was sent for a military course given by the British at the Sarafand (Tzrifin) army base for Jewish guards. When he returned to his home kibbutz after completing the course, he told his good friend Sini: "It was simply great. I enjoyed every day. Except for one thing: There was this one guy who was unbearable, who spoiled the whole course for me. His name was Moshe Dayan."[12]

History placed both Allon and Dayan at the center of Israeli security and political events. Conflicts between them were frequent and seemed compulsive; they peaked in June 1967, when Dayan was appointed defense minister, over Allon, to take Levi Eshkol's place. Israel's victory in the Six-Day War elevated Dayan to fame, and Allon was left in his shadow. Israel did not adopt Allon's creative and daring political course of action for the areas captured from Jordan, known as the Allon Plan, to no small extent because Dayan had developed his own plan for the territories of the West Bank: the "Five Fists Plan," to place outposts on the mountain ridge. When Dayan resigned from the government following the Yom Kippur War, Allon was appointed foreign minister in the Rabin government and held the position until the 1977 political upheaval. Menachem Begin, who formed the new government in 1977, chose Dayan as foreign minister to replace Allon. Dayan led Israel to a peace agreement with Egypt, which Allon had difficulty supporting as an opposition Knesset member. Sini lived much longer than Allon or Dayan and in one of the conversations I enjoyed with this unique individual at his kibbutz, Yiron, during the last years of his life, he remarked, "The State of Israel would have looked completely different if Dayan and Yigal had known how to cooperate during all of the events of their lives."

The period of the High Holy Days that preceded the Yom Kippur War is one example. For four critical days of Egyptian and Syrian preparation for war, and through many warnings about its proximity, Meir was outside Israel. During that period, Dayan avoided initiating governmental security-political consultations. Allon, filling in for Meir as deputy prime minister, would have had to head such meetings; it seems logical that this

---

[12] Armoni 2008, 105. Sini (Arnan Azaryahu), who was, together with Allon and Dayan, one of the founding members of the Palmach, later served as personal assistant and confidant to Yisrael Galili, as head of the national headquarters of the Haganah, and, later, as a government minister during the Six-Day War and the Yom Kippur War.

would have been difficult for Dayan to accept. The difficulty was compounded by the fact that Dayan knew that Allon was not a full party to the secret proceedings between Kissinger and Meir and between Kissinger and Sadat and that he had not seen all of the reports from military intelligence and the Mossad. Before the prime minister left Israel, Dayan had requested that Galili organize such a meeting—but only upon her return.[13]

Along with this obstacle and the absence of orderly work patterns for discussion and decision-making at the elite level of Israeli politics, there were additional difficulties during those critical days. Dinitz had to return to Israel upon the death of his father to "sit shiva," the seven-day Jewish mourning period. Dinitz's deputy, Mordechai Shalev, conducted contacts between Israel and the United States but lacked the intimacy required to maintain this secret channel, which had been based on intimate and confidential talks. Kissinger stayed in New York most of the time, occupied with diplomatic meetings during his first days as secretary of state, which made it difficult to carry on steady and routine discussion. If that was not enough, the three parties to the knowledge of the secret contacts had carefully distanced Abba Eban, the Israeli foreign minister, from any of this information, and he was now visiting the United States. All of these factors significantly affected developments in the following days.

## Monday, October 1: "The Arabs Talk and Talk"

On the night between September 30 and October 1, Israel's leaders received a number of conflicting warnings, all from reliable sources.[14] "On October 1, after two o'clock, a telephone message reported that the armies of Egypt and Syria, under Egyptian command, were planning to open hostilities in the morning," Aryeh Shalev testified. He added that, following that message, which came from a senior officer in the Egyptian army, "a check of Egyptian ground and air forces had been carried out and it became clear that none of the steps necessary to prepare for the initiation of battle had been taken; thus, it would be impossible for them to open hostilities on the first of the month." Military intelligence analysts attributed the information to a military

---

[13] Bartov 1978, 301.

[14] The events of that day have been discussed by Braun 1992, 45–48, on the basis of his private notes, and by Bartov 1978, 299–301, as well as Bartov 2002, 316–21, which relied on and quoted the discussion. This section relies on their accounts. The following were based on and added to his version: Shalev 2006, 118–22; Arbel and Neeman 2005, 2004–2009; Asher 2008, 50–52; Bar-Yosef 2001, 258–66.

exercise about to begin in Egypt. "I did not think that we had to distribute information at night that, in our opinion, lacked any basis. There is time enough to do that in the morning, along with an evaluation of its significance," Zeira told Dayan, explaining why he had waited five hours before informing him of the message.

On the following day, when war did not break out, the original source of the information provided an update that this was an exercise that could lead to war if Israel took military steps. Two days later, on October 4, the source again confirmed that his error had been due to an incorrect analysis of the exercise order.

Another intelligence source who often reported on the Egyptian military system transmitted information at the end of September about Egypt's decision to cross the canal and gain control of the Sinai passes. However, this source had transmitted twenty reports of focused alerts for war in five years: the first in November 1968, six additional reports in 1970, six more in 1971, five in 1972, and three during 1973. Military intelligence therefore doubted the twenty-first.

Simultaneously, on the night between September 30 and October 1, military intelligence received a focused report from a source known as "Kotesh" who had good access to information from the Egyptian army leadership and who was considered high-quality, trustworthy, and reliable. According to this information, on October 1, a large Egyptian military exercise that would simulate a canal crossing would begin. The exercise would end in an actual crossing. In retrospect, with the wisdom that comes *post factum*, this was correct information. It even fit the reports coming from the field about Egypt clearing land mines from the canal. However, its intensity was lost—it was first misinterpreted, then was lost in a sea of other reports. The heads of military intelligence continued to maintain that this was just an exercise. The information was distributed to the commands, but with an emphasis on that appraisal.

Allon, Dayan, and Elazar were notified of these alerts. In the morning, the third and final summary discussion of strategic matters took place in Dayan's office (as noted, the first two had taken place one week and two weeks previously). At the beginning of the discussion, Zeira referred to the alerts he had received. In addition, he outlined the unusual Syrian deployment and the information from important sources that the Syrian army was organized for war. Dayan and Elazar heard all of this, along with Zeira's appraisal that Syria would not go to war without Egypt and that there was no sign that Egypt was planning to open hostilities.

Dayan, guided by his political assessment, accepted this appraisal as additional support for his evaluation: "The Arabs talk and talk, but they don't fire much . . . . On the way to peace, or at least, to non-renewal of war, I expect that there will be a kind of ebbing of hatred, or not fanning the flames into something active."[15] However, Dayan did not hide his fear of Syrian action: "We are sitting on Syrian land and, for the Syrians, that is painful. They have a case for carrying out various actions."[16] He explained that "if the Syrians get into our settlements and slaughter people there, it will mean complete disaster for us."[17] Bartov testified about Dayan's observations, "The election-eve psychological atmosphere permeated the consciousness of a public who had for weeks been hearing that war was not expected in the coming years. Consciously or unconsciously, Dayan feared panic."[18]

Later in the day, an additional piece of information similar to Kotesh's was received. In retrospect, it too turned out to be true: The Egyptians had decided to cross the canal and take the passes, expecting the superpowers to intervene. Egypt intended to open the canal to shipping and conduct negotiations on a permanent settlement.[19] The source reported that Egypt was concentrating crossing equipment in the area of the canal and had breached openings in the earth embankment on the canal bank in order to lower bridging equipment to the water. Military intelligence summarized the situation in a report distributed on the same day:

> Egypt—A military exercise involving many branches of the army began at 8:00 and the army went on highest alert, while the operations centers were staffed at full complement. On the night between October 1 and October 2, soldiers were about to be called up for reserve service; in Syria, the state of heightened preparedness continued. This included the air force.[20]

Israeli newspapers devoted their October 1 headlines to the terror incident in Vienna, Golda Meir's speech in Strasbourg at the European Assembly discussions, and her trip from there to Vienna for a meeting with the chancellor of Austria. Nothing was written or said about security matters, nor were decision-makers quoted discussing the security situation.

---

[15] Bartov 2002, 317.

[16] Braun 1997, 47.

[17] Bartov 2002, 318.

[18] Ibid., 334.

[19] Arbel and Neeman 2005, 209.

[20] Braun 1992, 48.

## Tuesday, October 2: "Israel Will Be Acting Foolishly If It Rejects the Kissinger Plan"

In the absence of Meir, who had continued on from Strasbourg to Vienna, despite the information still flowing in about troop deployments on both the Golan and Suez fronts, Dayan made do with a discussion of the situation with Elazar. When they met in Dayan's office that evening, Elazar summarized the day's information:

> The conclusions are that in Egypt, an exercise is going on and that can be said with certainty. . . . In Syria, in contrast to the information, there are no signs of opening fire. . . . Why they are deployed that way, I don't have an explanation. Either they are afraid that we will initiate or they are preparing themselves, and my assessment is that they are not going to open fire.[21]

"At the moment, I don't propose anything else," Dayan said, and advised Elazar to take only passive, defensive steps in the near future, including laying mines, digging antitank ditches, and paving a road—actions which, by their nature, would take more than a few days.

The Israeli intelligence compilation of October 2 detailed Egypt's continued deployment at the canal which deviated from any known past exercise activity and testified to an intent to attack. The interpretations of the information that continued to come in aroused an internal dispute among military intelligence, but the research department and Zeira continued to adhere to their assessment that these moves were part of the Egyptian exercise; this evaluation was distributed to military and defense system elites. The compilation detailed information about Syrian forces' continuing concentration at the front and the transfer of fighter planes to frontal airfields. However, it determined that at this stage there were no signs that Egypt was ready to renew the fighting, which the Syrians would consider a condition for significant military success; the intelligence organization continued to assume that Syria's intentions were defensive.

Almost all of the newspaper headlines that day concentrated on the events in Austria, their significance, and Israeli and American pressure to change the Austrians' decision to close the transit camp for immigrants to Israel. The front pages even noted that the Soviet Union had defeated Israel 101 to 78 in the European basketball championship in Spain. Four

---

[21] Researchers of the events of that day in the military and intelligence realms rely on Braun 1992, 48–51; Bartov 1978, 303–304; Bartov 2002, 322–23; Bar-Yosef 2001, 267–72; Arbel and Neeman 2005, 210–14.

days before the war broke out, not even one word was reported about the security situation.

If decision-makers had fully read the news, they would have discovered a clear message from Kissinger under the headline "*Times*: Israel Will Be Acting Foolishly If It Rejects the Kissinger Plan." The article quoted a London *Times* editorial:

> If it becomes clear that the Arab states are willing to conduct negotiations, even indirectly, on the basis of proposals which have been raised by the American Secretary of State Dr. Kissinger for settling the Middle Eastern dispute, it will mean that Kissinger has achieved an unusual diplomatic breakthrough. Israel will be very foolish if it tries to prevent an agreement with the procedural arguments or territorial demands.[22]

The article also explained that "according to these proposals, which were published in the *Times* last week, Israel would retain its sovereignty over East Jerusalem, would evacuate only a part of the Golan Heights and would retain a presence in a good part of Sinai for a long period." Even if Dayan skipped this report, he knew its content well. Kissinger's plans and intentions had been central in his mind when he formulated his own approach.

## Wednesday, October 3: "To Share the Picture Rather Than to Make a Decision"

Golda's kitchen group met at 10:00 on Wednesday morning at the prime minister's home. The participants were Meir, just back from Vienna, Dayan, Galili, and Allon, as well as Elazar, Peled, and, taking the place of Zeira, who was ill, Aryeh Shalev, who was participating in the ministers' forum for the first time. Also participating in this consultation were Mordechai Gazit and Avner Shalev, directors of the Prime Minister's Office and that of the chief of staff, and Arie Braun, Dayan's adjutant.[23]

Dayan opened by explaining that he had called the meeting "due to the changes at the fronts, especially in Syria and to a certain extent, in Egypt." He asked Aryeh Shalev, who lacked experience in presenting information in that forum, to present an intelligence review. Later, in testifying about the

---

[22] *Times* of London, October 1, 1973, as reported in *Ha'aretz*, October 2, 1973.

[23] The events of that day in Israel have been described by Shalev 2006, 147–48; Braun 1992, 51–55; Bartov 1978, 306; Zeira 2004, 165–75; Nakdimon 1982, 67–71; Agranat Commission Report, 14–20. The following sources were based on and added to their descriptions: Bar-Yosef 273–86; Arbel and Neeman 2005, 215–25.

meeting, Shalev mentioned the participants' impatience at the lengthiness of his report; except for Allon, all of them knew the information he was presenting. He noted in particular that Dayan was perusing the newspapers during his review. Dayan, as mentioned, had his own explanation, different from that of military intelligence, for his assessment that Egypt was not intending to attack. He did not take the trouble to share his explanation with the others; he apparently considered the many details Shalev reported bothersome.

Nevertheless, if Dayan was listening to the report—and, considering his comments during the presentation it appears that he was listening—he heard Shalev fully detail the information received; a precise picture of Egyptian and Syrian troop deployments; King Hussein's warning (though he did not cite the source); the Syrian war plan; the report of September 30 about the intentions of Egypt and Syria to start a war on October 1 (which had already passed); the military exercise being conducted, stressing that from these positions, both Egypt and Syria could immediately initiate an attack; the alert, which had stated that the exercise would end with an actual crossing of the canal; and Shalev's appraisal that war, even if it was possible operationally, did not seem to be reasonable. Meir also heard all of this.[24]

After Shalev had completed his report, Elazar, perhaps because of the impatience he discerned in Dayan and the others, immediately opened with the conclusions: "At this stage, I think that we are not facing a joint attack by Egypt and Syria, and I believe that Syria alone is not going to attack us without the cooperation of Egypt." Elazar attributed less importance to the intelligence warnings; he considered them not unusual and even less alarming than past warnings about actions that did not take place. He reminded his listeners, "From time to time, we have also known about dates. What we knew about previous dates—sometimes they were more realistic than what we know now,"[25] referring to war warnings from intelligence agents during the past year. But, in contrast, this time no warning had been received from Marwan, which "lessened" the importance of other alerts.

Regarding the possibility of a cooperative Egyptian-Syrian attack, Elazar said, "I don't see a concrete danger in the near future—that is, not as a

---

[24] In February 2011, I visited Aryeh Shalev at his home in Ramat Gan to interview him about the events of those days. His ill health made it difficult for him to answer my questions. After a number of questions, I gave up and asked him to try to tell me what seemed important to him. With tears in his eyes, he succeeded in murmuring, "I told her. I told her. On October third I told her." He could not manage any more than that. There was no doubt that, for the past thirty-eight years, Shalev had been living with the burden of those days—all the more intensely during his last days.

[25] Bar-Yosef 2001, 279.

function of the present deployment." Nevertheless, he stated that in their present deployment the two armies could immediately attack and stressed that the Syrians could cross the ceasefire line under cover of their missiles. Should that happen, Elazar recommended deploying reinforced regular army forces (more than a hundred tanks instead of sixty or seventy), and eight artillery batteries instead of four, without calling up the reserves. He estimated that the air force could participate in the holding action, attack, and be the decisive factor even if "we lose two or three planes." He seemed to have internalized the obvious or implied message of the policymakers: to try to calm the atmosphere and not intensify the tension by calling up the reserves.

After the chief of staff presented his viewpoint, Dayan explained that the objective of the discussion he had initiated was "to share the picture rather than to make a decision."[26] It was evident that Dayan saw fit to update those present about the military developments of the past days—especially the prime minister, who had been absent from Israel—but had determined that it was not necessary to react to these developments. He disagreed with the military intelligence appraisal and examined Egypt and Syria's intentions with a comprehensive viewpoint, combining military analysis with political thinking. His view of the situation was that of a politician examining the train of thought of the decision-makers on the other side, weighing political benefit in contrast to abilities and military danger. It is no coincidence that the only one who understood him was Meir.

Dayan, as mentioned, accepted military intelligence's assessment that the probability of an attack by Egypt was low, but he did not agree with their explanation. In April he had already rejected Zeira's explanation that Egypt would avoid attacking because its leadership did not see itself as ready for a comprehensive war in which Egyptian forces could advance deep into Sinai. At that time, Dayan had well understood that Egypt was interested in attacking in order to set a political process in motion. "That's also a way of getting things moving," he had said then to the chief of staff, and had ordered the IDF to prepare for such an attack.[27] Now Dayan believed that because Sadat had been promised that a diplomatic process would begin in the near future, he had no need for a war "to get things moving." It was certainly not in his interest to initiate a military conflict in which Egypt was expected to lose and which would give Israel additional cards at the negotiating table in the form of conquered territory on the west side of the canal. At most, Sadat could gain from arousing tension in order to demonstrate the need for political steps, just as he had done in the past.

---

[26] Nakdimon 1982, 70.
[27] Braun 1992, 19.

Regarding Syrian intentions, Dayan completely disagreed with military intelligence. He believed that the Syrians had a strong motive for instigating quick action in order to gain immediate territorial benefit. With regard to the massive missile deployment, he responded during Shalev's report, "Almost the only significance for this internal division of missiles is that they want to reinforce their line and their ability to act in the Golan Heights under the umbrella of missiles, as the heights are covered to a greater extent than Damascus. That is not normal defense."[28]

In other words, Dayan understood Syria's hope that, with the present deployment, it could succeed in capturing the Golan, or part of it, with a swift action:

> And here the Syrians are facing a situation in which everything that it lost in the Six-Day War it can theoretically capture in one step, protected by a missile deployment and the artillery it presently has, and after that, it has a relatively good defensive line, a natural obstacle—the Jordan—and it has solved its national problem in freeing the Golan Heights from our control.[29]

Despite the Syrian deployment, like the others, Dayan did not disagree with the plan Elazar presented for defending the Golan—100 Israeli tanks against 600 Syrian tanks and a striking inferiority in the number of artillery batteries facing more than 500 Syrian batteries. This would be in a battle arena defended by surface-to-air missiles, which might limit the assistance of the Israeli air force.

Afterward, Dayan examined the situation with regard to the Egyptians:

> If the Egyptians cross the Suez tomorrow, in one blow, ten, twenty kilometers and up to the Mitla pass, forty kilometers. If the Egyptians are thinking about a move like that, they will find themselves in a very uncomfortable position after that first step. There are many traveling expenses in crossing the canal, and afterwards, working in an area which has no end and we are coming at them from all sides . . . a situation in which the Egyptians . . . are not solving

---

[28] Ibid., 52; Zeira 2004, 172.

[29] After the war, it became clear that, at first, the Syrians had planned "to establish their defense lines along the Jordan or on the Golan slopes," but a short time before the attack, they changed plans and decided "to be satisfied with holding the line of cliffs on the Golan inclines and to establish their defense lines there against reinforcements." It appears that the Syrians avoided nearing the lower areas of the Golan, outside of the defensive range of Syrian surface-to-air missiles. When the commander of the Syrian tank force, in the excitement of battle, deviated from these instructions, he was ordered to retreat immediately (Asher 2008, 81–86).

anything (they don't receive any political benefit for the effort—they are not regaining Sinai) and they are in a much more difficult situation than they are now, when the Suez Canal is protecting them. If they cross the Suez . . . they are exposing themselves, so that there are quite a few people who are not stupid saying: "Let them come, because if they cross—all of the tanks will advance on them," etc.[30]

There were those who saw Dayan's final words as evidence that he wished for an Egyptian attack.[31] This conjecture was an attempt to explain his indifferent behavior in the hours before the war. But Dayan did not want war. His words echoed his "political conception," but that was not clear to those present except to the prime minister herself. Dayan's understanding was that Egypt was aiming to regain its sovereignty over the territory it had lost in 1967 by a political agreement; thus it would be a mistake on Egypt's part to initiate a war at the present time. It would lose from both a military standpoint and a political standpoint. In contrast, the Syrians were, in any case, not aiming for a political process but rather for a surprising and swift military achievement. If they could manage to break through the ceasefire line and advance a few kilometers from the line in the direction of the Jordan, they would be regaining areas they had lost in 1967 and would be establishing a more convenient line for themselves. That was the reason Dayan continually related with great alertness to the danger posed by the Syrians and concluded that this danger did not exist in Egypt's case and that a coordinated attack was even less likely.

The prime minister understood Dayan's analysis. She said to those present at the briefing,

> I accept the "conception" of the difference between Egypt and Syria one hundred percent. I think that no argument can be made against it. To cross the canal, the Egyptians can and will be farther from their base and what will it give them in the end? On the other hand, the situation is completely different with the Syrians. Even if they wish to take all of the Golan, if they succeed in holding on to a few settlements, for each step over the line, if they can succeed in holding on to it—it exists in their hands.[32]

Dayan's "conception," which Meir accepted, was clear: Sadat did not have the military ability to regain Sinai, but he did have a feasible political

---

[30] Zeira 2004, 173.

[31] Arbel and Neeman 2005, 221.

[32] Agranat Commission Report, Arguments and Supplements to the Partial Report, 19; Zeira 2004, 175.

option that might soon be realized with the help of Kissinger's initiative. On the other hand, the Syrians did not have a political possibility of recovering the Golan. This line of thinking was also supported by military deployment—Egypt's success in crossing the canal would be disastrous for it, as it would lose the natural defense line of the canal which protected it and the forces that crossed would be destroyed. On the other hand, the Syrians could advance a few kilometers in a surprise attack and establish a new defense line, under the protection of missiles, along the cliffs that controlled the water obstacles of the Jordan River and Lake Kinneret.

Meir, surrounded by intelligence and military experts, later testified that "nobody at the meeting thought that it was necessary to call up the reserves and nobody thought that war was imminent."[33] It appeared that, in assessing the military situation, the prime minister could not have been expected to come to a different conclusion than the military experts. But this was not the case regarding her ability to read the political state of affairs.

After the consultation in the "kitchen," a cabinet meeting was called. The unusual security situation that had so occupied the security-political leadership, was not discussed at all at this meeting. Allon had proposed a separate discussion on this issue at a cabinet meeting on October 7, and the prime minister had agreed.

At exactly the same time, in Damascus, the president of Syria was agreeing to the Egyptian war minister Ismail Ali's proposal not to postpone the date of the first attack and to attack on Saturday at 14:00. At the two fronts, Egyptian and Syrian forces were continuing in their preparations, which could not be camouflaged from the Soviets in Egypt. In Cairo, Ashraf Marwan heard wonderment at the fact that Israel had not taken any steps in anticipation of the coming war. In the evening, he had to travel to Libya to deal with the transfer of the Egyptian navy and air fleets, a sign for him that war was imminent.

Israel took several military actions: it put the reserve mobilization system on high alert in case it would be needed. Northern Command was instructed to carry out additional moves, creating obstacles to a possible Syrian incursion—laying four thousand land mines and digging an anti-tank ditch six kilometers long. These were to be completed by October 9.

And what of the media?

---

[33] Meir 1975, 406–7.

Three days before the war, the front-page headlines were mostly devoted to the discussion between the prime minister and the chancellor of Austria, the implications of the terror event in Austria, and the Israeli basketball team's stinging loss to Turkey, 93 to 94 in overtime. Regarding the security situation, the Israeli government had held a press briefing for military affairs reporters a day earlier, on October 2, asking them to play down the reports of concentrations of Egyptian and Syrian forces. *Ha'aretz* reported marginally that "no tension was to be seen yesterday on the banks of the canal." This was a new item intended solely to refute "the information from Cairo that a state of alert had been announced in the Egyptian army units along the Suez Canal."[34]

The following evening, at an election campaign assembly in Givatayim, the prime minister proclaimed, "In a few more years, the Arabs will receive less territory from us in return than what they could have received at present."

## Thursday, October 4: "This Month We Will Not Transform the World"

The defense minister's viewpoint continued to dictate Israel's approach to its situation.[35] In the morning, Dayan summoned to his office Chief of Staff Elazar; Tal, his deputy; Hofi, the head of Northern Command; and Shalev, still filling in for Zeira. The participants and contents of the discussions are evidence that the IDF was being guided by Dayan's way of thinking, according to which Egypt would not attack and attention should thus only be devoted to the Syrian sector. Even with regard to Syria, Dayan did not speak in terms of a comprehensive war or even an urgent situation due to an immediate, specific threat.

Dayan asked those present, the IDF elite responsible for the Syrian sector, for a solution that would prevent a pointed, opportunistic Syrian thrust to harm one or more settlements in the Golan Heights.

> My trauma is not about the [Golan] Heights but about the settlements there whether they [the Syrians] break through or not, I think it is worthwhile and necessary for the State of Israel, for the IDF, to invest a large amount of money and much work, and more money and more work . . . to create a situation so that they [the Syrians] cannot just get up and go, so that they will have to work on it. If we have three days, we can delay them, call up the reserves; even one

---

[34] All of the information in this paragraph appeared in *Ha'aretz*, October 3, 1973.

[35] About the events of the first part of the day: Braun 1992, 55–56; Bartov 1978, 311–12; Bartov 2002, 329–31.

day, just not a surprise. . . . I'll buy any idea: fish ponds, land mines, anything anyone can think of.[36]

Those were Dayan's words. After the participants discussed preparing ground impediments, Hofi spoke: "If we are well-organized with our tanks, even without the air force, we won't have any problem with the Golan Heights." But that was not what Dayan meant. "In a situation where you don't mobilize the reserves?" he asked. Dayan was hoping for a deployment plan that would not require Israel to maintain a reinforced armored corps. He summarized these consultations:

> The general assumption is that they [the Syrians] will not take action without Egypt, and the Egyptians are not going [to initiate a war]. Let's say for the sake of argument that they will. This month [October, with the elections planned at the end of the month] we will not transform the world. After this month, winter will begin. In winter, it is clear that no serious war takes place. . . . If I summarize: what can be done this month should be done. What is impossible, a plan should be made of how much it has to cost. "[37]

It is a bit difficult to believe, but on the same day, two days before the war, the general staff held a routine meeting to discuss army discipline; no outline of the military situation was given. Perhaps this stemmed from the desire not to initiate a discussion that could arouse argument regarding the need to mobilize the reserves. In the summer of 1967, the general staff had been drawn into a conflict with decision-makers, demanding to initiate hostilities before all of the political steps had been completely explored. Calling up the reserves in the face of the Egyptian and Syrian threat led Israel to a dead end and forced it to initiate war in order to extricate itself from that decision. Neither did Meir, who appeared that day in the Foreign Affairs and Defense Committee, speak of the military situation; instead she discussed the humiliating treatment she had received from the Austrian chancellor.[38]

Three incidents that took place later in the day were convincing enough to indicate that Egypt was intending to go to war—and therefore that the war

---

[36] Braun 1992, 55.

[37] Ibid.

[38] Meir's assistants testified that "Kreisky had not even offered her a cup of water during their meeting, not to mention coffee" (Medzini 2008, 541).

would be a comprehensive one. Information accumulated gradually and the security elite were apprised of the full picture only after midnight. They discussed its implications the following morning, October 5.

The first piece of information resulted from an aerial reconnaissance sortie over the canal.[39] Toward nighttime, it became clear from the photographs that the crossing equipment had been brought closer to the canal. The reinforced Egyptian armored and artillery corps were deployed at battle positions and a dense battery of surface-to-air missiles could be seen. This information fit reports from the observation points at the canal, but it might also have been interpreted as part of the Egyptian military exercise. What was lacking was an expert personal view from the senior level of leadership. The Agranat Commission found that, during the week before the war, the head of the Southern Command, Shmuel "Gorodish" Gonen, and his intelligence officer only visited the canal line once. Perhaps his physical distance from the front explains why he did not receive a firsthand impression.

The second piece of information was a preliminary report of the evacuation of Soviet advisors' wives and children, who began to arrive from Syria in the afternoon hours. The information indicated that the families had received instructions to wait, with limited luggage, for bus transportation and evacuation by sea from the port of Latakia. It was later reported that the evacuation would be carried out by air; the first planes arrived in Damascus shortly before midnight. Information also arrived about preparations for an air evacuation from Cairo, where the first plane arrived shortly after midnight.[40]

The third event also took place toward midnight. Mossad agent Ashraf Marwan made contact with his handlers and warned them in code about accelerated preparations for war, but did not provide information about the date and even avoided using the code word that was meant to announce it. He asked to meet the head of the Mossad on the following evening in London.

Zeira and Zamir cross-checked all of this information and transmitted it to Elazar, Dayan, and Meir. It was presented to the political and defense leadership in the early hours of the morning, and as mentioned, set a chain of discussion in motion, beginning on the following morning, a shortened work day for Yom Kippur Eve.

And the media?

---

[39] Agranat Commission Report, 310–11.

[40] Information passed on by Shalev, filling in for Dinitz, to the White House on October 5, 1973, 17:00, NA RN, NSC, Country Files, HAK, Box 136; for more about this see Ben Porat 1991, 60–61; at length, Zeira 2004, 177, 179–82.

Two days before the war, loyal to the censor's instructions, newspaper editors avoided reporting on the situation. Military reporters discussed this after the war, testifying that

> in the ten days that preceded the war, there was a clear orientation in Israel to prevent any possibility of warning in the state media. Information that indicated Egypt's and Syria's intent to initiate large-scale hostile action was systematically and consciously prohibited from being published. The experiences of the Israeli military correspondents who inspected the ceasefire lines and came in contact with the low-level command during these ten days prove this.[41]

Only one short news item referred to this: Dado Elazar had warned the Egyptians and Syrians, who were concentrating their forces at the front, at a paratroopers' conference the day before at Kfar Maccabiah.

The following morning, readers of *Ha'aretz* read the front-page headline: "Kissinger Is Opening Discussions with Eban and Arab Foreign Ministers." The sub-headlines added: "The United States' Good Offices Will Be Offered to Guide the Sides Toward Negotiations to Settle the Conflict."

## Friday, October 5: "The Russians Know That the Egyptians and Syrians Are Going to Attack"

The short workday of Yom Kippur Eve turned out to be particularly long.

The rush of events began in the early hours of the morning. At about midnight, a message reached Israel from Marwan's contacts, along with his request to meet with the head of the Mossad. As noted, Marwan did not use the agreed-upon code word for war, but rather gave a general warning about preparations for one.[42] The wording of Marwan's request and the fact that it had not opened the report arriving from Paris moderated its urgency. It appears that this was why Zamir did not sense an emergency situation and not hurry to update anyone outside the Mossad about it. The unusual thing about the incoming information from the secret agent was

---

[41] Ben Porat et al. 1974, 53–55. A short time after the war, Yeshayahu Ben Porat, Yonatan Gefen, Uri Dan, Eitan Haber, Hezi Carmel, Eli Landau, and Eli Tavor, all newspaper reporters and among them experienced military commentators, contributed to a book about their personal views of the events that preceded the war and the war period. See also Bartov 1978, 317.

[42] Regarding the report from Marwan and the events that followed until his meeting with Zamir on the night of October 5: Zamir 2011, 146–47; protocol of the testimony of Freddie Eini, Mossad bureau chief, to the Agranat Commission, available at http://www.archives.mod.gov.il/Pages/Exhibitions/Agranat2/AlfredEini/15/mywebalbum/index.html.

the dictated date and time of the meeting with the head of the Mossad, which did not fit the pattern of communication up to that point.

A short time later, at 01:00 Israeli time, Zeira telephoned his colleague Zamir. According to his later testimony, this was the first time since being appointed a year earlier that Zeira had done so at such a late hour. The information about the Soviet evacuation marked a dramatic change for him in the level of tension. During this call, Zamir did not mention Marwan's request, nor did he note that he would leave that evening for London to determine the meaning of Marwan's warning.[43] It seems that Zamir was still not aware of the urgency in Marwan's request for a meeting.

About two hours later, Zamir's telephone rang again. His bureau chief, Freddie Eini, spoke to him for a second time, and only now did Zamir understand that the reference was to war. He then transmitted to Eini the news of the evacuation of Soviet families. Zamir then called Zeira and updated him about Marwan's request. "This means war; we don't have a date because a hint is not a date," said Zamir. He saw the fact that Marwan did not cite an exact date as evidence that an immediate step was not to be expected.

Zamir's flight to London was scheduled for that afternoon. Only after he had taken Zamir to the airport and returned to his office at the Mossad did the bureau chief call the prime minister's military secretary, Yisrael Lior. The secretary was unavailable, so he left a message asking him to call back. Meir found out about Zamir's trip to London at the cabinet meeting from Dayan, who had been informed of the trip by Zeira.

Marwan himself supplied an explanation for the unhurried conduct of affairs. He stated that, when he had called from Paris and asked to meet with Zamir, he had not known that war would break out within forty hours and had even doubted that it would take place at all. "In my opinion," Zamir testified years later, "Marwan did not want to say that war would break out without adding the background and the complementary factors, as well as the possible reservations according to which, if conditions changed at the last moment, Sadat might retreat from his warlike intentions."[44]

If Marwan's information still did not testify to an immediate war, the hasty Soviet evacuation should have been evidence of the highest probability of an attack in the coming hours.

Military intelligence reported the following:

---

[43] Eini testimony.
[44] Zamir and Mass 2011, 147.

Between 23:50 on October 4 and 03:30 on October 5, five Soviet Aeroflot IL–18 passenger planes landed at the international airport in Damascus. Two of the planes arrived from Budapest. All five took off later on October 5 and flew north. The tail numbers on the planes were 75676, 75602, 75516, 75465, and 75454. According to one report, Russian families (women and children) were seen at the airport, apparently being evacuated from Syria. Between 00:20 and 04:30 on October 5, six Aeroflot passenger planes landed in Cairo. Four of them were IL-18 and two were IL-62. Four of the six took off a few hours later (starting from 07:10) and flew to the Soviet Union. The tail numbers of the IL-18 planes were 75894, 74261, 75784, 74262, and those of the IL-62 were 86699 and 86698. In addition, it is known that seven ships of the Soviet fleet were scheduled to leave in the morning of October 5 from the port of Alexandria. Likewise, on October 4, a Soviet ship left the harbor of Port Said and a military landing craft left on the morning of October 5. An additional Soviet sea craft anchored in Marsa Matruh was also due to leave the port.[45]

A military intelligence compilation disseminated at 05:45 that morning summarized an aerial reconnaissance photograph of the Suez Canal front with the comment: "The Egyptian army at the canal front is in emergency deployment, one we have never seen in the past."

Israeli military intelligence followed a large volume of information in real time and reported its essence to decision-makers, who pondered its significance over the next few hours but did not succeed in understanding what should have been obvious—even when, as we shall see, Zeira presented this conclusion as the only possible reasonable explanation: the Soviets were expecting a coordinated Egyptian and Syrian attack in the coming hours. Israeli decision-makers found it convenient to maintain the illusion that Marwan would supply an exact warning a reasonable time in advance; as he had still not done that, the warning light of the Soviet evacuation and the accompanying alert siren could be ignored.

"Just looking at the numbers could bring on a stroke," Dayan commented that morning as he looked at the military intelligence report on Egyptian and Syrian deployment.[46] Whether due to external or internal political

---

[45] Intelligence report that included the Israeli assessment of low probability for war, Shalev to Nixon, October 5, 1973, 17:00, NA RN, NSC, Country Files, HAK, Box 136.

[46] Descriptions of the events of that day have been presented by: Braun 1992, 57–67; Bartov 1978, 315–24; Agranat Commission Report. Relying on these descriptions and

considerations, even on Yom Kippur Eve, the Israeli media obeyed the military censor and made no mention of the situation. However, no one who heard Dayan speak at the discussion held in his office could have had any doubt that he well understood the military significance of the information reported to him.

What Dayan said next, which did not receive great attention, testified to his train of thought and line of action, based on the political dimension: "You are not taking the Arabs seriously. I am dealing with the Labor Party platform, where they are taken extremely seriously." Not only was this a reprimand to the army commanders, but it was also an explanation that the military threat would be dealt with in the political arena. But while military intelligence was using the new information to gradually crack the assessment of low war probability, Dayan remained unchanged in his belief that Kissinger's diplomatic steps would satisfy Sadat, who would therefore avoid opening fire. This line of thought also led Dayan not to take steps such as mobilizing the reserves, which could only intensify the tension and lead to an unavoidable military conflict.

The discussions in Tel Aviv were conducted in a number of rounds. The first was in Elazar's office at 08:25. The second was held in Dayan's office at 09:00. The third took place in Meir's office at 09:45. Next, at 11:30, there was an improvised cabinet meeting with a limited number of government ministers. And finally, at 12:30, Elazar called an urgent discussion.

At 08:25, Elazar conducted a short and concise discussion with his deputy Tal, Zeira, and Peled. They decided to recommend that Dayan declare a full red alert of the entire standing army for the inception of war (which meant cancelling all vacations), to reinforce all of the fronts with a regular division of the armored corps, and to prepare for a general mobilization of the reserves.[47]

Elazar, Tal, and Zeira rushed on to the Ministry of Defense to a discussion called for 09:00 with Dayan's advisor, ex-chief of staff Zvi Tsur; the secretary-general of the Ministry of Defense, Yitzhak Ironi; the minister's assistants, Aryeh Braun, Yehoshua Raviv, and Avner Shalev; and other generals. The talk focused on the new situation, particularly on attempting to understand the Soviets' motive for evacuating and on what steps to take on Yom Kippur Eve. This was the last discussion of the security leadership before the war.

---

adding information were: Bar-Yosef 2001, 295–340; Zeira 2004, 177–208; Arbel and Neeman 2005, 235–56; Shalev 2006; 150–60. Agranat Commission Report, available at http://www.archives.mod.gov.il/pages/Exhibitions/agranat/agranat_commission.asp.
[47] Bartov 2002, 332.

Elazar told Dayan that, considering the information, he "was choosing the stricter way"—meaning that, since he did not have enough evidence that war would not break out, he was acting on the assumption that there would be an attack. Elazar explained that this was why he was using the standing army, which was under his command, and detailed what had been decided some minutes earlier in his own office. In other words, the entire standing army would be on full alert and all vacations would be cancelled. This applied not only to units at the front, but also to the air force staff and all forces that could be used in reserve. Mobilizing the reserves was not under the authority of the chief of staff, and at this point Elazar did not propose mobilization to Dayan.

The next speaker, Zeira, had up to that point continued to assess that there was a low probability for war. Against the backdrop of the dramatic events that had unfolded during the night, his position had changed. What undermined his certainty was the hurried evacuation of the Soviet families. "Of all of the things that Elazar has mentioned, I feel that the most problematic and serious is the Soviet issue," he said. "If the Russians hadn't done anything, the signs would have indicated that the Egyptians and the Syrians were not going to attack, but rather were anxious about us, and we have recently carried out a series of actions which could have caused them anxiety."[48] But the Russians were leaving and that could not be denied. Zeira enumerated three explanations which had been raised in military intelligence, only one of which seemed reasonable to him: "The bottom line is, the Russians know that the Egyptians and the Syrians are going to attack."

Zeira also reminded those present that "Zvika [Zamir] had received an announcement that night from a good source who warned that there was going to be something, and he requested that Zvika come to meet him. Tonight at ten p.m. he will see him, so prepare a list of questions."[49] On the basis of these factors, Zeira expressed his opinion that "it is certainly justified to do everything proposed by Elazar."[50] He was now less determined in his appraisal of the low probability of war, but was also encouraged by the "general feeling . . . that the regular army and the air force would hold them back." However, he concluded with a momentary return to his former assessment: "I don't see the Egyptians and the Syrians attacking."[51]

---

[48] Zeira 2004, 181; Bar-Yosef 2001, 300.

[49] Braun 1992, 59; Arbel and Neeman 2005, 237. In contrast to them, Bar-Yosef not only ignores this quote, but blames Zeira for not reporting to the forum about Zamir's trip to meet Marwan. Bar-Yosef 2001, 303–304. He bases his assertion on the oral testimony of the head of the Bureau of the Chief of Staff, Avner Shalev. It is possible that Shalev was not alert during Zeira's report.

[50] Zeira 2004, 184; Bar-Yosef 2001, 302.

[51] Zeira 2004, 184.

Ironically, Zeira's skepticism matched Marwan's as he expressed it to Zamir about twelve hours later. Marwan reported on preparations for the war that would break out the following day, but added his doubts that Sadat would actually implement the decision.

Dayan followed the presentations alertly and did not disapprove of their content. It was clear that he knew the details well and was very particular about their accuracy. "In all of the traffic between lines in Egypt, there hasn't been anything special?" he asked. "Complete quiet," replied Zeira. They were referring to the listening devices the Israeli Matcal special unit had installed on the Egyptians' telephone lines. Earlier, at midnight, following the information about the Soviet evacuation, Zeira had approved their activation and they began operating at 01:45.[52] At 02:00, Yoram Dubinsky (Dubi), the individual in charge of activating them, sent a telegram to Menahem Digly, the head of the collection department in military intelligence, reporting on their operation and detailing which lines were monitored and the few insignificant messages received.[53] The Egyptians were using wireless communication, not telephone lines, which the Israelis picked up freely and continually. The telegram sent to Digly also stated that the monitoring was carried out until 11:00. The ten hours during which the "special devices" were operating did not provide any information about Egyptian preparations for war. In actual fact, the "special devices" continued to work for many more hours, but after 11:00 no one was listening to them any longer. All of the other listening devices had signaled that war was imminent. While these devices did not pick up the information for which they had been designated, it was not the devices which failed, but the person who misled decision-makers in Israel to believe that they were an insurance policy for an advance warning of war.

At the meeting with Dayan, Zeira brought up another source of surprise: "Regarding the military exercise, as well, I have a dilemma. Is it a tactical exercise? Is it a telephone exercise? Is it a command exercise? Is it an exercise of the forces? Up to now, we have no indication about what

---

[52] The approval was given in a telephone conversation with Colonel Yoel Ben Porat, the commander of the collection unit, after a request from Ben Porat. In his book, Bar-Yosef (2010, 237) argues that Zeira "chose to lie to those in charge and tell them that the devices were operating, and there is no doubt that, in this way, he personally and significantly contributed to the lack of perception by the chief of staff and the minister of defense during those hours." Up-to-date information indicates that Bar-Yosef's argument about Zeira on this point has no basis in fact.

[53] Colonel Yossi Langotsky, who commanded the unit responsible for operating the "special devices," testified that his commander, Yoel Ben Porat, ordered him to activate the devices only for a trial. See Ha'aretz, December 19, 2005. It is possible that Langotsky was not aware of the fact that they were operating for more than ten hours.

kind of an exercise it is. In most places, forces are not being moved."[54]

At this stage, Dayan had already rejected Zeira's explanation that the Egyptian activity was an exercise and taken into account that "their exercise was only a cover, so that we would think it was a cover."[55]

*Eli Zeira, July 2011*

Photo: flash 90, Israeli Defense

He also correctly interpreted the Soviets' rushed evacuation when he determined that "what we previously viewed as being less probable we now view as having greater probability." As expected, Dayan supported and approved of the military's actions: "This Yom Kippur, everything you have done is well and good."[56] He had one request regarding the preparations for possible war: to prepare a helicopter, just in case one of them had to make a flight. On the other hand, he rejected Elazar's expressed intention that "if something happens, we want, in plain language, to begin to concentrate forces or to give alerts." Dayan responded to that immediately: "Don't move forces unless it actually begins. The roads are empty today."

Considering his new assessment of the situation, Dayan was facing two important questions: Whether to try to prevent the war, and if so, how? The person who raised these questions for discussion was Zvi Tsur, Dayan's advisor and perhaps his only confidant. As a positive answer to the first question was clear, it only remained to discuss how this could be done. Tsur presented two possibilities: first, to intimidate the Egyptians and let them know via the media that their intentions were known and that Israel was prepared to react; second, to do this more secretly, indirectly, and deliberately via the Americans.

Dayan's reaction indicated that he had already considered the question. He explained that, as a rule, Israel was not interested in deterring the Egyptians from attacking because if they did, "we will take care of them." However, this time the timing was unsuitable: "The whole business is not convenient for us." What was different this time? The probable reason for the "inconvenience" was the imminent elections. A war or a state military alert would require calling up the reserves on a wide basis and disrupt the

---

[54] Braun 1992, 59.

[55] Zeira 2004, 184.

[56] Braun 1992, 58.

routines of life, and that would have been unsuitable at that point in time. So it was important to try to stop the Egyptians from attacking and to calm the situation and clarify to them that there would be no surprise and that Israel was ready.

Dayan did not choose the direct and rapid deterrence method—using the media—although ten days earlier in the Golan Heights, when referring to the northern front, he had made use of the media to deter the Syrians. This time, he was not only aiming for deterrence, but also to tempt Sadat politically—and to do that secretly. Thus, he determined, "Considering our relations with Kissinger, we can tell him that Israel has not done anything and ask him what is going on with his clients. On the superpower level, not only won't they [the Russians] lie to them [the Americans], but they are not interested in a Russian-American conflict."[57] The other participants in this discussion did not know that the Israeli leadership had promised Kissinger that Israel would not escalate the tension. The days of escalation at the end of May 1967, during which Israel had mobilized the reserves when facing the threat of war with Egypt and Syria, were seared into Dayan's consciousness.

The discussion continued for about forty-five minutes and when it was finished, the forum went on to the Prime Minister's Office to update her on their conclusions and receive her approval. At that meeting, speakers solidified their positions and presented them more succinctly. Zeira again reported on the updated information but also repeated that an Egyptian-Syrian attack was completely improbable in his opinion and that "our feeling is that they are not going to attack." However, he also again noted that Zamir had left to have a personal meeting with the source of the alert, who had reported that something was about to happen.

Elazar distinguished between his interpretation that "they are not yet going to attack" and the fact that "technically they could do it." He thus explained that the IDF was on high alert, but he hoped that "there would be an additional early indication" before an attack. It is difficult to ignore the feeling among the partners to the secret of Marwan's existence that, as long as he had not transmitted focused information about the timing of a hostile attack, the tension was not yet substantial. What Elazar had not emphasized, Dayan completed: "Preparations have been made, except for a call-up of the reserves." He proceeded to present the reason for this: "We are not worried at the Egyptian front, and in the Golan Heights, we are worried all year round."

Zamir was absent from this consultation, as he was already on his way to London. At this stage, his position remained unvoiced. A short time

---

[57] Zeira 2004, 185.

after the war, Dayan asked him what he had been thinking on that day. According to Dayan's military secretary, who wrote the minutes, "Zvika replied that he too did not think that war was a probability before October 6. On the other hand, he thought that a high alert should be initiated and deployment reinforced."[58]

At this point, Dayan took over leadership of the discussion. He had already rejected Elazar's and Zeira's analyses and determined that the Egyptians were not carrying on a military exercise, but getting ready to cross the canal. Yet this did not worry him. Dayan declared Elazar's military steps satisfactory and refused to make any further military moves. Elazar himself still had not asked to mobilize the reserves, and like many of the security elite, Dayan too felt that the regular army and the air force could hold off an attack, if it took place, until reserve forces could arrive.

Dayan still retained his "political conception." September, Sadat's target date for an agreement, had come and gone, but within less than a month Dayan intended to begin an accelerated political process. Perhaps now Sadat was building additional leverage for pressure, escalating the threat to renew fighting and making it concrete.[59] More seriously, Dayan was concerned that this step might cause Israel to call up the reserves and to reach the elections while the country was paralyzed, in which case Israel might be pressured by the United States into making exaggerated concessions. There might be a return to the nerve-wracking "waiting period" of the summer of 1967, as Meir would mention later. In the discussion in his office, Dayan himself had said, "If a situation like 1967 begins to develop, and no one knows who suspected whom, we must now try to break the vicious circle and tell the Americans."[60]

Dayan clung to a line of secret political action that would enable him to dismantle the threat without revealing it to the public, and of course, without mobilizing the reserves. He assumed that there was still time for an enticing diplomatic step to prevent Sadat from initiating a war and time to make preparations on the northern border in order to prevent an opportunistic attack from the Syrians, who were not interested in a political process. "I propose telling the Americans that signs are accumulating

---

[58] Braun 1992, 54. He was relying on the minutes taken by Colonel Yehoshua Raviv, Dayan's military secretary, of the conversation between Zamir and Dayan on November 15, 1973.

[59] Of course, Dayan erred in assessing Sadat's calculations. His error was based on Kissinger's intentions and his own willingness to lead negotiations likely to satisfy Sadat. Dayan had already planned a trip to Washington at the beginning of December, immediately after formation of the new Israeli government. Kissinger demanded that Israel present its position for reaching an agreement by January 10.

[60] Zeira 2004, 184.

which make an Arab attack more realistic than in the past," he stated during the discussion in Meir's office, adding,

> We should request that the Americans speak to the Russians and make it clear to them, and have the Russians make it clear to the Arabs, that we do not intend to attack, but to warn them that if the Arabs initiate war, "they will find themselves in hot water," and we should ask the Americans to get the Russian reaction. If that calms things down, good. If not, we will request more equipment. . . . We have information that the probability now is greater and there is a deployment at present that is heading toward a definite canal crossing. . . . If we could tell Kissinger, but Simcha [Dinitz] is here [in Israel].[61]

Dayan knew that Kissinger had a direct channel to the Egyptians intended for political moves—but to activate it, Dinitz needed to be in Washington, not Israel. At the time, Abba Eban, the Israeli foreign minister, was in New York, in close proximity to Kissinger; they had even conversed twice the day before. Dayan did not even consider asking Eban to help in this mission, however, because he was not a party to the secret political moves.

It is difficult to assume that the others present, except for the prime minister, were aware of the significance of what Dayan had started to say. That is also true of researchers of the period. But Golda Meir did know what Dayan was referring to. She immediately interrupted him, saying that they could use the services of Mordechai Shalev, Dinitz's assistant. Shalev had accompanied Dinitz to his meetings with Kissinger and knew of the secret contacts. For Dayan that was sufficient. Only he and Meir understood what was being said and, as noted, Meir accepted Dayan's position "one hundred percent." She had even made use of the term "conception." This time she reinforced Dayan's line of thinking, viewing the Egyptian preparations as an attempt to improve Egypt's position in advance of the expected political process. She now said, "Perhaps their crooked thinking tells them that they have to force the [UN General] Assembly to face the fact that the region is not dormant, but active."

As we shall see, it turned out that the Israelis' message reached Kissinger only after the war had broken out. The US secretary of state, on whom Meir and Dayan had pinned their hopes of making Sadat put down his weapons, went to bed in New York secure in the assessment by all of the US and Israeli intelligence organizations that the probability of war in the Middle East was low, including a calming report from the CIA issued that very day which was

---

[61] Ibid.

identical to the assessment he had received from Israel.[62] Kissinger became aware of the impending war only ninety minutes before it broke out. He later admitted that he had not managed to evaluate the situation well and had not felt the proper sense of urgency, acknowledging that "policymakers cannot hide behind their analysts if they miss the essence of the issue . . . for that the highest officials—including me—must assume responsibility."[63]

After the discussion in the Prime Minister's Office, Elazar issued a written order to initiate Alert C, which meant that "the entire standing army and the reserves that have previously been mobilized should be in a state of high alert for war activity." In keeping with these orders, on the morning of October 6, there were about 300 tanks and their crews in Sinai and about 180 tanks in the Golan Heights. A high command post was prepared for action. But not all of the military networks were informed and aware that Alert C meant that war could break out at any moment. This was due in no small measure to the advance in the timing of the initial attack. Elazar also failed when he assumed, like almost all of the security apparatus elite, that the regular army alone could block the attack. These issues fell within the purview of the military establishment. However, these omissions and failures did not lead to the breakout of war. They could not have prevented it.

At 11:30, six government ministers who were spending Yom Kippur Eve in the Tel Aviv area gathered in Meir's Tel Aviv office of the prime minister: Bar-Lev, Galili, Dayan, and ministers Shlomo Hillel, Michael Hazani, and Shimon Peres.[64] In this incomplete assemblage, the cabinet held a meeting that included Elazar, Zeira, Gazit, Tsur, and a few more bureau chiefs.

---

[62] Central Intelligence Agency, *1973 Arab-Israeli War*, 44: "Judgment [Redaction] that Syrian Military Preparations are Defensive in Nature". See also Central Intelligence Agency, "Judgment [Redaction] that Syria Military Preparations are Defensive in Nature," October 3, 1973, 45; United States Intelligence Board, Combined Watch Report, October 4, 1973, 45: "We continue to believe that an outbreak of major Arab-Israeli hostilities remains unlikely for the immediate future, although the risk of localized fighting has increased slightly as the results of the buildup of Syrian forces in the vicinity on the Golan Heights. Egyptian exercise activity under way since late September may contribute to the possibility of incidents" (quoted in ibid.). For a description of the events of that day, see Kissinger 1982, 462–67.

[63] Kissinger 1982, 467.

[64] Minister Sapir was in Tel Aviv, but the government secretary-general could not locate him. Ministers Kol and Moshe Haim Shapira were not called to the meeting and later protested this omission. Nakdimon 1981, 90.

Since not all of the members of the government were cognizant of the situation, Dayan opened with a general summary. Listening to him, the ministers learned for the first time of the security tension, which had become more serious during the last twenty-four hours with the information that the Egyptians and the Syrians were about to renew hostilities. He completed his summary by saying, "We still are not completely sure that this is war, but the assessment was sufficient to invite you here."

Zeira presented to the ministers the information accumulated from the beginning of September until that moment. Regarding the deployment of Egyptian and Syrian forces, he said,

> It is suitable for both defense and attack. In the past, there has been information about thoughts of a coordinated Syrian-Egyptian attack in October; actually, today the Syrian and Egyptian armies are in position to be able to implement these attacks or to defend themselves against us from the same positions.[65]

Zeira finished his review with his assessment: "We still feel that there is a high probability that the Syrian and Egyptian states of alert stem from fear of us, and that there is a low probability that their real intentions are to carry out attacks with limited aims." He pointed out, though, that "the unusual thing about all of this is the fact that eleven [Soviet] planes reached Egypt and Syria, for which we have no explanation." He added that "almost all of the Russian vessels which were stationed in Alexandria have left the port . . . and the significance of that act is—Soviet reservations about an Egyptian attack."

None of the listeners asked the obvious question about the Soviet airlift: Why had the Soviets not approached the United States, if they were actually afraid that Israel was about to attack? Zeira had already analyzed this previously, in the more limited consultations: the only explanation for the rushed Soviet evacuation was fear of a coordinated Egyptian-Syrian attack. The fact that the evacuation had taken place by airlift testified that the attack was imminent.

Nevertheless, Elazar supported Zeira's assessment:

> The fundamental assessment of military intelligence that we are not facing a war is the more probable evaluation in my opinion. . . . However, I must mention that a defensive deployment according to Soviet military doctrine is also an attack deployment

---

[65] The discussion that follows relies on the protocol of military-political consultation at the Prime Minister's Office in Tel Aviv, October 6, 1973, at 11:30, 1.

and can become war. Thus, this deployment has all of the qualities required for attack. As I don't deal in interpretation, . . . I
must admit that they have the technical ability to attack from this
deployment. First, I have no proof that they do not want to attack.
Second, they are able to attack. As a result, we have taken comprehensive preparatory steps.[66]

In answer to a question from Galili, Elazar replied, "We are holding up
the mobilization of the reserves and other means until we have additional
indications." No one objected to the decision not to call up the reserves.

"I want to add one more thing," Meir interjected, after listening to
Dayan, the minister of defense and the highest level of the IDF leadership, with whose military authority she could not disagree. Her words
show that her difficulty regarding mobilization of the reserves was not
military but political. "There is one thing, there are the similarities which
are repeated from June 5, 1967. . . . It reminds me of what happened at
the end of May or the beginning or middle of May, until June 5, which
also should tell us something."

Meir did not want the scenario of summer 1967 to recur. At that
time, Israel reacted to Egyptian and Syrian deployment on the borders
with full mobilization. The following three weeks had seemed like an
eternity, with the economy at a standstill, the security leadership's
nerves on edge, and a loss of faith in relations between the government
and the military. Those three weeks led to dramatic developments in
the political system, leaving Israel with no alternative but to initiate
the war. The lengthy mobilization had been what led Israel to attack.
This time—when the enemy was stationed far from the borders of the
state, when the army held "defensible borders" of the Suez Canal and a
line of missiles in the Golan, when Kissinger and Nixon had agreed not
to compel Israel to retreat—Israel was obligated to the United States
not to mobilize. A development like what had taken place in summer
1967—military tension, general mobilization, and an escalation to the
threshold of war—was undesirable to a governing party during the days
before the elections.

Minister Hazani, who was present at the meeting and learned for the first
time of the situation, received the impression that the motive for not mobilizing the reserves was "so as not to create panic." Others chose to interpret
Meir's words as having an opposite meaning—as though her summary was
inviting the chief of staff to call up the reserves.[67] "Our intentions were to

---

[66] Ibid.

[67] Bar-Yosef 2001, 317. Bar-Yosef's interpretation was: "The feeling was that if the chief of
staff had proposed such a mobilization, the prime minister would have supported it."

prevent the eruption of the war," Meir herself declared thirty hours later.[68] This explained her summary at the cabinet meeting, twenty-four hours before the war broke out, better than any other interpretation.

The marathon of consultations concluded with a meeting of the general staff at 12:30 in the afternoon. Elazar called the meeting to present the general staff with the essence of what had been said throughout the morning and his assessment regarding the question of whether war would break out: "I see the danger of war breaking out today or tomorrow as less probable than war not breaking out."[69] He continued, "I don't think that this is the zero hour. I hope that we will receive a warning." Elazar knew that Zamir was on his way to meet Marwan and that Marwan was able to transmit a number of days' warning. While he was talking, Zeira interrupted him to give an update of about the accelerated evacuation of the Soviets from Egypt and Syria.

The discussions that day received practical expression in military deployment. At the Golan Heights front, the number of tanks was doubled by returning the Seventh Division to the Golan, including three tank battalions. An additional artillery battalion was added at this front. In Sinai, three divisions of the regular armored corps were stationed in the area between the canal and Refidim-Bir Gafgafa, and the artillery force was increased at the canal zone. The reserve mobilization system was on high alert to implement an order to mobilize. The air force mobilized additional reserves in order to be ready to assist in holding a defensive position; these were mostly technicians and supervisory units. The elite military command post was operating.

The Prime Minister's Office asked Mordechai Shalev, acting as Dinitz's representative in Washington, to arrange an urgent meeting with Kissinger in order to convey a dispatch they had worded.[70] The dispatch included three clauses.

---

[68] Golda Meir's address to the nation the night of Yom Kippur, October 6, 1973, was broadcast on radio and television. Available at: http://www.jewishvirtuallibrary.org/jsource/History/meir73.html.

[69] Braun 1992, 64.

[70] NA RN, NSC, HAK, Dinitz, Box 136; FRUS XXV, 284–85; Gazit to Shalev, Vav Lamed/760, October 5, 1973, Aleph-4996/3, ISA; Shalev to Gazit, Lamed Vav/952, October 5, 1973, Aleph-4996/3, ISA; Shalev to Gazit, Lamed Vav/956, October 6, 1973, Aleph-4996/3, ISA; Kissinger 1982, 464–65.

Photo: CIA, Hulton-Deutsch Collection/CORBIS

*Israeli tanks move through the Sinai, October 1973*

The first stated that Jerusalem was attributing the military alert in Syria and Egypt and the deployment along their front lines with Israel to one of two possibilities:

> A. A bona fide assessment by both or one of these countries, for whatever reason, that Israel intends to carry out an offensive military operation against them or against one of them. B. The intention on their part—or on the part of one of them—to initiate an offensive military operation against Israel.[71]

The second clause of the message related to the first possibility. Israel promised that it had no such intentions and that the opposite was true:

> We wish to assure you personally that Israel has no intention whatever to initiate an offensive military operation against Syria or Egypt. We are, on the contrary, most eager to contribute towards an easing of the military tension. Inform the Arabs and the Soviets of our attitude, with the view of allaying their suspicions and the aim of restoring calm to the area.[72]

---

[71] NA RN, NSC, HAK, Dinitz, Box 136; FRUS XXV, 284–85.
[72] Ibid.

The third cause was a warning to clarify in advance to Egypt and Syria that if one of them intended to attack, Israel would react powerfully and with great strength.

The military implications of the message, which promised to contribute to the restoration of calm in the region, included Israel not mobilizing the reserves and not attacking first. As noted, this was the price demanded from Israel for the "Understandings of December 1971": "To wait longer than two hours."[73]

The message was transmitted to the embassy in Washington, where Shalev waited for the intelligence report to arrive. The Israeli embassy tried to arrange a meeting in New York between Kissinger and the foreign minister. The intelligence report arrived at the embassy in Washington at 16:30; Shalev passed on the message and the intelligence report to Kissinger's assistant at the White House at 17:30 (near midnight in Israel) and they were immediately sent to Kissinger's people in New York. Kissinger himself received the message and the report only after the war had broken out.

The quiet that characterized the end of the short workday on Yom Kippur Eve left the main players of that day time for thought. Golda Meir later testified that she had remained in her office for some time to consider the discussion earlier in the day, during which she had not disagreed with the certainty expressed by Dayan, Elazar, and the other members of the defense and political leadership that they had taken the necessary steps to deal with the situation. "I sat in my office, thinking and agonizing until I just couldn't sit there anymore and I went home."[74]

Dado Elazar remained at work in his office until 17:00 that night.[75] When he left to go home, he was still deliberating about whether it had been an exaggeration to declare Alert C on Yom Kippur Eve.

Eli Zeira testified that his thoughts wandered to the meeting abroad and to Zamir's coming report about his meeting with Ashraf Marwan; he was waiting for an "additional indication."

The information that continued to accumulate from intelligence sources to military intelligence headquarters during the Friday afternoon hours strengthened the signs of approaching war, but there was still nothing to indicate its timing. The messages only increased the operatives'

---

[73] Report on the meeting between Rabin and Kissinger on December 24, 1971, Lamed Vav/416, Aleph-7052/20, ISA.

[74] Meir 1975, 411.

[75] Bar-Yosef 2001, 320, based on an interview with Avner Shalev; Bartov 1978, 324.

internal argument about the probability assessment and whether they needed to disseminate the information flowing in. Zeira, who received the information at 23:00, decided to put off distributing it and did not inform Elazar. "From my standpoint and from that of the minister of defense, the IDF was prepared and ready for war," Zeira later testified about his thinking. It can certainly be assumed that Zeira, along with Elazar, Dayan, and Meir, all of whom knew that Zamir was then meeting with Marwan, put his trust in the ability of the Egyptian agent who was close to Sadat to indicate the exact timing of the war in advance, before it was too late.

# 8

# Yisrael, What Do We Do Now?

*"Yisrael, what do we do now?"*

**—Golda Meir to her military secretary, Yisrael Lior,
upon receiving word that war would break out
at the end of the day[1]**

On Saturday, October 6, the day the war broke out, events began in London.

The head of the Mossad, Zvi Zamir, landed there on Friday afternoon, the night after Ashraf Marwan communicated with his contact, Dubi, and in the second part of a short conversation, as Zamir later testified, transmitted "information directed toward setting up an urgent meeting with me in London to discuss the matter of war. Marwan had indicated the necessity for the meeting, its location and its timing. And that was it."[2] The wording of the message testified to the absence of any sense of alarm appropriate to the situation. Zamir even testified to the Agranat Commission that the warning had been general and thus he did not see fit to report it personally to the prime minister. Thirty-eight years later, Zamir was still pondering why Marwan had not reported to his contact that war would break out in another forty hours.

Zamir set out for the meeting; his sole aim, as he testified, was to find out about the date and time of the war. In Israel, despite all of the signs, it was still difficult for the political leadership to reconcile itself to the possibility that war was imminent; those who knew about the meeting were

---

[1] Haber 1987, 13, 24.
[2] Regarding the meeting in London: Zamir and Mass 2011, 146–49.

primed to hear what Marwan had to say. Nevertheless, and in accord with the conditions the Egyptian agent dictated, Zamir and Dubi had to wait a few more hours to meet him. In retrospect, it became clear how much each of the twenty-four hours that passed before they met could have been significant to decision-makers in Israel.

During their previous meeting, a month earlier in Rome, Marwan had reported that war would not break out until perhaps toward the end of the year. As noted, based on this information, Zamir had estimated only a few days earlier that "if we analyze their inclinations, I must assume that if we are referring to an assessment framework of a year, their inclinations are, in fact, not to go to war."[3] Now Marwan had received completely different information, and in Zamir's opinion, he had made an effort to clarify it completely before he reported it. In Israel, decision-makers had understood that Marwan would know enough about the date of a war to warn about an attack weeks in advance.

Somewhat surprisingly, the imminent war did not come up immediately at the beginning of the conversation in London—only after they had discussed the thwarted rocket attack in Rome and its implications for Marwan's activity. When the two men moved on to the essence of the discussion, Marwan reported that a war coordinated by Egypt and Syria would break out on the following day, that it would be conducted according to an agreed-upon plan, and that it was still not clear whether Egyptian forces would halt after capturing a strip of ten kilometers west of the canal or whether they would continue on in the direction of the passes. Marwan added this reservation to his report: "I must tell you that if political or military conditions were different, if there were a decisive and important change in the military or political conditions, Sadat could stop everything."[4]

Marwan told Zamir that his hurried trip to Libya to deal with concealing the Egyptian air and sea fleets was a sign for him that war was on the way. But Zamir received the impression that Marwan had already heard in Cairo that the military leadership had been amazed not to have seen changes in military deployment on the Israeli side, considering the concentration of Egyptian forces in the canal area. He perceived the contradiction in what the agent was saying, but "I did not ask him how long he had known, both because it would not have made any difference and also because I did not see any point in initiating a discussion that

---

[3] Agranat Commission Report, additional partial report, explanations and substantiations, Vol. 1, 167.

[4] Zamir and Mass 2011, 148.

would create tension between us."[5] Zamir explained this by considering that Marwan never imagined that the war would be a surprise for Israel. Knowing Marwan well, Zamir did not see the logic in delving into the military details, and at the end of the discussion, he hurried to carefully convert the details into code and to communicate them in a telephone conversation with his bureau chief in Tel Aviv. He then transmitted the full protocol of the discussion, as taken down by Dubi, by teleprinter. This report arrived at the Prime Minister's Office before the ministers assembled on October 6.

## "The Entire IDF Should Not Be Mobilized Because of Zamir's Stories"

At 02:30 Israeli time on October 6, about twenty-four hours after Zamir received Marwan's request to meet, information reached Israel about the war scheduled to start just before dark.[6] One telephone call from London set Israeli agitation in motion. Marwan had not reported that the hour of attack had been moved forward. So Zamir understood the time to be set in accord with a war plan he had known in advance, at sunset. His lack of information about the timing of the attack, which began at 13:50 and not at sunset, greatly affected the ensuing chaos in the IDF, especially in the air force, during the fateful hours of that day. Later, this added to the arguments that Marwan had intended to deceive Israel.

Zamir was careful to report all of the details Marwan provided. He included the possibility that Sadat could stop everything if political conditions changed. This was enough to reinforce Dayan's opinion that mobilizing the reserves was unjustified. "The entire IDF should not be mobilized for Zamir's stories," he told Elazar when they met at 05:50 to discuss the significance of Zamir's information.[7] Dayan responded to the information by saying,

> We have received information like that in the past. Afterwards, when the Arabs have not attacked, we get the explanation that "at the last minute" Sadat changed his mind. This time, too, we have heard that if Sadat understands that we have found out about it and he has lost

---

[5] Ibid.

[6] According to the testimony of Freddie Eini to the Agranat Commission, Protocol of Commission Discussions, Session 15.

[7] Gordon 2008, 267, based on the protocol written by Shlomo Gazit, who was at the discussion.

the element of surprise, there is a chance that he will cancel or at
least put off the date of the attack.[8]

Dayan's words and deeds in the following hours testified to the fact that
this was how he continued to see the situation unfolding. However, even
though he thought that neutralizing the element of surprise was likely to
prevent war, he did not attempt to announce publicly and immediately that
Israel knew about the coming attack, but rather put his trust in the secret
channel with Kissinger. Perhaps he was correct in choosing a political step,
but he was much too late, weeks and months overdue, in the timing of its
implementation.

Dayan, like Meir, Elazar, and Zeira, received Zamir's information at
about 04:00.[9] Elazar summoned Tal, Peled, and Zeira for a preliminary
discussion at 05:00. From that moment Peled became a central partner in
coordinating the developments of the day.

At 05:50, a consultation took place in the minister of defense's office
with the participation of Dayan, Elazar, Zeira, Shlomo Gazit (brother of
Mordechai and coordinator of operations in the Occupied Territories,
who later replaced Zeira as head of military intelligence), and the director-
general of the Ministry of Defense, Yitzhak Ironi. "Dayan did not look
especially tense," testified Gazit. According to Gazit, the atmosphere during
the discussion was good, even lighthearted. A sense of happiness prevailed;
the fighting would begin that evening.[10]

The discussion itself focused on a disagreement between Dayan and
Elazar regarding Israel making a preventive strike by and calling up the
reserves. Elazar considered the situation from a military standpoint,
assuming that war was certain, and he wanted to prepare accordingly—to
mobilize a large reserve force of four divisions and anticipate the enemy
attack with a preventive strike by the air force. On the other hand, Dayan,
who was considering the situation both politically and militarily, assumed
that the secret contacts with Kissinger would appeal to Sadat's judgment
and logic; thus, there was no reason for Israel to attack or mobilize the
reserves; at most, a small number could be called up without increasing the
tension. Dayan also knew that this was what Israel had promised Kissinger.
"If Egypt starts, we will begin earlier in the Golan. If Syria begins, we will
not initiate an attack on Egypt," Elazar instructed. Regarding the reserves,
he announced, "I will bring a proposal to the prime minister to mobilize

---

[8] Dayan 1976, 575.

[9] Gordon 2008, 224; Bartov 1978, 324; Dayan 1974, 575; Braun 1992, 68.

[10] Author's discussion with Shlomo Gazit, May 8, 2012.

*Aluf Avraham Adan explaining a map to Golda Meir, Moshe Dayan, and Israel Galili, October 29, 1973*

Photo: Ron Frenkel, Israeli National Photo Collection

only defensively." Dayan then asked Zeira, "If we announce it [that we know about the war] and we mobilize, will that deter them from attacking?"[11]

Elazar demanded a mobilization of about two hundred thousand reservists—the entire fighting and support force—while Dayan, considering the situation, was ready to approve about twenty to thirty thousand. After an additional argument, Dayan agreed to enlarge the scope of the call-up to fifty to sixty thousand: two divisions, one for each front. When it was clear that there would be no compromise, they passed the decision to the prime minister. In the end, Israel carried out no preliminary mobilization at all, even though Elazar and Dayan had agreed on two divisions.

Dayan also vetoed a possible preliminary strike by the air force: "Our political situation does not enable us to do what we did in 1967."[12] Elazar did not give in on this issue, even after Dayan declared that "under no circumstances" would he agree. Elazar continued to argue that the air force was prepared to attack, and Dayan was forced to explain to him that there was no chance of a preemptive strike: "Even if the Americans are one hundred percent sure [that Egypt and Syria will attack], they will not let us attack first."[13] He told Elazar that the prime minister would definitely oppose an Israeli

---

[11] Gordon 2008, 258, based on the protocol written by S. Gazit.

[12] Braun 1992, 69–70.

[13] Ministry of Defense Archives, minutes of discussion between Dayan and Elazar, October 6, 1973, at 05:45.

attack. There was one thing on which both Dayan and Elazar agreed: If war broke out, the air force's reaction would focus on Syria.

On this point, the Syrian issue, the cheerfulness of the meeting reached its peak:

> Elazar: We can stop worrying about that this morning, like the story of the man . . .
>
> Dayan: What story?
>
> Elazar: A man was seen leaving a brothel at seven in the morning. When he was asked what was going on—why so early?—he replied, 'I have such a full day today that I wanted to get that out of my head first thing in the morning.'[14]

## "Zvika's Source Says That the War Can Be Avoided By an Information Leak"

"Yisrael, what do we do now?" the prime minister asked her military secretary, when he gave her the information Zamir had communicated just before four that morning. She did not reach her office, a short distance from her home in Ramat Aviv, until seven. Few people would have been willing to stand in the prime minister's shoes that morning.

At 08:05, a consultation was held in the Prime Minister's Office with the participation of Ministers Dayan, Bar-Lev, Galili (who was a bit late), and Allon (who joined them toward the end of the meeting). Also present were Elazar, Zeira, Tsur, Mordechai Gazit, and other participants.[15] Although most of the meeting was devoted to the decision about calling up the reserves, the issues that came up—and, specifically, what Meir, Dayan, and Galili said—reveal a bit more about the considerations guiding the decision-makers.

At the beginning of the meeting, Dayan suggested allowing the Arabs regular activity in the Occupied Territories and free movement through the transfer points on the Jordan bridges. He continued:

> I propose evacuating the children today from the Golan Heights, the South Sinai Solomon Region, and Abu Rodeis [the oil fields in

---

[14] Discussion with Shlomo Gazit, May 8, 2012. Quoted from the protocol of the discussion between Dayan and Elazar.

[15] This discussion is based on the minutes of the meeting as written by Eli Mizrahi, head of the Prime Minister's Office, ISA, available at http://www.archives.gov.il/NR/rdonlyres/66FC5A72-27F7-41A6-9969-7ED71A097F57/0/yk6_10_0805.pdf.

Sinai]. In the Golan there are only thirty children in all. If they have other ideas, that is their business. Toward evening or in the afternoon, propose that they take the children out for a trip. Bring them down. The women, if they want to stay—let them stay.

Golda Meir replied, "I know the people there. They won't send their children. I think it has to be an order." Dayan responded: "Tell them to go down—let them be brought down. Tomorrow they can make their objections to you."

So while Chief of Staff Elazar was waiting impatiently for approval to call up the reserves in order to stop the Egyptians and Syrians, who were about to attack, Dayan was discussing a trip for the Golan children and Meir was concerned about the self-image of the settlers—subjects that, at least during those moments, should have been the concern of junior workers in their offices.

Only after he had asked to tighten the intelligence coordination with the United States and considered how to relate to Jordan did Dayan turn to the question of a preventive attack. He knew that the prime minister would not confirm such a move in light of her promise to the United States, so he summarized briefly: "Regarding a preemptive strike: we cannot allow ourselves to do that this time. . . . In principle, if they don't open fire, we will not open fire."

Dayan did not request approval to call up the reserves upon which he and the chief of staff had already agreed, but presented his viewpoint:

> Dado [Elazar] wants a bigger call-up; I disagree. If things get more serious and fire breaks out, we will call up a full alignment. Otherwise [if we call up the reserves] this will mean that we are making war. . . . If I thought that there was no alternative, I would mobilize everyone. Up until nightfall, a limited call-up, and these forces will prepare to go into action tomorrow morning. If we want to continue the call-up tonight, we will continue to mobilize. On this issue, perhaps the chief of staff has a different opinion.

Elazar, who spoke after Dayan, opened with the main subject of disagreement, the question of the extent of the mobilization:

> The reserves we do not call up now will not be able to take part in the war by tomorrow. They will go into action only on Monday morning. The reserves that we do not call up now mean the loss of a day. So I am in favor of a large call-up. I favor a call-up of two hundred thousand soldiers. . . . If we don't have a large call up, then I don't see less than seventy-eighty thousand. From the standpoint

of international political impact, it doesn't matter if we call up seventy thousand or two hundred thousand. . . . It's better if they say that we started it and then we win. That is what they will say in any case. I am in favor of a large call-up. That's it for the call-up. . . . With regard to a preventive strike, that would save many lives. . . . To me, that's very tempting from an operative standpoint. We don't have to decide about that now. We have four hours to consult with the Americans.

In answer to Minister Galili, who asked how much advance time the air force would need to carry out such a decision, Elazar responded, "We'll be ready at 12:00 to go ahead. Between the air force [bombing the airfields] and missiles [attacking the missile system] we'll need three hours." He also explained that if they put off the preventive strike on the airfields to 13:00, they could not begin striking the missile system. At that stage, Elazar was still assuming that it would take a relatively short time to destroy the missile system.

It appears that Zeira now began to understand that his "low probability" assessment had been incorrect. He intervened in the discussion only after Meir asked for a situation report. Zeira sounded more hesitant than usual, but still found it difficult to entirely abandon his original position:

> They are technically and operationally prepared for war in accord with the plan we know about. Everything is ready, but despite the fact that they are ready, in my opinion, they know that they will lose. Sadat today is not in a position in which he has to go to war. Everything is ready, but there is no urgency. And he knows that the balance will not improve.

When Meir asked how, in his opinion, Sadat would behave, he answered exactly like Marwan: "He has not yet given the order to proceed. Perhaps at the last moment he will draw back. We may be able to influence what he does or decides."

In answer to a question from Galili, Zeira explained that deterrence might help. It could be achieved in two ways: "One, calling up the reserves. Two, if, for example, we activate the Americans." To a great extent, he aimed to explain what Marwan had intended when he maintained that Israeli political or military moves could yet stop Sadat. Like Elazar, Zeira's thinking was military, but while Elazar was primarily concerned with military defense and an ultimate counterattack, Zeira was focusing on deterrence. This was in contrast to Dayan, who was still adhering to his political intention to make use of the American track and retaining his belief that threat or political temptation would succeed in halting an Egyptian attack. After all, if Dayan had wanted to create military deterrence, he too would have supported a massive reserve mobilization.

Galili, who had arrived at the Prime Minister's Office early but joined the meeting later,[16] continued trying to hold onto the element of doubt Marwan had expressed and did not give up: "Zvika's source said that we can prevent the war using an information leak. Zvika proposes that we try it." Galili immediately suggested making public the great amount of intelligence information Israel had accumulated: "We can use it and mention all of the details, except for the change in the whereabouts of the president and his advisors." This remark revealed two bits of very great significance that were not known by the others, or at least, not by Elazar and Zeira. The first was the secret information that Sadat had moved to work in a "war room" so secret that Israel could not divulge that it even knew about it.[17] Indeed, as Sadat wrote later in his memoirs, "On Thursday, the eighth day of Ramadan [October 4], I moved my workplace to the Al-Tahara Palace, which was temporarily established as a war command headquarters."[18] The additional and, at this moment, most important piece of information: Galili knew that Zamir, who only a few hours earlier had spoken to Marwan, the person perceived as knowing Sadat's most intimate secrets, had suggested trying non-military ways to prevent the war.

Zamir had not transmitted proposals; Galili based his own suggestions on the complete protocol of the conversation between Marwan and Zamir as written down by Dubi, which had been sent to Israel by teleprinter immediately after Zamir had transmitted his preliminary summary report. Regarding its contents and their implications, Zamir testified:

> Up until the end, he [Marwan] did not know about the timing since he did not know the extent to which he could rely on what Sadat had said. In his opinion, Sadat was a manipulator. He didn't know whether, after he had spoken with me, it [the war] would take place, that Sadat would not do some kind of manipulation. . . . He didn't tell me, "Listen, leave everything, this is war!" He didn't say that. He knew that there could be a political statement from some source—American, Russian, Israeli—that would divert him [from

---

[16] Haber 1987, 25.

[17] "The most significant warning arrived at the research department only about three months after war had broken out. This was the news from a good source on October 4 who reported the urgent preparations of President Sadat's operations room" (Shalev 2007, 122).

[18] Sadat 1978, 187.

his move to war] and he would say, "So let's wait. So we won't do it." That would be his good excuse toward his public, the Egyptians, for putting off his decision.[19]

Like Dayan, Galili tried to hold on to the hope of a possible escape from the situation, as Marwan had suggested. It appears that, later, Meir also joined them in this. But the defense minister believed that the war could be prevented by a secret political move rather than by leaking Israel's information held about Egypt's and Syria's intentions. As it was clear that a preventive attack had been vetoed and Elazar knew that he would not receive approval for such a step, Dayan requested to return the discussion to the mobilization issue. In his opinion, a call-up, like an information leak, would pose an obstacle to secret political measures. He wanted to prevent mobilization—or, if that was impossible, to limit its scope.

Prime Minister Meir was still deliberating between Dayan and Elazar. She tried to include another factor in her considerations, one that supported Dayan's stance against mobilization. "I am considering. Another aspect is the effect of a call-up on the economy tomorrow," she said, but immediately continued with an argument supporting Elazar's position: "If this is really war, [mobilization] is no disaster. If there is a war, we will not understand why there was a delay of twelve hours." But before she decided, she quickly skipped to the question of a preemptive strike; she had already promised Kissinger, in coordination with Dayan and in accord with his recommendation, that she would not attack in advance. Now she said: "My heart is drawn to it; we'll see." Perhaps she was trying to soften her negative determination for Elazar, but this just increased his illusions that ultimately perhaps such an attack would be approved, and heightened the pressure and confusion in the air force.

Here again, Meir stopped and returned to Galili's train of thought about the possibility of preventing the war using an information leak:

> What would happen if we accept the advice of that friend [Marwan, whom she sometimes called "Zvika's friend"]? Why don't we use the BBC, CBS, and the others to announce that the Russians are evacuating Syria and Egypt and assess why they are leaving? Second, perhaps we can at least leak to the news

---

[19] Author's discussion with Zamir on February 19, 2012. "I wouldn't have written it if I hadn't thought that it was important," testified Zamir about the doubts Marwan had expressed, which were included in Marwan's message reporting on his meeting with Zamir, transmitted on the day the war began.

*Egyptian forces cross the Suez Canal, seen here from the west side, October 7, 1973*

agencies a bit of what is going on at the borders—that is to say, to destroy their illusions of surprise. In 1967 they didn't try to hide anything. This time they are hiding on the assumption that we don't know.[20]

It appears that the prime minister feared that she had already slid into military matters, the realm of expertise of those who were sitting opposite her, and she continued with her reservations: "Inasmuch as this doesn't harm us, if they know that we know, does that make things difficult for us or not?"

Dayan returned to the question of mobilization. This time he left room for a compromise: "If you approve a large call-up, I will not resign," he said unwillingly. That led Elazar, this time much more aware of the precious time that had gone by, to send his adjutant Avner Shalev to call up the two armored divisions on which they had agreed, numbering about seventy thousand soldiers. The time was 09:00. The final decision, approved by Meir, was to call up 100,000 to 120,000 reservists. "I haven't changed my opinion," Dayan responded to the decision. "What is your number?" asked the prime minister. "Less than half," replied Dayan. He made sure that the protocol stated: "The chief of staff will mobilize the entire number as proposed by the chief of staff."

---

[20] Protocol of the consultation in the Prime Minister's Office, Yom Kippur, October 6, 1973, 08:05, http://www.archives.gov.il/NR/rdonlyres/66FC5A72-27F7-41A6-9969-7ED71A097F57/0/yk6_10_0805.pdf

Dayan seems to have intended that, if war should not break out, the complaints about the extreme mobilization would be directed to the chief of staff and not to him.

The meeting was adjourned.

About six months later, the Agranat Commission placed the responsibility for the delay in mobilizing the reserves that morning on Elazar. The text of the discussions makes it difficult to accept that determination, as do Dayan's later statements, such as: "Even if we had known with certainty four days before the war broke out [that the Arabs were going to attack], we would not have called up the reserves earlier."[21] Indeed, Dayan's insistence was based on the IDF's assessment that the regular army would be able to halt the attack with the assistance of the air force, but his reasoning was political rather than operational.

## Planes Lacking a Political Captain

While these difficult decisions were being made, Elazar and Peled were operating in the vain hope that an early preemptive attack on the missile system and the airfields in Syria would be approved. The two thought that this could most logically be done in the afternoon. In a telephone conversation at five in the morning, Elazar had authorized Peled to take the necessary steps in the air force for an attack on the Syrian missile system, the on-site timing of which was determined as 11:00.

From the moment Benny Peled received the call from Elazar and activated his men, the airforce had focused on preparing to carry out the attack. At 06:45, it became clear that problematic weather would prevent an attack on the Syrian missile batteries; Peled received Elazar's approval to change the mission and prepare to attack Syrian airfields. This change demanded not only preparations by the aircrews but also altering the scheduling, munitions, and airplane formations. From this stage on, the air force and its command center, bases, squadrons, and units can be compared to a line of ants whose route is disturbed again and again. Its constituents tried, after each disturbance, to realign and make their way to the alternative destination dictated to them. Thus, the timing of the alternative assignment attacking Syrian airfields was set for noon.

Ran Pecker, the commander of the air force base at Tel Nof, described the attack planes taxiing to their take-off positions:

> From every direction, Phantoms and Skyhawks were appearing, heavy with bombs and full gas tanks, moving in sequence and

---

[21] Nakdimon 1978, 187.

joining the growing convoy, slowly moving along the taxiway towards the runway. Everything was carried out precisely and in complete radio silence. Not a word was heard in communications. A surrealistic drama. Suddenly an inspector in the tower broke the radio silence and ordered all of the planes to move back and return to their underground stalls. The announcement of the operation's cancellation caught us out of the blue.[22]

Even though Elazar and Peled knew that, due to political considerations, there was little chance that Dayan and Meir would change their minds and approve the preventive strike, they held to their original plan until the last moment. The chaos that took over the decision-making apparatus also led to mistaken decisions in the air force, which stymied its ability to carry out these missions.

Thus, at 13:00, when Peled understood that no preventive attack at all would be approved, he ordered a change in the Phantom formations from airfield attack to interception formation, preparing to defend the airspace over Israel. When the war actually did break out, this greatly harmed the planes' ability to return to base and rearm in order to assist in the ground forces' holding action and attack airfields. As Shmuel Gordon described:

> The chief of staff remained faithful to offensive attack even after the war had broken out, but he was not aware of the chaos that had engulfed the air force. Although the chief of staff had been told that he could prepare for an operation, thirty minutes later, when he asked again, most of the Phantoms had been launched into the air, wasting their time on mostly pointless patrol missions after their bombs had been unloaded or their pilots had ejected them into the sea.[23]

Gordon conducted a comprehensive and in-depth investigation of air force activity, published in 2008.[24] Regarding these hours, he wrote: "The air force command had never been shaken to this extent. Never had it had to struggle for balance as it did on that fateful day."[25]

## Waking Kissinger: "We May Be in Trouble"

At 10:15 Israeli time, Kenneth Keating, US ambassador to Israel, reached the prime minister's office at her invitation. Gazit and Dinitz also joined

---

[22] Ronen 2002, 330–31.

[23] Gordon 2008, 269. Based on Amir 2000, 225, and Ronen 2002, 332.

[24] Gordon 2008, 223–96.

[25] Ibid., 272.

the meeting just before Dinitz's executive jet was to take off for Rome, on his way back to Washington.

"We may be in trouble," the prime minister opened the discussion.[26] After briefly summarizing recent developments, she requested the United States' aid in clarifying to the Soviets and Egypt that Israel did not intend to attack Syria or Egypt but was preparing to defend itself if attacked, and was therefore calling up part of its reserve forces. In addition, she requested that the United States warn Egypt and Syria about the results of the war if Israel was attacked. Here Meir was adopting Dayan's strategy—deterrence via the secret political track rather than via the media. She was also acting on the basis of what she had understood as Marwan's recommendation to transmit "a political statement from some source—American, Russian Israeli—which would divert him [from his move to war] and he would say: 'So let's wait. So we won't do it.'"[27]

Keating requested assurance that he had understood the promise and the prime minister again confirmed that Israel would not conduct a preventive strike. Keating summarized his report to Washington with his impression that Meir sincerely wanted to prevent unnecessary bloodshed. The 06:00 telegram alarmed Joseph Sisco, Kissinger's assistant for Near Eastern and South Asian affairs, enough to lead Sisco to burst into Kissinger's suite at the Waldorf Astoria Hotel in New York early Saturday morning.[28]

The evening of October 5 was the first time Kissinger had taken for himself since he had been appointed Secretary of State on September 22. Without working papers, he shut himself up in his hotel suite for a private supper. His assistants knew that, to every extent possible, they should avoid disturbing him. When the message from the prime minister of Israel reached New York from the White House with an accompanying intelligence report, his assistants did not see fit to disturb him, especially since the message indicated that Israel was not panicking and had not fully called up the reserves. The message ended with: "We consider the probability of military action by two armies against Israel as low."[29] Even if the situation

---

[26] Tel Aviv 7766, October 6, 1973, 10:33, NSC, NA RN, 1173. A copy of the original flash cable can be found in the National Security Archive at George Washington University: http://www.gwu.edu/~nsarchiv/NSAEBB/NSAEBB98/octwar-09.pdf.

[27] Author's interview with Zamir, February 19, 2012.

[28] Kissinger 1982, 466–67; Kissinger 2003, 13–14.

[29] Message transmitted by Shalev to the White House, October 5, 1973, 17:00, NA RN, NSC, HAK, Box 136; National Security Archive, http://www.gwu.edu/~nsarchiv/NSAEBB/NSAEBB98/octwar-07.pdf. Even the next morning, a short time before the war broke out, the CIA, perhaps influenced by Israeli appraisals, assessed that "for Egypt, a military initiative makes little sense at this critical juncture of President Sadat's reorientation of domestic and foreign policy" ("President Nixon and the Role

had been different, it can be assumed that Kissinger would not have taken any action vis-à-vis Moscow, other European capitals, or the Middle East at this time. In retrospect, he assessed that anything he might have done then would have been useless.[30] The die had already been cast.

The failure that day was not administrative; it did not stem from delays in transmitting the message. It was a failure of thinking by Israeli decision-makers, who were unable to understand that the Soviets' urgent evacuation from Egypt and Syria at the same time could have had only one explanation—they knew the imminent timing of the coordinated Egyptian-Syrian attack on Israel. Kissinger later wrote: "Policymakers cannot hide behind their analysts if they miss the essence of an issue. They can never know all the facts, but they have a duty to ask the right questions. . . . We knew everything but understood too little. And for that the highest officials—including me—must assume responsibility."[31]

When Sisco broke into his room with the news, Kissinger did not know that he had only ninety minutes to act.[32] At the beginning, he considered the situation a misreading of one side by the other. More than eight months had passed since he had found out about Sadat's aspiration to motivate a political process; he was aware of Sadat's demand to reach an agreement by September. More than a few times during the last few months, Kissinger had urged Israel to let him launch his initiative—and he had been refused. It appears that Kissinger thought his intention to begin acting energetically to reach an agreement the following month, immediately after Israeli elections, was clear to both sides. He had prepared Israel and informed the Egyptians; this had been publicized in the mass media as well. Only a day earlier, he had discussed it with Mohammed el-Zayyat, the Egyptian foreign minister, and Sadat and Hafez Ismail knew about the discussion. In addition to the lack of military logic in attacking Israel, Kissinger, like Dayan and Meir, did not see the sense in Egypt initiating a military move precisely at this time. Sadat's move taught Kissinger an informative lesson in statesmanship. After the war, he knew how to appreciate it and did not hide his admiration for the Egyptian president.

Now, however, Kissinger was still trying to prevent the use of weapons and begin diplomatic moves. His first act was to wake his nearest interlocutor, Soviet ambassador Anatoly Dobrynin, to inform him of the seriousness of the situation and coordinate developments with him. At

---

of Intelligence in the 1973 Arab-Israeli War," *Central Intelligence Bulletin*, October 6, 1973, 45).

[30] Kissinger 1982, 466.

[31] Ibid., 467.

[32] Regarding Kissinger's actions and words before and during the early hours of the war: Kissinger 2003, 7–37.

06:40, Dobrynin sounded groggy. His short, meaningless answers caused Kissinger to remark, "If this keeps up . . . there is going to be a war before you understand my message." In any case, they succeeded in agreeing to take all measures necessary to prevent the war, if possible.

At 06:55 Kissinger spoke by telephone to Mordechai Shalev, Dinitz's deputy in Washington. The gist of their discussion was Kissinger's message that "we are in touch with the Soviets and the Egyptians, urging the utmost restraint. Dobrynin has said they will cooperate with us. We are setting up special communications. We would like to urge you not to take any preemptive action because the situation will get very serious if you move."[33]

At 07:00 he called Zayyat, who was in New York at the time. Zayyat sounded surprised at the developments; perhaps he really was. He had left Egypt before Sadat began to gradually inform officials about the war; even then, Sadat had only apprised those closest to him. He had avoided updating his foreign minister even the day before the war broke out to prevent him from being uncomfortable during his meeting with Kissinger on October 5, a few hours before the first attack. (This was the meeting during which Kissinger informed Zayyat of his intentions to begin negotiations after the elections in Israel).[34]

Now, one hour before the start of the attack, Kissinger told Zayyat of Israel's announcement that it had no intention of attacking, the warning that it would "take extremely strong measures" if Egypt opened fire, and the uncompromising warning he had transmitted to Israel not to make a preemptive strike. He requested that Zayyat communicate this to the government of Egypt as urgently as possible and ask them to show restraint so that he, Kissinger, would have the opportunity to deal with the situation. "I will do this immediately, although I am very apprehensive that this is a pretext on Israel's part." replied Zayyat; Kissinger responded with the promise that "if it is a pretext, we will take strong measures against them."[35]

Zayyat passed the message on to Cairo immediately. The time was then 13:25 in Cairo, about twenty-five minutes before the beginning of the war. Sadat was not free to speak, and Kissinger's message was received by Hafez Ismail.[36]

---

[33] NA RN, HAK, Telcons Box 22; see also Kissinger 2003, 17–18.

[34] Zayyat had been scheduled to speak at the General Assembly meeting the day before, on October 5, but at the last minute, asked to change the date and speak on October 11. Regarding the decision not to inform him of the impending war, see Heikal 1975, 15–16.

[35] NA RN, HAK, Telcons Box 22; FRUS XXV, 292.

[36] Heikal 1975, 31.

At 07:15, Kissinger spoke to his deputy, General Brent Scowcroft. At 07:25 he spoke with the Russian Embassy to reiterate the messages to Moscow, with which Dobrynin was speaking at that very moment. At 07:30, he spoke with Roy Atherton, Sisco's deputy, at his office in the State Department. At 07:35, he again spoke to Zayyat. He calmed him by saying that Israel had "given formal assurances that they will not launch [an] attack nor initiate military operations." Zayyat thanked him but added: "This seems like what happened in 1967." He ended with a marginal question that few have noticed: "May I ask how you are contacting [the Israelis]? Is Eban here?" Kissinger was unsurprised by the fact that, although war was approaching, the Israeli foreign minister, who was then in New York, was not at all in the picture as to events in the political arena. He replied to Zayyat that communications were with the embassy in Washington and that they were very good.[37]

At 07:45, Kissinger reported to Mordechai Shalev that he had transmitted the Israeli announcement, that he was in direct contact with the Egyptians, and that the Americans were asking Zayyat to communicate with Cairo. On the other hand, there was no direct contact with the Syrians; messages were being communicated via the Soviets.[38]

At 07:47, Kissinger again talked with Dobrynin. They updated each other on the fact that all of the messages had been sent. Kissinger asked what was going on with the Syrians since he had no direct contact with them, and then surprised his Soviet colleague by telling him that he had talked directly to the Egyptian foreign minister. "You spoke with him on the telephone?" wondered Dobrynin. Kissinger had decided that, under these circumstances, he could reveal something of the secret talks he had been conducting with Egypt: "He is in New York. We had a good conversation in New York. Yesterday we had a friendly meeting, but inconclusive. As I told you, we are not going to play any games. You will be told what we do. You can reassure Moscow on that point."[39]

At 07:51, he spoke to Commander Jonathan Howe, who was handling communications in the Situation Room of the White House. "When I ask you to do something, it must be done that second," he rebuked Howe, who he said was transmitting messages too slowly.[40]

At 08:15, Zayyat called and said: "I could not get the president. He is in the operations room. I got this following information: At six o'clock this morning, there was [sic] some navy units and airplane units—Israelis took

---

[37] Kissinger 2003, 19–21.

[38] Ibid., 22.

[39] Ibid., 22–23.

[40] Ibid., 23.

[i.e., instigated] some provocation on the Egyptian borders. We have actually tried to repel them and are doing so."[41]

This was how Kissinger found out that the Yom Kippur War had broken out, using the wording on which the Egyptians and the Syrians had agreed, meant to disguise the attack as a reaction to alleged Israeli provocation.

## "They'll Be Sorry"

At 11:00 Israeli time, a meeting took place in Elazar's command headquarters ("the pit") with the participation of Dayan, Elazar, Tal, the heads of the Commands, and the commanders of the branches. It was meant to frame an action plan for the IDF against Syria's and Egypt's war plans as they were known to Israel. During the meeting, Elazar asked to send planes into the air for a defensive patrol, as a message of deterrence. Dayan again expressed opposition to demonstrating open deterrence. He still had faith in the covert diplomatic moves. He explained:

> If the only reason for the air patrol is to deter them, it is unnecessary. But if it is good for you to be in the air, then be in the air. Because, regarding deterrence, we have told the American ambassador to notify the Egyptians and Syrians that we know that they are going to attack and that we are ready.[42]

Later, Dayan led a roundtable discussion to present the expected scenarios on each of the fronts and in the air, while asking difficult questions. It could be seen that he was in control of both the military details and military theory. He accepted the deployment plan Elazar presented. At the end of the discussion, Dayan returned to examine another scenario:

"What happens if, on the night following Yom Kippur, at midnight, it becomes clear that there is no war?"

"The release of the reserve soldiers will not take place less than forty-eight hours later," Elazar responded.

"A hundred thousand men will wander around for a full day before being sent home?" asked Dayan.

"They won't just wander around; they will also be sent to the front. If it becomes clear that there is no war, we will release them within forty-eight hours," Elazar replied in an impatient tone—three hours before the

---

[41] Ibid., 24–25.
[42] Braun 1992, 78.

opening attack, he was still being forced to deal with Dayan's doubts that the war would break out at all.[43]

Elazar later conducted separate discussions with the generals of the Commands and the commander of the navy. The beginning of the war found Head of Northern Command Hofi on his way to his command post and the head of Southern Command, Shmuel Gonen, giving out deployment orders.

"We did our best to prevent the outbreak of the war," Prime Minister Golda Meir stated in a broadcast to the confused nation on the evening of the first day of the Yom Kippur War. In saying "our best," she was referring to the urgent report that had woken Kissinger ninety minutes before the outbreak of battle. She did not, of course, refer to the fact that, during the seven months preceding the war, she had distrustfully rejected Sadat's initiative to open peace negotiations and Kissinger's proposal to lead these negotiations, and had reacted with scorn to the threat that accompanied the Egyptian proposal.

After ten days, when the war was at its height, Meir stated in the Knesset: "We have no doubt that the battle has been renewed over the very existence of the Jewish state. This is a war which is about our very existence as a state and as a nation." She said this about a war taking place far from the borders of the State of Israel, across the Sinai desert and deep within territories captured from Egypt and Syria—a war that could have been prevented if only Israel had recognized their sovereignty over these territories, or at least Egypt's sovereignty over Sinai. Meir was chastising herself for decisions she made in the days preceding the war. Some have even claimed that she expressed suicidal thoughts.[44] However, it is not known whether she was also chastising herself about the many months during which she acted to maintain the stagnation.

Even four years later, when Sadat announced his wish to come to Jerusalem in a dramatic step that paved the way for a peace agreement, Meir refused to trust his declaration. "If he comes to Jerusalem, hair will grow on the palms of my hands," she said.[45]

Assessing the probability of war occupied many people in the intelligence and military systems during this period; after the war it occupied those who wrote about the period. However, this was not the important

---

[43] Bartov 1978, Vol. II, 30.

[44] Nakdimon 1982, 145.

[45] Stein 2003, 91. Based on the author's interview with Mordechai Gazit.

question for decision-makers that year. Golda Meir and Yisrael Galili determined Israel's political conduct. Dayan was a partner, but at moments of dispute, it was Meir's viewpoint that determined what policies would be carried out. Other senior ministers, like Allon, Sapir, and Eban, who held different views, had no status in making political decisions; vital information was even kept from them. Meir also avoided seeking Yitzhak Rabin's assistance, although he had been chief of staff and ambassador to the United States and knew all of the details of Sadat's initiative and Kissinger's views in that regard.

Israel's security conduct was determined solely by Dayan. Meir and Galili did not intervene and the army and intelligence elites had almost no influence on Dayan. He did not adopt their assessments, nor did he reject them, but he appraised the situation and formulated a line of action by himself. He listened to the information they supplied and communicated his instructions, which were formed independently without depending solely on military intelligence assessments.

Dayan, Meir, and Galili viewed the situation politically. They knew that Sadat was aiming for political action but, at least during an election year, they were not ready to accept its territorial requirement: namely, Israeli recognition of Egyptian sovereignty of Sinai, along with an Israeli presence at key points in Sinai for a period of years.

Dayan analyzed the political situation correctly during that year and understood the developments taking place. He already knew, even in the early stages, that if there were no political moves, Sadat would take military steps with limited aims during the second half of the year in order to motivate such moves. Dayan rejected the military intelligence assessment of low war probability early on. In the spring, he led Meir's "kitchen cabinet" to prefer war—a war in which Egypt would dictate the conditions and Israel would be limited in its military deployment, even if it knew what was to occur—rather than participating in the process Kissinger wished to set in motion.

In June, Dayan began to understand that Israel would not be able to continue with an indefinite stalemate. He suited his viewpoint of a peace agreement with Egypt to the principles Sadat proposed and Kissinger supported. In September, Dayan revealed this publicly, in the media, and personally prepared to begin such a process immediately after the elections. These developments formed the basis of his belief—and his gamble—that Sadat would not attack during the election period, as he would lose both the war and the political process.

The information about Syrian military preparations, on the other hand, concerned the minister of defense; the Syrians were not interested in a political process and a sudden short attack could have gained them territorial advantage. However, in his information about Egypt Dayan did not perceive moves that would lead to war. His viewpoint was supported by significant factors:

- Marwan's September report stating that a war would perhaps take place only toward the end of the year (i.e., after the elections).

- King Hussein's warnings hinting that war would break out if there was no significant political movement.

- Intelligence information that attributed Egyptian troop deployments to a military exercise.

- Zamir's report from London during the final hours before the war broke out. According to the head of the Mossad, even a few hours before the war, Marwan was still qualifying his focused warning of attack and believed that if there was a significant change in political conditions, Sadat could stop everything.

Dayan assessed the situation independently according to the information that was supplied to him by intelligence and in accord with the information only he and Meir knew with regard to the secret contacts—information about which military intelligence had no knowledge. While in May he had rejected the military intelligence assessment of "low probability" of war and ordered the chief of staff to prepare for war, this time, in October, the assessment that continued to predict a low probability of war, on the basis of military factors, reinforced Dayan's own line of action—which he had adopted in any case. In addition, the internal political consideration that "this whole business is not worth it for us at this point in time" no doubt added weight to his decisions.[46]

Thus in all of the final days before the war, particularly on the last day, Elazar wanted to prepare in the best possible way militarily, on the assumption that war would break out. But Dayan dictated a line of action intended to make every attempt to prevent the war in secret, even at the price of raising obstacles to military deployments. Meir agreed with him. If it was she who led the policy of political inaction all year, now, when she was forced to make a military decision, she supported Dayan's line.

Dayan was wrong. He erred in his assessment of the timing. Sadat was of the opinion that the political moves had to take place before the Israeli elections, not after them, as Dayan had gambled. Dayan's character, which led him to act without including others in his considerations and his

---

[46] At a consultation on Friday, October 5, 1973. He was referring to the coming elections in Israel (Zeira 2005, 187).

thinking, prevented him from soliciting feedback about his conclusions. It also prevented these conclusions from being checked or supervised.

At 11:30 Israeli time on Saturday, Yom Kippur, the Israeli government met with partial ministerial attendance at the Prime Minister's Office in Tel Aviv. Some of the ministers who were present were surprised to hear for the first time about the military tension of the last few days; Dayan was forced to devote quite a bit of time to describing the events that had led to the brink of the coordinated Egyptian-Syrian attack about to take place. At 14:05, while they were discussing how events had reached this point and what actions were being taken, they heard the noise of rising and falling sirens announcing the beginning of the war. Folklore has it that Golda Meir murmured ironically in Yiddish: *"Nur dos falt mir ois."* ("That's all I needed.") Then she added in English: "They'll be sorry for this."[47]

---

[47] Medzini 2008, 548.

# Appendix

# The Story of Ashraf Marwan and the Yom Kippur War

In the story of the Yom Kippur War, the name Ashraf Marwan has come up again and again. Forty years after the war and about six years after his mysterious death, Marwan's story continues to fascinate the Israeli public and arouse disagreement and tension. Perhaps his secret will never be known and he will continue to intrigue the imaginations and pique the curiosity of authors and researchers.

The question of whether Marwan was the best spy Israel has ever had or a double agent for Egypt whose goal was to lead Israel astray about the timing of the war is peripheral to the main concern of this book, which is to turn the spotlight from the intelligence domain to the political arena, which was no less secretive. Indeed, as this book has shown, it is on the political level rather than on the intelligence level that the deeper answers and explanations for the surprise of the Yom Kippur War can be identified. In any case, Defense Minister Dayan related to military intelligence forecasts with skepticism and adopted them only to the degree that they matched his own view of Middle Eastern political events. The prime minister followed his lead. Dayan's reaction to the crucial information that reached him on the morning the war broke out was: "We don't call up the entire IDF because of Zamir's stories."

An examination of the events of 1973 challenges the myth that "Ashraf Marwan was the best spy Israel ever had in an enemy country and one of the best in history."[1] Nor does historical research confirm the determination that the warning Marwan transmitted on the eve of the Yom Kippur

---

[1] Bar-Yosef 2010, back cover.

*Ashraf Marwan*

Photo: Public domain

War about Egypt's and Syria's intention to initiate war on the following day "was the most fateful in the history of the state. Without it, the reserve call-up would have begun only after war had broken out, and the Golan Heights would have totally fallen to the Syrian army."[2] In actuality, the general mobilization of the reserves took place only three hours before the outbreak of the war.

The disagreement between those who still support Marwan's reliability (led by the former head of the Mossad and Marwan's controller, Zvi Zamir) and those who support the double-agent theory (most prominently the former head of military intelligence, Eli Zeira) is a footnote to the historical research of the war and its causes. But this footnote still manages to elicit excitement and to torture those involved in the affair far more than the weightier questions that have been neglected in Israel's still-ongoing process of national self-scrutiny. Thus, it seems fitting to investigate the Ashraf Marwan riddle, even if this still cannot be done using the methods of historical research.

On Sunday, December 29, 2002, Dr. Ahron Bregman was in the backyard of his home in London when his wife Dana called him to the telephone. "I am the man you have written about," said an unfamiliar voice.[3]

"How can I be sure?" Bregman asked the caller, who did not identify himself by name.

"You have sent me your book on Israeli wars with the dedication 'To Ashraf Marwan, Egyptian hero,'" replied the person on the other end.

"How are you?" asked Bregman.

Marwan replied that he was then recuperating from three open heart surgeries and added that he wanted to tell Bregman three things: "One, I am not challenging you. Two, you have got your enemies and I have got my

---

[2] Ibid.

[3] Bregman's testimony to the London police, Document 1, LHCMA, Bregman Files.

enemies. Don't listen to my enemies. Three, we should meet up when I am a bit better . . . but don't listen to my enemies." The two exchanged wishes for the new year and ended their short conversation.[4]

Dr. Bregman, an Israeli historian teaching at King's College in London, immediately understood what Marwan was talking about. Eight days before this surprising conversation, he had for the first time revealed Marwan's name and identified him as a Mossad spy from the Egyptian elite whose identity had been hidden for years behind code names, pseudonyms, and hints. Ostensibly, Marwan had every reason to be furious at the revelation, and certainly to distance himself from any contact with the Israeli researcher, but instead, he had chosen to telephone.

Four and a half years later, on Tuesday, June 24, 2007, Ashraf Marwan called Bregman's cell phone.[5] Since their first talk, they had remained in contact, a contact rather strange in its very existence as well as in the ways it was conducted. It was based primarily on consultation and exchanging information for the book Marwan was writing. Uncharacteristically, this time Marwan left three short, urgent messages on Bregman's answering machine asking him to call immediately. The first had been left at 13:52 London time, the second an hour later at 14:51, and the third twenty minutes afterward, at 15:11. About fifty minutes after the last message, Bregman called back. Marwan told him that he was about to finish writing his book, *What Happened in October 1973.*[6] During this conversation he claimed that his contacts with the Mossad in 1973 were part of an Egyptian plan to deceive Israeli intelligence. He even boasted that Sadat had said that if not for him, Egypt could never have won the war. At the end of the long conversation they planned a meeting for the next day.

That meeting never took place. The next day, Marwan was dead. He had jumped or had fallen from the terrace of his home—or had been thrown from it. His body was found in the garden below. The manuscript he was talking about has never been found.

But his end, like his confession about his part in the Egyptian deception the day before he died, did not solve the mystery of his life. After all, Marwan was interested in portraying himself as an Egyptian patriot and as an agent who had defrauded Israel, whether or not this was true, and the question of his suicide/fall/murder has never been clarified; neither its motive nor who was responsible (if anyone was) has ever become known. The clues must be sought in the past—in 1973 and before.

---

[4] Ibid.

[5] Bregman's testimony to the London police, Document 6, LHCMA, Bregman Files.

[6] Ibid.

## For Whom Was Marwan Acting?

Ashraf Marwan was not recruited as a spy on the Mossad's initiative. In the spring of 1969, on his own initiative, he visited the Israeli Embassy in London and proposed his services to Israeli intelligence. This in itself would be enough to cast the suspicion of his being a double agent. Marwan's background—as President Nasser's son-in-law and confidant to Nasser's successor, Sadat—and the quality of the information he transmitted even at his first meetings, increased that suspicion many times over. "This looks too good to be true," Zamir said of Marwan.[7] It is clear that the decision to make him a Mossad operative was made after a meticulous investigation to rule out the possibility that Marwan had proposed his services to Israel in order to defraud it. The information he transmitted to his handlers, rare in its quality, strengthened this assumption. Even Zeira testified that, before the war, he had not doubted Marwan's reliability.

Much of the information Marwan provided to Israel remains unknown to the public; it is doubtful that it will ever be revealed. However, it is known that this information, received during the period preceding the Yom Kippur War, centered on Egypt's rearmament, its plans for war, and warnings about the war's initiation. Most of these warnings were simultaneously reported to Israeli intelligence through other sources and information-gathering methods, which attested to their credibility.[8] However, from a certain stage, particularly in 1973, quite a bit of the information Marwan supplied misled Israeli assessment organizations and decision-makers. This fact does not mean that the deception was done intentionally, just as the important and credible information he supplied previously does not testify that his aim was to earn the trust of the intelligence bodies in Israel in order to mislead them later, at the critical point of the outbreak of war. Perhaps Marwan did not intentionally deceive but simply, like the consumers of the information he transmitted, erred himself, both in assessing the real intentions of Sadat and in estimating his own ability to obtain credible information about these intentions in real time.

In contrast to the conventional wisdom, Marwan's ability to provide information with important implications for decision-making in Israel was low. In Israel, intelligence leaders were temporarily blinded by the quality of the previous information Marwan had provided and thought that he could be a source of secret information of great value. As is frequently the

---

[7] Zamir and Mass 2011, 130.

[8] Five conversations with Zeira between January 22, 2011, and January 15, 2012; Bar-Yosef 2011, 148. Bar-Yosef wrote that the war plans Marwan communicated "reinforced what was already known in Israel."

case with good sources of information, they found it difficult to accept the fact that Marwan's information could be incorrect, partial, or too late.

Zamir, as head of the Mossad, more than once joined Marwan's regular contact person at their meetings and if one asks him personally, he still defines Marwan as the "best of the Mossad's human sources."[9] "The arguments proving that Marwan was actually a credible source and not a double agent of Egypt," he wrote, "are set out in detail and informatively in Uri Bar-Yosef's book *The Angel*." However, the more Bar-Yosef goes into detail, explaining that Marwan "did not leave one secret in Egypt which was not revealed to Israel"[10] and that he "was one of the most effective spies in history," the more his explanations raise doubts when it comes to the critical year of 1973.

After the war, Marwan played an important role in the political steps Kissinger took to remove the oil embargo imposed by the Arab states and to achieve Israel's disengagement agreements with Egypt and Syria. At the same time, Marwan remained in contact with the Israeli Mossad. Did Marwan share Sadat's secrets with Israel during that period? It is also doubtful whether that can be answered; in any case, it is outside the framework of this discussion.

Before we turn to an investigation of Marwan's role in the events of 1973, it is important to clarify the question at the center of the argument: for whom was Ashraf Marwan working? In opposition to Zamir and Bar-Yosef, whose apologetic approach maintains that Marwan was serving Israel, Zeira is no less decisive. Even before Marwan's name was publicly revealed or the very existence of a human agent was known, Zeira wrote: "The 'information' served the program of deception by the president of Egypt, perhaps guided under the personal direction of Anwar Sadat himself."[11] Zeira strongly argues that Marwan "volunteered" to serve Israel with the aim of deceiving it at the decisive moment, and presented this position in his book, *Myth versus Reality: The Yom Kippur War*. The two researchers who have investigated this issue in depth coincidentally have similar family names: Ahron Bregman and Ronen Bergman. Both have tended to accept Zeira's evidence and have expressed this approach in their writings. Since the Hebrew edition of the book you are now reading was published, doubts about Marwan's credibility as an Israeli agent have increased among senior intelligence and military personnel in Israel.

However, no one has unequivocal proof to determine whom Marwan was really representing. This is even true for the most senior

---

[9] Zamir and Mass 2011, 141.

[10] Bar-Yosef 2010, 11.

[11] Zeira 2004, 158.

Israeli intelligence figures of the time, Zeira and Zamir. Their two extreme positions are not backed up by unambiguous proof. Indeed, if the events of 1973 cast doubt on Bar-Yosef's and Zamir's thesis, they do not necessarily lead to the conclusion that Zeira is correct. Between these two extreme positions a wide range of possibilities exists. For example, Marwan might have been an agent who simply attempted to maneuver between the two sides, Israel and Egypt. Or as Zamir, who knew Marwan well, has suggested: "He did not think in terms of Egypt and Israel. He was serving Ashraf Marwan and nothing more than that concerned him."[12]

Another possibility is that, at the beginning, Marwan made contact with the Mossad and acted to serve Israel and himself, but that, at a certain stage, his loyalties changed and in 1973 he acted in coordination with Sadat. Thus he enjoyed both worlds; he continued to receive a large commission from Israel and saved himself from the danger of being uncovered as a spy for Israel by ultimately serving Egyptian interests. It is also possible that, like other spies in the past, he tried to "launder" his activities and to offer his services to his country with some measure of sincerity, without revealing the depth of his original disloyalty. It seems we will never be able to determine to whom Ashraf Marwan was loyal in the depths of his heart. But we can examine who was served by the information he transmitted and who was deceived, if we trace his activity in 1973.

## Did Marwan Knowingly Deceive Israel?

We will examine Marwan's credibility by focusing on three groups of events:

1. The "false warnings" focusing on the outbreak of war, which Israel received during the first half of 1973.

2. Marwan's reports after the US-Soviet summit, when Sadat began to feel that the only alternative left to him for setting a political process in motion was the military one. During this period, preparations for war and coordination between Egypt and Syria intensified.

3. Marwan's reports during the days and hours preceding the war, after D-Day and the zero hour for the Egyptian and Syrian coordinated attack had been determined.

---

[12] Zamir and Mass 2011, 141.

## The False Warning Period

During the early months of 1973, Marwan transmitted a number of focused warnings to Israel about an imminent outbreak of war. These warnings were not followed by the envisaged action. In fact, each report included dates for attacks that Sadat had no intention of carrying out, at a time when the armies of Egypt and Syria were not yet ready to do battle and before the details of attack had been worked out.

- In November 1972, Marwan reported on Sadat's decision to open hostilities in December, primarily making use of the air force, with artillery support and commando raids by helicopter, in order to inflict losses on Israel. He also reported that a general attack would begin in January, after heating up the front, in coordination with the Syrians.

- On January 17, 1973, he repeated a similar warning.[13]

- On April 11, 1973, Marwan reported that war would break out in mid-May in coordination with the Syrians, with the aim of reaching the Sinai passes. This was before possible dates for a coordinated war had been discussed. Sadat and Assad discussed these dates later, at their meeting in Alexandria.[14]

- On April 24, 1973, he reported that Sadat and Assad had met and decided to delay the attack until the end of May or the beginning of June.

- On May 25, 1973, he reported that Sadat had put off the war by at least two months.

- Between June 14 and June 16, 1973, Marwan reported to his contact person that Assad and Sadat had agreed to start the war at the end of September or the beginning of October. This information was partially borne out by events. Taken alone, it would have been decisive proof of the quality of Marwan's information. But in the general context of the number of warnings he transmitted, there was almost no month about which he had not warned that hostilities would begin. In addition, the end of September as a date for attack had never been proposed at any stage by the commanders of the armies.

---

[13] The only one to mention a report on that date was Bar-Yosef 2011, 200.

[14] Gamasy 1994, 157.

Did this series of warnings mean that Marwan was trying to deceive Israel, as Zeira has claimed? Not necessarily.

However, the series of incorrect warnings also makes it difficult to call Marwan "the best spy that Israel had in an enemy country and one of the most successful spies in history." Bar-Yosef, who has stubbornly defended this declaration, explained that, at each of the dates, Egypt had actually intended to begin warfare, but Sadat had each time changed his mind. Is that true?

It has already been mentioned that only on August 23, 1973, were possible dates for war determined; D-Day was set only on September 12, while Marwan had given Israel the series of "false warnings" long before that. Moreover, Egypt was not prepared militarily and was not making real preparations to go to war on the dates about which Marwan warned. A comparison of the deployment of Egyptian and Syrian forces toward the real date of October 6, 1973, and their deployment during the period of false warnings reinforces this argument. As a matter of fact, during the period of false warnings, Sadat often made threatening public pronouncements about war, but these became fewer and fewer as preparations for war and coordination with Syria took a more practical turn.

Zamir also feels that Sadat never intended to initiate a war on the dates Marwan reported. Each time that Marwan transmitted such a warning, he added his assessment that it was doubtful whether Sadat would actually carry out the attack. He had always been right, except for his assessment on October 5.

If Marwan was not a double agent, how can his many specific war warnings be explained? Perhaps the explanation lies between what was occurring in the secret political channel and Sadat's internal needs. Sadat had to act to motivate the United States to advance in the secret channel with Kissinger, and he wanted to prevent foot-dragging. The threat of war was a useful tool. He threatened publicly with statements to the media, but those became ineffective after two years of announcing that this was "a year of decision" while, in practice, nothing happened. Now he had to intensify the threat, both toward the Americans and through them, toward Israel and his own home audience. He began to speak to his close associates about dates for an attack in order to demonstrate his serious intentions, doing so each time Kissinger seemed to be moving too slowly in the secret channel. The "false warnings" thus came from Sadat himself. Marwan, as one of Sadat's close associates, was exposed to these threats and quickly reported them to Israel, perhaps without even knowing whether they were feasible. Marwan's status and proximity to the Egyptian president enabled him to obtain information in Egypt, but Sadat did not share all of his decision-making considerations with Marwan.

This was the case at the end of 1972. Kissinger did not hurry to determine a date for the meeting with Hafez Ismail, and Sadat wanted to create the impression that war was imminent. In November 1972 Marwan warned his Israeli contact of warlike activity toward the beginning of 1973. At the same time, the entire Egyptian senior military command was being replaced; Sadat was occupied with eliminating a military conspiracy to prevent this from occurring. In addition, the new military leadership had only just begun to work together.[15] Indeed, this false war threat evaporated when, at the end of January, Kissinger and Ismail set a clandestine meeting for the end of February.

A similar scenario took place on April 11, 1973. The date for the second meeting between Kissinger and Ismail came and went; they neither met nor rescheduled. On April 5, Sadat assembled his new government, which, in Gamasy's words, decided that "there is no alternative but to open a military campaign. . . . Thus, he [Sadat] asked General Ismail Ali to investigate the possibility of breaking the ceasefire, simultaneously presenting his case to the General Assembly and increasing the intensity of our diplomatic offensive."[16] The threat was lifted temporarily on April 24, after a date was set for a secret meeting between Kissinger and Ismail (which took place in Paris on May 20). However, the threat was only postponed and was later used to press Nixon and Brezhnev for a decision on the Middle East at their summit meeting at the end of June. On each of these occasions, Marwan echoed the false threats emanating from the president's office in Cairo, but this does not mean that he knew the gun Sadat was waving was not loaded, nor that his actual mission was to dull Israeli vigilance when the real danger approached.

## Syria and Egypt Prepare for War

Sadat's tactics changed drastically at the end of June, after the US-Soviet summit, when it appeared that the possibility of political movement before Israeli elections no longer existed. Sadat then began accelerated preparations for military action while tightening his coordination with the Arab states—Libya, Saudi Arabia, Qatar, Kuwait, and of course Syria. Marwan's role in this coordination was central.

Together with Sadat, he met on August 16 with Kamal Adham, advisor to Saudi King Faisal. Immediately afterward, on August 17, Marwan left for

---

[15] Shazly 1987, 132–43; Gamasy 1994, 135–36.
[16] Gamasy 1994, 153. Based on Hafez Ismail, *The National Security of Egypt*, 267–69. This is not a description of a focused preparation.

Libya on a mission for Sadat and met with Qaddafi. He returned to Cairo and left immediately for Kuwait and, from there, Jeddah.[17]

The first peak of Marwan's activity occurred between August 22 and August 27. Marwan was then in close contact with Sadat and was spending most of his time with him. During the first days, on August 22 and 23, the senior echelons of the Egyptian and Syrian armies met in Alexandria and determined two possible periods for the outbreak of the war (September 7 to 11 and October 5 to 10). Marwan reported to Israel that this meeting had taken place but did not disclose its content or the dates determined.

On August 24, Marwan participated in a discussion between Sadat and Faisal in which Sadat informed the Saudi king that a war would break out in the very near future. Marwan included this statement in his report to Israel. On August 25, Marwan returned to Cairo to meet Qaddafi. Afterwards, he joined the talks between Sadat and Assad in Damascus, where they discussed the war and its opening date. On September 2 in Rome, Marwan reported to his contacts that Sadat had requested that they initiate the war at the end of the year.

These reports might be termed deficient and obstructive. The information he provided that war would not take place before the end of the year remained unrevised until the eve of the actual fighting. When the obvious sight of Syrian and Egyptian troops being deployed provoked the Israeli intelligence system, the head of military intelligence and his research department expressed harsh reservations. Here Zeira's argument that Marwan's reports led to a mistaken assessment is significantly reinforced.

But did Marwan intentionally deceive Israel?

Marwan left Egypt with Sadat on August 23, and thus he was not present for the summary of the officers' meeting. The few partners to the secret of this meeting strictly maintained their silence. Sadat did not even tell Faisal the date of the first attack, because it had not yet been decided. What Sadat did tell Faisal, Marwan faithfully reported to Israel. In Sadat's discussions with Assad, Marwan had been present only partially, as he had returned to Cairo for one day. From the second part of the discussions, he could have understood that an understanding had not yet been reached about the opening of hostilities.

Marwan reported on those meetings in Rome at the height of the "rocket affair," which could be interpreted two ways. On one hand, the fact that Marwan averted a terrorist attack could attest to his loyalty and his obligation to act for Israel. On the other hand, this event could be seen

[17] Cairo 2494, August 17, 1973; Cairo 2540, August 22, 1973. Report of the United States Interests Section in Cairo, NA, http://aad.archives.gov/aad/createpdf?rid=57586 &dt=2472&dl=1345 and http://aad.archives.gov/aad/createpdf?rid=59677&dt=2472& dl=1345.

as evidence that he was acting with the full knowledge of Sadat and as his emissary, since Sadat had an interest in thwarting a terrorist attack; he could have sent Marwan to eliminate the threat.

The second peak of coordination for the approaching war was the meeting between Sadat and Assad on September 10 through 12 in Cairo. These discussions were publicly known and reported by the media. At this meeting, October 6 was determined as the day hostilities would begin, but Marwan did not report this. It is possible that he simply did not know.

## The Last Days before the War

On September 22, two weeks in advance, as had been promised, Sadat informed the heads of the army that he and Assad had decided to initiate war on October 6. Preparations accelerated. Marwan was in Egypt at the time and it is likely that, at the very least, even if he did not know the exact date, he was aware of the following events.

On September 27, a full army mobilization was declared; additional circles in the chain of command were gradually informed about the impending war. On October 1, a military exercise began in Egypt which included deploying forces to the canal front. Marwan knew that Sadat had reported to the members of the National Security Council that he would soon break the ceasefire and had updated the senior army echelon that war was imminent without informing them of the specific date. He also knew about the report Sadat had transmitted to the Soviets; because he had accompanied Qaddafi during his stay in Cairo on October 1, he also knew about the messages and hints Sadat had passed on to the Libyan leader. "It is a matter of hours," Sadat had said to his Libyan guest when urging him to accelerate the shipment of military equipment from Libya to Egypt.[18] Marwan witnessed the troop movements as well as the talk in the upper political ranks. This was the impression Zamir received on the night of October 5 when he met with Marwan, about fourteen hours before the war broke out. Zamir testified that Marwan told him the Egyptian army command had been amazed that Israel had not reacted to the Egyptian deployment.[19]

Perhaps it may be assumed that Marwan also knew about Defense Minister Ismail Ali's trip to Damascus on October 3 for final coordination of war matters, but he did not know the details of what was agreed upon there. On October 3 Marwan, whom Sadat had appointed to supervise coordination with Libya, was busy accompanying Libyan prime minister

---

[18] Heikal 1975, 14; El-Saadany 1994, 121.
[19] Zamir and Mass 2011, 149.

Abdel Salam Jalloud, who had arrived in Cairo for a visit.[20] On this visit, Sadat told Jalloud "to rush back to Tripoli to inform 'his Moammar' that the battle Qaddafi had always questioned was to begin in a few days. Without telling him the exact date, he confided that when Egypt Air planes arrived in Libya for safety, the war would begin the following day."[21] On the same day, and to this end, Marwan left for Libya. This indicates that on October 3, Marwan knew that war would break out in the coming days.

Marwan told Zamir that he then understood that war was going to break out in the very near future—thirty-six hours from the moment he would arrange for the transfer of the Egyptian naval and air forces to Libya. In Israel, decision-makers knew at that stage about the force deployment but were still in doubt about how to evaluate Egypt's intentions. The agent who usually transmitted war warnings to Israel weeks and months in advance, and who passed on secret details from the discussions of the Egyptian governmental elite, still had not reported anything to Israel this time.

"I am leaving reserve mobilization for additional indications." This was Elazar's reaction to intelligence reports about Egyptian force deployment.[22] He consoled himself a few days before the war by, apparently, counting on the missing information Marwan would supposedly supply. Indeed, Israeli decision-makers considered Marwan to be providing them with an intimate peek into the inner rooms of the Egyptian government. But at the most crucial moment of all, Marwan did not supply the most vital piece of information.

On October 4, Marwan reached Paris. Only then, in the late evening hours, did he first communicate with his contact Dubi; well into the conversation, Marwan transmitted his general warning about preparations for war. This was still not a focused warning, and he did not use the agreed-upon code word for a certain outbreak of war. Consequently, the report Dubi passed on to Israel reflected this lack of urgency, opened with other issues, and focused on those matters. Only at the end of the report did it mention war preparations and Marwan's request to meet with Zamir the following evening in London. When he received the report in the early hours of the morning on October 5, Zamir had the impression that the warning was not extremely urgent and acted accordingly. It was certainly logical to assume that, if Marwan had put off the continuation of his report for twenty-four hours, it probably was not greatly urgent.[23]

---

[20] *Ha'aretz*, October 5, 1973. The article includes a photograph of them with President Sadat dated October 3, 1973.

[21] Saadany 1994, 121.

[22] Braun 1992, 63.

[23] About the feeling that Zamir was not serious enough about the significance of the warning, see the testimony of Freddie Eini, director-general of Zamir's office, who

Considering these events, it is difficult to avoid the argument that Marwan was operating to thwart the Israeli government, even if there was no "smoking gun." Zamir's complete confidence in Marwan's credibility, authentic as it may be, does not provide proof that Marwan was indeed reliable.

We may here propose explanations for the question which puzzled even Zamir: Why didn't Marwan move more quickly in reporting his warning? Marwan actually knew that the force movements were not an exercise, but perhaps he believed these military movements were so visible that he had no doubt that Israel was aware of what they really meant; maybe reporting earlier would have put him in danger of being revealed; maybe he did not wish to report until he had precise information. But all of these are only conjectures made in retrospect.

## Last-Day Question Marks

Marwan and Zamir had both been in London for about twenty-four hours before the war broke out, but they met about eight hours after they had arrived there. Marwan dictated the timing of the meeting. Zamir later explained the interval by reporting that Marwan wanted to clarify additional details before he transmitted his report. Those hours of delay had severe implications, considering the subsequent race in Israel to mobilize the reserves about three hours before the first attack. Perhaps if Zamir had met Marwan immediately after reaching London, in the afternoon hours of October 5, he would have known the correct questions to ask in order to transmit an early report to Israel.

But this does not end the question marks.

When they finally met, at the beginning of the day the war broke out, Israeli time, Marwan gave a double report. Zamir testified that, in answer to his question about when the war would break out, Marwan replied that "it would break out on the following day, October 6, and would begin with a coordinated attack by Egypt and Syria."[24] However, in the same breath, Zamir testified in Marwan's defense:

> During the conversation, Marwan added reservations: "I must tell you that if political or military conditions change, if there is a decisive and important change in military or political conditions, Sadat can stop everything."[25]

communicated Marwan's announcement. Minutes of the Agranat Commission discussions, Meeting 15, http://www.archives.mod.gov.il/Pages/Exhibitions/Agranat2/AlfredEini/15/mywebalbum/index.html

[24] Zamir and Mass 2011, 148.

[25] Ibid.

Perhaps Marwan still believed that, even at this late stage.

The mistaken information about the zero hour also adds to the doubts about Marwan's reliability. Zamir reported, as he understood from Marwan, that the war would break out at dusk. But the attack actually began at 13:50, a fact that added just one more surprise and made it even more difficult for the Israeli army to deploy. In answer to the accusation that Marwan deceived Israel about the opening hour of the war, the defenders of his credibility argue that the opening hour was changed only on October 3, the date Marwan set out in the evening for Libya, so perhaps he did not know of the change. They will have to deal with a new question.

On December 7, less than two months after the war, Hassanein Heikal, editor of the Egyptian newspaper *Al-Ahram* and a close associate of Sadat, revealed details about the hours before the attack.[26] His report was credible and testified to his acquaintance with the secret details, including messages exchanged during those hours between the United States and Egypt. Those details that can be crosschecked with other sources confirm their validity. One instructive detail, which was also quoted in the Israeli press, has escaped the notice of researchers: "According to the preliminary program," Heikal related, "the war was supposed to break out at twilight but it was brought forward by the army high command because on the evening of October 4 Israel had received information about the zero hour." This revelation, assuming it is credible, immediately poses two questions:

1. How could Heikal have known, two months after the war and years before Marwan's story began to leak out to the media, that on October 4 Israel had actually received a warning about the outbreak of the war?

2. A no-less-bothersome question: The zero hour was changed on October 3. If Heikal's explanation is true, how did the Egyptians know in advance that Israel would receive information about the outbreak of war?

On the face of it, these questions seem to supply ammunition for the double-agent theory. If Marwan had coordinated his steps with Sadat, the Egyptian president would have known in advance that the Israelis would receive this information and Heikal, his close associate, would have been able to report that immediately after the war. This explanation might appear even stronger when, in 1975, two years after the war, Heikal published his book about the Yom Kippur War, *The Road to Ramadan*, which omitted the

---

[26] *Ha'aretz*, December 9, 1973, quoting *Al-Ahram*, December 7, 1973. Heikal said that twenty minutes before the war broke out, Sadat received a dispatch from Nixon.

previously stated reason for the change in times. It offered instead an explanation that has since been adopted in the research literature: that the attack hour was brought forward as a compromise with the Syrians, who were pushing to begin the war in the morning, when the low sun at their backs would blind the Israeli pilots. For exactly the same reason, the Egyptians, who would be attacking from the west, wanted to begin the battle in the late afternoon. In the end, they compromised on two in the afternoon.

How can we account for these two explanations? Did Heikal or someone from the upper echelons of Sadat's government realize the danger in the first explanation and hurry to censor it, in order to maintain Marwan's credibility in the eyes of the Israelis, who still did not suspect him? Was it an innocent and coincidental newspaper error by an editor very close to Sadat, which was later corrected? We will probably never know.

Even without Heikal's slip of the pen, Zeira views Marwan's late report and the mistake in the zero hour he reported as additional proof of the double-agent theory. Zeira developed a complex argument in an attempt to explain why, if Marwan really was a double agent, he attempted to supply advance warning to the Israelis—incomplete, late, and insufficient as it was. In his opinion, the optimal scenario for Sadat would be if Israel attacked Egypt or Syria while Egyptian forces were already prepared for an immediate canal crossing. In that case, Israel would be presented as the aggressor for initiating the war while the Egyptians would be perceived as reacting. Israel would be unable to prevent their reaction, crossing the canal, considering the extent of the Egyptian attack force under the umbrella of surface-to-air missiles. Marwan's warning, according to Zeira, was meant to achieve that end and to motivate Israel to attack under inferior conditions a short time before the zero hour of the Egyptian and Syrian attack. Unsurprisingly, in retrospect, this explanation makes Dayan's foot-dragging appear to be a positive calculation that prevented Israel from falling into the trap of a preventive attack, rather than hesitation leading to a critical delay in fully mobilizing the reserves.

On one point there is no disagreement: The fact that Israel did not initiate the war operated in its favor among US decision-makers. But this was cold comfort.

## To What Extent Did Marwan Affect Israeli Decision-Making?

The circle of those privy to Marwan's information and its source was a very limited group. It included Prime Minister Golda Meir, Ministers Dayan and Galili, Chief of Staff Elazar, Zeira, and of course, Zamir. This group was given the raw material; the information given to others was distributed so

Photo: CIA

*The aftermath of a tank battle in the Valley of Tears, Golan Heights, October 1973*

as to give the impression that it came from a number of sources. In this limited group, no one was in doubt about the source's reliability at that point in time, but not all of its members related to Marwan's information in the same way.

There were those who were amazed at the information and blinded by its high quality. Others investigated it with a businesslike, critical approach, judging it by how it integrated with additional information to which they had access and by the general picture it provided, and now and again came up with a different evaluation than the one Marwan's report implied. Dayan and Zeira stood out among those who related to the information critically.

Even though Marwan operated directly under the auspices of the Mossad and the military intelligence professionals did not know the source of the information, they continued to wonder at the quality of his information: "There is no precedent in history for such a source which has opened Egypt to us so transparently," said one; added another, "Information of quality so high that all of the intelligence bodies have been waiting for it all of their lives and get it once in many generations . . . is more precious than gold."[27]

---

[27] Bar-Yosef 2010, 145–46.

Israel paid for Marwan's information not in gold, but in cash—lots of it. Folklore has it that Marwan received sums so high for his series of meetings that he could have bought an apartment in the most expensive part of Tel Aviv.[28] But Israel paid a much higher price for the complacency created by this abundance of quality information received from an agent who was part of the Egyptian elite. Most of the details Marwan transmitted were military in nature: war plans and armaments. Much of this was known to intelligence from other sources and different methods of information gathering. Marwan added to this information and, primarily, reinforced the picture military intelligence had created before his reports. In this way, he removed doubts and simultaneously complimented the professional ego of the intelligence operatives: "Until now [when information began to come from Marwan] we analyzed and saw what we could. Now we hear the information 'from the horse's mouth.' We can see a picture which is a bit fuller."[29]

This was dangerous. In their great enthusiasm about information they were getting from Marwan, analysts did not pay enough attention to the possibility that it was not always full or correct. They did not properly consider, for example, the overabundance of incorrect war warnings. What they were lacking was a timely and in-depth investigation of whether Sadat was prepared to initiate war on the many dates Marwan warned about: in December 1972, at the beginning of 1973, in mid-May, at the end of May or the beginning of June, after July, and at the end of September or the beginning of October. Such an investigation could have led intelligence analysts to relate more carefully to the "calm before the storm" in the weeks before the war, during which Sadat made fewer public threats and Marwan reported postponement of the war by a few months. But the intelligence people could not make an educated analysis that would take into consideration developments or constraints in the political track, because not even the highest levels were party to what was occurring in the secret track between Kissinger, Sadat, and Meir.

Simply considering the large number of false warnings should have been enough to direct the intelligence and political echelons into giving greater consideration to the readiness of the Egyptian army and the deployment of Egyptian forces at the front when analyzing the probability of war. Up until September 1973, they acted accordingly when what they saw did not testify to a proximate war. But during the days preceding the war, they preferred to give more weight to the various explanations for

---

[28] Ibid., 149.
[29] Bar-Yosef 2011, 150. Quoting the head of air force intelligence research.

army preparations in Egypt and Syria and chose to wait for "additional indications," like a delayed warning from Marwan.

A salient issue here is Marwan's contribution to Israeli intelligence's understanding of the "conception" of the Egyptian conditions for going to war. On this topic, as well, there is a serious dispute: did Marwan bring Israel up to date that the Egyptian war plan had been limited or did he let Israeli decision-makers continue in their mistaken evaluation?

There is no disagreement that Marwan played a central role in Israel's perception of the Egyptian approach, according to which a condition for initiating a war was the ability to cause harm to the Israeli home front in order to deter Israel from attacking deep into Egypt. There is also no disagreement that "the new Egyptian plan, known only to a few Egyptians, was unknown to Israel."[30] Thus, despite the warnings Marwan relayed at the beginning of 1973, Israeli military intelligence determined that "the probability that the Egyptians will open hostilities is not great . . . the chances that they will succeed in crossing the canal are close to zero."[31]

The dilemma is whether Marwan ever reported that there had been a change in the Egyptian approach. Here, opinions are divided.

Those who argue that he did rely on Marwan's report of the Supreme Council of the Armed Forces meeting on October 24, 1972. The meeting minutes Marwan transmitted were not detailed and did not mention the "change in approach." However, Marwan's later oral report implied that Sadat would not avoid giving the order to open fire even if he had not completed equipping the army, and that the army would not refuse such an order. This was understood by Zamir and also by Dayan, who read the raw material Marwan communicated in November 1972. At a meeting in "Golda's kitchen" on December 1, 1972, Dayan said: "We must assume that Egypt will renew its fire over the canal at the beginning of 1973." As mentioned, even later, in May, Dayan did not accept Zeira's assessment that the Egyptians would not open fire because they were not ready, believing that Sadat was planning a limited war that did not require him to complete Egypt's rearmament. "I have a different assessment than his," Dayan said, after Zeira had expressed his original assessment. "I think their objective in continuing the war is to gain political achievements. . . . The Egyptians assume that, in the end, when the operation is finished, they will have succeeded in setting foot on the eastern bank of the canal."

In contrast, military intelligence, with Zeira at its head, argued that they did not know of any change in the Egyptian approach until the date the war broke out. They did know that, in contrast to accepted thinking with

---

[30] Zeira 2004, 111; Bar-Yosef 2010, 137–43.
[31] Braun 1992, 18.

regard to the "Egyptian conception" Marwan had communicated in the past, beginning in November 1972, Marwan had begun to transmit warnings of renewed fighting. They saw this only as information he had uncovered and not as a change in approach to the actual issue of war. Moreover, Marwan always made sure to add his reservations as to whether the threat would be carried out, and stated that in any case, even if there was fighting, it would not deviate from attacks by the air force and commando raids in the canal sector.

In the political domain, to which it might have been expected that Marwan, who was close to Sadat, could contribute significantly, he was never asked to supply information. "Political information did not come in," testified Zamir. "We were dealing with an enemy and not with a partner for peace." When, during our discussions, I mentioned the details of the secret channel between Sadat and Kissinger, about which Zamir had been ignorant, he lamented: "Why didn't they tell me? I could have tried to obtain information about that, too. I had ways to do that."[32]

We will now examine the importance attributed to Marwan in real time by each of the senior army, intelligence, and political echelon representatives in Israel.

## The Chief of Staff

Dado Elazar related critically and carefully to the information Marwan transmitted, as befits someone who is responsible not only for forming an intelligence assessment but also for providing a response. Thus, even if in early 1973 Elazar presumed that the Egyptians would not initiate a war, he acted with what he understood to be the required care after Marwan's false warnings. Therefore, in December, he argued:

> It is not plausible that they will start a war in the near future. . . . Nevertheless, this does not mean that we should not be making preparations . . . so I will not say that there is no chance that war will break out and we can sleep soundly.[33]

He took this line in April as well:

> I do not want to estimate in percentages, but we must act on the assumption that it could happen. Not that I have analyzed this situation differently than military intelligence . . . but there is internal logic supporting war. . . . So we have to make preparations for it, and

---

[32] Author's interview with Zamir, February 19, 2012.
[33] Braun 1992, 18.

that does not mean that we have to become panicky and mobilize; we must do staff work and preliminary preparations.[34]

Elazar was faithful to this line even in October. His great error was that he thought the steps he had taken would provide an adequate military response to the situation at the canal and in the Golan Heights. In truth, even if he had insisted on reinforcing the troops and mobilizing the reserves before October 6, he would have been refused. But he did not make this demand. The approach of the chief of staff, which seems to have been "not to cause panic by mobilizing the reserves," held true in October, as well. It was influenced to a great extent by the fact that, in contrast to the past, Marwan communicated his total warning less than twelve hours before the war. At a consultation which took place at the Prime Minister's Office on October 3, Elazar stated: "From time to time, we also knew of dates. What we knew about dates then was sometimes more positive than what we know now."[35]

## The Head of Military Intelligence

Eli Zeira was appointed head of military intelligence in October 1972; during his first few months in office, he did not know about Marwan's status. Perhaps for this reason, he related to Marwan's information, particularly to the series of warnings, with the required critical approach and gave them balanced and impartial weight in his assessments. In December 1972 he justifiably argued that, despite Marwan's warning,

> the chances that Egypt will initiate war are not great . . . the chances that they will try to cross the canal are close to zero. . . . Sadat [according to Marwan] has given an order to prepare and to complete preparations by the end of December. He did not give a date for the opening of fire and has not decided on a plan.[36]

On April 18, Zeira rejected Marwan's warning about war in mid-May and at the end of May; this time, too, he was right. He logically stated that

> it would be a mistake for the Egyptians to start a war. . . . But let's say that Sadat's logic is different. . . . About that, we . . . have changed our assessment and we check indicators in the field daily and hourly to see whether he is doing anything or not. The truth is that we are

[34] Bartov 2002, 259.

[35] Bar-Yosef 2001, 79.

[36] Braun 1992, 18.

finding more indications that he does not intend to start a war than those testifying that he intends to attack.[37]

However, the test of "indicators in the field," defined by Zeira so clearly in reference to Marwan's early warnings, was completely pushed out of his deliberations by the end of September and the beginning of October, when he decided to continue to wait for a clear warning from Marwan when all indications in the field testified to an impending war.

## The Head of the Mossad

Zvi Zamir was not an official assessor of intelligence and security matters. His status was determined by the prime minister's need to keep him close by as a balance against Dayan in decision-making; she greatly respected him personally. In his professional role, Zamir was not exposed to the full intelligence picture. So it can be assumed that the information from Marwan, whom Zamir knew better than anyone else, would play a major role in his assessments. The false warnings were credible, in his opinion, as were the reservations Marwan always added. Even though these warnings were never realized, they led Zamir to the conclusion that Egypt intended to attack each time Marwan warned.

At the beginning of the series of warnings, Zamir said in December, "Relying on the material we have we must operate under the assumption that there may be firing. When I say fire it's not renewing war all along the canal, but rather harassment here and there."[38] Zamir also was more aware and understood the change in Egypt's conditions for going to war—the change in "conception." So for example, on April 18, 1973, he stated: "We are acquainted with the thesis of preliminary conditions for war: an in-depth reaction; proper air defense; bridges to cross the canal, electronic equipment. . . . [Sadat's] preliminary conditions have apparently been fulfilled."[39]

Zamir's appraisal should have had great importance, since he was personally involved in the relationship with Marwan. But perhaps because of that, he also expressed reservations at that meeting: "I am not sure and I am not predicting. I am not saying that there is any certainty that it will happen"—the same reservations Marwan had expressed.[40]

---

[37] Bartov 2002, 257–58.
[38] Braun 1992, 18.
[39] Bartov 2002, 259.
[40] Ibid.

However, to the same extent, Zamir's confidence in Marwan and his adherence to the information Marwan provided led him to assume, two weeks before the war, that war would not take place before the end of 1973. In addition, the fact that Marwan's alarm was restrained during the hours before the war dictated that Zamir act as Marwan did and transmit the late, focused warning, with its "yes/no." Zamir's emphasis on the "yes" was to a great extent his own personal decision, as he testified:

> [Marwan] did not tell me to "stop everything, this is war." [He said] it is possible that a move by the Soviets and the Americans can stop Sadat. Perhaps [Sadat] is even waiting for it. We spoke for an hour and I decided from everything he said that this was war. He wasn't sure. But for me this is war and we should take this risk [viewing it as war] because, between the two possibilities this is the most serious.[41]

Zamir took the risk seriously, and this seriousness preceded the Israeli military preparations by ten hours. But the unclear message Marwan had transmitted also enabled a different interpretation, a less severe one, which suited the positions of military intelligence and Defense Minister Dayan.

### The Prime Minister

"But how is that possible?"[42]

This was Golda Meir's surprised reaction when she personally received the report containing intimate details of discussions among the Egyptian elite. Meir was amazed, but accepted the information with no uncertainty or doubts. It appears that this was also true of her confidant, Minister Galili. Even in the very few hours before the war broke out, both tried to grasp at the doubtful aspect of the report communicating an imminent war and, relying on Marwan's advice, attempted to prevent it.

Meir acted as though the secrets of Sadat, her primary enemy, were being made clear to her. Zamir personally communicated to her what Sadat said and what he thought. This intensified her confidence in the source of information and became an alternative to an organized evaluation of the situation based on an integration of information sources.

Regarding security, the prime minister did not have or pretend to have the capability to judge the quality of Marwan's information. She had to apportion weight to the assessments of the people surrounding her. In these situations, Dayan had the deciding voice. Meir could only have tried

---

[41] Author's discussion with Zamir, February 19, 2012.
[42] Zamir and Mass 2011, 138.

to balance his influence on her and on decision-making in security matters by adding others, especially Elazar, Zamir, and Zeira in army matters and Galili in political questions.

With regard to politics, Meir was determined to prevent any negotiations. Dayan once called her "one of those people that God has graced with a worldview in colors of black and white and has freed them from shades of twilight and quandaries about dusk. Her answer to a question was either-or."[43] For her, Sadat was the enemy and not to be believed. She did not investigate the seriousness of Marwan's intentions.

Even when in April 1971 Israel discovered, apparently from Marwan, that Sadat was interested in a full peace agreement, with no conditions regarding the Palestinian issue. Meir did not clarify this. She considered communicating this information to Nixon and Kissinger, but immediately pulled back.[44] She viewed such information as an opening that could lead to American pressure on Israel for moves that Israel was unwilling to make. The fact that Israel preferred even then to hide this information from the Americans hints that it was not only election considerations that motivated Meir to refuse Kissinger when he tried to advance negotiations in March 1973 on the basis of Sadat's initiative.

This information from April 1971 could also be interpreted in two contrasting ways. Those who believe in Marwan's credibility can find additional proof as to the high quality of the information he communicated about Sadat's intentions without Sadat's knowledge. Those who suspect him of being a double agent can identify more evidence that Marwan was serving the clear interests of Sadat, his real operator, in communicating messages to Israel.

### The Defense Minister

Dayan was the central figure and sole determiner of Israel's security and political conduct. He was the only person in Israel with full security and political information concentrated in his hands. His experience enabled him to construct an independent appraisal of the situation and his character determined that he did not justify this appraisal to others. His public and political status empowered him to direct security and political moves according to his assessments. He listened to the military intelligence analysis of the situation, but acted according to his own evaluations and guided the chief of staff to do so as well. The prime minister did not feel that she could disagree with Dayan unless he left her an opening.

---

[43] Dayan 1976, 576.
[44] Rabin 1979, 345–46.

Dayan insisted that he directly receive the raw material Marwan transmitted; he was aware of the availability of what defined as "very concrete intelligence information that we thought was the best that could be obtained."[45] This implies that although he respected its credibility and importance, he knew that it was only "the best that could be obtained"— thus, not always correct. In fact, Dayan never hesitated to maintain his own assessment, even when it conflicted with Marwan's information.

Even before Kissinger accepted Ismail's request to meet, Dayan reached the conclusion, *inter alia* on the basis of Marwan's reports, that Sadat might renew the fighting. He reacted by making use of the political channel:

> We must tell the Americans two things: 1. We have reliable information that the Egyptians are planning to renew hostilities at the beginning of 1973. 2. We have no intention of entering a new war of attrition, and if they renew the war we will hit them hard. We must be as one with the Americans. We must warn them [Egypt] and threaten and caution them against renewing fire.[46]

Dayan repeated this reaction throughout 1972 and until the war actually began. The prime minister accepted his advice.

In April, Dayan rejected Marwan's warnings of war in May. He believed that the Egyptians could only initiate a war after that time. Political events indicated that they would not open fire before July, so he ordered war preparations for the second half of 1973. With regard to the Americans, he said:

> Now it is too early [to talk of war], when we must tell them about our assessment and information and tell them that as far as we are concerned, the issue is in doubt. . . . Let's say that there is information and if there is information from the field we will formulate an opinion and will let them know about it.[47]

In other words, not only did Dayan reject Marwan's warning, he even refused to share it in full with the United States so the US government would not pressure Israel to participate in negotiations on the basis of Sadat's initiative.

The information Marwan communicated in September, according to which Sadat would not initiate hostilities before the end of the year and which implied that this would take place only after the elections, supported

---

[45] Bergman and Meltzer 2003, 182.

[46] Braun 1992, 18.

[47] Bartov 2002, 262.

Dayan's thinking that Sadat preferred a political process which would begin before the end of the year, accompanied by American pressure on Israel. As mentioned, Dayan intended to visit Washington at the beginning of December, immediately after the formation of the new Israeli government.[48] The military intelligence assessment of a low probability of war, based on completely different factors, did not add or subtract anything from Dayan's considerations. The fact that, in contrast to the past and despite rising security tensions, Marwan did not transmit any new warnings suited Dayan's perception of the situation.

This also determined the way Dayan related to Marwan's final message on the last day of peace. Until the last moment, Dayan believed that Egypt would not initiate a war. In opposition to Zamir, who stressed the "yes" (war) in Marwan's message in London fourteen hours before the war broke out; to Elazar, who demanded action in accord with this assumption; and to a certain extent even to Zeira, for whom the evacuation of the Soviets had cast doubt on his certainty of "low probability," Dayan only feared a surprise attack by the Syrians and did not even want to mobilize the reserves for deployment at the southern front.

Dayan did not want war. He certainly did not want war before the elections. So he proposed ideas for a peace agreement with Egypt that would suit Sadat's expectations. He communicated these ideas to the Americans as early as June and expressed them publicly in September. He planned to lead these moves and even thought that Sadat was aware of this, and thus would not be interested in initiating a war but was just creating pressure by raising military tension. Dayan preferred to remain skeptical about Zamir's report of his meeting with Marwan. Sadat succeeded in surprising Dayan—and perhaps Ashraf Marwan as well.

## Who Revealed Ashraf Marwan's Identity?

Those who first wrote about 1973 mentioned Marwan only as an unnamed, authorized, and very reliable information source, or as one who knew Egypt very well. Naturally, as time went by, more identifiable details about him were whispered. At the end of the 1980s the question of the identity of the elite Egyptian spy aroused the curiosity of an inquisitive, diligent young newspaper reporter, Aluf Benn, today the editor-in-chief of *Ha'aretz*. The hints he had heard led him to search a news database for "Egypt," "Great Britain," and "businessman." The search immediately led him to an article in the *Financial Times* that mentioned Ashraf Marwan, a

---

[48] Dinitz to Gazit about his discussion with Kissinger, September 30, 1973, Lamed Vav/934, Aleph-4996/2, ISA.

name he remembered from Shazly's book *The Crossing of the Suez* (1980). The article referred to Marwan as an advisor to President Sadat. The reporter understood that he had solved the riddle.

Books about the Yom Kippur War continued to appear, and they never omitted the role of the super-agent. His name, of course, was never mentioned. Among those books was the one published by Eli Zeira in September 1993, twenty years after the war. Zeira's decision to write was influenced by his discussions with Moshe Vardi, the editor of *Yedioth Aharonoth*, and the newspaper's military correspondent, Eitan Haber, who encouraged him to bring his version of events to the public. By the end of 1992, the manuscript was ready. Zeira's argument that the "source of quality information" had actually been working to deceive Israel was a major focus of his book, *Myth versus Reality* (2004). He explained that his suspicions had increased after he read the books written by the two Egyptian chiefs of staff, Shazly (*The Crossing of the Suez*) and Gamasy (*The October War*), as well as Jeffrey Robinson's book about the Saudi oil minister Yamani (*Yamani: The Inside Story*).

In his book, Zeira called Marwan "the information." His name was not mentioned, nor were there any identifying details about him. The censor approved the manuscript. In April 1993, journalist Rami Tal of *Yedioth Aharonoth* was asked to edit the book, with the goal of publishing it in time for the twentieth anniversary of the war and to use its contents in the newspaper's Jewish high-holiday seasonal magazines. The manuscript was also sent for approval to the ministerial committee, as required. It appears that, somewhere in this process, the manuscript was seen and read by others who were not involved in the publication process.

During the editorial work, Tal too was curious about who "the information" was. He read the books Zeira mentioned as having aroused his suspicions about the credibility of the source and concluded correctly that the man was Ashraf Marwan. Zeira later faced criticism that he should only have mentioned Robinson's book in order to protect Marwan's identity, even though the censor approved the manuscript. Was the decision by the censor and the ministerial committee correct in allowing an open discussion about whether the elite Egyptian agent was working to deceive Israel? This question is worth pondering. But after approval had been given for such a discussion, Zeira should not have been the lightning rod for arguments on the issue.

As mentioned, Zeira's book was published in September 1993, in a form even more heavily edited than the one the censor had approved. During the following years, the book did not generate interest in the name of the Mossad agent. A few months later, in 1994, the Egyptian military attaché in Libya, Salah el-Saadany, published a book (most probably not in coordination with Zeira), *Egypt and Libya from Inside, 1969–1976*, that described relations between the two countries during these years. Marwan's name appeared prominently in the story as someone who had been an effective Egyptian emissary. The book referred for the first time, extensively and in depth, to the story of Qaddafi's attempt to down an El Al plane in Rome, the attack which was foiled by Marwan (see chapter 6).

On December 2, 1994, an article based on Saadany's book was published in *Ma'ariv* by another young reporter, Oded Granot. His long article centered on Marwan's character and featured a photo of Marwan's picture, putting a ring on the finger of his wife Mona, Nasser's daughter. It appears that Granot knew more than he wrote even then, as the final paragraph, which dealt with the thwarting of the attempt to down the plane, testified:

> And only one question actually remains open and arouses curiosity: How was the terrorist cell exposed? And was it only the Israeli Mossad that was operating here, or did the Egyptians prefer to act so that the terrorist attack would not take place? The answer could be no less surprising than the affair itself.[49]

Aluf Benn, who had already solved the "riddle of the name" on his own years earlier and had kept the secret, met Granot (ironically, in Cairo), talked with him about his article, and learned that Granot had not chosen to complete his article as he did by chance. He knew who the hero of the story was—and his connection with the Mossad.

Five more years passed without additional details being exposed which might give Marwan's identity away. In September 1999, as the Jewish high holidays were approaching, Hanoch Marmari, then editor of *Ha'aretz*, called a meeting in his office to brainstorm articles for the special holiday magazines. Aluf Benn suggested an article about the Mossad agent who communicated to Israel information about the opening of the Yom Kippur War. "He is now living in London and his story has never been exposed," he said.[50] "And you know who he is?" asked the surprised Marmari. Benn admits that he hesitated for a minute and then revealed the details to those present: "Yes. His name is Ashraf Marwan."

There and then, they decided to ask reporter Ronen Bergman to prepare an article for the holiday magazine. To that end, Bergman requested an interview with Zeira. "As you know, most of the discussion will be about Marwan and about your argument that he was a double agent,"[51] Zeira

---

[49] *Ma'ariv*, December 2, 1994.

[50] Aluf Benn, "How I Found the Spy," *Ha'aretz*, December 26, 2004.

[51] Interview with Zeira, January 15, 2012.

quoted Bergman's opening remarks at the beginning of their interview. Zeira says that he replied, "In this discussion names will not be mentioned. That is the condition for its taking place. If not, it has just ended." He states that he did not even ask Bergman how he knew the name. The discussion took place in line with Zeira's conditions and the article was published in *Ha'aretz* on September 17, 1999, with no mention of Marwan's name and no identifying details except to call him "a senior source operated by Israel in Egypt and one of the most important sources in general."[52] The article focused on whether the source was a double agent. Most of the details in the article that deviated from this question had already been published in the literature or in newspapers.

At the same time, at King's College London, Ahron Bregman was writing a book about Israeli history. Two years earlier, in 1998, following his work on a BBC television series reviewing Arab-Israeli wars, he had published another book (*War and Israeli Society Since 1948*) dealing with Israel's fifty years of war that included interviews with personalities such as Shimon Peres, Ariel Sharon, Yisrael Tal, and Eli Zeira. The Yom Kippur War took its appropriate place in the book, but Marwan was not mentioned at all.

This time, for his new book, Bregman took up the challenge Oded Granot had posed in his *Ma'ariv* article in 1994 to investigate the connection between Marwan and the Mossad. With no special difficulty, he too found the answer Benn had discovered more than ten years earlier, followed by reporters from *Yedioth Aharonoth*, *Ha'aretz*, *Ma'ariv*, and perhaps other media outlets.

In May 2000, a long time before he completed his book, Ahron Bregman published an article in the weekend magazine of *Yedioth Aharonoth* based on the material he had accumulated. The article still did not mention Marwan's name, but described him as "very close to President Nasser and later, the right-hand man of Nasser's successor, Sadat."[53] This article also discussed the argument that a Mossad agent was actually working to deceive Israel.

Before the publication of the book, in September 2002, Bregman presented another article on the subject to the *Yedioth* weekend magazine. This article did not mention the name Marwan either—but this time, Bregman stated that in Israel the intelligence agencies had termed their agent "the son-in-law" because of his family connection to Nasser, as well as "the doctor." Bregman knew that the assertions about the use of the terms were untrue, as he himself had originated the nickname "son-in-law," but he wished to publicly challenge the limitations on publication

---

[52] *Ha'aretz*, September 17, 1999.

[53] Rami Tal, "Egyptian Double Agent," *Yedioth Aharonoth*, May 9, 2000.

posed by censorship, and he succeeded. Even though these deliberate hints were clear enough, the censor approved the article. "They shrugged their shoulders," stated the email Bregman received telling him that the article had been approved.[54]

Two additional researchers who tried to solve the name riddle in their research and writing about the Yom Kippur War were Dr. Ephraim Kahana from Israel (*Ashraf Marwan, Israel's Most Valuable Spy: How the Mossad Recruited Nasser's Own Son-in-Law*) and Howard Blum from the United States (*The Eve of Destruction: The Untold Story of the Yom Kippur War*). Both of these researchers interviewed Zeira. Kahana also published an article "Early Warning versus Concept: The Case of the Yom Kippur War 1973" in summer 2002. His details about Marwan were those published two years earlier in Bregman's article in *Yedioth Aharonoth*. Kahana had talked with Bregman, who claimed that in that first conversation, Kahana had already guessed the identity of the Mossad agent and that the discussion between them strengthened that assumption. About six years later, Kahana testified in an affidavit to Justice Theodore Or that he heard Marwan's name and details about him from Zeira. Blum's book was published in 2003, after Marwan's name had become public knowledge. There is no disagreement that he learned Marwan's identity from Ahron Bregman.

In 1998 a book called *Who Killed Diana?* was published following Princess Diana's death in an automobile accident.[55] It provided an expanded picture of Marwan's deeds and affairs, as a business rival of the Egyptian tycoon Mohamed al-Fayed, the father of Princess Diana's boyfriend Dodi, who was killed with her in the accident. Whether the book's information was true or false, it was later quoted as an inexhaustible source for writings about Marwan in the press and in literature. The book maintained, among other things, that Marwan had served as a secret agent for the intelligence organizations of a few countries, among them the Israeli Mossad.

In the meantime, the last barrier to revealing Marwan's name had been breached. In May 2002, after the publication of the article in *Yedioth Aharonoth*, Ahron Bregman tried to contact Marwan but received no reply. Nor did Marwan react when Bregman sent him a copy of his soon-to-be-published book, with a personal dedication. But Bregman's persistence finally bore fruit. A short time later, on December 2, 2002, in an article in the Egyptian newspaper *Sawt al-Umma*, Marwan described Bregman's book as a "ridiculous detective story."[56] Bregman reacted in an interview

---

[54] Mail from Rami Tal to Ahron Bregman, September 15, 2002, LHCMA, Bregman Files.

[55] Regan 1998.

[56] *Sawt al-Umma*, December 2, 2002; Bregman's police testimony, January 25, 2008, LHCMA, Bregman Files.

with the reporter Khalud el-Gamal published in *Al-Ahram* on December 21, 2002, in which he confirmed that Marwan was the Mossad agent about whom so much had been written. For the first time, the agent's full name had been revealed to the public.[57] Eight days later, on December 29, Bregman sent Marwan a fax in which he detailed why he had disclosed his name.[58] He added that in the coming year, many books would be published to commemorate the thirtieth anniversary of the war. Therefore, he wrote, as his name was already known to many, Bregman had no doubt that it would be published in the future. He preferred to be the first to do that and to highlight his own version, which held that Marwan had been operating for Egypt rather than Israel. Bregman also requested Marwan's help in dealing with his own critics by answering the question of whether Nasser also knew of his ties with the Israeli Mossad. He explained that this point was the weak link in the double-agent thesis.

Immediately, on that same day, Marwan telephoned Bregman at home in London and they spoke for the first time. The contacts between them continued, mostly by letters and faxes to Marwan in London and in telephone calls Marwan initiated.[59] These always took the same form: Marwan would call, listen to make sure that Bregman was on the line, and hang up. He would then call again and they would talk. By June 2003 Bregman had sent Marwan three letters apologizing for publicizing his name at such an inconvenient time, when Marwan was occupied with health problems. He said that he intended to write a book about him and tried to convince Marwan to cooperate. He also informed him about Howard Blum's book, which was about to be published in the United States, and about preparations for a segment on the popular television program *60 Minutes*.

On June 6, 2003, Bregman sent Marwan a fax: "There have been developments—some good, some bad. I want to speak to you. Please contact me as soon as possible." On the same day Marwan telephoned him. "I want it to die," he told Bregman, who responded without hesitation: "It will not!" "Why do they do this revenge?" Marwan protested in English that he seemed to be paying a price for something that was not connected to him: "They are at war there." He promised to meet with Bregman after he had resolved his health problems.

On October 23 the two met in London at the Intercontinental Park Lane Hotel, where Marwan informed Bregman that he was planning to write his own book. "It will take time. I will consult with you from time to time," he

---

[57] *Al-Ahram*, December 21, 2002.

[58] Bregman to Marwan, fax, December 29, 2002, LHCMA, Bregman Files.

[59] Ibid. Bregman transmitted the text of his conversations and correspondence with Marwan to the police as part of his testimony after Marwan's death.

told Bregman, who did not want to leave empty-handed from the meeting and asked, "Why did you warn about war at six p.m. when, in reality, it began at two p.m.?" Marwan downplayed the importance of the error: "A few hours. What difference does it make?" He then repeated his inner feelings: "I wish the matter would die."[60]

In the meantime, the publication of Marwan's name had aroused a storm in Israel about whether he had been a double agent. In April 2005, Zeira filed a libel suit against Zvi Zamir, who had accused him of betraying the most important Israeli agent in the Egyptian elite. The Marwan story had returned to the headlines.

On Friday, May 6, 2005, Ronen Bergman published another article on the affair in *Yedioth Aharonoth*.[61] Under a series of photographs of Marwan with Hosni Mubarak on October 4, 2004, celebrating the anniversary of the "October War," a sub-heading stated: "That's not the way a traitor is hugged in Egypt. That's the way a national hero is embraced." Ahron Bregman sent Marwan an envelope with a photocopy of the article. The following day, on Saturday morning at 09:45 London time, Marwan telephoned Bregman's home.[62] They talked for about twenty minutes. Bregman wanted to know more about the book Marwan was working on. Marwan said that he intended to focus on the events of 1973, ending in January 1974 with Israel and Egypt signing the disengagement agreement in which Marwan had played such an important part.

Again there was a long break in contacts between the two. The next telephone call took place at 13:05 London time on October 6, 2006, thirty-three years after the war.[63] Marwan said that he was in the United States and that for the last three years he had been having health problems. He asked about the book written by Aryeh Shalev, the former head of the research department of military intelligence, which had just been published (*Israel's Intelligence Assessment before the Yom Kippur War: Disentangling Deception and Distraction*) and discussed the orientation of his own book, to be called *October 1973: What Happened*. Marwan hinted that the book would say that he had not been a spy at all, but rather part of a staff of forty people engaged in deceiving Israel—and that there had not been one double agent, but many. "They can say whatever they want; the outcome speaks for itself . . . Golda Meir wanted to commit suicide. Israel lost hundreds of tanks during the first days of the war. . . . I'm not a superman," he said. Bregman interpreted this as a hint that the deception

---

[60] Ibid.

[61] *Yedioth Aharonoth,* May 6, 2005.

[62] Bregman's police testimony, Document 5, Bregman Files, LHCMA.

[63] Bregman's police testimony, Document 4, Bregman Files, LHCMA.

had not been carried out by Marwan alone. In other words, at least some of the abundance of information that flowed to Israeli intelligence was initiated by the Egyptians and was directed at deceiving Israel. Marwan said that the only mistake Sadat had made was to order an advance (referring to the attack on October 12, in the direction of the Sinai passes). He explained that the Egyptian president had reacted to Assad's rage when he understood that Egypt was going to stop the attack much further back than had been agreed. Marwan was proud of the medal he had received from Sadat for his part in the victory. "Keep updating me," he requested at the close of the forty-minute conversation.

As mentioned above, the last conversation between the two took place a day before Marwan's death.

## Was the Timing of Marwan's Death Coincidental?

The publication of Marwan's name in January 2003 stimulated a flood of articles in the Israeli press. In addition, his full name began appearing in books. This combined with the voices supporting Zeira's argument that Marwan had deceived the Mossad motivated senior military intelligence operatives to take legal action against Zeira, who they said had "revealed secrets about intelligence sources and in doing so, did great harm to national secrets."[64] The first to take action in October 2003 were Amos Gilboa and Yossi Langotsky. After the defense minister at the time, Shaul Mofaz, rejected their petition, they applied to the state attorney.

In September 2004, an updated edition of Zeira's book was published that repeated his arguments that Marwan had been a double agent, this time using his real name. Zeira presented his arguments in detail in two sequential interviews with reporter Dan Margalit on the television program *The Final Supplement* that September.[65] Zamir reacted in an interview with Margalit on the same program.[66] He accused Zeira of leaking Marwan's name to the press and to various researchers and argued that he deserved to stand trial. Zeira sued Zamir for libel. The case was heard by Justice Theodore Or, sitting as arbitrator. "The deliberation results in the rejection of the plaintiff's suit," the judge determined in a thirty-six-page decision issued on March 25, 2007.[67]

---

[64] Gilboa was a former head of the military intelligence research department; Langotsky was a former head of the military intelligence collection department (Bar-Yosef 2010, 351).

[65] *Final Supplement,* Israeli television, September 10, 2004; Or 2006, 2.

[66] *Final Supplement,* Israeli television, September 23, 2004.

[67] Or 2006, 36.

As agreed and requested by the parties, publication of the testimonies or of any part of the protocol of discussion in the arbitration is forbidden due to national security considerations. My assumption is that the publication prohibition also falls on this arbitration ruling.[68]

This was how the arbitration ruling began. Nevertheless, Or's ruling was published three months later, on June 23, 2007. When this became known to Marwan, he viewed it as the first official confirmation by the State of Israel that he had been a Mossad agent. Three days later, he contacted Bregman in that urgent and unusual telephone call during which they agreed to meet on the following day. The next day, Marwan was dead.

Marwan had lived for thirteen years under the shadow of Granot's hint about his connection with the Mossad in *Ma'ariv* in December 1994. Five years had passed since that relationship had become public after Ahron Bregman's revelation. Three years had gone by since Zeira had confirmed the information. During that entire period, Marwan had not felt threatened. His defense had been the argument by Zeira and others that Marwan had actually been Sadat's emissary and part of an Egyptian plan of deception that preceded the Yom Kippur War. During this period, Marwan's daughter had married the son of Egyptian foreign minister (and later secretary-general of the Arab League) Amr Moussa. He had been received with exceptional honor by Egyptian government figures, among them President Mubarak, and was a good friend of Mubarak's son and expected heir.

Marwan had been in the United States during the arbitration, concerned with his heart problems and far from events. He returned to London concerned that the official legal proceedings in Israel had explicitly confirmed him as a spy operating for Israel. He tried urgently to make contact with Bregman and left him three messages on his answering machine. When they spoke later, the conversation focused on the arbitration ruling, and they determined to meet on the following day. "And, in general, how are you?"[69] Bregman asked at the end of the conversation. "Just fine, except for this headache," Marwan replied, referring to the Or arbitration ruling. "Okay, my friend, best wishes and goodbye," Bregman ended the conversation. The following day Bregman waited in his office for a telephone call to arrange the meeting. Instead, he received a call from his sister in Israel telling him of Marwan's mysterious death by falling from the terrace of his home.

---

[68] Ibid., 1.
[69] Bregman's testimony to the police, Document 7, LHCMA, Bregman Files.

Perhaps the proximity of the arbitration ruling to Marwan's death was coincidental. But Marwan's conversation before his death proves that, for the first time, he was worried. "At least two respected Egyptians who had become a source of embarrassment to the government elite . . . met their deaths under similar circumstances in London," wrote Bar-Yosef.[70] But, ironically, if the timing of Marwan's death was not coincidental, those who fought for Marwan's honor and argued stubbornly against Zeira created the conditions that hastened the death of the person they themselves called the best spy Israel had ever had. That is certainly not what they intended. But the publication of Justice Or's ruling, in contrast to what it determined, led to later events. The very fact that the arbitration ruling caused Marwan to feel threatened might testify to his not having worked in the service of Egypt—or, at least, not always in its service.

In this story, there are no completely guilty parties. Since the centrality of political conduct in the events of 1973 has still not been expressed in research, the role of the intelligence apparatus has been emphasized in considering the dramatic failure of the Yom Kippur War. Facing such a heavy burden of guilt, it can be understood why, in retrospect, Israelis' misgivings about whether the intelligence system should have trusted the elite Egyptian agent finally became an overly emotional public controversy between the former heads of the Israeli intelligence system. It would have been preferable if these misgivings had remained within the four walls of the intelligence organizations. In that case, it may be said that the Israeli public would have gained the privilege of not knowing about them. Perhaps they led to the revelation of Marwan's identity.

But after his identity had been publicized, Zeira's position—that Marwan had acted as Sadat's emissary to deceive Israel—actually elevated Marwan's status in the eyes of the Egyptians. That is what served to protect him from denunciation as a traitor even after his name was publicly revealed. The official ruling against Zeira created the impression that those who attacked Zeira and argued decisively that Marwan had acted for Israel and against Egypt had been right. Perhaps this impression was what led to his death shortly after the ruling. Or's decision may have been the final legal word on the question of who leaked Marwan's name, but it is not certain whether this was the real truth. It is doubtful whether those involved, in the fervor of blind justice, ever took into consideration the possible implications of his public exposure.

In Israel, the affair died away. In July 2012 the attorney general decided to close the case against Zeira for exposing Marwan's identity. The significant questions remained outside the discussion.

---

[70] Bar-Yosef 2011, 13.

The Egyptians, in any case, fabricated a suitable burial for Marwan and gave him a funeral ceremony befitting a national hero. The media coverage emphasized his role in the Egyptian deception plan. President Mubarak himself, who in 1973 was a member of the small circle of war planners, testified to Marwan's central role in these plans and his great contribution to their success. Did he really mean that? It appears that there is almost no one left to ask.

# Dramatis Personae

The following is a list of major players in this book and their positions during the period leading up to the Yom Kippur War.

## Israel

**Yigal Allon** (1918–1980): Deputy prime minister of Israel under Golda Meir; acting prime minister during her illness. Author of the Allon Plan.

**Menachem Begin** (1913–1992): Chairman of the Gahal political bloc and head of the opposition in the Knesset in 1973; took leadership of the newly formed Likud party shortly after the war and was elected prime minister in 1977.

**Moshe Dayan** (1915–1981): Israeli minister of defense from 1967 to 1974; later served as minister of foreign affairs under the Begin government.

**Simcha Dinitz** (1929–2003): Director-general of the Prime Minister's Office and political advisor to Golda Meir before being named Israel's ambassador to the United States in 1973, replacing Yitzhak Rabin.

**Abba Eban** (1915–2002): Israeli foreign minister from 1966 to 1974.

**David "Dado" Elazar** (1925–1976): Chief of General Staff of the Israel Defense Forces from 1972 to 1974, when he was forced to resign in the wake of the Yom Kippur War.

**Yisrael Galili** (1911–1986): Minister without portfolio under Golda Meir and a member of her "Kitchen Cabinet."

**Mordechai Gazit** (1922–): Golda Meir's chief of staff before succeeding Simcha Dinitz as director-general of the Prime Minister's Office in 1973.

**Yitzhak Hofi** (1927–): Head of Northern Command for the IDF.

**Golda Meir** (1898–1978): Fourth prime minister of Israel; elected in 1969 and resigned in 1974 in the aftermath of the Yom Kippur War.

**Benny Peled** (1928–2002): Israeli general; named commander of Israel's air force in 1973 and advised Golda Meir during the war.

**Yitzhak Rabin** (1922–1995): Israeli ambassador to the United States from 1968 to 1973, when he was replaced by Simcha Dinitz; succeeded Golda Meir as prime minister in 1974 in the wake of the war.

**Aryeh Shalev** (1928–2013): Head of research the IDF military intelligence; was rebuked by the Agranat Commission after the war and retired in 1976.

**Avner Shalev** (1939–): Advisor and bureau head to Chief of Staff Elazar during the war.

**Mordechai Shalev**: Deputy to Ambassador Dinitz and charge d'affaires at the Israeli embassy in Washington, D.C.

**Ariel Sharon** (1928–): Head of Southern Command until his resignation from the IDF in July 1973; later served as prime minister from 2001 until his stroke in 2006.

**Yisrael Tal** (1924–2010): IDF general, assistant head of general staff, and deputy to Chief of Staff Elazar during the war; highly influential in the development of Israeli military doctrine.

**Zvi Tsur** (1923–2004): Chief of General Staff of the IDF from January 1961 to December 1963; in 1973 served as advisor to Moshe Dayan.

**Gad Yaacobi** (1935–2007): Knesset member and assistant transportation minister; close associate of Moshe Dayan.

**Zvi "Zvika" Zamir** (1925–): Director of the Mossad (the Israeli intelligence agency) from 1968 to 1974.

**Eli Zeira** (1928–): Director of Israeli military intelligence (AMAN) from 1972 to 1973, when he was rebuked by the postwar Agranat Commission and resigned.

## Egypt

**Ahmad Ismail Ali** (1917–1974): Defense minister of Egypt during the war.

**Mohamed Abdel Ghani el-Gamasy** (1921–2003): Head of Egyptian military operations during the Yom Kippur War; appointed chief of General Staff in December 1973.

**Mohamed Hassanein Heikal** (1923–): Editor-in-chief of Egypt's *Al-Ahram* from 1957 to 1974; worked closely with Anwar Sadat during the Yom Kippur War.

**Hafez Ismail** (1919–1997): National security advisor to Anwar Sadat.

**Ashraf Marwan** (1944–2007): Egyptian intelligence operative; son-in-law to Egyptian president Gamal Abdel Nasser; Mossad agent (see Appendix). Died under mysterious circumstances in 2007.

**Anwar Sadat** (1918–1981): President of Egypt from 1970 until his assassination by Islamists in 1981.

**Saad el-Din el-Shazly** (1922–2011): Chief of staff of the Egyptian armed forces during the war; resigned in December 1973.

**Mohammed Hassan el-Zayyat** (1915–1993): Egyptian minister of foreign affairs from 1972 to immediately after the Yom Kippur War.

## United States

**Joseph Greene** (1920–2010): Head of US interests section in Cairo until June 1973.

**Alexander Haig** (1924–2010): White House chief of staff to President Nixon beginning in August 1973.

**Richard Helms** (1913–2002): Director of the CIA until February 1973, then US ambassador to Iran.

**Kenneth Keating** (1900–1975): Served as US ambassador to Israel from August 1973 to 1975.

**Henry Kissinger** (1923–): National security advisor to the White House from 1969 to 1975; sworn in as US secretary of state on September 22, 1973, just before the start of the war. Controlled the United States' secret channels of communication.

**Richard Milhous Nixon** (1913–2004): President of the United States from 1969 to 1974, when he resigned rather than face impeachment over the Watergate scandal.

**Peter Rodman** (1943–2008): Member of the National Security Council and assistant to Henry Kissinger.

**William P. Rogers** (1913–2001): US secretary of state under President Nixon from 1969 until September 1973; author of the Rogers Plan.

**Harold Saunders** (1930–): Member of the National Security Council and assistant to Henry Kissinger.

**James Schlesinger** (1929–): Director of the CIA from February to July 1973, when he was appointed secretary of defense by President Nixon.

**Brent Scowcroft** (1925–): US Air Force general and deputy assistant for national security affairs to President Nixon; later served two terms as national security advisor.

**Joseph Sisco** (1919–2004): Assistant secretary of state for Middle Eastern affairs under Kissinger.

## Soviet Union

**Leonid Brezhnev** (1906–1982): General secretary of the Central Committee of the Communist Party of the Soviet Union from 1964 to 1982; made efforts toward détente with Richard Nixon.

**Anatoli Dobrynin** (1919–2010): Soviet ambassador to the United States from 1962 to 1986.

**Andrei Gromyko** (1909–1989): Foreign minister of the Soviet Union from 1957 to 1985.

**Vladimir Vinogradov** (1921–1997): Soviet ambassador to Egypt from 1970 to 1974.

## Other

**Hafez al-Assad** (1930–2000): President of Syria from 1971 to 2000.

**Moammar Qaddafi** (1942–2011): President of Libya from 1969 to 2011.

**King Faisal bin-Abdulaziz al-Saud** (1906–1975): King of Saudi Arabia from 1964 to his death in 1975; led modernization efforts and exerted great influence in the region, particularly with regard to inter-Arab relations.

**King Hussein bin Talal** (1935–1999): King of Jordan from 1952 to 1999.

**Kurt Waldheim** (1918–2007): Secretary-general of the United Nations from 1972 to 1981; later served as president of Austria.

# Timeline of Events

All times given are local times at the location being discussed.

## 1972

July 17: Sadat publicizes his decision to remove Soviet military advisors from Egypt.

July 19: Sadat contacts the United States with a request to begin talks in order to turn over a new leaf in US-Egypt relations.

October 6: Kissinger and Rabin meet in the White House.

October 24: Sadat participates in a meeting of the Supreme Council of the Armed Forces in Egypt.

November 14: Dayan meets with Kissinger as well as Rogers in Washington.

December 1: Golda Meir's "kitchen cabinet" meets to discuss warnings that Egypt will initiate renewed fighting.

December 19: Message from Ismail to Kissinger.

December 20: Message from Kissinger to Ismail.

December 22: Kissinger and Rabin meet at the White House.

## 1973

January 12: Sadat and President Tito meet in Yugoslavia.

January 23: Message from Kissinger to Ismail.
The Vietnam ceasefire agreement is initialed in Paris.

January 24: Meeting between Kissinger and Rabin at the White House.

January 25: 11:00 President Nixon and Rabin meet at the White House.
16:10 Discussion between Kissinger and Rabin.

January 27:    Message from Ismail to Kissinger.

February 3:    Message from Kissinger to Ismail.

February 5:    Kissinger and Rabin meet at the White House.

February 6:    Kissinger and King Hussein meet in Washington.

February 7:    Hafez Ismail visits Moscow and meets with the Soviet leadership.

February 15:   CIA director Schlesinger meets with Rabin in Washington.

February 18:   Meir and Dayan consult at Glilot.

February 20:   Hafez Ismail and British foreign minister Alec Douglas-Home meet in London.

February 21:   Kissinger and Rabin meet.

The Israeli Air Force shoots down a Libyan passenger plane over Sinai. One hundred and eight passengers and crew members are killed.

February 22:   Kissinger and Rabin meet, then speak later by telephone.

February 24:   Telephone conversation between Kissinger and Rabin.

February 25:   Kissinger and Hafez Ismail meet secretly in Armonk, New York.

February 26:   Second secret meeting between Kissinger and Ismail in Armonk.

18:00 President Nixon and Kissinger meet in the White House.

19:15 Kissinger and Rabin speak by telephone.

February 27:   Sadat meets with senior media figures in Cairo.

Meir, Rabin and Zamir meet with Schlesinger in Washington.

11:42 Kissinger and King Hussein meet secretly in Washington.

15:30 Kissinger and Rabin meet.

February 28:   Egyptian defense minister Ismail Ali visits Moscow.

08:15 Kissinger, Meir, and Rabin meet at Rabin's Washington home.

12:30 Deputy Secretary of State Kenneth Rush meets with Meir.

16:00 Defense Secretary Richardson meets with Meir.

19:30 Kissinger and Rabin meet at the White House.

23:30 Kissinger and Rabin speak by telephone.

March 1:　09:47 President Nixon and Kissinger meet to prepare for Nixon's meeting with Meir and Rabin.

10:30 Kissinger and Rabin speak by telephone.

11:00 Nixon and Kissinger meet with Meir and Rabin.

15:06 Kissinger and Rabin speak by telephone.

March 2:　Ismail Ali meets with Soviet leaders in Moscow.

March 9:　Message from Kissinger to Hafez Ismail.

18:40 Kissinger and Rabin meet; Kissinger outlines to Rabin an agreement with Egypt and a schedule to reach it, and asks for Meir's consent.

March 10:　Meir and Rabin speak by telephone.

15:15 Kissinger and Rabin speak by telephone; Rabin delivers Meir's negative reply.

March 13:　Meir reports to a small group of ministers on her discussions in the United States.

March 20:　Message from Ismail to Kissinger.

March 22:　Message from Kissinger to Ismail.

March 26:　Sadat makes a speech in Cairo and announces changes in his government.

March 30:　Kissinger meets with Dinitz, Rabin's replacement as Israeli ambassador to the United States.

April 1:　*Newsweek* correspondent de Borchgrave interviews Sadat.

April 6:　Kissinger and Dinitz speak by telephone.

April 7:　Message from Ismail to Kissinger.

April 10:　The IDF begins Operation Spring of Youth in Lebanon.

April 11:　A message from Kissinger to Ismail is delayed on Meir's demand.

Kissinger and Dinitz meet at the White House.

|            | Ashraf Marwan passes to Israel intelligence information and a warning that Sadat intends to open hostilities in mid-May. |
| April 12:  | Ismail receives Kissinger's message suggesting a date for their next meeting. |
| April 13:  | Kissinger and Dinitz speak by telephone. |
| April 18:  | "Golda's kitchen cabinet" meets to discuss warnings that Egypt plans to renew hostilities. |
|            | Kissinger and Dinitz meet in the White House. |
|            | Sadat presides over an Egyptian cabinet meeting to discuss war against Israel. |
| April 20:  | Message from Ismail to Kissinger. |
| April 21:  | The National Assembly meets in Cairo to discuss war with Israel. |
| April 23:  | Ismail sends Kissinger a message to confirm their May meeting. |
|            | Sadat meets with Assad in Alexandria to coordinate a war against Israel. |
|            | Marwan reports that the war will be postponed to the end of May or the beginning of June. |
| April 24:  | Gazit, director general of the prime minister's office, meets with Soviet representative Yuri Primakov in Geneva. |
| April 26:  | Gazit and Primakov meet again. |
| May 3:     | Kissinger and Dinitz meet in the White House. Dinitz tells Kissinger about Hussein's warning to Meir about Egypt's and Syria's intention to renew hostilities. |
| May 7:     | Message from Kissinger to Ismail. |
| May 8:     | Kissinger and Soviet foreign minister Gromyko meet in Zavidovo, Soviet Union. |
| May 9:     | Hussein meets with Meir and Dayan in Tel Aviv. |
|            | Kissinger meets with Soviet leaders in Zavidovo and Moscow. |
| May 12:    | Kissinger meets with Israeli foreign minister Abba Eban at the White House. |
| May 13:    | Kissinger and Dinitz meet at the White House. |

| | |
|---|---|
| May 14: | The IDF General Staff meets with Dayan in Tel Aviv to discuss Israeli war objectives. |
| May 15: | Kissinger and Dinitz meet at the White House. |
| May 18: | Gad Yaacobi communicates Dayan's intentions regarding a peace treaty to the United States. |
| | Kissinger and Eban meet at the White House. |
| May 20: | Kissinger and Ismail meet near Paris. |
| May 21: | Summary at the IDF General Staff meeting with Dayan regarding preparations for war in the coming months. |
| May 25: | Marwan reports on the postponement of the war. |
| May 26: | Message from Kissinger to Ismail. |
| | |
| June 2: | Kissinger and Dinitz meet at the White House. |
| | President Nixon offers Kissinger the post of Secretary of State. |
| | Message from Ismail to Kissinger. |
| June 5: | Message from Kissinger to Ismail. |
| June 10: | Message from Ismail to Kissinger. |
| June 14: | Discussion between Kissinger and Dinitz. |
| | Kissinger submits a memorandum to the president regarding summit discussions between Nixon and Brezhnev. |
| | "Golda's kitchen cabinet" to discuss the US-Soviet summit. |
| | Marwan reports that the war has been postponed to the end of September or the beginning of October. |
| June 15: | Kissinger and Dinitz meet in the White House. |
| June 18–23: | Summit meeting between President Nixon and Secretary-General Brezhnev in Washington. |
| June 28: | Rogers sends a memorandum to Nixon proposing the initiation of a secret political process between Israel and Egypt. |
| | |
| July 1: | Joe Alon, Israeli air attaché, is murdered near Washington. |
| July 3: | Kissinger and Dinitz meet in San Clemente, California. |
| July 4: | Kissinger and Dinitz speak by telephone. |

July 6:        Dayan and Elazar decide to reduce compulsory
               IDF service.

July 7:        Message from Kissinger to Ismail.

July 11:       Message from Ismail to Kissinger.

July 13:       Hafez Ismail visits Moscow and meets with Brezhnev.

July 16:       Sadat's speaks in Egypt to the National Assembly regard-
               ing the situation following the summit meeting between
               Nixon and Brezhnev.

July 20:       Kissinger and Dinitz meet in the White House.

August 3:      Kissinger and Dinitz meet in the White House.

August 8:      Kissinger and Dinitz speak by telephone.

August 10:     Israel intercepts an Iraqi passenger plane in an attempt to
               capture George Habash, head of the Popular Front for the
               Liberation of Palestine.

August 12:     Israel decides to end the war deployment according to the
               "Blue-White Plan."

August 13:     Kissinger transmits a message to Ismail via the Iranian
               ambassador in Washington in another attempt to set a
               secret political process in motion.

August 14:     Kissinger and Dinitz meet at the White House.

August 15:     Kissinger meets with the Iranian ambassador in
               Washington.

               Kissinger and Dinitz speak by telephone.

August 16:     Marwan and King Faisal's advisor meet in Cairo.

August 17:     Marwan leaves for Libya on a mission for Sadat and meets
               with Qaddafi.

               Marwan returns to Cairo, then leaves for Kuwait and
               Saudi Arabia.

               Kissinger and Eban meet at Dinitz's home in Washington.

August 20:     Kissinger and Dinitz meet.

August 21:     Senior representatives of the Syrian army arrive in
               Alexandria for discussions of the Supreme Joint Council of
               the Armed Forces in order to coordinate plans for the war.

August 24:     Sadat and Marwan meet with King Faisal in Saudi Arabia.

Sadat and Marwan meet with Emir Khalifa in Qatar.

August 25–26: President Sadat and President Assad meet in Baludan near Damascus.

Marwan meets with Qaddafi in Cairo, then leaves for Damascus to meet with Sadat and Assad.

August 30: Kurt Waldheim, secretary-general of the United Nations, visits Jerusalem and meets with Meir.

September 2: Marwan reports on Sadat's trip; he says that war is planned only toward the end of the year. He also provides details to the Mossad of Libyan-operated terrorists' plans to use missiles to shoot down an El Al plane in Rome.

September 4: The Central Committee of the Israeli Labor Party adopts the "Galili Document," the governing party's policy for settling the territories occupied in 1967.

September 8: Kissinger and Dinitz meet.

September 10: Kissinger and Dinitz meet at the White House.

Dinitz leaves for consultations in Israel.

Sadat, Assad, and King Hussein meet in Cairo.

September 12: Sadat and Assad determine October 6 as the date for initiating the war. Sadat reports to his close associate, journalist Mohamed Hassanein Heikal, that war will begin the following month.

September 13: Thirteen Syrian MiGs are shot down during an air skirmish above northern Syria. Israel loses one Mirage.

September 14: *Ma'ariv* publishes Dayan's political intentions regarding a peace agreement with Egypt.

September 15: Kissinger meets with the Iranian ambassador at the White House.

September 17: First of three strategic discussions in the IDF general staff with Dayan in Tel Aviv.

September 20: The US embassy in Tel Aviv issues a report on Dayan's political intentions.

September 22: Kissinger is appointed US secretary of state.

Sadat and Assad give their armies' chiefs of staff the date of the opening of hostilities—October 6.

September 23: Dinitz returns to Washington after a series of consultations in Israel.

September 24: Second discussion in the IDF general staff, dealing with strategic thinking. This time Zvi Zamir, director of the Mossad, also participates.

Kissinger gives a speech at the UN General Assembly in New York.

Kissinger receives a memorandum from his assistant Bill Quandt dealing with the chances for an Israeli-Arab agreement.

September 25: King Hussein meets Meir at Glilot.

Kissinger meets with Arab foreign ministers in New York.

September 26: Eve of Rosh Hashanah.

The London *Times* reports on Kissinger's plan for an agreement between Israel and Egypt.

In Tel Aviv, Dayan and IDF General Staff hold a series of discussions about the military situation. Dayan visits the Golan Heights and publicizes the military situation to representatives of the press.

September 27: First day of Rosh Hashanah.

Egypt proclaims a full military call-up exercise, the twenty-third in nine months.

September 28: Third anniversary of Nasser's death.

Nixon and Kissinger meet in the White House with Gromyko, who warns of a flare-up in the Middle East.

September 29: Terror attack in Austria against a train carrying Jewish immigrants from the Soviet Union.

Sadat assembles the National Security Council and reports that war will break out in the near future. He does not cite a date.

Sadat informs Vinogradov, Soviet ambassador in Cairo, that Egypt is about to break the ceasefire with Israel. Marwan does not report this until the night of October 5.

September 30: Meir leaves for Strasbourg for discussions at the European Council.

Kissinger and Dinitz meet at the White House.

The IDF General Staff meets to discuss the situation at the Syrian front.

October 1:     After making a speech at the European Council, Meir leaves for Vienna to deal with the closing of the immigrant transit camp.

October 2:     Dayan and Elazar meet to discuss the security tension.

October 3:     Libyan prime minister Abdel Salem Jaloud visits Egypt and meets with Sadat and Marwan.

Ismail Ali leaves for Damascus to coordinate the time the war is to begin.

Marwan leaves for Libya to coordinate moves connected to the war initiative.

"Golda's kitchen cabinet" meets to discuss the military situation.

October 4:     The Egyptians update Vinogradov on the date the war will begin.

Dayan holds consultations in his office about the security tension.

The IDF General Staff meets to discuss army discipline.

Marwan leaves Libya for Paris and reports on preparations for war. Asks to meet Zamir on the following evening in London.

Reports begin arriving in Israel in the evening that the Soviet advisors' families are being evacuated from Egypt and Syria.

Journalist Yosef Harif reports in *Ma'ariv* on Dayan's attitude toward political steps after the Israeli elections; the US embassy in Israel reports this to Washington.

October 5:     Yom Kippur Eve.

08:25 Discussion in Elazar's office.

09:00 Discussion in Dayan's office.

09:45 Discussion in Meir's office.

11:30 The Israeli government meets, with a number of ministers absent.

12:30 The IDF General Staff holds an urgent discussion in Tel Aviv.

Kissinger meets with Egyptian foreign minister Zayyat in New York.

17:30 Message from Meir to Kissinger delivered to the White House.

22:00 In London, Zamir meets Marwan, who tells him that the war will begin on the following day at sunset.

October 6:

In Israel:

02:30 Zamir reports that war will break out that evening.

03:50 Zamir's message is communicated to Meir and Dayan.

05:00 Elazar meets with Zeira and Peled.

05:50 Dayan meets with Elazar.

08:05 Consultation in Meir's office.

10:15 Meir meets with the US ambassador Keating.

11:00 Dayan participates in a consultation at the IDF command post.

12:00 Government ministers meet in Meir's Tel Aviv office.

13:50 First sightings of Egyptian attack planes. The attack begins.

14:05 Alert sirens heard in Israel.

In New York (six hours behind Israel and Egypt):

06:30 Kissinger is informed that war will break out in the coming hours and calls Dobrynin, Soviet ambassador to the United States.

06:55 Kissinger telephones Mordechai Shalev, Dinitz's deputy.

07:00 Kissinger speaks with Zayyat.

07:25 Zayyat speaks with Hafez Ismail in Cairo.

07:35 Kissinger speaks again with Zayyat.

07:45 Kissinger speaks again with Shalev.

07:47 Kissinger speaks again with Dobrynin.

08:15 Kissinger speaks again with Zayyat and learns from him that war has broken out.

# Bibliography

## Archives

Bregman Files. Liddell Hart Centre for Military Archives. King's College, London. http://www.kcl.ac.uk/library/collections/ archivespec/collections/lhcma.aspx

Central Intelligence Agency Library. https://www.cia.gov/library

Ford Presidential Archives. Gerald R. Ford Presidential Library and Museum. Ann Arbor and Grand Rapids, Michigan. http://www.fordlibrarymuseum.gov

Israel State Archives. Ginzach Ha-Medina. Jerusalem, Israel. http://www.archives.gov.il

Library of Congress. Washington, D.C. http://www.loc.gov/index.html

National Archives of the United States. US National Archives and Records Administration. Washington, D.C. http://aad.archives.gov

National Security Archive. George Washington University. Washington, D.C. http://www.gwu.edu/~nsarchiv/

Nixon Presidential Archives. US National Archives and Records Administration. Nixon Presidential Library and Museum. Yorba Linda, California. http://www.nixonlibrary.gov/

## Books

Agranat Commission. *The Partial Report of the Israeli Commission of Inquiry*. 1974. Hebrew.

Arbel, David, and Uri Neeman. *Shigaon L'lo Kipurim [Unforgivable Delusion]*. Tel Aviv: Yedioth Aharonoth, 2005. Hebrew.

Armoni, Ora. *Haver V'Ish Sod, Sikhot Im Sini [A Confidant and a Friend]*. Tel Aviv: Ha'Kibbutz Ha'Meuchad, 2008. Hebrew.

Asher, Daniel, ed. *Ha-Surim al Ha-Gderot [The Syrians on the Borders: The IDF Northern Command in the Yom Kippur War]*. Tel Aviv: Maarakhot, 2008. Hebrew.

Bartov, Hanoch. *Dado, 48 Shanim V'Od 20 Yom [Dado, 48 Years and 20 Days]*. Or Yehuda: Dvir, 1978. Hebrew.

———. *Dado, 48 Shanim V'Od 20 Yom [Dado, 48 Years and 20 Days]*. 2nd ed. Or Yehuda: Dvir, 2002. Hebrew.

Bar-Yosef, Uri. *Ha-Tzofeh Nirdam [The Watchman Fell Asleep: The Surprise of Yom Kippur and Its Sources]*. Tel Aviv: Zmora Bitan, 2001. Hebrew.

———. *Hamalakh [The Angel]*. Tel Aviv: Kinneret, Zmora-Bitan, 2010. Hebrew.

———. *Hamalakh [The Angel]*. Revised ed. Tel Aviv: Kinneret, Zmora-Bitan, 2011. Hebrew.

Ben Porat, Yishayahu, Yehonatan Geffen, Uri Dan, Eitan Haber, Hezi Carmel, Eli Landau, and Eli Tavor. *Hamekhdal [Kippur]*. Tel Aviv: Special Edition Publishers, 1974.

Bergman, Ronen, and Gil Meltzer. *Milkhemet Yom Kippur: Zman Emet [The Yom Kippur War: Real Time]*. Tel Aviv: Yedioth Aharonoth, 2003. Hebrew.

Braun, Aryeh. *Moshe Dayan B'Milkhemet Yom Kippur [Moshe Dayan and the Yom Kippur War]*. Tel Aviv: Yedioth Aharonoth, 1992. Hebrew.

Caspit, Ben, and Ilan Kfir. *Ehud Barak*. Tel Aviv: Alpha Tikshoret, 1998. Hebrew.

Central Intelligence Agency. *President Nixon and the Role of Intelligence in the 1973 Arab-Israeli War.* Washington, D.C.: Central Intelligence Agency, 2013. May 14, 1973. Released January 30, 2013. Available at https://www.cia.gov/library/publications/historical-collection-publications/arab-israeli-war/nixon-arab-isaeli-war.pdf.

Dayan, Moshe. *Avnei Derekh [Story of My Life].* Jerusalem: Edanim; Tel Aviv: Dvir, 1976. Hebrew.

Dinitz, Simcha. Untitled. Unpublished manuscript. 2003. Hebrew.

Ezov, Amiram. *Tzlikha [Crossing].* Tel Aviv: Kinneret, Zmora-Bitan, Dvir, 2011. Hebrew.

Gamasy, Mohamed Abdel Ghani el-. *Milkhemet October 1973 [The October War: Memoirs of Field Marshal El-Gamasy of Egypt].* Tel Aviv: Special Edition Publishing, 1994. Hebrew.

Golan, Matti. *Ha-Sikhot Ha-Sodiot Shel Henry Kissinger [The Secret Conversations of Henry Kissinger].* Tel Aviv: Schocken, 1976. Hebrew.

Gordon, Shmuel. *Shloshim Sha'ot B'October [Thirty Hours in October].* Tel Aviv: Sifriat Ma'ariv, 2008. Hebrew.

Haber, Eitan. *Ha-Yom Tifrotz Milkhama [Today War Will Break Out: The Reminiscences of Brig. Gen. Israel Lior].* Jerusalem: Edanim Publishers, 1987. Hebrew.

Heikal, Mohamed. *The Road to Ramadan.* New York: Ballantine Books, 1975.

Kipnis, Yigal. *Ha-Har She-Haya K'Mifletzet, Ha-Golan Bain Suria V'Yisrael [The Mountain Which Was as a Monster: The Golan Between Syria and Israel].* Jerusalem: Magnes, 2009. Hebrew.

Kissinger, Henry. *White House Years.* New York: Little, Brown and Company, 1979.

———. *Years of Crisis.* London: Weidenfeld and Nicolson, 1982.

————. *Crisis: An Anatomy of Two Major Foreign Policy Crises.* New York: Simon and Schuster, 2003.

Maoz, Moshe. *Asad: Ha-Sphinx M'Damesek [Asad: The Sphinx of Damascus].* Tel Aviv: Sifriat Ma'ariv, 1988. Hebrew.

————. *Yisrael, Suria, Sof Ha-sikhsukh?! [Syria and Israel: From War to Peacemaking].* Tel Aviv: Sifriat Ma'ariv, 1996. Hebrew.

Medzini, Meron. *Golda: Biographia Politit [Golda: A Political Biography].* Tel Aviv: Yedioth Aharonoth, 2008. Hebrew.

Meir, Golda. *Khayai [My Life].* Tel Aviv: Sifriat Ma'ariv, 1975. Hebrew.

Meital, Yoram. *Hitpatkhut Mediniuta Shel Mitzraim B'Yakhas L'Sikhsukh Im Yisrael 1967–1977 [Egypt's Struggle for Peace: Continuity and Change, 1967–1977].* Ph.D. dissertation, Haifa University, 1991. Hebrew.

Nakdimon, Shlomo. *Svirut Nemukha [Low Probability].* Ramat Gan: Revivim, 1982. Hebrew.

Quandt, William B. *Peace Process: American Diplomacy and the Arab-Israeli Conflict since 1967.* Washington, D.C.: Brookings Institution Press, 2001.

Rabin, Yitzhak. *Pinkas Sherut [The Rabin Memoirs].* Tel Aviv: Sifriat Ma'ariv, 1979. Hebrew.

Robinson, Jeffrey. *Yamani: The Inside Story.* New York: Simon and Schuster, 1988.

Ronen, Ran (Peker). *Netz Ba-Shama'im [Hawk in the Sky].* Tel Aviv: Yedioth Aharonoth, 2002. Hebrew.

Saadany, Salah el-. *Egypt and Libya from Inside, 1969–1976: The Qaddafi Revolution and the Eventual Break in Relations.* Jefferson, NC: McFarland, 1994.

Sadat, Anwar. *Sippur Khayai [In Search of Identity: An Autobiography].* Jerusalem: Edanim, 1978. Hebrew.

Seale, Patrick. *Assad: Ha-Ma'avak al Ha-Mizrakh Ha-Tikhon [Assad of Syria: The Struggle for the Middle East]*. Tel Aviv: Ma'arachot, 1993. Hebrew.

Shalev, Aryeh. *Kishalon V'Hatzlakha B'Hatra'a [Success and Failure in Advance Warning: Israeli Intelligence Assessments before the Yom Kippur War]*. Tel Aviv: Ma'arachot, 2006. Hebrew.

Shamir, Shimon. *Mitzraim B'Hanagat Sadat [Egypt under Sadat]*. Or Yehuda: Dvir 1978. Hebrew.

Shazly, Saad Mohamed el-Husseiny el-. *Khatzi'at Ha-taala [The Crossing of the Suez]*. Tel Aviv: Ma'arachot, 1987. Hebrew.

Shlaim, Avi. *Ha-Melekh Hussein, Biographia Politit [Lion of Jordan: The Life of King Hussein]*. Or Yehuda: Dvir, 2009. Hebrew.

Stein, Kenneth. *Medini'ut Amitza [Heroic Diplomacy: Sadat, Kissinger, Carter, Begin and the Quest for Arab-Israeli Peace]*. Tel Aviv: Ma'arachot, 2006. Hebrew.

Zamir, Zvi, and Efrat Mass. *Be-enayim Pekukhot [Eyes Wide Open]*. Tel Aviv: Kinneret, Zmora-Bitan, 2011. Hebrew.

Zeira, Eli. *Mitos Mul Metsiyut [Myth versus Reality: The Yom Kippur War]*. Revised ed. Tel Aviv: Yedioth Aharonoth, 2004. Hebrew.

# Acknowledgments

Writing this book was a long journey: provoking, demanding, fraught with difficult decisions, but nonetheless enjoyable and exciting.

I was accompanied by friends, researchers, and academics, some from the beginning stages of gathering materials and studying them, and others from the actual writing. Their interest, their attentiveness, and their reactions to the information that was accumulating, the conclusions derived from the material and the manuscript that evolved, were of great help to me. This is my opportunity to thank them again. They were joined by many others, some whom I do not personally know, who reacted to the Hebrew version of the book published in September 2012, who contacted me to thank me, to comment, to express appreciation, and at times to share a personal experience or to add information.

In addition to the documentation collected in archives in Israel and in the United States, I received additional information and guidance on how to get this information in personal conversations and interviews. The people I approached cooperated willingly and to the best of their abilities and I am grateful for their contributions. Special thanks go to two of those who played central roles in the events of 1973: the head of the Mossad, General Zvika Zamir, and the head of military intelligence, General Eli Zeira. Both of them devoted long hours to discussing events with me, listened to the discoveries I presented, and related to them with serious consideration. During my discussions with them, I received the impression that, despite the well-known hostility between them, they still have a great deal in common, more than they are willing to admit. I continue to believe this despite the polemic that developed after the publication of the book in Israel.

The English version was prepared on an almost impossibly tight schedule. The animated discussion in Israel around the book and its findings, which found expression in the media, at academic conferences, and in lectures and meetings with interested audiences, was concurrent to the preparation of the English manuscript and created an additional burden for me. It would not have been possible to complete the project in time to mark the fortieth anniversary of the Yom Kippur War without the work of the wonderful, hard-working team of Barbara Doron in Israel and Bill Quandt, Helena Cobban, and Kimberly MacVaugh at Just World Books and Sarah Grey at Grey Editing in the United States. They deserve my thanks.

A special word of thanks to Bill Quandt, who listened, read, and initiated the publication of the English version of the book and who used his rich knowledge as a player in the events of that year and as an academic and researcher of the period in order to edit the book comprehensively and meticulously.

Another word of special thanks goes to Barbara Doron. Her excellent translation of the Hebrew manuscript is only one component of her contribution to the publication of the English version. Her wide knowledge of the book's topic, her diligence, and her motivation to deal with the tight schedule of the editing process led to her being a full partner in all of the other aspects of the publication process.

It is difficult to describe how this journey would have taken place without the support of Mira, my wife, who enabled the research and its main figures to become part of our lives for a number of years. She listened, read, clarified, commented and encouraged. Noa, Alon and Roni, Dror and Nira joined her to complete the family environment and they took interest, participated, became expert in the material, debated, and supported. My thanks to you are not only for your assistance but also for the happiness you have given me.

CPSIA information can be obtained at www.ICGtesting.com
Printed in the USA
BVOW08s2108091013

333310BV00001B/61/P